THE PLURALIST CHARACTER OF THE EUROPEAN ECONOMIC CONSTITUTION

This monograph intervenes in the long-standing and controversial debate on the socio-economic orientation of the European Union. Arguing that the European economic constitution is pluralist in the sense that it does not favour any specific socio-economic paradigm, it shows that European law allows the pursuit of very different regulatory projects by the European and the national legislators. This pluralist character of the European economic constitution stands in an uncomfortable relationship with the policies currently pursued by the European Union, which are often neoliberal in their orientation. The book takes an interdisciplinary approach: it analyses the Treaty on the Functioning of the European Union as interpreted and developed in the case law of the Court of Justice, its history, and its regulatory purpose in the light of conflicting socio-economic paradigms.

By challenging the orthodoxy, the book makes a bold proposition that will likely resonate in both European economic law scholarship and European law in general. With the ongoing economic crisis triggering a significant interest in economic questions among legal scholars it is particularly timely and topical.

Volume 67 in the Series Modern Studies in European Law

Modern Studies in European Law

Recent titles in this series:

The EU Accession to the ECHR
Edited by Vasiliki Kosta, Nikos Skoutaris and Vassilis P Tzevelekos

The European Court of Justice and External Relations: Constitutional Challenges
Edited by Marise Cremona and Anne Thies

A Critique of Codification
Leone Niglia

Protecting Vulnerable Groups: The European Human Rights Framework
Edited by Francesca Ippolito and Sara Iglesias Sanchez

EU International Relations Law Second Edition
Panos Koutrakos

Fundamental Rights in the EU: A Matter for Two Courts
Edited by Sonia Morano-Foadi and Lucy Vickers

What Form of Government for the European Union and the Eurozone?
Federico Fabbrini, Ernst Hirsch Ballin and Han Somsen

The UK and European Human Rights: A Strained Relationship?
Edited by Katja S Ziegler, Elizabeth Wicks and Loveday Hodson

The European Union in International Organisations and Global Governance: Recent Developments
Edited by Christine Kaddous

Nudge and the Law: What Can EU Law Learn From Behavioural Sciences?
Edited by Alberto Alemanno and Anne-Lise Sibony

Fundamental Rights in EU Internal Market Legislation
Vasiliki Kosta

Uniformity of Customs Administration in the European Union
Kathrin Limbach

The Impact of Union Citizenship on the EU's Market Freedoms
Alina Tryfonidou

Equal Citizenship and Its Limits in EU Law
Päivi Johanna Neuvonen

For the complete list of titles in this series, see 'Modern Studies in European Law' link at www.hartpub.co.uk/books/series.asp

The Pluralist Character of the European Economic Constitution

Clemens Kaupa

•HART•

OXFORD • LONDON • NEW YORK • NEW DELHI • SYDNEY

HART PUBLISHING
Bloomsbury Publishing Plc
Kemp House, Chawley Park, Cumnor Hill, Oxford, OX2 9PH, UK

HART PUBLISHING, the Hart/Stag logo, BLOOMSBURY and the Diana logo are trademarks of Bloomsbury Publishing Plc
First published in Great Britain 2016

First published in hardback, 2016
Paperback edition, 2019

A catalogue record for this book is available from the British Library.

Library of Congress Cataloging-in-Publication Data

Names: Kaupa, Clemens, author.

Title: The pluralist character of the European economic constitution / Clemens Kaupa.

Description: Oxford ; Portland, Oregon : Hart Publishing, an imprint of Bloomsbury Publishing Plc, 2016. | Series: Modern studies in European law ; volume 67 | Includes bibliographical references and index.

Identifiers: LCCN 2016015258 (print) | LCCN 2016015748 (ebook) | ISBN 9781849467698 (hardback : alk. paper) | ISBN 9781509901098 (Epub)

Subjects: LCSH: European Union countries—Economic policy. | Law—Economic aspects—European Union countries. | European Union—Constitution.

Classification: LCC KJE6415 .K38 2016 (print) | LCC KJE6415 (ebook) | DDC 343.2407—dc23

LC record available at https://lccn.loc.gov/2016015258

ISBN: HB: 978-1-84946-769-8
PB: 978-1-50992-644-2
ePDF: 978-1-50990-108-1
ePub: 978-1-50990-109-8

Series: Modern Studies in European Law, volume 67

Typeset by Compuscript Ltd, Shannon

Acknowledgements

This book is based in parts on my dissertation, which I wrote at the University of Vienna ('Dealing with competing socio-economic paradigms in Internal Market Law', 2013), and my LL.M. thesis, which I wrote at Harvard Law School ('Towards a distributive analysis of ECJ decisions', 2011). I would like to thank my supervisors, Professor Friedl Weiss, Professor Alexander Somek and Professor Gráinne de Búrca for their help and their patience. I am grateful for all the support I have received from my parents and my family, from my friends and colleagues, and from Leo and Moises.

Amsterdam, in May 2016

Contents

crisis in 2008, and after the brief phase of irritation that it created, this dominance was re-established and in fact has deepened.[4] Most notably, neoliberalism has come to shape the European polity in the form of austerity politics.

However, the crisis of 2008 also brought a renewed consciousness of the ideological nature of the socio-economic policies that the Western countries as well as the Union had followed over recent decades. What, given the hegemonic status of the neoliberal worldview, had for a long time been considered to be the only correct way of thinking about the economy, is now subjected to renewed scrutiny. Today, there is a greater awareness that neoliberalism constitutes but one way among many to conceptualize how the economy works and to define a society's objectives and the policies necessary to achieve them.

Within this context, the present book picks up a specific topic of both legal and political relevance, namely the socio-economic orientation of the Union's constitutional framework. It addresses the question of whether the legal framework of the European Union must be assumed to imply a choice in favour of any specific socio-economic paradigm that is of normative relevance in the interpretation of European law.[5] In other words, must European law be interpreted along the lines of any specific economic worldview? The answer I propose in this book is that this is not the case: the Union's legal framework cannot be held to constitute a comprehensive choice in favour of any specific ideological position that would have to be taken into account in the interpretation of European law. Rather, it will be shown that the Treaty[6] is a pluralist framework, by which I mean that it provides a scope

[4] Crouch (n 1), vii–viii.

[5] A socio-economic paradigm is a set of political and scientific assumptions, research methods and policy propositions relating to the socio-economic sphere, usually associated with specific academic currents (eg specific economic theories) and possibly (but not necessarily) related to political movements (eg certain parties). A socio-economic paradigm provides its adherents a coherent understanding of society and the economy and proposes a comprehensive set of policy prescriptions. In short, a socio-economic paradigm describes a specific way of thinking about the role and functioning of the economy in society. Currently, two major socio-economic paradigms can be identified: neoliberalism on the one hand, which I defined in n 1, and 'Keynesian' (maybe better: 'left-social-democratic/post-Keynesian') on the other. Keynesianism assumes an intrinsic interdependence between markets on the one hand, and the state on the other. The latter engages directly in the socio-economic sphere, most notably through macroeconomic management, the provision of public services and strategic investment, eg in infrastructure. Equality is considered a relevant concern, and the state engages in redistributive policies. The paradigm draws from post-Keynesian economic theory, and is associated with a left social democratic movement (which may be found in social democratic, green and socialist/communist parties). Currently, neoliberalism constitutes the hegemonic view, and Keynesianism the main alternative paradigm. I believe that other alternative views and practices, such as Marxism, radical libertarianism or post-growth thinking currently do not function fully as 'socio-economic paradigms' in the above-defined sense, most notably because they do not provide a comprehensive policy toolbox. However, in this book I will argue that the Treaty is open towards various socio-economic paradigms in a more general sense and not just towards the two main paradigms just defined. This would imply that, for example, a future post-growth paradigm may possibly rely on the Treaty as a basis for its policies.

[6] The book covers the entire period from the Union's formation up to today. During that period, the Treaty establishing the European Economic Community (EEC Treaty) was amended multiple times, becoming the Treaty establishing the European Community (EC Treaty) and ultimately the Treaty on the Functioning of the European Union (TFEU). For reasons of clarity the book will uniformly refer to it as the 'Treaty', unless it is necessary to refer to a specific version.

of discretion for the implementation of a multiplicity of socio-economic projects that remains undetermined (or underdetermined) in central aspects. However, this potential openness is often obscured by hegemonic historical, political and economic narratives that enter, explicitly or implicitly, the interpretation process. In order to identify the pluralist character of the Treaty, these narratives must be addressed in detail. The question as to the normative orientation of the Union's legal framework will thus serve as the basis for an extensive inquiry into the historical, economic and doctrinal views that shape our understanding of European law today.

The book's guiding question is a recurring theme in European law scholarship; most notably, it found expression in the concept of the 'European economic constitution'.[7] In the early years of the Community's existence, German ordoliberal scholars had argued that the Treaty of Rome established an 'economic constitution' that had to be read as a comprehensive programmatic choice (*Gesamtentscheidung*) in favour of a specific socio-economic paradigm, and which in turn was claimed to have normative implications insofar as European law had to be interpreted in the light of it.[8] Since then, the concept of the 'European economic constitution' has been repeatedly employed to inquire into the socio-economic orientation of European law.[9] The concept is referred to in this book in order to relate to this debate, though it will be shown that any positive claim as to an alleged comprehensive choice in favour of any specific paradigm must be rejected. This point has been made repeatedly in the past, most notably by Miguel Poiares Maduro, who speaks of the 'open' character of the European economic constitution.[10] It is one

[7] The term refers not only to constitutional law in the formal sense, but to all rules that shape the economic structure of society. From a perspective of European law, it would thus include primary as well as secondary law.

[8] See the programmatic explanations in Franz Böhm, Walter Eucken and Hans Grossmann-Doerth, 'Unsere Aufgabe' in Franz Böhm (ed), *Die Ordnung der Wirtschaft als geschichtliche Aufgabe und rechtsschöpferische Leistung, 1* (Kohlhammer, 1937) xix.

[9] See for example Manfred Streit and Werner Mussler, 'The economic constitution of the European community: From Rome to Maastricht' (1994) 5 *Constitutional Political Economy* 319; Miguel Poiares Maduro, *We the Court. The European Court of Justice and the European Economic Constitution: a critical reading of Article 30 of the EC Treaty* (Hart, 1998); Wolf Sauter, 'The Economic Constitution of the European Union' (1998) 4 *Columbia Journal of European Law* 27; Christian Joerges, 'What is left of the European Economic Constitution? A melancholic eulogy' (2005) 30 *European Law Review* 461; Stefano Giubboni, *Social Rights and Market Freedom in the European Constitution* (Cambridge University Press, 2006) 15–29; Kaarlo Tuori and Klaus Tuori, *The Eurozone Crisis* (Cambridge University Press, 2014) xii and 13; Christian Joerges, 'The European economic constitution and its transformation through the financial crisis' ZenTra Working Papers in Transnational Studies No 47/2015; Herwig Hofmann and Katerina Pantazatou, 'The Transformation of the European Economic Constitution' University of Luxembourg Law Working Paper 2015-01.

[10] Poiares Maduro (n 9), 159. In his book, Poiares Maduro argued that different interpretations of Art 34 TFEU exist, which correspond to competing normative models of the European economic constitution. In particular he identified three models, which are broad paradigms or visions of how the EU works and should work, and which are also connected to different modes of governance, and different modes of legitimation. These three constitutional models are: centralization, competition and decentralization. The first model holds that negative integration through the application of the Treaty freedoms should be followed by positive integration on the European level, which is legitimated

of the objectives of the present book to update this claim in regard to the Union's most recent developments. However, the book's central, and distinct, function is to establish an analytical framework that allows us to identify the multiple historical, political and economic narratives that shape the dominant understanding of the European economic constitution, especially after the crisis of 2008 put into question many of the previously hegemonic assumptions, while at the same time giving rise to new ones.

The European socio-economic system has been and continues to be a capitalist one. The mutation of capitalism from its corporatist post-war version to its current neoliberal form shaped the Union's legal and institutional setup and its political practices, just as it shaped the law and politics of other international regimes and all Western countries. The way the Union's legal and institutional structure and its policies have been defined by neoliberal thinking, how they have come to facilitate neoliberal outcomes and undermined the pursuit of alternative socio-economic projects, has been highlighted by numerous scholars over the past decades. The contributions made by the various authors to understanding the complex dynamics of this process cannot be discussed at length here. However, some of the more important insights shall be highlighted. The most obvious starting point is Fritz Scharpf's finding that the Union's institutional setup is liable to facilitate neoliberal outcomes. In that regard, Scharpf has recently argued that 'European integration has reduced the capacity of democratic politics to deal with the challenges of global capitalism, and it has contributed to rising social inequality.'[11] According to Scharpf, these phenomena are effected by 'asymmetries' in European policy-making, namely 'the priority of negative over positive integration and of monetary integration over political and social integration',[12] which are in turn rooted in the legal and institutional setup of the Union.[13] This asymmetry undermines the Union's ability to establish a social-democratic form of governance in which liberalized markets are embedded in a sufficiently strong regulatory framework on

by European democratic means. The second model is one of pure negative integration with no subsequent re-regulation at the European level, with the market providing sufficient legitimation. The third model is based on the understanding that the democratically regulated nation states are the primary source of legitimacy. According to Poiares Maduro, 'all models have played, and will continue to play, a role in the shaping of the European Economic Constitution' (ibid, 150). Accordingly, 'Treaty rules such as Article [34 TFEU] should be understood and interpreted in light of these models.' At the same time, 'all models present institutional malfunctions varying according to the set of factors and values described.' Poiares Maduro therefore conceptualized EU law and its institutions—themselves shaped by different economic-constitutional visions—within a context of competing economic and constitutional aspirations. The role of the CJEU lies in identifying 'the different institutional malfunctions'. Poiares Maduro emphasized the political dimension of judicial review, as it is required to balance competing interests. Based on what he called the 'open character of the European Economic Constitution', Poiares Maduro identified the CJEU's internal market adjudication as a space where the upsides and downsides of different models of the European economic constitution can be evaluated (ibid, 159).

[11] Fritz Scharpf, 'After the crash: A perspective on multilevel European democracy' (2015) 21 *European Law Journal* 384, 384.

[12] ibid, 384.

[13] ibid, 385–86.

the European level.[14] The accuracy of Scharpf's diagnosis has become particularly manifest since the outbreak of the economic crisis. Authors like Mark Dawson, Floris De Witte and Augustín Menéndez have shown that the measures enacted by the Union in response to the crisis have undermined not only the rule of law and democratic governance, but also the ability of both the Union and the Member States to pursue alternative socio-economic projects.[15] Lukas Oberndorfer has described the unfolding model of European governance as one of 'authoritarian competitive statism' (*autoritärer Wettbewerbsetatismus*), in which regulatory competition between the Member States is enshrined in the Union's constitutional framework through authoritarian means.[16] Beyond the institutional difficulties of re-establishing a form of social-democratic governance on the European level identified by Scharpf, it has been argued by authors such as Martin Höpner and Armin Schäfer that the divergent character of the Member States makes the development of redistributive instruments on the European level, most notably tools of taxation and transfer, difficult.[17] It has been held that, because of these structural conditions, the European Union today conforms in many aspects to the model of 'interstate federalism' that Friedrich Hayek hoped would be the result of international economic integration.[18] The dynamics of how neoliberal thinking enters the law- and policymaking process have been extensively mapped. For example, Marija Bartl has shown how neoliberal thinking has come to shape the technocratic rationality that underlies European policymaking.[19] Alexander Somek has described how the Union's legal setup, largely based on individual rights, has undermined collective forms of organizing society.[20] The historical process of the Union's neoliberal transformation has been extensively documented. Referring to Ruggie's concept of 'embedded liberalism' that built on Polanyi's work, the Union's post-war form has been described as one where international trade

[14] Fritz Scharpf, 'The asymmetry of European integration, or why the EU cannot be a "social market economy"' (2010) 8 *Socio-Economic Review* 211.

[15] Mark Dawson and Floris de Witte, 'Constitutional Balance in the EU after the Euro-Crisis' (2013) 76 *Modern Law Review* 817; Agustín José Menéndez, 'The Existential Crisis of the European Union' (2013) 14 *German Law Journal* 453.

[16] Lukas Oberndorfer, 'Die Renaissance des autoritären Liberalismus? Carl Schmitt und der deutsche Neoliberalismus vor dem Hinrergrund des Eintritts der "Massen" in die europäische Politik' (42) 168 *Prokla* 413, 414.

[17] Alexander Somek, 'From Workers to Migrants, from Distributive Justice to Inclusion: Exploring the Changing Social Democratic Imagination' (2012) 18 *European Law Journal* 711, 713 and 716; Höpner and Schäfer argue that the economic and institutional heterogeneity of EU Member States stands in the way of re-establishing a functioning welfare system on the European level. The Member States differ markedly, both in their levels of prosperity and in their institutional setup. This leads to conflicts of interest between the Member States, which make the re-embedding of markets in redistributive regulations on the European level unlikely. Martin Höpner and Armin Schäfer, 'Embeddedness and Regional Integration: Waiting for Polanyi in a Hayekian Setting' (2012) 66 *International Organization* 429, 431–32, 436–38.

[18] Höpner and Schäfer (n 17).

[19] Marija Bartl, 'Internal Market Rationality, Private Law and the Direction of the Union: Resuscitating the Market as the Object of the Political' (2015) 21 *European Law Journal* 572.

[20] Alexander Somek, *Individualism. An Essay on the Authority of the European Union* (Oxford University Press, 2008).

METHODICAL CONSIDERATIONS

The book attempts to establish the socio-economic orientation of the Treaty on the basis of extensive historical, economic and doctrinal analyses. This interdisciplinary approach raises a number of methodical issues, which are addressed in this section in the form of four methodical considerations.

The first consideration is that there are two types of claims to be encountered in the discussion on the socio-economic orientation of the Union, which should be distinguished for analytical reasons. The first type relates to the question of whether the Union's legal or institutional setup produces or facilitates outcomes that conform to a specific socio-economic paradigm. The second—which is the subject of this book—is whether such outcomes are legally *required*. The former type of claim may be described as concerned with identifying 'causal' relationships (in the sense of identifying causes for a specific observable phenomenon), and the latter with normative ones.[26] Because we are dealing with social phenomena, the term 'causal relationships' is not meant in a narrow, mechanistic sense. Instead, I employ it to describe scholarship concerned with identifying legal and institutional structures that constitute contributory causes for certain socio-economic outcomes, without arguing any monocausal relationship. A well-known example of an author who strives to identify 'causal' relationships between the Union's legal and institutional framework and certain socio-economic effects in the sense just defined is Fritz Scharpf, whose arguments we briefly discussed in the introduction. Of course, normative and causal relationships are intertwined in important ways, many of which we will address further below and throughout this book. And yet, the two types of claims are still different propositions: a legal framework may be open to different interpretations, and yet have the structural tendency to produce certain outcomes. Ignoring this distinction has problematic consequences, insofar as a certain observable effect may incorrectly be assumed to be also normatively required. However, if the law itself is ambiguous, then other factors than the norm itself must account for systematic biases. One such factor may be power: the reason why lawmakers, administrators or courts opt for a specific outcome may find explanation in the prevailing power relations. Moreover, hegemonic political, economic and legal narratives may shape the outcome, as will be discussed further below. Distinguishing between the normative content of legal provisions and the outcomes they effect is an analytical precondition for identifying choices by lawmakers, administrators and judges, as well as for recognizing how the power structure or hegemonic assumptions shape legal outcomes. For example, parts

[26] This difference obviously mirrors Kelsen's distinction between legal and sociological claims, which in turn draws from Hume's is/ought distinction. I will propose further below that the distinction is still analytically useful if conceptualized in a constructive and not an essentialist form. Because Kelsen's vocabulary is liable to be misunderstood in the latter sense, I reconceptualize the dichotomy as a distinction between 'legal' and 'causal' relationships. See Hans Kelsen, *Über Grenzen zwischen juristischer und soziologischer Methode* (Mohr, 1911).

of the CJEU's internal market case law have been criticized for their ideological biases.[27] Whether such biased outcomes are legally *required* or merely factually *enabled* or *facilitated* by the Union's legal and institutional structure makes a significant difference: in the former case, the Court would in fact be acting correctly when issuing biased judgments; in the latter case, the bias must be assumed to have another cause than the Treaty provisions themselves, eg it might be the result of a discretionary choice of the Court, or of the socio-economic views it has adopted. I will describe the choice to follow a specific interpretation among multiple options as 'political' in nature. Such 'political' choice can in turn be contested, and 'political' justification be demanded. I understand this need for justification in a broad sense, including all types of (eg economic or moral) arguments that support the claim that one among a number of possible interpretations of the Treaty should be preferred over others. For example, it is quite clear that, far from merely engaging in the technocratic implementation of fully determined Treaty obligations, the ECB in fact enjoys a broad discretionary choice in its actions, which consequently requires *political* justification.[28]

The use of this law/politics distinction as an analytical device has a critical potential, if employed in constructive and not essentialist terms. By this I mean the recognition that the law/politics distinction is established and constantly reconstructed within legal discourse, and is not based on some alleged intrinsic difference. Contemporary law as a historically contingent institution is characterized by its relative autonomy vis-à-vis political, economic and other societal processes, which is a precondition of its very functioning.[29] Surely law serves power. At the same time, however, the legal system's relative autonomy implies that the former may not always be fully congruent with the latter. Following Sonja Buckel, the legal system may be held to exhibit a double character: it realizes hegemonic power, but also provides tools that may potentially be turned against it.[30] The present book aims to show that the dual character also characterizes the European economic constitution.[31] While it may be structured in a way that

[27] See for example Clemens Kaupa, 'Maybe not activist enough? On the Court's alleged neoliberal bias in its recent labor cases', in Bruno De Witte, Mark Dawson and Elise Muir (eds), *Judicial Activism at the European Court of Justice: Causes, Responses and Solutions* (Edward Elgar, 2013).

[28] In this sense Streeck (n 2), 227–28.

[29] Niklas Luhmann, *Das Recht der Gesellschaft* (Suhrkamp, 1995) 60; this is also the underlying assumption of Kelsen's theory of law. Hans Kelsen, *Reine Rechtslehre* (Deuticke, 1934) iii; Hans Kelsen, *General Theory of Law and State* (Harvard University Press, 1949) 121.

[30] Sonja Buckel, *Subjektivierung und Kohäsion* (Velbrück Wissenschaft, 2007) 312–15.

[31] Expressing what I believe is a similar idea: Michelle Everson and Christian Joerges, 'Reconfiguring the Politics–Law Relationship in the Integration Project through Conflicts–Law Constitutionalism' (2012) 18 *European Law Journal* 644; Everson and Joerges argue that 'European law is neither "conservative" nor hostile to the new conflict situations … On the contrary, European law can appear to be far more liberal than political sentiment; a progressive force for institutional change within a world of altered identities' (ibid, 655). Everson and Joerges refer to a potential of European law, rather than to its actual application: 'With its recent jurisprudence, however, the CJEU has now prised open national constitutions and alienated the national constitutional jurisdiction without, however, being able to offer anything in return other than a neo-liberal European perspective' (ibid, 651).

facilitates specific outcomes, it is yet not completely determined by any specific socio-economic paradigm.[32]

The second proposition is that, as just mentioned, the interpretation of law is strongly shaped by hegemonic historical, political, economic and legal narratives. The influence of such hegemonic narratives is rarely addressed in the regular interpretation process, often because they are not recognized as such: instead of being one view on history, economics or legal doctrine among others, they are mistaken for an objective description, or a statement of commonsensical positions.[33] For example, the interpretation of internal market law is necessarily based on assumptions about how and under which conditions trade is beneficial. Such assumptions are sometimes explicit, but most of the times implicit. It can be argued that lawyers will tend to base their views on economic assumptions that they hold to be uncontroversial because, to employ a term coined by Galbraith, they constitute the 'conventional wisdom'.[34] However, the conventional wisdom is usually the hegemonic socio-economic paradigm, so that the attempt to base legal arguments on seemingly commonsensical economic views in fact perpetuates the hegemonic position. To identify hegemonic narratives, alternative views in history, economics or legal doctrine must first be established which enable a competing reading of the law. Against such a background, hegemonic narratives that shape our understanding of the law can be identified. This is a constructive effort in the sense that these alternative narratives are not readily available in legal discourse and must be actively re-established, a task that usually transcends the limited purview of doctrinal argumentation. The book engages extensively in historical, economic and legal studies to identify alternative narratives relating to the socio-economic orientation of the European economic constitution. For example, a historical analysis of the 1962 Commission Action Programme uncovered a reading of the Treaty of Rome that stands in stark conflict to the interpretation of the Treaty in much of today's literature, and supports the claim that the Treaty of Rome must be considered as a pluralist instrument. Similarly, our analysis of

[32] US constitutional history provides an illustrative analogy: the body of constitutional judgments that form part of the 'Lochner era' shows how the US constitution was mobilized on the basis of a liberalist ideology in the interest of capital against labour protection, thereby functioning as a tool of hegemonic power. Only a few years later, however, the same constitution served as the basis for Roosevelt's New Deal legislation, after the Supreme Court had initially still squashed early measures. The 'Lochner era' received its name from the infamous decision *Lochner v New York* 198 US 45 (1905), and ended with *West Coast Hotel Co v Parrish* 300 US 379 (1937). As possible entry points to the discussion see for example John Forsythe, 'Legislative History of the Fair Labor Standards Act' (1939) 6 *Law and Contemporary Problems* 464; Laura Kalman, 'Law, Politics, and the New Deal(s)' (1999) 108 *Yale Law Journal* 2165.

[33] Addressing a similar issue, Bartl has identified 'the emergence of "isles" of uncontested knowledge (assumptions) in the EU policy and law-making, which substitute political debate on socially and economically salient matters.' Bartl (n 19), 574. At another point, Bartl speaks of 'the perception of "obviousness" of [functionalist entities'] goals and purposes', Marija Bartl, 'The Way We Do Europe: Subsidiarity and the Substantive Democratic Deficit' (2015) 21 *European Law Journal* 23, 42.

[34] See John Galbraith, *The Affluent Society* (Houghton Mifflin Company, 1998) 6–17.

the Commission's harmonization programme in the 1960s and 1970s allows us to challenge the common representation of the so-called 'new approach' of the 1980s in contemporary literature, and to question the normative implications that are usually projected onto it. Finally, a close analysis of the economic literature on issues such as trade and growth puts into question the common understanding of the Treaty freedom provisions, and the doctrinal system developed on its basis. By identifying and challenging hegemonic discourses that shape our understanding of the law, and actively reconstructing alternative interpretations of the Treaty, new arenas for political contestation are opened up,[35] which in turn may be beneficial from a perspective of democratic governance.[36]

The third consideration is that the analytical concepts of European law scholarship are shaped by present-day political assumptions. Our tools are not necessarily neutral: by employing these instruments we are liable to project today's political views onto the European legal framework and its development, yet misconceive the resulting, ideologically shaped representation as a factually correct depiction. Just as the emerald city in Frank Baum's *Wizard of Oz* appears green, not because it actually is green, but because all visitors are required to wear green-tinted goggles, a legal structure that appears to conform to our analytical categories may do so because it is structured this way through the analytical process. Maybe the most problematic, yet pervasive analytical frame employed in European law scholarship today is the dichotomic distinction between 'economic' and 'non-economic' concerns, as well as related dichotomic concepts that we will discuss further below. The analytical frame is truly hegemonic in the sense that it is employed by authors of both left and right affiliations.[37] As a descriptive concept, the dichotomic pair implies that some of society's activities belong to an 'economic' realm, whereas others do not. Such dichotomic description must be recognized as ideological in the sense that it belongs to a specific worldview, whereas it is rejected by others. For example, within the dichotomy between 'economic' and 'non-economic' concerns, social, labour or consumer regulation are frequently conceptualized as 'non-economic'. It has been proposed, however, that the welfare state in fact forms

[35] Many authors have called for a politicization of the European polity in some form. See eg Bartl (n 19), 575; Mark Dawson and Floris De Witte, 'Self-Determination in the Constitutional Future of the EU' (2015) 21 *European Law Journal* 371, 382; Marco Dani, 'Rehabilitating Social Conflicts in European Public Law' (2012) 18 *European Law Journal* 621; Damian Chalmers, 'The European Redistributive State and a European Law of Struggle' (2012) 18 *European Law Journal* 667, 667; Gareth Davies, 'Democracy and Legitimacy in the Shadow of Purposive Competence' (2015) 21 *European Law Journal* 2.

[36] Bartl points out that one significant dimension of democratic governance is the ability of the electorate to engage in substantive choices, for which the reconstruction of the possibility of political contestation is an important precondition. Bartl (n 19), 24; Gareth Davies similarly argued that '[t]he essence of a political debate is the possibility of choice between outcomes', Davies (n 35), 14; Scharpf has similarly held that political conflicts on the substantive orientation of European policies may increase the political legitimacy of the European polity. Scharpf (n 11), 404.

[37] This is illustrated for example by the demand for a 'social Europe', which is often invoked by the European left, and manifestly refers to the dichotomy between 'social' and 'economic' objectives.

1

Interpreting the Treaty in its Historical Context I: The Treaty of Rome

INTRODUCTION

THE LAW, IT may be argued, is constituted by its history. The stories we tell about what the law once was shapes our view of its scope and limits today; the accounts we give of the law's development influence our present understanding of it. This is true for any field of law, though the extent to which historical narratives play a role in the self-understanding of a legal field may of course vary. The use of historical arguments in the interpretation of law finds doctrinal expression in the common interpretative techniques of national law as well as of international law. Most notably, Article 31 of the Vienna Convention on the Law of Treaties requires the interpretation of the treaty on the basis of the ordinary meaning given to the terms employed by the treaty, in their context and in the light of the Treaty's object and purpose. Article 32 defines supplementary means of interpretation which include preparatory work of the treaty as well as 'the circumstances of its conclusion'. Article 32 therefore opens the door for the use of historical materials and historical arguments. While the Court of Justice of the European Union (CJEU) does not usually make use of the Vienna Convention for the interpretation of the Treaty,[1] its own style of interpretation, often termed 'purposive', equally allows it to draw upon historical considerations in its interpretation of the Treaty text. In *CILFIT*, for instance, the Court described its interpretative approach as follows:

> [E]very provision of Community law must be placed in its context and interpreted in the light of the provisions of Community law as a whole, regard being had to the objectives thereof and to its state of evolution at the date on which the provision in question is to be applied.[2]

The emphasis of the Court tends to rest on the context and regulatory objectives of the Treaty, with an eye on the evolutionary character of European law. Accordingly, Advocate General Fennelly argued that '[t]he achievement of the common

[1] Richard Gardiner, *Treaty Interpretation* (Oxford University Press, 2010) 121.
[2] Case 283/81, *CILFIT v Ministry of Health* [1982] ECR 3417 (hereinafter *CILFIT*), para 20.

market consists of a programed and intentionally obligatory agenda for change'.[3] Any attempt to establish the purpose of the Treaty as well as its 'state of evolution' necessarily raises historical questions, such as the following: what was the Treaty's purpose at the time of its ratification, and did this purpose change over the following decades, and if so, how?[4] A purposive interpretation of the Treaty provisions requires us to identify the objectives and means of the Treaty as understood by those who drafted it and by those it was addressed to, and to comprehend how this understanding evolved over time. While the meaning of the Treaty as understood by its drafters and their contemporaries is certainly important in the Treaty's interpretation, no European law scholar would claim that this should be the sole authority for the interpretation of the Treaty today. Rather, European law is commonly understood to be an evolving legal order: employing US constitutional terminology, we could speak of the Treaty as a 'living document'.[5] Therefore it is not only the 'original intent' of the drafters that must be taken into account, but also the subsequent changes that the Treaty was subject to, which will be discussed in later chapters.

The present chapter investigates whether a historical reading would suggest that the Treaty of Rome should be understood as a normative choice for a specific socio-economic paradigm, which is of contemporary relevance in the interpretation of European law. The answer provided in this chapter will be in the negative: the Treaty must be considered to be pluralist in the light of different present-day socio-economic paradigms. It must be emphasized that, while the chapter deals with historical material, the ambition of the chapter ultimately lies not in the field of history, but of law, and the research question remains *normative* and *contemporary*. It is asked whether the Treaty's history and evolution reveal a specific socio-economic preference that has normative relevance in the light of present-day legal conflicts. This question is *contemporary* because it attempts to clarify the Treaty's meaning in regard to current legal conflicts. It is *normative* because it attempts to establish how legislators and courts are supposed to act today, whereas it is ultimately not interested in causal explanations of past events, the latter being the focus of historical studies proper. The chapter moves in an interdisciplinary field at the intersection of history and law, which raises certain methodical challenges. In many ways, the history of the European Economic Community appears as almost contemporary to us: the regulatory concerns that were at issue in, for example, the

[3] Nial Fennelly, 'Legal Interpretation at the European Court of Justice' (1996) 20 *Fordham International Law Journal* 656, 671.

[4] Ulrich Everling held in this regard: 'It is common to refer to "teleological" interpretation, and that presents relatively few problems if it is understood as meaning the purpose-oriented application of technical provisions. However, the word means more than this; the Greek term "telos" in this context signifies the ultimate objective and the deeper purpose of the entire process of European integration. But what is the "telos" of the Community today? Is it still that of the founders, if even they were agreed in that respect?' Ulrich Everling, 'The Court of Justice as a decisionmaking authority' (1984) 82 *Michigan Law Review* 1294, 1305.

[5] See for example Thurgood Marshall, 'The Constitution: A Living Document' (1987) 30 *Howard Law Journal* 915.

1950s or the 1980s appear still relevant to us today, and the terminology remains comprehensible. Legal scholars may find themselves immediately familiar with material from the early days of the EEC. However, such apparent familiarity is also deceptive: in many relevant regards the economic and the political context of the Treaty of Rome was fundamentally different from today. If we apply a contemporary mode of thinking to the historical material, we will likely ignore significant and fundamental differences between the 1950s and now. If historical debates are read on the basis of a contemporary political understanding, we merely project our current views onto the past, and we are then liable to misunderstand the normative implications of Europe's most fundamental legal text. In order to establish the normative meaning of the Treaty of Rome and to avoid projecting contemporary concepts into the past, the present chapter attempts to reconstruct the Treaty within the context of the legal, economic and political debate that accompanied its inception.

The book looks at the Treaty at three points in time: during its inception in the 1950s, during the reforms of the 1980s and 1990s, and at the present moment. The first two parts are the subject of the present chapter and the next, whereas the discussion of the most recent reforms follows in the final chapter. In this chapter, we will first attempt a contextualization of the Treaty of Rome, and discuss the process of trade liberalization that was ongoing in the 1940s and 1950s within which the EEC was conceived. Today the Treaty of Rome is sometimes discussed against the backdrop of the protectionism of the inter-war period. However, such a representation invokes a dichotomic conception in which the Treaty is assumed to express a political choice for free trade and against protectionism, and which sometimes is implied to have a normative dimension insofar as a Treaty preference against national regulation with restrictive effects on inter-European trade is assumed. It will be argued, however, that this merely constitutes a projection of a contemporary socio-economic position onto the Treaty of Rome, and does not correctly depict the specific character of the Community in the light of other, both global and regional, projects of economic integration, most notably those pursued under the auspices of the Organization for European Economic Cooperation (OEEC; now OECD—Organization for Economic Cooperation and Development) on the European level and under the General Agreement on Tariffs and Trade (GATT) on the global plane. It is proposed that the Treaty of Rome must instead be understood as a specific form of economic integration, which differed in significant aspects from the existing liberalization projects.

The main part of the chapter will argue that, if the Treaty of Rome is conceptualized as a regulatory choice, then it is best described as having a two-part objective of liberalizing the movement of goods, services and productive factors within a framework of normalized economic, fiscal, and social policies and coordinated macroeconomic policies, all of which should ensure 'undistorted competition'.[6]

[6] See EC, 'Memorandum of the Commission on the action programme of the Community for the second stage' COM(62) 300 6; see also Hans von der Groeben, 'Competition Policy in the Common Market and in the Atlantic Partnership' (1965) 10 *Antitrust Bulletin* 125, 126–27.

The pursuit of this dual, interconnected strategy by the Treaty of Rome found expression in the objective—frequently referred to by the Commission in the early years—of establishing an 'economic union'. Distortions of competition were assumed to arise from both private actors—eg through the formation of cartels—and public actors, either by granting distorting state aid, or by the existence of an unharmonized regulatory framework that created undue benefits for certain operators.[7] In the discourse of the 1950s and 1960s, competition was considered to be 'undistorted' not if it is free of regulation, but if it was undistorted by influences that were deemed to be unwanted. This did not exclude regulatory differences and did not aim at levelling all factual disparities; instead, it sought to establish competition among European producers that was based on their innovative efforts as well as the productive advantages of the various regions, but not on artificial benefits caused by regulatory differences not justified by underlying structural differences, or by a lenient or protectionist regulatory structure that facilitated rent-seeking behaviour.[8] The question of what kind of competition was desirable, and which form of regulation was necessary to enable it, however, was not determined by the Treaty. As we will see, through its open structure as a 'framework treaty' the Treaty enabled, yet did not require, far-reaching harmonization, and also did not significantly limit the options in harmonization in substantive terms. The Treaty thus provided a potentially limitless regulatory scope, and yet remained underdetermined in substantive terms. Consequently, I believe that it is best described as a pluralist instrument.

Before we take a closer look at the Treaty of Rome, we will briefly discuss three analytical concepts commonly employed in discussions on the Treaty of Rome: the dichotomy between 'economic' and 'non-economic' objectives; that between 'negative' and 'positive' integration; and 'neoliberalism'. In today's scholarship it is frequently implied that the Treaty of Rome provided significant harmonization competences only in the 'economic' realm, whereas competences in other areas—correspondingly conceptualized as 'non-economic'—remained limited.[9] I have

[7] See for example Jelle Zijlstra, *Economische politiek en concurrentieproblematiek in de EEG en de lid-staten* (Staatsdrukkerij- en Uitgeversbedrijf 1966) 39.

[8] The Commission speaks for example of 'undesirable movements of production factors' that may be the consequence of differences in taxation. See EC (n 6), 26.

[9] By way of example see Kaarlo Tuori and Klaus Tuori, *The Eurozone Crisis* (Cambridge University Press, 2014), 13, who hold that '[i]n the first decades of its history, say, up to the Maastricht Treaty, integration was almost exclusively an economic project'. See also Joerges and Rödl, who argue: 'The ordo-liberal European polity consists of a twofold structure: at supranational level, it is committed to economic rationality and a system of undistorted competition, while, at national level, re-distributive (social) policies may be pursued and developed further … Then, we become aware of the Wahlverwandtschaft with German ordo-liberalism, in that only the European market-building project was juridified through supranational law, whereas social policy at European level could, at best, be said to have been handled through intergovernmental bargaining processes'. Christian Joerges and Florian Rödl, 'Informal Politics, Formalised Law and the "Social Deficit" of European Integration: Reflections after the Judgments of the ECJ in Viking and Laval' (2009) 15 *European Law Journal* 1, 4; along similar lines, Majone holds that the 'possibility of separating economics and politics' was an 'assumption of the founding fathers'. Giandomenico Majone, *Rethinking the Union of Europe Post-Crisis—Has Integration Gone Too Far?* (Cambridge University Press, 2014), 151.

rarely only required to disapply a certain measure; rather, they usually face implicit or explicit positive obligations as well (eg to provide for a system that is capable of establishing the equivalence of product requirements, or to reorganize their national labour law in a certain way). This means that the application of the Treaty freedoms is always an act of (judicial) law making and entails not only negative, but also positive obligations for the Member States. From a legal perspective, then, there is no qualitative difference between 'negative' and 'positive' integration. The use of the dichotomy in *legal* analysis is problematic in at least two ways: first, the concept of 'negative integration' obscures the degree of substantive discretion that is available to the courts, and the political nature of their choices. The application of European law by the courts may be represented as a quasi-technical endeavour, when in fact it constitutes an act of (judicial) lawmaking.[16] Second, it is liable to be charged with ideological meaning along the lines of the two-sphere fallacy discussed above: for example, redistributive concerns could easily be considered to fall under 'positive integration', from which it could (incorrectly) be deduced that they do not or should not play a role in 'negative integration', eg in the application of the Treaty freedoms by courts. However, there is no reason why distributive concerns should not be taken into consideration in the adjudicative process, for example as part of proportionality balancing. Thus, while the distinction between negative and positive integration as an analytical framework has been an important one when speaking about the dynamics of European integration, I believe that it should not be imported into legal discourse proper.

Finally, it is sometimes asserted in today's literature that the Treaty of Rome implemented a neoliberal programme. Neoliberalism of the 1950s is held to have been characterized by the view that strong regulatory structures are required for the functioning of the market (in delineation from the laissez-faire views of early liberalism), and by competition as the key driving force.[17] If neoliberalism is defined in such a way, then, as we will see in this chapter, it is certainly plausible to argue that the Treaty of Rome conforms in many aspects to this programme; in this sense, neoliberal thinking of the 1950s clearly shaped European law. However, such a finding should not easily be assumed to have normative implications for either the interpretation of the Treaty of Rome or of European law today, for at

Viking Line ABP and OÜ Viking Line Eesti [2007] ECR I-10779 (hereinafter *Viking*); Case C-341/05, *Laval un Partneri Ltd v Svenska Byggnadsarbetareförbundet, Svenska Byggnadsarbetareförbundets avdelning 1, Byggettan and Svenska Elektrikerförbundet* [2005] ECR I-11767 (hereinafter *Laval*); Case C-319/06, *Commission/Luxembourg* [2008] ECR I-4323; Case C-346/06, *Dirk Rüffert v Land Niedersachsen* [2008] ECR I-1989 (hereinafter *Rüffert*).

[16] Duncan Kennedy has argued in this regard that '[t]he European Court of Justice is neoformalist in its interpretation of the canonical "freedoms" of movement of goods and persons in a "single market" in part, as is widely recognized, in order to drape its legislative power in the cloak of necessity'. Duncan Kennedy, 'Three Globalizations of Law and Legal Thought: 1850-2000' in David Trubek and Alvaro Santos (eds), *The New Law and Economic Development* (Cambridge University Press, 2006) 69.

[17] See eg Colin Crouch, *The strange non-death of neoliberalism* (Polity, 2011) 7.

least three reasons. First, as we will see in this chapter, the Treaty was a pluralist instrument, and could be—and indeed was—interpreted in multiple ways, including ways that were not to the liking of the neo- or ordoliberals[18] of that time: this is amply illustrated by the interpretation of the Treaty as forwarded by the Commission in the 1962 Action Programme, which we will discuss extensively in this chapter. Even if ordo- or neoliberal scholars were in fact able to shape the Treaty of Rome,[19] this does not mean that others would have to interpret the law the way they preferred.[20] Moreover, while competition certainly was (and continues to be) a guiding theme of the Treaty, it should not be ignored how underdetermined that concept was:[21] for example, as we will see, it was a significant issue of debate what kind of regulatory harmonization would be necessary to enable a beneficial form of competition. In principle, the need to ensure 'undistorted competition' could very well have justified a broad harmonization of social regulation, as the Commission in fact proposed in the Action Programme. The significant influence of neo- or ordoliberals on the Treaty of Rome, or the fact that its architecture corresponds to a certain degree to their programme, does not allow the conclusion that it also should, from a normative perspective, be interpreted along such ideological lines.[22] This view is also supported by the fact that both the left and the right saw the regulatory structure established by the Treaty as a possible vantage point to pursue their respective socio-economic projects, as Leon Lindberg showed in his study.[23] A second point of caution is that the ideological positions of the 1950s and 1960s should not uncritically be assumed to correspond to contemporary political positions in any straightforward way. I would propose that many social democrats of today would agree with significant parts of the writings of neo- and ordoliberals like Franz Böhm, Alexander Rüstow, or Hans von der Groeben.[24] By contrast, some neo- or ordoliberal propositions, for example relating to the need for a strong regulatory framework and the importance of social justice, would probably not sit well with contemporary liberalists. Ordo- or neoliberal positions of the 1950s can thus not be uncritically equated with neoliberal positions of today. Thus, even if

[18] These terms are defined below (nn 24 and 25).

[19] Joerges, 'The European economic constitution and its transformation through the financial crisis' (n 9), 6.

[20] See in this sense Wolf Sauter, 'The Economic Constitution of the European Union' (1998) 4 *Columbia Journal of European Law* 27; see also Tuori and Tuori (n 9), 16.

[21] For a discussion of competing views on competition law see for example Crouch (n 17), 52–62.

[22] A somewhat comparable point is made by Majone, who points out that neoliberal figures such as Röpke or Erhard were in fact opposed to the EEC, and that the general economic atmosphere of the 1950s was characterized by an economic policy that was quite distant from the neoliberal ideal (nationalization of industries, economic planning, etc). Majone (n 9), 154–60.

[23] Leon Lindberg, *The political dynamics of European economic integration* (Stanford University Press, 1963), passim, in particular 107–11, 287–95.

[24] I employ the term ordoliberal in a broad way to include scholars like Wilhelm Röpke, Alfred Müller-Armack, Alexander Rüstow or Hans von der Groeben who are not, strictly speaking, part of the 'Freiburg school' of Walter Eucken and Franz Böhm which constitutes the 'ordoliberal' group in a narrow sense. However, they form part of a broader intellectual movement which developed in response to the pre-war laissez-faire liberalism, so that a uniform designation is justified.

we can identify a considerable influence of neo- or ordoliberals on the Treaty of Rome, the normative implications of such a finding from today's perspective are far from straightforward. And third, there is a risk of hindsight bias, in which those aspects conforming to an ordo- or neoliberal programme are seen as the Treaty's decisive characteristics because of the Union's subsequent development.[25]

The chapter aims to show that the Treaty of Rome ultimately cannot be understood as implementing or favouring any specific socio-economic paradigm in a way that is of normative relevance from today's perspective. Not only is the Treaty of Rome ambivalent as regards the quality of harmonization that is to accompany economic integration, it is also open as to which economic objectives it aims to pursue through market integration. It is in this sense that the Treaty of Rome is best described as a pluralist project in the light of competing socio-economic paradigms.

TRADE LIBERALIZATION PRIOR TO 1957

Trade liberalization had already been in full swing for almost a decade, on both a European and a global level, when the Treaty of Rome was signed.[26] Immediately after the war, trade had been resumed on the basis of bilateral agreements among the European countries.[27] However, these agreements soon proved to be a highly limiting framework for trade, most notably because of problems relating to the balance of payments among the trading countries.[28] The balance of payments, a central concern to economists in the 1950s (as it still is today), describes the relationship between a country's payments for imports and its receipts from exports.[29] Trade imbalances were assumed to have significant negative effects: a trade deficit drained a country of gold and dollar reserves; a trade surplus could potentially have inflationary effects.[30] As the European currencies were not convertible until

[25] To avoid confusion, I will from here onwards uniformly refer to the stream of post-war thinking associated with scholars like Eucken, Böhm and Müller-Armack as 'ordoliberalism", and reserve the term 'neoliberalism' for the intellectual positions commonly described under this designation from the 1980s onwards.

[26] See on this for example Gordon Slynn, 'Aspects of the Law of the European Economic Community' (1985) 18 *Cornell International Law Journal* 1, 1–2; see however Myrdal's more ambivalent depiction of the post-war economic system, which he described in 1956 as being in a state of disintegration. Gunnar Myrdal, *An international economy: problems and prospects* (Harper & Brothers, 1956) 1–4.

[27] Jan Tumlir and Laura La Haye, 'The Two Attempts at European Economic Reconstruction After 1945' (1981) 137 *Zeitschrift für die gesamte Staatswissenschaft/Journal of Institutional and Theoretical Economics* 367, 382.

[28] Frederic Boyer and JP Sallé, 'The Liberalization of Intra-European Trade in the Framework of OEEC' (1955) 4 IMF Staff Papers 179, 182; see also UN, *The European economy from the 1950s to the 1970s* (Secretariat of the Economic Commission for Europe, 1972) 6.

[29] See Robert Marjolin, 'Prospects for the European Common Market' (1957) 36 *Foreign Affairs* 131, 136; see also James Meade, *The theory of international economic policy*, vol 1: The Balance of Payments (Oxford University Press, 1954) 3ff.

[30] See Wilhelm Röpke, *Die Lehre von der Wirtschaft* (Eugen Rentsch Verlag, 1961) 173; It was assumed in Germany that a trade surplus would lead to 'imported inflation'. See on this Otmar Emminger,

the late 1950s, trade deficits with one country could not be outbalanced with trade surpluses with other countries. Because countries strived to achieve balanced trade flows in order to protect their reserves in gold and dollars, bilateral agreements could potentially result in 'downward bilateral balancing':[31] states would reduce the overall level of trade in order to prevent a trade deficit.[32] For a number of reasons—one probably being this highly restrictive system of trade relations—the European economies collapsed in 1947.[33] The Marshall Plan (or European Recovery Programme) was conceived as a loan programme in reaction to this collapse, and was to be administered by the OEEC (now OECD).[34] It was decided that this effort should go hand in hand with the establishment of a multilateral system of trade in Europe.[35] Gunnar Myrdal commented:

> The basic commitments to economic integration were, in the first instance, made by the West-European governments to the United States as a sort of counterpart to American aid and only incidentally to each other. Moreover, the big plans and the splashy appeals were usually aimed not at Western Europe but at the American public and the American Congress.[36]

Efforts to reduce quantitative restrictions and tariffs on a multilateral level started with the signature of the Convention for European Economic Cooperation in April 1948.[37] The Convention established the OEEC, and was signed by 17 European countries. Article 4 thereof held:

> The Contracting Parties will develop, in mutual cooperation, the maximum possible interchange of goods and services. To this end they will continue the efforts already initiated to achieve as soon as possible a multilateral system of payments among themselves, and will cooperate in relaxing restrictions on trade and payments between one another, with the object of abolishing as soon as possible those restrictions which at present hamper such trade and payments.

The Convention also proposed the formation of a customs union or a free trade area as a possible way of achieving these objectives.[38] From the outset, the aim

The D-Mark in the conflict between internal and external equilibrium, 1948–75 (Princeton University, Essays in International Finance No 122, 1977), 1.

[31] Boyer and Sallé (n 28), 207.

[32] As examples for the discussion on the balance of payments in the 1950s see James Meade, 'The Balance-of-Payments Problems of a European Free-Trade Area' (1957) 67 *Economic Journal* 379; Fritz Machlup, 'Three Concepts of the Balance of Payments and the so-called Dollar Shortage' (1950) 60 *Economic Journal* 46; Friedrich Lutz, 'Europäische Währungsprobleme: 1946–1950' [1951] *ORDO: Jahrbuch für die Ordnung von Wirtschaft und Gesellschaft* 299, 300.

[33] Tumlir and La Haye (n 27), 368–69.

[34] For a brief account of the early years of the organization see OEEC, *The Organisation for European Economic Cooperation: history and structure* (Chateau de la Muette, 1953); see also Henry Lintott, 'The Organization for European Economic Cooperation' (1949) 3 *International Organization* 269; Lincoln Gordon, 'The Organization for European Economic Cooperation' (1956) 10 *International Organization* 1.

[35] OEEC (n 34), 12.

[36] Myrdal (n 26), 65.

[37] OEEC (n 34), 11.

[38] Art 5.

was to establish something coming close to a 'single market' among the member countries.[39] The OEEC's trade liberalization programme started in the summer of 1949,[40] with the first trade agreements under the auspice OEEC being concluded in November 1949.[41] The OEEC's Council decided that the Member States should remove at least 50 per cent of their quantitative restrictions on imports on private account (ie, imports by private traders, as opposed to governmental agencies) by 15 December 1949.[42] In the following years, intra-European trade quickly expanded, even surpassing the optimistic projections of the OEEC secretariat.[43] In 1950, the OEEC devised its 'Code of Liberalization of Trade',[44] which obliged Member States to progressively eliminate quota restrictions and to abstain from discrimination in the administration of their import policies.[45] Further reductions of quantitative restrictions, of 60 per cent and 75 per cent of the trade, were scheduled for October 1950 and February 1951, respectively.[46] By the mid-1950s, the scope of quantitative restrictions had been greatly reduced,[47] which means that the OEEC had succeeded in a far-reaching liberalization of trade among its Member States (though the statutory limits to the liberalization obligation was set at 75 per cent of imports on private account and exceptions applied in regard to imports by government monopolies,[48] and some commentators were more ambivalent about the true extent of the liberalization reached).[49]

[39] Boyer and Sallé (n 28), 181.
[40] Tumlir and La Haye (n 27), 386.
[41] ibid, 381.
[42] The goal was achieved by most countries, not least because the Council decision merely formalized the situation that had already been reached in practice. Boyer and Sallé (n 28), 183.
[43] Tumlir and La Haye (n 27), 384–85. The following table shows the development of trade of the OEEC Member States (billions of dollars, 1948–49 prices; based on data provided by Tumlir and La Haye (n 27)).

	1947 Actual	1948/49 Programme	1948/49 Realized	1952/53 Programme	1952/53 Realized
Intra-OEEC imports (including their overseas territories)	7.9	9.35	11.35	11.80	18.40
Imports from overseas world	12.5	12.40	13.55	12.85	13.75
Exports to overseas world	5.4	6.20	7.30	10.60	10.70

[44] On the Code of Liberalization see Boyer and Sallé (n 28), 182.
[45] Arts 1 and 7; see ibid, 185.
[46] Art 2; see ibid, 185.
[47] Dennis Swann, *The Economics of the Common Market* (Penguin Books, 1992) 97; see also Boyer and Sallé (n 28), 203. Commentators in the 1950s and 1960s generally agreed that the liberalization programme of the OEEC was a success. See for example Leslie Nemes and Andre Aversa, 'Legal Aspects of the European Economy since World War II' (1961) 36 *Notre Dame Lawyer* 111, 128.
[48] See Boyer and Sallé (n 28), 187.
[49] Gunnar Myrdal argued in this regard: '[T]he "liberalization percentages," by which progress was commonly measured, implied a large overstatement of the true degree of trade liberalization reached. It turned out to be particularly difficult to make real progress with the abolition of quantitative restrictions on agricultural products. In many cases liberalization from quantitative restrictions has been accompanied by increases in tariffs'. Myrdal (n 26), 58.

The OEEC's programme of trade liberalization was complemented with the European Payment Union (EPU), which was signed by the OEEC Member States in 1950, the same year that the Code of Liberalization of Trade came into force.[50] The EPU was created to address the problem of trade balances at a time when currencies were not convertible other than to the dollar. Without currency convertibility, the European countries were essentially forced to keep trade flows in balance with every single trading partner, as there was no possibility to balance a trade deficit with one country with the trade surplus with another. This, in turn, increased pressure for trade discrimination.[51] Moreover, upholding currency exchange controls could undermine the liberalization of trade.[52] With the establishment of currency convertibility an important rationale for trade discrimination disappeared, and non-discrimination could be established as a basic principle under the Code.[53] Under the EPU, the Member States would periodically report their trade balance to the Bank for International Settlements, and the accounts of the various countries would be offset against each other.[54] Countries with an overall trade deficit within the EPU area would become debtors to the EPU for the part of the debts that could not be offset, whereas countries with surpluses would become creditors. While countries would be granted a credit for smaller trade deficits, they would have to clear parts of the debts with payment in gold. A similar system applied to creditor countries: a smaller trade surplus would be treated as a credit to the EPU, whereas a larger trade surplus would be cleared by a payment in gold by the EPU. However, only half of the surplus would be paid in gold, whereas the other half would be considered an automatic credit to the EPU. This system was designed to induce both debtor and creditor countries to eliminate trade imbalances within the EPU. This feature of the EPU is interesting from a contemporary perspective, in the light of the ongoing discussion whether countries with a consistent trade surplus should be under an obligation to reduce it.

At the same time that trade was successfully liberalized under the auspices of the OEEC in Europe, trade liberalization progressed at a similarly high-paced speed on the global level. Although the Havana Charter for the projected International Trade Organization failed to pass the US Congress, the General Agreement on Tariffs and Trade (GATT) came into force in 1948, having been signed by 23 countries (which together accounted for 80 per cent of world trade).[55] By 1956, four (of the GATT's total eight) trade rounds had been successfully concluded. It was

[50] See Hanns Küsters, *Die Gründung der Europäischen Wirtschaftsgemeinschaft* (Nomos Verlagsgesellschaft, 1982) 176–77; on the EPU and a critique from an ordoliberal perspective, see Lutz (n 32), 330–38.

[51] Boyer and Sallé (n 28), 187–88; see also UN (n 28), 23.

[52] Henry Schloss, 'The European Payments Union' (1951) 17 *Southern Economic Journal* 465, 465.

[53] Boyer and Sallé (n 28), 187–88.

[54] On the functioning of the EPU, see Schloss (n 52).

[55] Douglas Irwin, 'The GATT in Historical Perspective' (1995) 85 *American Economic Review* 323, 325.

in this environment of general trade liberalization and expansion that the Treaty of Rome was conceived. By the late 1950s, at the point when the Treaty of Rome was signed, all the fundamental impediments to international trade had been cleared. Multilateral trade regulation had been established, currency convertibility had been ensured, and, according to an UN economic survey, 'by the end of the 1950s relatively few [quantitative restrictions] remained on trade among member countries'.[56] The choice between protectionism and trade in Europe had already been made in favour of the latter, and had been given a relatively solid and successful institutional framework in the form of both the OEEC and the GATT. From a normative perspective, it is too simplistic to conceptualize the Treaty of Rome as a choice in favour of trade over protectionism, because the European countries had been engaged in successful projects of trade liberalization for almost a decade prior to its inception. Instead, the decisive issue relevant for answering the question of whether the Treaty of Rome constituted a choice for a specific socio-economic paradigm is what *kind* of economic integration the Treaty of Rome pursued, as compared to other integration projects that were implemented around the same time. It is interesting to note in this regard that the Treaty of Rome initially faced significant scepticism, as it was argued that the form of integration it envisioned stood at odds with liberalization projects such as the GATT and the OEEC programme, and that the EEC was liable to pursue a protectionist agenda, or at least to have such effect.[57] The EEC was perceived as a deviation from the policy prescriptions of traditional trade theory, a point that we will further look into in the following sections.

THE REGULATORY APPROACH OF THE TREATY OF ROME: ENABLING 'UNDISTORTED COMPETITION' IN AN 'ECONOMIC UNION' THROUGH MARKET-MAKING AND HARMONIZATION

The Means and Ends of the Community: Article 2 EEC

Any inquiry into the specific quality of integration pursued by the Treaty of Rome should start with Article 2 EEC, which defined the goals of the Community as well as the regulatory instruments to realize them. The provision held:

> The Community shall have as its task, by establishing a common market and progressively approximating the economic policies of Member States, to promote throughout the Community a harmonious development of economic activities, a continuous and balanced expansion, an increase in stability, an accelerated raising of the standard of living and closer relations between the States belonging to it.

[56] UN (n 28), 24.

[57] For a discussion of this issue, see for example Hans von der Groeben, 'Gemeinsamer Markt und Euratom—Stand der Entwicklung' in Hans von der Groeben (ed), *Europa—Plan und Wirklichkeit* (Nomos, 1967), 97.

Article 2 EEC defined five dynamic goals: four of a socio-economic, and one of a non-economic nature (closer relations between the Member States).[58] To achieve these goals, Article 2 EEC proposed two distinct means: the establishment of a common market on the one hand, and the coordination and harmonization of economic policies among the Member States on the other. The provision thus lays down a specific relationship between the common market and the Community's regulatory objectives, as well as between the two instruments of market-making and harmonization. We will now take a closer look at each of these two relations, as they shine a light on the specific regulatory approach pursued by the Treaty of Rome.

The first relation that requires a closer look is that between market-making and the Community's regulatory objectives. While the establishment of a common market was among the central policies to be implemented by the Community, it was conceptualized as a means to reach the Community's goals, and not as an end in itself. The implications of this distinction may not be completely clear from a contemporary perspective, where the beneficial effects of a market-based organization of economic activities, though critically discussed, are rarely questioned as such. By contrast, markets as instruments of coordinating production and distribution were facing heavy criticism from both the left and the right in the 1940s and 1950s.[59] The ability of markets to, for example, increase living standards, or to do so in a balanced and stable fashion, was hardly taken for granted at that point in history. This meant that both the left and the right (if they did not oppose market-based organization as a matter of principle) supported a market-based organization of the economy only if it was structured in such a way that it would actually further society's goals. Such conditionality of support for a market-based organization of the economy found expression, for example, in the discussion on inequality, which was termed the 'social question'.[60] In the 1940s and 1950s, the 'social question' was a central concern for policymakers of all colours. The inability of the European countries to ensure a minimum of balanced distribution of income in the first half of the twentieth century was seen as an important cause for the rise of authoritarian regimes in the 1920s and 1930s.[61] After WWII, it was acknowledged that the future success of polities based on democratic representation would depend on their ability to ensure (at least a minimum of) equity. Moreover, the economic and (non-left) political elite was alarmed by the possibility of a left revolution or communist takeover, so that the 'social question' could no longer be safely ignored even by those who had no genuine interest in equitable

[58] Paul Kapteyn and Pieter verLoren van Themaat, *Introduction to the Law of the European Communities* (Sweet & Maxwell, 1973) 49.

[59] For an extensive discussion see for example Joseph Schumpeter, *Capitalism, Socialism, and Democracy* (Harper Colophon Books, 1975) 59–163.

[60] Röpke (n 30), 322.

[61] Alan Milward, *The European Rescue of the Nation-state* (Routledge, 2000) 26.

distribution. Michael Heilperin, a liberalist who was initially critical of the EEC, justified his conversion to European integration the following way:

> Only if European capitalism can become socially acceptable, i.e., be regarded by the man in the street as the economic system which serves European masses best, will communism really be defeated in those western European countries where, as in Italy and France, it continues to keep large sectors of the population spellbound.[62]

Ordoliberals voiced similar thoughts: for example, von der Groeben argued that a 'liberal order will prevail only if it is perceived as just'.[63] As ordoliberals saw markets as moral institutions in the sense that they provided the framework within which individuals could exercise their freedom,[64] and as a satisfactory solution to the 'social question' was believed to be a precondition to their continued existence, they deemed the raising of living standards to be a central political issue.[65] Beyond such political calculations, inequality was also commonly understood to undermine the functioning of the system in purely economic terms. James Meade, for example, argued that inequality made the pricing system inefficient, so that the preservation of its function necessitated of taking 'the radical measures to ensure a tolerably equitable distribution of income and property'.[66] The importance of equitable distribution for the functioning of the economy was equally emphasized by ordoliberal scholars such as Walter Eucken or Wilhelm Röpke.[67] These authors did not support just any market-based form of organization, but only those which had a specific quality, namely that of increasing living standards in an equitable way. Eucken emphasized, for example, that the question of equitable distribution should not be separated from issues of general economic policy.[68] It is in this historical context that the characterization of the common market as one of two

[62] Michael Heilperin, 'European Integration: Commercial and Financial Postulates' in Grove Haines (ed), *European Integration* (Johns Hopkins Press, 1957) 129.

[63] Hans von der Groeben, 'Die Bedeutung der EWG für Europa', in Hans von der Groeben (ed), *Europa—Plan und Wirklichkeit* (Nomos, 1967) 33; see also Böhm, who criticized the 'classic' liberal claim that a society free of state intervention would automatically develop a harmonious economic system. Böhm predicted that a 'laissez-faire, laissez-aller' system would create adverse social effects, which in turn would lead to a political backlash against liberalism. Franz Böhm, 'Die Idee des ORDO im Denken Walter Euckens: Dem Freunde und Mitherausgeber zum Gedächtnis' [1950] *ORDO: Jahrbuch für die Ordnung von Wirtschaft und Gesellschaft* 15, 41–44.

[64] Hans von der Groeben, 'Vier Jahre Gemeinsamer Markt' in Hans von der Groeben (ed), *Europa—Plan und Wirklichkeit* (Nomos, 1967), 115. On the moral dimension of markets in ordoliberal thinking see for example Röpke (n 30), 42–44, 46, 214, 292, 306–07, 323; see also Böhm (n 63), 11; von der Groeben (n 63), 32.

[65] According to Lell, the Treaty of Rome was in agreement with the ordoliberal view because it 'combines the market principle and the social principle'. Hans-Joachim Lell, *Die soziale Harmonisierung in der Europäischen Wirtschaftsgemeinschaft und ihre wirtschaftlichen Auswirkungen* (Duncker & Humblot, 1966) 22.

[66] James Meade, *Planning and the price mechanism: the liberal-socialist solution* (Allen & Unwin, 1948) 35.

[67] Walter Eucken, *Grundsätze der Wirtschaftspolitik* (Mohr & Siebeck, 1952) 11–13, 140–41; Röpke (n 29), 277, 322.

[68] Eucken (n 67), 13.

means to achieve the Community's goals must be understood: the Treaty of Rome did not aim at the establishment of just any common market; rather, this common market was supposed to be one that furthered the Community's objectives, such as the raising of living standards.

This leads us to the second relationship of interest, namely that between the two means established by Article 2 EEC. Following Article 2 EEC, the approximation of the economic policies of the Member States is as important as market-making.[69] The drafters of the Treaty of Rome assumed that the Community's goals of increasingly stable, harmonious and balanced growth required an increasing level of coordination of the Member States' economic policies.[70] They believed that the beneficial effects of competition, set in motion through the increasing mobility of goods and factors of production, could unfold only if competitive conditions were normalized, and ensuing macroeconomic instabilities, such as trade imbalances, were properly managed.[71] In this sense the two goals of establishing a common market and of progressively approximating the economic policies of the Member States are intrinsically intertwined.[72] The specific quality of European integration may thus be defined by the dual goal of establishing a common market within a framework of approximated economic policies in order to achieve the Community's regulatory objectives.

Economic Union

The project pursued by the Treaty of Rome was frequently referred to as the creation of an 'economic union'.[73] The term describes a form of integration that relies on market-making in conjunction with harmonization to normalize productive conditions in order to achieve the Community's objectives. The 'economic union' that the EEC was supposed to become was often distinguished from more traditional forms of economic integration such as free trade areas or customs unions. European Commissioner Robert Marjolin wrote in 1957: '[t]he European Economic Community is more than a customs union; it is a real economic union, in which conditions of production and trade will be progressively equalized'.[74] The term was thus meant to emphasize the difference to integration projects based on traditional free trade thinking, which were much less far-reaching in their

[69] See for example EC, 'First General Report on the Activities of the Community (January 1958 to September 1958)' (1958) 12.

[70] See for example von der Groeben (n 6), in particular 129, 138–47.

[71] See for example Marjolin (n 29), 136; on the relation between market integration and macroeconomic coordination in the Treaty of Rome, see for example Kapteyn and verLoren van Themaat (n 58), 52–53.

[72] See von der Groeben (n 6), 128–29.

[73] See for example Hans von der Groeben, 'Die nächsten zehn Jahre' in Hans von der Groeben (ed), *Europa—Plan und Wirklichkeit* (Nomos, 1967), 155; the term 'economic union' is usually associated with the influential book by Bela Balassa, *The Theory of Economic Integration* (George Allen & Unwin Ltd, 1961).

[74] Marjolin (n 29), 132.

ambition. Inspired by the United States, the biggest and most successful single market at that time, the Treaty of Rome aimed at full factor mobility within a framework of normalized economic, social, and fiscal policies as well as coordinated macroeconomic policies, all of which would trigger 'dynamic' gains from trade.[75] These 'dynamic' gains that were expected from the formation of an 'economic union' stood in contrast with the merely 'static' gains that were promised by traditional trade theory. We will further discuss the concepts of 'static' and 'dynamic' gains in a later section. The underlying idea of the Treaty of Rome—expressed in the concept of the 'economic union'—was that economic integration required an institutional framework that would enable full market integration, the harmonization of competitive conditions, and the coordination of economic policies among the Member States.

The ambition to trigger dynamic growth effects through market integration within harmonized regulatory conditions set the Treaty of Rome apart from competing integration projects pursued at the same time, most notably the project for a free trade area put forward by the UK.[76] The project was initially proposed by the UK to derail negotiations for the Treaty of Rome, and ultimately led to the creation of the European Free Trade Association (EFTA).[77] The EFTA was presumably based on arguments derived from traditional free trade theory (though the UK planned to uphold the preference system within the Commonwealth,[78] which was hardly reconcilable with the free trade vocabulary employed).[79] It aimed at the liberalization of trade in industrial goods alone, and did not provide for the harmonization of regulation among the Member States, with the exception of a very general prohibition of restrictive practices liable to frustrate the provisions of the EFTA Convention.[80] An alternative view that illustrates the specific character of the EEC was the position of Ludwig Erhard, who opposed the formation of the EEC and supported the British project instead.[81] Erhard preferred to pursue tariff reductions without the establishment of a customs union, without free factor movement, without a regulatory integration of the national economies into a common market, and without a strong institutional framework.[82]

[75] Milward (n 61), 108; see also von der Groeben (n 73), 155; Myrdal (n 26), 60.

[76] Küsters (n 50), 280–94.

[77] George Schopflin, 'EFTA: The Other Europe' (1964) 40 *International Affairs* 674, 674–75.

[78] Küsters (n 50), 165–66, 283; many authors proposed that the British opposition should not be read in terms of conflicting intellectual concepts alone. Rather, the UK pursued specific national interests, most notably upholding the commonwealth preference system, for which EFTA provided a better framework. For this argument see for example Hans von der Groeben, *Aufbaujahre der Europäischen Gemeinschaft. Das Ringen um den Gemeinsamen Markt und die Politische Union (1958–1966)* (Nomos, 1982) 63–64.

[79] On the economic rationale of the seven Member States which joined the EFTA, see Miriam Camps, *Britain and the European Community* (Princeton University Press, 1964) 219–20; on the EFTA's self-presentation within the intellectual context of free trade, see ibid, 228.

[80] Schopflin (n 77), 682.

[81] Camps (n 79), 116–17; see also Küsters (n 50), 287; on Ludwig Erhard's view on integration see 80–82.

[82] See Küsters (n 50), 79–86, 142–44.

In contrast to such views, the Treaty of Rome envisaged the abolition of tariffs and quantitative restrictions within a context of normalized conditions that would ensure 'undistorted' competition. Trade under unharmonized competitive conditions is always liable to arise on the basis of competitive advantages deriving from regulatory differences alone. The competition that the drafters of the Treaty of Rome sought, however, was one that pushed producers to do as best as they could on a level field that was not distorted by regulatory differences.[83] Producers should be successful not because they were subject to relatively more beneficial regulatory conditions than their competitors, but because they tried harder to succeed. The goals of the EEC of establishing 'a common market with conditions similar to an internal market', including the mobility of productive factors, competition law and sufficient and balanced growth could not be pursued through the classical means of international trade alone—namely the abolition of tariffs and quantitative restrictions.[84] Beyond that, given the extensive regulatory differences in the Member States, the liberalization of trade in sectors like services or agriculture—excluded from other free trade projects such as the EFTA—depended on a harmonized regulatory basis.[85] Harmonization was thus not merely a facilitator, but a precondition to market integration in those sectors. The Treaty of Rome must therefore be conceptualized as a qualitatively distinct project from other forms of economic integration, which has been described as 'economic union'. It was characterized by the ambition to integrate the European markets in all sectors on the basis of harmonized competitive conditions, which was supposed to help achieve the Community's regulatory goals.

THE COMMON MARKET WITHIN AN 'ECONOMIC UNION'

In this section we take a closer look at the economic debate that informed the creation of one of the Treaty's central projects, the establishment of a common market among the six Member States. It will be shown that the EEC was established in a phase when very diverse views on economic integration were discussed among policymakers and scholars, which all shaped the Treaty of Rome to different degrees. The traditional understanding of economic relations between states had been informed by what is often called 'orthodox' or 'standard' trade theory, which draws from Ricardo's concept of 'comparative advantage'. The central concern of orthodox trade theory was to show that tariffs and quantitative restrictions distorted trade flows, and thereby prevented the optimum division of labour between trading countries. After the war, orthodox trade theory provided

[83] Along these lines see for example von der Groeben (n 63), 23; see also von der Groeben (n 57), 100.

[84] Von der Groeben (n 63), 22, 63.

[85] Camps (n 79), 117.

the intellectual backbone of early trade liberalization. However, the negotiations on the Treaty of Rome took place against the background of a shifting economic debate, which put increasing emphasis on the issue of economic growth. Economists and policymakers became concerned with the preconditions of economic growth, on which orthodox economic theory had little to say.[86] In post-war debate, growth was increasingly conceptualized as a 'dynamic' process based on innovation and change, while the analytical framework of orthodox trade theory was seen as 'static', as it dealt with the optimal distribution of a given set of resources and knowledge. This paradigm shift deeply affected the policy debate on European integration. On the following pages, we will look at the 'static' and the 'dynamic' view on economic integration, and discuss their significance for the interpretation of the Treaty. In a later chapter, we will take a more detailed look at competing economic views on growth and trade.

'Static' Gains from Integration

Orthodox trade theory postulates that, under conditions of free trade, production is divided in an optimal form between the trading countries.[87] Tariffs and quantitative restrictions distort this system, as they (in the case of tariffs) increase the price of goods from abroad or (in the case of quantitative restrictions) restrict or prohibit the acquisition of goods from abroad altogether. If tariffs and quantitative restrictions are reduced or abolished, this allows buying from cheaper sources abroad, which means that the same output is achieved with less input. From a perspective of orthodox trade theory, the reduction of tariffs and quantitative restrictions is always welfare-enhancing, and global free trade is the optimal solution. Orthodox trade theory provided the intellectual underpinning for the post-war project of global trade liberalization, most notably for the GATT. By contrast, the case for regional economic integration as pursued by organizations such as the OEEC and later the EEC was far more ambivalent. From the viewpoint of orthodox trade theory, regional trade integration projects were not necessarily beneficial, and were therefore disapproved of by free trade oriented economists.[88] The reason was that if tariffs were reduced only between the Member States of a customs union, but remained in place in relation with third countries, inefficient trade distortions might occur. This problem was first raised by Jacob Viner, who showed that customs unions might have both negative as well as positive welfare effects.[89]

[86] See for example Solow, who argued that '[g]rowth theory, like much else in macroeconomics, was a product of the depression of the 1930s and of the war that finally ended it'. Robert Solow, 'Growth theory and after' (1988) 78 *American Economic Review* 307, 308.

[87] For a traditional treatment of the gains from the division of labour, see for example Röpke (n 30), 66–69, 226–31.

[88] Milward (n 61), 107.

[89] Jacob Viner, *The Customs Union Issue* (Carnegie Endowment for International Peace, 1950) 43–45.

Depending on the circumstances, customs unions could be either 'trade-creating' or 'trade-diverting': trade creation occurs if national commodities are replaced by cheaper ones from a partner country, whereas trade diversion takes place if cheaper imports from third countries are replaced by more expensive commodities from a partner country for the sole reason that the latter benefit from lower tariffs. Customs union would therefore have the effect of replacing more efficient with less efficient production.[90] Because these effects depend on the specific circumstances, no prima facie judgment on the net welfare effects of regional integration was possible in Viner's view.[91] This ambivalent assessment of regional integration was shared by most orthodox scholars at that time.[92] Whether a customs union had positive or negative effects was believed to depend on a variety of factors, for example whether the participating countries had 'complementary' or 'competitive' economies.[93] Viner's claim was discussed very controversially, and various scholars attempted to qualify his findings: Lipsey, for example, tried to show that trade diversion may still have welfare-enhancing effects under certain conditions.[94] Ultimately, orthodox trade theory did not overcome Viner's initial verdict that regional economic integration, depending on the circumstances, could be either welfare-enhancing or welfare-reducing.[95] According to a later commentator, there was, however, 'a bias in the theoretical literature that at least one of the participating countries gains, the customs union as a whole gains and a third country is adversely affected'.[96] This meant that followers of orthodox trade theory could not and did not approve of regional trade integration on its

[90] However, some scholars in fact approved of replacing global with European trade. According to Tibor Scitovsky, increasing intra-European trade would make the coordination of national employment policies possible, which would in turn allow full employment without the risk of balance of payments difficulties. Tibor Scitovsky, *Economic theory and Western European integration* (Allen & Unwin, 1958) 17–18.

[91] Viner argued that '[c]ustoms unions are, from the free-trade point of view, neither necessarily good nor necessarily bad; the circumstances … are the determining factors'. Viner (n 89), 44, 52; see also Bela Balassa, 'Trade Creation and Trade Diversion in the European Common Market: An appraisal of the evidence' (1974) 42 *The Manchester School* 93, 1.

[92] See Balassa (n 73), 29; Michael Heilperin, 'Freer Trade and Social Welfare: Some Marginal Comments on the Ohlin report' (1957) 75 *International Labour Review* 173, 180; see also Milward (n 61), 107ff with further references.

[93] See generally Balassa (n 73), 33–35; Lipsey believed that customs unions between complementary economies were problematic, whereas Makower and Morton argued that they were beneficial. Richard Lipsey, 'The Theory of Customs Unions: A General Survey' (1960) 70 *Economic Journal* 496, 498; H Makower and G Morton, 'A Contribution Towards a Theory of Customs Unions' (1953) 63 *Economic Journal* 33.

[94] Lipsey argued that trade may lead to changes in consumption patterns (if substitution between commodities is assumed), which may result in overall welfare gains. Lipsey (n 93), 499ff; Corden attempted to model (internal) economies of scale within the framework of orthodox trade theory. Warner Corden, 'Economies of Scale and Customs Union Theory' (1972) 80 *Journal of Political Economy* 465.

[95] Melvyn Krauss, 'Recent Developments in Customs Union Theory: An Interpretive Survey' (1972) 10 *Journal of Economic Literature* 413, 417.

[96] W Haack, 'The Selectivity of Economic Integration Theories: A Comparison of Some Traditional and Marxist Approaches' (1983) 21 *Journal of Common Market Studies* 365, 368.

economic merits alone. If certain orthodox trade scholars nonetheless supported regional integration it was solely on the basis of the political assumption that it would constitute a step towards global trade liberalization.[97] From this perspective, regional tariff reductions might pave the way for future trade deals on a global level. This diagnosis, however, was based on a political expectation only, and was not shared by all scholars. Jacob Viner, for example, believed that customs unions would 'almost inevitably operate as a psychological barrier to the realization of the more desirable but less desired objectives of the Havana Charter—the balanced multilateral reduction of trade barriers on a non-discriminatory basis'.[98] This view found expression in the phrase that customs unions are always only 'second best' as compared to global free trade.[99] Only if free trade could not be achieved on a global level would regional integration constitute an acceptable alternative.[100] The ambivalence of orthodox trade theory towards regional integration also shaped the legal framework of the GATT. The GATT is based on the most-favoured nation principle (Article I GATT): advantages conceded to one trading partner must be granted immediately and unconditionally to all other Member States as well. Regional trade organizations like the EEC, however, grant benefits to members of their free trade or customs union that they do not grant to other GATT members, thereby applying discriminatory distinctions. Although Article XXIV.5 GATT allows for regional integration in the form of customs unions and free trade agreements, the provision was controversial.[101] While some believed that customs unions constituted a step towards broader trade liberalization, others disagreed, arguing that regional trade integration (which necessarily created discriminatory distinctions) contravened the spirit of the GATT.[102] Accordingly, orthodox trade scholars were initially critical about the EEC, as they feared that European trade integration would re-establish those barriers to global trade that the GATT sought to dismantle.[103] Studies conducted in the first years after the foundation of the EEC indeed found a significant change in trade patterns, towards increased

[97] Balassa (n 73), 35; Krauss (n 95) 413; Viner (n 89), 51; Lipsey (n 93), 497; Röpke (n 30), 79–80; see also Paul Wonnacott and Ronald Wonnacott, 'Is Unilateral Tariff Reduction Preferable to a Customs Union? The Curious Case of the Missing Foreign Tariffs' (1981) 71 *American Economic Review* 704, 704.

[98] Viner (n 89), 139.

[99] Richard Lipsey and Kelvin Lancaster, 'The General Theory of Second Best' (1956) 24 *Review of Economic Studies* 11, 13–14.

[100] See for example Röpke (n 30), 79–80.

[101] For a critical assessment see for example Viner (n 89), 120–27; see also Jacob Viner, 'Economic Foundations of International Organization' in Jacob Viner (ed), *International Economics* (The Free Press, 1951) 380; Majone (n 9), 157–58.

[102] See Kenneth Dam, *The GATT. Law and International Economic Organization* (University of Chicago Press, 1970) 274.

[103] Such ambivalence generally characterized the assessment of the EEC in the 1950s and 1960s. See for example Montgomery, who argued in 1965: 'Economists have always equivocated in their evaluation of the potential economic effects of the establishment of the European Economic Community (EEC). Beginning in 1950 with simultaneous writings on the subject by Maurice Bye, Herbert Giersch, and Jacob Viner, a body of literature has developed which recognizes that from a world viewpoint as

intra-European trade. However, they disagreed whether this phenomenon was caused by trade creation or trade diversion.[104] Whereas Lamfalussy argued that the evidence was not clear for assuming either trade-creating or trade-diverting effects, Balassa concluded that the overall effect was trade creation.[105]

By the late 1950s, however, a new generation of economists had started to question the relevance of the insights provided by orthodox trade theory.[106] This is illustrated for example by an article by Cooper and Massell, which showed that orthodox free trade theory had little explanatory value when it came to regional economic integration.[107] They held that under the assumptions of orthodox trade theory, customs unions would always constitute a sub-optimal choice. They argued that unilateral tariff reductions would always be more beneficial than the formation of a customs union, as they achieve all the possible benefits of a customs union (ie, tariff reduction) without its adverse effects (ie, trade diversion).[108] Cooper and Massell concluded that regional integration could thus never be justified on the basis of orthodox trade theory alone, so that alternative explanations had to be sought as to why states nonetheless engaged in regional economic integration projects. Moreover, a growing number of studies indicated that 'static' gains from integration—ie, those conceptualized on the basis of orthodox trade

well as from the outlook of the participants, an economic union has potential both for adding to and for lessening economic welfare.' Sarah Montgomery, 'The Potential Economic Effects of the European Economic Community' (1965) 6 *Boston College Law Review* 425.

[104] Balassa (n 91), 1.

[105] ibid, 2 and 15.

[106] See Bertil Ohlin et al, 'Social Aspects of European Economic Cooperation (Ohlin-Report, Summary)' (1956) 74 *International Labour Review* 99, 102. See also CA Cooper and BF Massell, 'A New Look at Customs Union Theory' (1965) 75 *Economic Journal* 742, 747; Scitovsky (n 90), 10; Jacob Viner, 'Conflicts of Principle in Drafting a Trade Charter' in Jacob Viner, (ed), *International Economics* (The Free Press, 1951), 352; For an example of the use of the framework of static and dynamic gains in literature on the EEC see Donald McLachlan and Dennis Swann, *Competition policy in the European Community: the rules in theory and practice* (Oxford University Press, 1967) 4–15.

[107] Cooper and Massell argued that '[w]hether a customs union is on balance beneficial (compared with the initial non-preferential tariff) will depend on whether the tariff-reduction effect outweighs the pure trade diversion effect. But this result implies that a customs union is necessarily inferior to an appropriate policy of non-preferential protection. Even without the option of forming a customs union, the home country already has the option of lowering its initial tariff and thereby reaping the beneficial effects that a customs unions would provide without the offsetting costs. Moreover, because a customs union is always purely trade-diverting compared with the best non-preferential tariffs, then the theory of second-best is not helpful in evaluating the welfare effects of the customs union per se; second-best theory is relevant only for evaluating the welfare effect of the tariff reduction component.' Cooper and Massell (n 106), 745f.

[108] ibid, 745; A critique of Cooper and Massell's argument can be found in Wonnacott and Wonnacott (n 97), 705. Petersmann explains that, even though unilateral trade liberalization would be beneficial, governments cannot engage in it because of the presence of a prisoners' dilemma and a 'protectionist trap', in which the general interests of consumers and taxpayers have no strong political representation, unlike those of specific interest groups. The opposition to free trade can be overcome only if reciprocal rights to market entry are secured for the exporting industry. Ernst-Ulrich Petersmann, 'Grundprobleme der Wirtschaftsverfassung der EG' (1994) 48 *Aussenwirtschaft* 389, 393–94.

theory—were a relatively insignificant aspect of regional economic integration. Tariffs constituted only a fraction of overall production costs, so that the direct gains from tariff reductions would not be very high in practice.[109] In reviewing a number of studies that had attempted to quantify the potential gains from free trade, Leibenstein concluded that realistic efficiency gains were a one-time effect of 1 per cent or less of the GDP (most of the reviewed studies estimated the potential gains at no more than 0.1 per cent).[110]

Economists of the 1950s had become interested in the topic of economic growth, which was understood as a complex, dynamic phenomenon. Consequently, the issue of economic integration was increasingly looked at from such a perspective as well, and the discussion turned to the so-called 'dynamic' effects of integration, ie, the effects that integration would have on growth. While 'static' gains from trade, as conceptualized by orthodox trade theory, remained an important narrative in support of trade and economic integration—Mundell argued in 1960 that the 'English classical model of foreign trade ... still survives as a basic tool of analysis'[111]—it was no longer believed to provide a sufficient understanding of the central economic issues of the day. Pinder, who reviewed the economic literature on European integration in the late 1960s, found that the majority of scholars held 'static' effects of integration to be mostly irrelevant, while 'dynamic' effects were believed to be of central importance.[112] Scitovsky, for example, argued that '[t]he free trader's stock argument, the beneficial reallocation of production between countries resulting from the freeing of trade, turns out to be of little significance in the case of Western Europe; and the main results of integration are shown to be various consequences of the increase of competition which the common market is almost certain to bring about'.[113]

'Dynamic' Gains from Integration

After the war, the United States was the most productive, most innovative and socially most advanced economy in the world. It became the role model for all efforts of economic development, and in particular for European economic integration.[114] One central advantage of the United States, it was believed, was the

[109] Alfred Müller-Armack, *Wirtschaftsordnung und Wirtschaftspolitik* (Verlag Rombach, 1966) 326.

[110] Harvey Leibenstein, 'Allocative Efficiency vs "X-Efficiency"' (1966) 56 *American Economic Review* 392–97.

[111] Robert Mundell, 'The Pure Theory of International Trade' (1960) 50 *American Economic Review* 67.

[112] Pinder (n 10), 93 and 95.

[113] Scitovsky (n 90), 10.

[114] See for example Paul-Henri Spaak et al, *Rapport des Chefs de Délégation aux Ministres des Affaires Etrangères* (Spaak-Report) (1956), 9; see also Küsters (n 50), 239; von der Groeben (n 73), 155.

massive size of its internal market.[115] It was speculated that increased market size would trigger 'dynamic' effects, such as increased innovation through competition and scale effects, which would have a positive long-term impact on the growth rate.[116] If the European economies wanted to catch up with the United States, it was believed, they had to emulate its internal market. However, such 'dynamic' effects of economic integration could not be easily reconciled with orthodox economic theory, which was concerned with the optimal allocation of a given set of resources. Accordingly, 'dynamic' effects of economic integration were either ignored or rejected by orthodox trade theory.[117] Viner and Meade, for example, dismissed the idea of 'dynamic' effects of integration, doubting, inter alia, the possibility that European integration could trigger beneficial scale effects.[118] In the mid-1950s, however, the issue of dynamic integration effects moved into the focus of economists, inspired by the growing interest in the process of economic growth.[119] Bela Balassa, who wrote an influential book on economic integration, commented: 'To the majority of observers … the liberalist ideal of integration is a relic from the past, and its application to the present-day economic life appears rather anachronistic'.[120] Orthodox trade theory, Balassa concluded, was unhelpful in conceptualizing the multiple and complex effects of economic integration on economic growth.[121] And in 1957 a study on the impacts of the common market on global trade published by the GATT dismissed the concerns of orthodox trade theorists about potential adverse effects of European integration. The study argued that in times of expanding trade, dynamic changes in trade volume would leave potential trade-diverting effects of regional integration projects such as the EEC largely irrelevant.[122] Robert Marjolin similarly claimed in an article from 1957 that the 'dynamic' growth effects of economic integration would surely outweigh the trade-diverting effects of the EEC for third countries.[123]

The increasing importance of 'dynamic' arguments is readily identifiable in both the Spaak and the Ohlin Reports, which were written in preparation of the negotiations over the Treaty of Rome. The Ohlin Report argued that 'the case for freer international trade as presented on the basis of orthodox classical theories is not quite adequate'.[124] Similarly, the Spaak Report rebuffed the core assumption

[115] Hans von der Groeben, 'Nationalstaat und Europäische Gemeinschaft im Lichte sozialen Wandels' in Hans von der Groeben (ed), *Europa—Plan und Wirklichkeit* (Nomos, 1967), 81–82.

[116] Mordechai Kreinin, 'On the dynamic effects of a customs union' (1964) 72 *Journal of Political Economy* 193.

[117] Balassa (n 73), 103ff.

[118] See ibid, 106, with further references.

[119] ibid, Intro, ix, and 103; see also Müller-Armack (n 109), 334.

[120] Balassa (n 73), 8–9; see also Scitovsky (n 90), 10; Milward (n 61), 108.

[121] Balassa (n 73), Intro, ix, and 8; see also Scitovsky (n 90), 10.

[122] GATT, *The Possible Impact of the European Economic Community, in Particular, the Common Market, upon World Trade* (Trade Intelligence Papers No 6, Geneva, 1957), quoted in Mordechai Kreinin, 'On the "Trade-Diversion" Effect of Trade-Preference Areas' (1959) 67 *Journal of Political Economy* 398.

[123] Marjolin (n 29), 139–40.

[124] Ohlin et al (n 106), 102.

of orthodox trade theory, arguing that '[i]n an expanding economy, the division of labour finds expression not so much in a replacement of existing production, but rather in a much faster development of the most efficient forms of production'.[125] The 'dynamic' benefits of economic integration that were at the centre of the policymakers' considerations included phenomena such as internal and external economies of scale, increased competition, lessening of uncertainty in inner-European trade, faster rate of technological change, and changes in the investment patterns.[126] In the following, we will take a closer look at some of these 'dynamic' effects.

Internal and External Economies of Scale

The concept of 'economies of scale' describes gains in productivity through additional output, or, in other words, increased returns from size.[127] If the marginal costs of production fall (meaning that every additional good costs less in production), products become cheaper if more are produced. 'Internal' economies of scale are increased returns to size that can be accrued by a single company (eg by building larger factories). 'External' economies of scale describe returns to size that are accrued by an industry or region as a whole.[128] Because size matters in this scenario, assuming internal economies of scale requires abandoning the idea of perfect competition (ie, that no market participant has enough market power to unilaterally influence the price of a product[129]), a core assumption in orthodox economic theory.[130] Scale effects were among the most frequently

[125] Spaak et al (n 114), 13 (my translation). The original text reads: 'Dans une économie en expansion, cette division du travail s'exprime moins par un déplacement des productions existantes que par un développement d'autant plus rapide, dans intérêt commun, des productions les plus economiques.'

[126] Balassa (n 73), 5–6; Franz Gehrels and Bruce Johnston, 'The Economic Gains of European Integration' (1955) 63 *Journal of Political Economy* 275, 281.

[127] Standard economic theory assumes constant or diminishing returns to scale, which for example Joan Robinson defined as follows: 'The concept of constant returns to scale, in the technical sense, means that each physical input required for a given output—man-hours of labor of specific skill and energy, machines of specific types, materials, sites, and so forth—can be regarded as homogeneous within itself, and that a given proportionate increase in each input will bring about an equal proportionate increase in output. Diminishing returns arise from the fact that some inputs, in particular those that are given by nature, cannot be increased at will. To produce a certain proportionate increase in output then requires a more than proportionate increase in *other* factors.' By contrast, increasing returns to scale are described as follows: '[T]he economies of large-scale production which give rise to increasing returns operate by changing the nature of the inputs. Output per man-hour grows as work becomes more specialized; equipment can be designed to produce a larger output at lower cost, larger supplies of materials can be more finely graded, and so forth. It is not a question of the proportions in which given physical inputs are used but rather a question of the specification of the inputs themselves.' Joan Robinson, *Economic heresies* (Basic Books, 1971) 52–53.

[128] On the development of external economies of scale in the EEC see for example Zijlstra (n 7), 40.

[129] See for example Eucken (n 67), 33.

[130] Corden (n 94), 465; the contradiction between the objective of realizing economies of scale and competition is addressed, for example, by Franz Böhm, 'Das Janusgesicht der Konzentration' in Franz Böhm (ed), *Freiheit und Ordnung in der Marktwirtschaft* (Nomos, 1980) 214; see also the author's

employed arguments in favour of European economic integration.[131] In an article from 1955, Gehrels and Johnston described the potential of internal and external economies in a single European market as follows:

> The process of reducing costs would, in all probability, be greatly accelerated by the creation of a single market of 160 million … By encouraging an increase in the size of individual plants as well as a concentration of industries in particular areas, the single market would permit the realization of both internal and external economies of scale. Larger plants could achieve better internal division of labor, and there would be greater scope for mass-production techniques utilizing specialized capital equipment. The external gains would result from the development of needed supplier industries in close proximity; from the improvement of transportation and handling services as increased traffic justifies investment in better facilities; and from the development of a plentiful supply of labor competent in the operations of the particular industry.[132]

Economists became concerned, for example, with questions such as the 'optimum plant size'. The idea—assuming economies of scale—was that mass production created the greatest benefits if large quantities were produced. Economists who compared the United States and the European economies found that the quantities produced per plant were often very different. Balassa showed, for example, that an average US plant produced 700,000 refrigerators, whereas a European plant produced only 65,000.[133] A similar disparity was found in many other industries, including automobiles, steel and synthetic fabrics.[134] It was believed that the larger US market could accommodate multiple production plants that could all run at optimum output levels, so that scale effects could be accrued while competition was maintained. In comparison, the plants located in the fragmented European markets all ran at sub-optimal production levels. In a unified European market, it was hoped, producers could attain optimum production levels by producing larger quantities in fewer facilities.[135] Achieving economies of scale was one of the primary goals of the policymakers of 1957.[136] The Spaak Report lamented, for

critical stance against large-scale company fusions in Franz Böhm, 'Die Kapitalgesellschaft als Instrument der Unternehmenszusammenfassung' in Franz Böhm (ed), *Freiheit und Ordnung in der Marktwirtschaft* (Nomos, 1980) 295; see also Ernst-Joachim Mestmäcker, *Europäisches Wettbewerbsrecht* (Beck'sche Verlagsbuchhandlung, 1974) 81–83. According to Mestmäcker, company size has come to be understood as synonymous with economic and political power. Accordingly, mergers among European companies were sought so that they could match their American counterparts in size. The Commission, Mestmäcker argued, had largely supported this concentration effort. Mestmäcker argued, however, that the question of whether these concentrations actually fostered greater productivity had largely been ignored.

[131] See for example Scitovsky (n 90), 24–26; Zijlstra (n 7), 40.

[132] Gehrels and Johnston (n 126), 283.

[133] Balassa (n 73), 131.

[134] Scitovsky (n 90), 25, fn 1; Balassa (n 73), 131.

[135] André Philip, 'Social Aspects of European Economic Cooperation' (1957) 76 *International Labour Review* 244, 246.

[136] See for example Robert Looper, 'The Significance of Regional Market Arrangements' (1959) *University of Illinois Law Forum* 364, 367.

example, that no European company was large enough to efficiently employ high-end production methods comparable to those employed by US automakers.[137] The fragmented character of European industry made it impossible, the report went on, to produce large airplanes, or to make efficient use of nuclear energy.[138] As we will see below, some 30 years later the Delors Commission similarly emphasized scale effects when advocating further market integration.

A central factor for accruing economies of scale is the trust of producers in the long-term existence and stability of the common market.[139] Only if investors were confident in the political commitment of the original six Member States to the continued existence of the European market would they invest in large-scale production of a European dimension. A relatively stable system of exchange rates was considered to be important in that regard: with fluctuating exchange rates, producers treat national markets as distinct, and may not adopt Community-sized production. Moreover, large-scale production required a certain approximation of production standards, so that goods could be sold across the Community. As quantitative restrictions prevented the concentration of production, their abolition was another central requirement for the attainment of conditions within which economies of scale could be realized. By contrast, measures that merely raised the cost of production or of trade—including tariffs, but also certain non-tariff barriers—would not hinder the realization of economies of scale as long as the productivity gains from increased production surpassed the costs created by these measures. Regulatory differences between the Member States that merely affected the cost structure, but did not restrict intra-Community trade as such, therefore did not constitute restrictions to the establishment of economies of scale. In fact, economies of scale may be one of the main reasons why production is often not located in areas where the factor costs—eg labour costs—are lowest. Industries such as the chemical industry in the Ruhrgebiet or the pharmaceutical industry in Basel are located in high-wage countries such as Germany or Switzerland because the gains from scale that can be accrued in these regions surmount the potential gains from locating production in areas where factor prices are lower.[140] It can already be seen that a common market that aims at fostering 'dynamic' gains such as economies of scale has different regulatory preconditions than a common market that aims at the realization of 'static' efficiencies alone: whereas the latter requires only the abolition of tariffs and quantitative restrictions, the former must take a far broader spectrum of regulatory concerns into account.

[137] Spaak et al (n 114), 9.

[138] See also von der Groeben (n 63), 63.

[139] Von der Groeben (n 73), 155–56.

[140] As already mentioned, however, the belief in economies of scale was not shared by all economists alike. For example, Jacob Viner and Harry Johnson doubted their existence. Johnson argued in 1957 that 'the economies of scale expected to be achieved … may be largely illusory'. See Harry Johnson, 'The Criteria of Economic Advantage' (1957) 19 *Bulletin of the Oxford University Institute of Economics & Statistics* 33, 35.

Competition

The founders of the EEC expected that increased competition among producers would force companies to permanently invest, to develop new technologies and production methods and to increase the quality of their products. Competition, the Spaak Report held, would help replace antiquated production methods that kept prices high and salaries low, and would prevent collusion among producers.[141] The beneficial effects of increased competition were largely ignored by scholars working in the orthodox tradition, as orthodox theory assumed efficient deployment of available resources by the market.[142] In particular, orthodox economic theory ignored how firms adopt and apply modern production and management techniques. By contrast, a newer generation of economists believed that European-wide competition had to put competitive pressure on producers to learn and to adopt new knowledge.[143] Gehrels and Johnson described the potential beneficial effects of competition as follows:

> As a result of integration, producers in each country would be exposed to increased competition and would become more fully aware of techniques and products available in neighboring countries. The less efficient producers, both in industry and in agriculture, would be under greater pressure to employ such techniques and to adopt product changes than is now the case in the smaller national markets.[144]

Moreover, European-wide competition would put pressure on widespread oligopolistic behaviour:

> The wider market would increase the number of oligopolists competing on a common basis and would weaken industry discipline. It would thereby increase the likelihood of aggressive firms seeking to increase their sales through lowering prices and costs and tapping new classes of consumers. These possibilities seem especially promising in the mass-production industries, where important further economies of scale could be realized.[145]

Lipsey described the expectations connected to increased competition as follows:

> Business firms may not be adopting methods known to be technically more efficient than those now in use due to inertia, a dislike of risk-taking, a willingness to be content

[141] The Spaak Report held: 'Dans un marché plus vaste, il n'est plus possible d'organiser le maintien de modes d'exploitation vieillis qui déterminent à la fois des prix élevés et des salaires bas; et les entreprises, au lieu de préserver des positions immobiles, sont soumises à une pression permanente pour investir, en vue de développer la production, d'améliorer la qualité et de moderniser l'exploitation: il leur faut progresser pour se maintenir. Ces avantages d'un marché commun ne peuvent cependant être obtenus que si des délais sont accordés et des moyens collectivement dégagés pour permettre les adaptations nécessaires, s'il est mis fin aux pratiques par lesquelles la concurrence est faussée entre les producteurs, et s'il s'établit une coopération des Etats pour assurer la stabilité monétaire, l'expansion économique et le progrès social'. Spaak et al (n 114), 14.

[142] Lipsey (n 93), 496; Gehrels and Johnston (n 126), 282.

[143] Scitovsky (n 90), 10.

[144] Gehrels and Johnston (n 126), 282–83.

[145] ibid, 283.

> sensitivity and lead to investment, expansion of capacity, and other structural changes which would otherwise seem to risky.[157]

Beyond that, it was believed that economic integration would have a positive impact on growth only if it actually led to investment in more innovative and cost-efficient production. Standard theory implies that the reallocation of resources is usually welfare-enhancing: if a producer relocates production to a location with lower costs, both the producer and the economy as a whole benefit from lower prices. This, however, is no longer the case if the gains are not passed on to the consumers because of insufficient competitive pressure, or because the producer relocates not to access cheaper productive factors, but to make use of lower taxes and social costs. In this situation the European polity as a whole does not benefit, as the relocation does not realize productive efficiencies, but merely exploits differences in taxation and social regulation. The Ohlin Report raised this issue in the following way:

> [A]ttention is also drawn to the possibility that differences in national social policies might give rise to international capital movements for which there would be no real economic justification, particularly if some countries went further or were more successful than others in redistributing their national incomes and if in consequence the rate of net profits after tax in the former group of countries were substantially lower than in the latter group ... It is difficult to judge how serious this problem is. Because of the shifting of incidence, rates of taxation on profits or social charges do not throw much light on the actual burden of taxation on net capital profits. Moreover, even if differences in national social policies do effectively influence the net yield of capital, it is not certain that any large volume of capital would move from one country to another for this reason alone.[158]

The Ohlin Report argued that the seriousness of capital movements that have 'no real economic justification' (from a social welfare perspective) was difficult to assess, partly because the overall tax burden was difficult to compare. The Report assumed, however, that capital movement for the reason of incurring advantages that stem solely from differences in taxation and social charges were relatively unlikely. This conclusion requires some contextualization: the Ohlin Report was devised at a time of legally and factually limited capital mobility.[159] It is on this basis that the experts concluded that capital movements for the sole reason of incurring benefits from differences in taxation and social regulation were likely to be of limited importance. Maurice Byé, one of the experts assigned to devise the Ohlin Report, advanced a different argument in his dissenting opinion that was attached to the Report.[160] Byé believed that there was a risk of regulatory competition between the Member States on the basis of different levels in social regulation,

[157] Gehrels and Johnston (n 126), 282.
[158] Ohlin et al (n 106), 121.
[159] ibid, 122.
[160] ibid, 121–23.

which created unfair advantages for producers from countries with lower wage and social standards.[161] The other experts who worked on the Report believed that—assuming continuing wage increases based on the productivity gains of each country, and assuming sufficient labour union power to realize them[162]—regulatory differences in the social field would generally not create unfair advantages.[163] By contrast, Byé held that harmonization of social legislation would be necessary, as otherwise 'the existence of economically unsound disparities imposed on the yield of capital by the legislation of different countries' would induce 'undesirable' (ie, unproductive) capital movements.[164] We will see later that the Commission took a view similar to that of Byé in its 1962 Action Programme. While the risk of capital movements that take advantage of regulatory differences but otherwise do not create productivity gains did not appear a realistic possibility to the majority of the experts of the Ohlin Commission, given the regulatory environment of that period, the discussion highlights that the experts did not take the positive effects of economic integration for granted. The possibility that producers could pursue rent-seeking (thus, socially unproductive) strategies was well-known. However, they assumed that the EEC's regulatory structure, most notably capital controls, would not create conditions so that such strategies could become prevalent. The dissent between Byé and his colleagues therefore illustrates the disagreement on the (structural) conditions necessary to realize the potential benefits of economic integration.

Normative Implications of the Debate on 'Static' and 'Dynamic' Gains from Integration

We have seen that the formation of the EEC was accompanied by a vivid debate on the benefits of economic integration. Orthodox trade theory provided the intellectual background for the trade liberalization projects that were initiated after the war. However, the case for regional integration remained ambivalent from its perspective, and this is why enthusiasm for the Treaty of Rome among many traditional scholars remained lukewarm at first. By contrast, a new generation of economists expected gains from integration that could be conceptualized only insufficiently in the language of orthodox trade theory. Inspired by the United States, it was assumed that regional integration would trigger economic growth in a 'dynamic' form by enabling the realization of economies of scale, increasing competition and changing investment patterns, thereby fostering innovation. The debate on 'static' and 'dynamic' gains from integration must be understood in the

[161] ibid, 122.
[162] ibid, 112.
[163] ibid, 103–13.
[164] ibid, 122.

context of the paradigm shift that took place in the debate among scholars and policymakers. They were increasingly interested in the topic of economic growth, which they understood as a complex and dynamic phenomenon.

The debate has certain implications for the interpretation of European economic law today. On a very general level, it can be argued that the EEC was shaped by a variety of economic perspectives, so that the Treaty of Rome may be best conceptualized as a pluralist instrument.[165] This raises the question of how such pluralism can be operationalized in, for example, internal market law doctrine. The 'static' view of the benefits of integration usually finds expression in a certain scepticism about all measures that constitute obstacles to trade and mobility. The assumption is that the realization of the benefits from trade mainly requires the elimination of trade barriers, which would then allow the most efficient allocation of resources. It has been shown, however, that many scholars believed that the immediate gains from increased allocative efficiency were limited, and that the beneficial effects of increased trade and factor mobility would in fact depend on its impact on growth. Yet the relation between trade and factor mobility on the one hand and growth on the other is indirect and not automatic. Most notably, the potential benefits of the common market can be realized only if investment patterns change, which requires (political) trust in the longevity of the Member States' commitment to the integration project.[166] Moreover, a central concern was to translate increased openness among the Member States into more competition and innovation so that the development of an oligopolistic and collusive environment on the European level would be prevented. This 'dynamic' view of the benefits from integration implies that the positive effects of trade and factor mobility are not automatic, and instead necessitate a regulatory and institutional structure that ensures that trade and factor mobility are in fact conducive to the general welfare. The 'dynamic' view would translate into internal market law doctrine in the form of an acknowledgment that economic mobility does not automatically translate into welfare gains. Rather, the regulatory and institutional framework of the Member States must be considered to be potentially important from an economic perspective, so that its disruption by a specific interpretation of the Treaty freedoms may in fact be welfare-reducing. It can thus be argued that the 'static' gains from integration find reflection in the broad interpretation of the Treaty freedoms according to the *Dassonville* formula, whereas the 'dynamic' gains from integration support the suggestion that the economic freedom of individuals must be balanced with competing regulatory objectives, and that the latter may in fact justify the restriction of the former. The proportionality analysis should thus not

[165] In post-war debate, the two perspectives—the traditional, 'static', free trade model as well as the post-war, 'dynamic' and growth-oriented model—were often used in conjunction. See for example von der Groeben (n 6), 129–30.

[166] Zijlstra argued, for example, that scale effects can arise only in the long run, as a consequence of long-lasting labour and capital movements. Zijlstra (n 7), 40.

only be conceptualized as the balancing of 'economic' and 'non-economic' concerns as it is frequently done, but also between different socio-economic perspectives on how the Union's welfare is best maximized.

COORDINATION AND HARMONIZATION

We now turn to the second main instrument provided for by Article 2 EEC to achieve the Community's goals, namely that of 'progressively approximating the economic policies of Member States'. In this section we will discuss the role of the coordination and harmonization of national policies within the regulatory framework of the Treaty of Rome. It is my central claim that the coordination and harmonization of economic policies was commonly seen as a precondition for realizing the potential benefits of the common market, so that the two instruments—market-making and harmonization—were conceptualized as being intrinsically connected.[167] The close relationship between the two means is already expressed in the Treaty's preamble, according to which the Member States are 'recognizing that the removal of existing obstacles calls for concerted action in order to guarantee steady expansion, balanced trade and fair competition'. Along the same line, Kapteyn and verLoren van Themaat argued in their textbook that '[t]he two concepts must be clearly distinguished, but on the other hand they form an indissoluble unity, like two sides of the same coin'.[168] Addressing a similar point in more general terms, German state secretary and ordoliberal theorist Alfred Müller-Armack argued that the institutional setup of the global economy that existed prior to 1914, which relied on a limited regulatory framework of low tariffs, market access and convertible currencies alone, was no longer sufficient in the light of the overall requirements of contemporary polities.[169] A modern, liberal system of economic multilateralism, Müller-Armack believed, would require a stable institutional framework to function: markets and regulation were thus not considered to be opposites, but understood to be intrinsically interwoven.

The need to coordinate and harmonize national policies followed from two central assumptions: first, it was believed that increased market integration would also increase the susceptibility of the European economy to macroeconomic instabilities, most notably balance of payments problems.[170] The Treaty of Rome created a variety of instruments aimed at coordinating the Member States' responses to

[167] See for example von der Groeben, who argued: 'As long as the Common Market is not completely established, the chief task of competition policy will be to make competition effective in inter-state trade. This cannot be done all at once, but only step by step. It requires harmonization and co-ordination of the various measures to promote competition, and calls imperatively for a unified and coherent policy in the face of the various types of public and private restrictions and distortions.' Von der Groeben (n 6), 152.

[168] Kapteyn and verLoren van Themaat (n 58), 51.

[169] Müller-Armack (n 109), 320–21.

[170] See Marjolin (n 29), 136; see also Kapteyn and verLoren van Themaat (n 58), 52–53; Müller-Armack (n 109), 337–38.

However, such restrictive political understanding could neither alter the fact that, from a legal perspective, the Treaty provided for broad coordination and harmonization competences on the European level, nor that the Treaty envisioned a dual regulatory approach of liberalizing economic activities within a framework of normalized competitive conditions.

The Path to 'Economic Union': The Interpretation of the Treaty of Rome by the Commission in the 1962 Action Programme

The path towards 'economic union' among the Community's six Member States was not uncontested in the years after the signature of the Treaty of Rome. Opposition arose in particular from De Gaulle's government, which assumed power shortly after the Treaty of Rome came into force, and which attempted to disarm the Community's supranational elements and to remake the EEC into a more traditional intergovernmental organization.[177] Liberalists such as Germany's finance (and later prime) minister Ludwig Erhard wished to water the EEC down into a more traditional customs union without any far-reaching approximation of economic, fiscal and social policies.[178] The call for the accession of the UK to the Community voiced by politicians like Erhard during and after the negotiations on the Treaty was motivated, some believed, not least by the hope that the accession would undermine any further-reaching integration.[179] The decision of May 1960 by the Member States to speed up by a year the implementation of the first stage of the transitional period was thus interpreted by some as an implicit choice against early enlargement and in favour of deeper integration of the Six.[180]

On the occasion of entering the second stage of the transitional period, the Commission issued an 'Action Programme' about its future regulatory projects. For us it serves as an illustration of how the Commission's envisioned 'economic union', as well as of how the Commission understood the competences granted to the Community by the Treaty.[181] The Action Programme aimed at a far-reaching coordination and harmonization of policies among the Six already within the transitional period. The Commission hoped that this would eventually lead to a

William Nicoll, 'The Luxembourg Compromise' (1984) 23 *Journal of Common Market Studies* 35; Ernst-Joachim Mestmäcker argued that the Luxembourg compromise showed, after a decade of hopes for a European federation, for the first time the 'political limits' of integration that stemmed from a traditional definition of state sovereignty. Ernst-Joachim Mestmäcker, 'Auf dem Wege zu einer Ordnungspolitik für Europa' in Ernst-Joachim Mestmäcker, Hans Möller and Hans-Peter Schwarz (eds), *Eine Ordnungspolitik für Europa: Festschrift für Hans von der Groeben zu seinem 80 Geburtstag* (Nomos, 1987) 9.

177 Von der Groeben (n 78), 163–70.

178 Lindberg (n 23), 125–31, 188–91; see also von der Groeben (n 78), 46, 66–67.

179 Von der Groeben (n 78), 171.

180 Lindberg (n 23), 141–42, 167–68, 177–78; see also von der Groeben (n 78), 143.

181 In this sense von der Groeben (n 78), 171.

general common economic policy.[182] As already mentioned, this process was usually described as the creation of an 'economic union' among the Member States, a term employed in explicit contrast to the concepts of 'free trade area' or 'customs union'. It implied the establishment of full factor mobility within a framework of coordinated and harmonized economic, fiscal, social and macroeconomic regulation.[183] In the introduction to the Action Programme, the Commission held:

> The Treaty of Rome, interpreting as it does the intention of its Contracting Parties to embark on full integration, and taking into account the economic conditions which govern the establishment of a unified economic area, provides for the economies of the Six to be welded into a real economic union. Within this general framework a distinction should be drawn between the customs union and the economic union (in the narrower sense of the term), which are complementary and interdependent.[184]

According to the Commission, the implementation of the first phase of the transitional period scheduled by the Treaty of Rome, with deep tariff cuts and the abolition of many quantitative restrictions had been successful and relatively uncomplicated. It had been facilitated by the significant economic growth and expansion of trade the Member States experienced in the 1950s and early 1960s. However, the Commission argued, this initial success would now have to be complemented with increased harmonization of national policies:

> The customs union has proved to be the right take-off point for a vigorous advance towards a unified economy. At the same time as it has provided a foundation for the Community economic power, it has acted as a unifying factor among the Member States. But this swift demolition of trade barriers has also confirmed that the Treaty was rightly heedful of economic requirements in prescribing that the establishment of economic union proper should proceed in parallel with the customs union, and not lag behind.[185]

The concept of 'economic union' was not understood as a mere intensification of previous steps of integration, but as a qualitatively different project, which, however, was believed to be a necessary correlate to the customs union: '[I]t will only be possible to create one big internal European market if integration extends to those aspects of policy and of State control which affect the economy'.[186] According to the Commission, 'a customs union that was not geared to a broader economic union would scarcely be viable'.[187] The Commission essentially aimed

[182] EC, 'First General Report on the Activities of the Community (January 1958 to September 1958)', 13.

[183] EC, 'Memorandum of the Commission on the action programme of the Community for the second stage', 4, 10; on this see von der Groeben (n 78), 206–09.

[184] EC, 'Memorandum of the Commission on the action programme of the Community for the second stage', 4.

[185] ibid, 5–6.

[186] ibid, 8.

[187] ibid, 7.

at establishing conditions presenting the 'characteristics of a domestic market'. Drawing from the example of the recently agreed-upon CAP, the Commission held that such conditions would exist only if there is a common regulatory policy. In other words, a true single market arises in a common regulatory framework:

> In order to grasp fully the true nature of the Community's task in settling the final shape of the common policies, and so of economic union, it must be remembered that an economic order based on freedom can only exist in the world of today at the price of constant State intervention in economic life. Such intervention takes a twofold form: in the first place, the State sets up a framework of controls covering every branch of the economy as well as every adjacent field; secondly, it is constantly altering the factors called into play, through the innumerable adjustments involved in its day-to-day economic activity: in short, by pursuing a 'policy' in the proper sense of the term. In speaking of economic union we refer specifically to both these aspects of State intervention. What is required is to harmonize and unify the influence exerted by the six Member States on the economy in such a way that the six countries find they are sharing a single new economic area within which their Governments will have a common set of economic regulations and pursue a common policy.[188]

The Commission took a stand in favour of a broad harmonization of social, fiscal and economic law. We have already seen that the Ohlin Report had advised against an extensive harmonization of such policies, but not because the authors found regulatory competition desirable, but because they did not believe that corporate mobility for the sole reason of taking advantage of regulatory differences was likely. In the 1962 Action Programme, the Commission took a very different position, and advocated in favour of harmonization to end 'the disparities in many fields which artificially favour or handicap businesses competing on the market'.[189] The underlying assumption was that the potential benefits from competition would be realized only if companies competed on a level regulatory playing field. Companies that could offer lower prices for the sole reason that they were subject to lower tax rates and social charges would undermine competition on the basis of efficiency and innovation. Factor movement towards its most efficient use would thereby be distorted, and the beneficial effects of economic integration undermined. Accordingly, the Commission stated in the Action Programme: 'Differences in direct tax systems and rates can lead to undesirable movements of production factors and distort competition within the Common Market.'[190] Thus, the Commission found it advisable to 'eliminate distortions of competition stemming from disparities in tax laws and administrative practice and to obviate economically unwarranted changes in production factors'.[191] This would help to 'secure greater neutrality in respect of competition in company law, tax law and the law on industrial property'.[192]

[188] ibid, 6.
[189] ibid, 27.
[190] ibid, 26.
[191] ibid, 24.
[192] ibid, 22.

The early years after the signature of the Treaty of Rome were characterized by a vivid debate on the degree of harmonization necessary for the functioning of the internal market, and in particular on the competences of the Community institutions in that matter. In regard to the latter, the 1962 Action Programme took a strong stance in favour of a broad reading. As the Treaty provisions were often phrased in an ambivalent form, and included a number of substantially unlimited general harmonization competences, such expansive reading was certainly not implausible from a legal perspective. As already discussed, however, the Commission encountered important opposition from the Member States, which did not always support the broad interpretation of the harmonization competences forwarded by the Commission. With increasing Gaullist opposition to further integration, a far more limited approach had to be taken.[193] While the Action Programme thus proposed a vision of European integration and an understanding of the competences granted by the Treaty that was clearly not shared across the board, it nonetheless provides an illustration of how the Treaty could have plausibly been understood, and was, in fact, interpreted by one of the central European institutions. The Action Programme assumed a close interrelation between market-making on the one hand and the harmonization and coordination of national policies on the other, read the Community's competences extensively and forwarded a broad understanding of which national policies should be coordinated or harmonized. On the following pages we will have a closer look at the different areas of harmonization and coordination provided for in the Treaty, and discuss their relation with the common market.

Competition Policy

As already discussed, it was assumed that competition would trigger dynamic growth effects within an integrated common market. European-wide competition was supposed to put pressure on prices and to force companies to modernize, innovate, cut costs, increase efficiency, and develop new supply and distribution networks as well as to enhance logistics. Fernand Spaak, director of the Cartels and Concentrations Division at the High Authority (and son of Paul-Henri Spaak), described the role of competition in the Treaty of Rome as follows: 'Competition has been chosen as the motive force of the economic revolution that is to promote the interpenetration of several national economies, prisoners for centuries of their different structures, different traditions and habits, and merge them in a new economic entity, the European Common Market'.[194] The Treaty of Rome

[193] On the Gaullist position in the 1960s, see for example Uwe Kitzinger, *The European common market and community* (Routledge, 1967) 19–24.

[194] Fernand Spaak and Jean Jaeger, 'The Rules of Competition within the European Common Market' (1961) 26 *Law and Contemporary Problems* 485, 487.

conceptualized competition as a dynamic process that would unfold only under conducive structural, institutional and regulatory conditions.[195] This understanding of competition differed in important aspects from orthodox economic theory, according to which markets were perfectly competitive. This would imply that competition would arise automatically from the workings of market forces alone, and would in particular not require any specific legal and institutional setup.[196] This assumption was no longer found convincing by most economists, in particular given the fact that a mono- and oligopolistic corporate structure visibly dominated the European economies.[197] Moreover, even with competition in place, its beneficial effects were not taken for granted. Ordoliberals like Walter Eucken or Wilhelm Röpke argued that competition between companies would not automatically increase the general welfare.[198] Instead, it required a conducive framework that ensured fair competition, and which translated the efforts of the competitors into gains for the consumer. According to Röpke, a 'strong state' was required to ensure a functioning system of competition.[199] Expressing the rift between orthodox theory on the one hand and the views that shaped the regulation of competition in the Treaty of Rome on the other, Wilhelm Röpke argued: 'The claim of archaic liberalism that the desirable state of free competition will be reached on its own if only the state would refrain from interfering in the economic life has turned out to be a grave error, though it retains a kernel of truth.'[200]

Impediments to competition were assumed to originate from two sources: 'specific' distortions of competition on the one hand, and 'general' distortions on the other.[201] Whereas the former describes distortions arising from state aid, fiscal and transport tariff preferences as well as restrictive practices by public and private enterprises, the latter covers distortions arising from regulatory differences and from macroeconomic imbalances.[202] 'Specific' distortions of competition constitute the realm of competition policy in the narrow sense, which was laid down in the Treaty's competition chapter: Articles 92–94 EEC targeted distortion of competition by subsidies, and Articles 85–90 EEC aimed at preventing behaviour of companies that undermined competitive conditions.[203] 'General' distortions

[195] See for example ibid, 486; Röpke (n 30), 46, 219–21, 317–18; However, there was some disagreement whether markets had a 'natural' tendency towards monopoly or towards competition. Röpke, for example, identified a tendency towards competition, and assumed that the ultimate cause of monopolies was often to be found in government policy. Ibid, 212, 218–19.

[196] We will discuss this more extensively in a later chapter.

[197] See the examples compiled by Perry Anderson and Stuart Hall, 'The Politics of the Common Market' (1961) I/10 *New Left Review* 1, 5.

[198] Eucken (n 67), 43; Röpke (n 30), 100–02.

[199] Röpke (n 30), 235–36, 302–05.

[200] ibid, 219 (my translation).

[201] These two aspects of competition were emphasized, for example, by Spaak et al (n 114), 132; Kapteyn and verLoren van Themaat (n 58), 56; McLachlan and Swann (n 106), 3–67; Mestmäcker (n 180), 52.

[202] Von der Groeben (n 78), 82.

[203] For an early treatment of European competition law see for example Walter Van Gerven, *Principes du droit des ententes de la Communauté Économique Européenne* (Bruylant 1966).

of competition required a competition policy in the broad sense of normalizing competitive conditions in the economic, fiscal and social realm, as well as the coordination of measures aimed at stabilizing macroeconomic imbalances. The beneficial effects of competition would arise, it was believed, if companies were forced to compete on the basis of their own efforts, and not on the basis of regulatory differences alone.[204] In this regard, the Spaak Report held:

> Beyond open discrimination and interventions aimed at favoring certain companies or production sectors, legal and administrative acts may affect production costs in a way that it should be studied with utmost attention whether, by their own effect or their difference between two or more countries, some of them may distort the conditions of competition between the national economies as a whole or between certain economic sectors.[205]

The Treaty provides numerous possibilities for the approximation of general policies that distort the conditions of competition, which will be discussed in the following sections. Competition policy therefore exemplifies the dual approach of the Treaty of Rome, which is based on the assumption that the benefits of market integration are realized only within a conducive regulatory framework that normalizes competitive conditions.

Approximation of Laws

As already mentioned, the approximation of national laws was understood to be one of two central instruments created by the Treaty of Rome to achieve the Community's goals. Harmonization would ensure competition under equal conditions.[206] According to competition commissioner Hans von der Groeben, 'the approximation of laws is not only an essential instrument of competition policy but also one of the most important means to European integration itself'.[207] This is why, according to von der Groeben, simple conflict-of-law rules were insufficient for establishing a common market:

> It is immediately clear that this aim cannot be reached by using the traditional rules on the conflict of laws. Within a common market it is not sufficient to know whether this or that municipal law is applicable. The decisive point is rather that the municipal law applicable to any given case shall conform substantively with the law applicable to

204 Groeben argued that distortions of competition 'may have the same effect as tariffs". Von der Groeben (n 64), 114.

205 Spaak et al (n 114), 60 (my translation). The original text reads: 'En dehors des discriminations ouvertes et des interventions destinées à favoriser certaines entreprises ou certaines productions, les dispositions d'ordre législatif ou réglementaire ont une incidence telle sur les prix de revient qu'il convient d'examiner avec le plus grand soin si, par leur incidence propre ou par leur disparité entre deux ou plusieurs pays, certaines d'entre elles n'aboutissent pas à fausser les conditions de la concurrence entre des économies nationales dans leur ensemble ou pour des branches d'activite déterminées.'

206 Von der Groeben (n 78), 86.

207 Von der Groeben (n 6), 142.

> competitors in other EEC countries to an extent sufficient to preclude concerned the appropriate measures to avoid the particular distortion.[208]

Differences between the economic regulations of the Member States were seen as potentially distorting the conditions of trade and competition.[209] As a remedy, the Treaty of Rome provided for numerous specific harmonization and coordination competences, as well as the general harmonization provisions in Articles 100 and 101 EEC, in Article 57(2) EEC,[210] the 'necessary powers' clause of Article 235 EEC, and the possibility to enact treaties among the Member States to complement the Treaty of Rome in Article 220 EEC. Article 100 EEC provided a general competence to approximate provisions that 'directly affect the establishment or functioning of the common market'. Article 101 EEC allowed for harmonizing measures if regulatory differences between the Member States are 'distorting the conditions of competition in the common market and that the resultant distortion needs to be eliminated'. Finally, Article 235 EEC allowed for legislation in all areas if such measure is 'necessary to attain, in the course of the operation of the common market, one of the objectives of the Community and this Treaty has not provided the necessary powers'. Whereas Article 100 EEC and Article 235 EEC required unanimity in the Council, Article 101 EEC required only qualified majority after the first stage of the transitional period.

Overview: The General Harmonization Competences and the'Necessary Powers' Clause

Article 100 EEC	General harmonization competence for the 'approximation of such provisions laid down by law, regulation or administrative action in Member States as directly affect the establishment or functioning of the common market' (unanimity).
Article 101 EEC	General harmonization competence if a 'difference between the provisions laid down by law, regulation or administrative action in Member States is distorting the conditions of competition in the common market and that the resultant distortion needs to be eliminated' (qualified majority after first stage).
Article 235 EEC	Residual[211] harmonization competence if 'action by the Community should prove necessary to attain, in the course of the operation of the common market, one of they objectives of the Community and this Treaty has not provided the necessary powers' (unanimity).

[208] ibid, 143–44.
[209] See for example ibid, 142.
[210] While the provision is not usually recognized as a general harmonization competence and is only acknowledged in its para 1, which deals with the recognition of qualifications, para 2 in fact allowed for the coordination of all national regulation 'concerning the taking up and pursuit of activities as self-employed persons'. According to Ivo Schwartz, Director for the approximation of laws at the Commission, this included any form of law regulating economic activities in every possible economic sector. Ivo Schwartz, '30 Jahre EG-Rechtsangleichung' in Mestmäcker, Möller and Schwarz (n 176), 334.
[211] Kapteyn and verLoren van Themaat (n 58), 243–44.

The general approximation provisions were understood to be potentially extremely broad in scope.[212] This is illustrated, for example, by the interpretation of Articles 100, 101 and 235 EEC provided in the 1973 textbook on European law by Paul Kapteyn and Pieter verLoren van Themaat, who would later take office at the CJEU as judge and advocate general, respectively. Concerning the scope of Article 100 EEC, for example, they held that regulatory fields which were affecting the functioning of the common market and were thus subject to potential harmonization included areas such as labour law, social legislation, fiscal legislation and parts of civil and commercial law.[213] The authors of an early German commentary on the Treaty of Rome, Wohlfahrt et al, proposed in its first edition from 1960 a comparably broad scope of Article 100 EEC, despite their generally more reserved stance regarding the regulatory competences of the Community.[214] And another commentator held:

> Article 100 of the EEC Treaty does not determine the material extent of the authority for harmonization by enumerating particular fields of law. The material extent of this authority granting provision depends on an interpretation of the concept and the requirements of the market.[215]

Article 101 EEC was commonly assumed to be of similarly extensive breadth: according to Kapteyn and verLoren van Themaat, the main cause of distorted competition is differences in regulation between the Member States, which lead to differences in the competitive position of the concerned economic actors.[216] Because such distortions stem from uncoordinated national legislation, they may arise even in absence of any discriminatory or restrictive legislation. According to the Spaak Report, differences in legislation that may distort competition and thus may justify harmonization included direct and indirect taxation, the methods of financing the social security systems, price regulation, income differences between men and women, working hours, overtime and paid holidays.[217] And according to Wohlfarth et al, distortions of competition are indicated if the different provisions of the various Member States lead to different production costs, which clearly is a far-reaching definition.[218] It was sometimes held that Article 101 was applicable

[212] See for example Ernst Wohlfarth et al, *Die Europäische Wirtschaftsgemeinschaft: Kommentar zum Vertrag* (Vahlen, 1960) 302; see also Vogelaar, who rejected the proposition that Art 100 could only be employed to harmonize distortive regulation if it had 'immediate' beneficial effects on the common market. Instead, Vogelaar proposed that '[t]he real borders of harmonization lie at the point where national law by reason of its territorial applicability is unfit to provide solutions for the Community problems which arise. At that point Article 100 can no longer provide the solution and recourse must be had either to Article 220 (which provides for dealing by agreement with certain specific legal situations within the Community) or to Article 235'. Theodore Vogelaar, 'The Approximation of the laws of Member States under the Treaty of Rome' (1975) 12 *Common Market Law Review* 211, 215.

[213] Kapteyn and verLoren van Themaat (n 58), 240.

[214] Wohlfarth et al (n 212), 304.

[215] M Seidel, 'The Harmonization of Laws Relating to Pharmaceuticals in the EEC' (1969) 6 *Common Market Law Review* 309, 311.

[216] Kapteyn and verLoren van Themaat (n 58), 244–46.

[217] Spaak et al (n 114), 62–63.

[218] Wohlfarth et al (n 212), 306.

only to 'specific' distortions, and could thus not be employed to rectify 'general' distortions arising from differences in regulation.[219] However, this was, as we just saw, certainly not the dominant understanding, especially in the Community's early years. Finally, Article 235 EEC was also assumed to be of extremely broad scope. Kapteyn and verLoren van Themaat held: 'Formally, one could derive from this article a general legislative power of the Community, especially in economic and social fields …'.[220] Article 235 EEC would in fact provide the legal basis for significant policy initiatives in the 1970s, most notably the EMS, consumer and environmental protection.[221]

Given this broad scope of Articles 100, 101 and 235 EEC, the other, more specific harmonization and coordination competences were sometimes read as implicit limitations to the general harmonization provisions because they allegedly provided a preliminary indication of the Community's competences. However, this was an implausible reading: the provisions were defined in a broad way precisely to complement the other, more specific harmonization competences. According to Kapteyn and verLoren van Themaat the general approximation competences were applicable in all 'those spheres where the specific provisions are deficient'.[222] And Dennis Thompson commented: 'These articles apply in all cases where the functioning of the Common Market is impaired without any limitation on the subject-matter of the laws involved'.[223] Thus, the general harmonization provisions were commonly conceptualized in purely functional terms, and as essentially not limited in any substantive sense. It is in this sense that early commentators called the Treaty of Rome a 'framework treaty': it left the substantive design of the Community open to the legislators, speaking to the pluralist character of the European economic constitution.

Tax Harmonization

The example of turnover taxes provides a clear illustration of the Treaty's dual approach of pursuing market integration within a framework of normalized

[219] In the early 1970s the Commission forwarded the view that Art 101 could be employed only for 'specific' distortions; see EC, 'First communication of the Commission about the Community's policy on the environment' SEC (71) 2616 final, 9. However, a different reading of the provision was proposed by other Community institutions. A report by the Economic and Social Committee held, for example, that Art 101 could be employed for the harmonization of technical standards, thus for 'general' distortions. *Etude du Comité économique et social sur les problemes concernant le rapprochement des législations relatives aux entraves techniques* (CES 469/72 1972), 6.

[220] Kapteyn and verLoren van Themaat (n 58), 244; Wohlfahrt et al refer to the Preamble and Arts 2 and 3 EEC, arguing that the question whether a certain measure is 'necessary' to reach these goals lies in the discretion of the competent institutions alone. Wohlfarth et al (n 212), 608.

[221] Sauter (n 20), 32.

[222] Kapteyn and verLoren van Themaat (n 58), 48.

[223] Dennis Thompson, 'Harmonization of Laws' (1965) 3 *Journal of Common Market Studies* 302, 303.

competitive conditions.[224] The adverse effects of differences in turnover taxation were considered to be among the most urgent concerns to be corrected by harmonization.[225] The Treaty of Rome specifically authorized the harmonization of turnover taxes in Article 99 EEC. The distortive aspect of unharmonized systems of turnover taxation lay not so much in differences in tax rates, as turnover taxes of the country of production were refunded upon export, and then charged at the importing country's tax rate.[226] Rather, the problems arose from the tax system employed by most Member States, the so-called 'cascade system', which distorted competition in a number of ways.[227] In the 'cascade system' the turnover tax was to be paid on the basis of the product's price at the occasion of every sale that took place. This meant that a product that was processed in stages by different companies accumulated a higher tax burden then when the same process took place within a vertically integrated company.[228] This put large, vertically integrated enterprises at an arbitrary advantage in comparison to non-integrated (eg specialized) businesses, thereby distorting competition between the former and the latter.[229] Moreover, the 'cascade system' tended to burden higher-processed goods more than lower-processed goods, thus distorting competition in favour of the latter.[230] Finally, the 'cascade system' made the calculation of the compensatory levy to be charged on imports or refunded for exports difficult, and thereby facilitated discrimination by the importing country (see Article 97 EEC).[231] The harmonized system that was ultimately introduced, the VAT, required companies to pay tax only for the value added, which did not distort competition between integrated and non-integrated companies or between higher- and lower-processed goods. Moreover, because it was much easier to calculate, it prevented a distortion of competition by Member States through the imposition of an unduly high compensatory levy. By contrast, it did *not* harmonize VAT rates among the Member States.[232] The case of indirect taxation thus illustrates how the Treaty of Rome conceptualized the benefits from market integration to arise only within a framework of normalized competitive conditions, which sometimes made significant harmonization measures necessary.

[224] On the effects of an unharmonized system of indirect taxation on competition, see for example McLachlan and Swann (n 106), 26–37.

[225] See for example Schwartz (n 210), 339–40; see also Zijlstra (n 7), 42.

[226] Kornél Vilmos Antal, 'Harmonisation of Turnover Taxes in the Common Market' (1963) 1 *Common Market Law Review* 41, 48.

[227] All with the exception of France, which already used a VAT system.

[228] On the different national systems, see Antal (n 226), 44–48.

[229] Von der Groeben (n 6), 141; see also Kapteyn and verLoren van Themaat (n 58), 199; Schwartz (n 210), 340.

[230] Antal (n 226), 45.

[231] ibid, 44; see also von der Groeben (n 6), 141; Kapteyn and verLoren van Themaat (n 58), 199; Schwartz (n 210), 340; von der Groeben (n 78), 85–86.

[232] Majone (n 9), 306.

the Protocol expected such approximation to occur automatically within the first years of the transitional period, it allowed France (which at that point had more progressive labour and social regulation than the other Member States) to take 'protective measures' in case it did not, unless the Council took action.[242]

However, the degree of harmonization considered to be necessary was a significant issue of disagreement.[243] It is important to understand the debate within its historical context: this means, in particular, that opposition to harmonization of social policies in the 1950s should not be equated uncritically with today's arguments in favour of regulatory competition. The Ohlin Report, which we discussed in an earlier section, provides a telling example: the majority of the authors of the report assumed that a comprehensive harmonization of social policies would not be necessary to prevent relocation based on regulatory differences alone. Given the general economic and political situation as well as the existence of far-reaching restrictions on capital mobility, the report's assumption that differences in tax and social charges alone would probably not trigger widescale relocation of production is not implausible. Thus, the report's scepticism about comprehensive harmonization of social policies is not based on the authors' preference for regulatory competition; rather, they did not believe that relocation based on regulatory differences was, given the circumstances, a likely risk. Another illustration for the complexity of the debate on the harmonization of social policies is the views voiced by Hans von der Groeben. Von der Groeben acknowledged that wage increases should follow 'productivity advances', which means that wages should rise in proportion with productivity gains. He assumed, however, that competitive pressures alone would achieve this task, so that European coordination in that regard would not be necessary.[244] Of course von der Groeben's position coincided with the economic interests of German industry of that time, as Germany's social costs were

[242] Heading II of the the Protocol to the Treaty of Rome 'on certain provisions relating to France' concerned payment for overtime, and it held in its first paragraph that '[t]he Member States consider that the establishment of the common market will result, by the end of the first stage, in a situation in which the basic number of hours beyond which overtime is paid for and the average rate of additional payment for overtime in industry will correspond to the average obtaining in France in 1956'. It thus suggests that a levelling of overtime regulation in the Member States is assumed to take place in the first years after the signature of the Treaty of Rome. In case this does not occur by the end of the first stage, however, the second paragraph allows France to take 'protective measures' unless the Council takes action itself.

[243] See for example von der Groeben (n 57), 101–02; Scholars discussed, for example, whether social costs were 'natural costs' justified by underlying economic fundamentals related to the location of production, or 'artificial costs', explained by regulatory differences alone. Only in the latter case would differences in social benefits distort competition. As an example see Wohlfarth et al (n 212), 363–65; For a rather negative assessment of harmonization effirts in the social field see for example Lell (n 65), 144–53; Majone argued more recently: 'In fact, the Treaty of Rome never mandated that social policies should be harmonized prior to, or concurrently with, trade liberalization inside the common market. Rather, it suggested that social harmonization should be regarded as a possible corollary rather than a requirement for the common market.' Majone (n 9), 150.

[244] Von der Groeben (n 6), 140; see also Lell (n 65), 114–53.

assumed to be low in comparison to those of the other Member States. However, the assumption that dynamic forces would ensure sufficient wage increases even without harmonization was not unrealistic in the political and economic situation of the 1950s: economic growth was strong, and labour supply scarce, which indeed gave unions the power to negotiate considerable wage increases. Moreover, Groeben's critical view of harmonization was not motivated by the belief that companies from different Member States should compete on the basis of different social costs; rather, he was explicit that companies should have the same 'starting conditions', which in particular prohibited 'artificial' distortions of competition originating in differences in legislation.[245] However, he argued that, rather than attempting to equalize the various cost factors through the arduous harmonization of a multitude of (social, tax, labour, etc) measures, a general equalization of costs could be achieved much simpler through a correct currency valuation. Under a 'realistic' exchange rate, von der Groeben held, differences in social charges would no longer distort competition.[246] Thus, von der Groeben did not reject harmonization in social policies as a matter of principle, and did not view regulatory competition as a virtue. Rather, he did not see the need for approximating social regulation, given the socio-economic situation of that time and the availability of other regulatory instruments to achieve the same goal. Most commentators took a moderate position, and understood the regulatory compromise of the Treaty as one where harmonization should accompany the developments triggered by market integration.[247] German *Staatssekretär* Alfred Müller-Armack, for example, acknowledged that the expected gradual approximation of social conditions through market integration should be complemented by coordinative policies.[248]

In regard to regulatory competences in the field of social policy, the Treaty of Rome provided a complex picture. The Treaty included numerous provisions relating to a high level of employment, which tended to be worded in relatively precise terms, and the Commission could propose legislation in those areas.[249] These provisions included the measures relating to the free movement of workers, the freedom of establishment as well as the tasks of the ESF such as retraining measures or the common vocational training policy (Article 128 EEC). The ESF was established for the length of the transitional period, though it could be—and indeed later was—charged with new tasks by unanimous decision (Article 126(b)). It was assigned with 'the task of rendering the employment of workers easier and of increasing their geographical and occupational mobility within the Community' (Article 123 EEC). The fund covered 50 per cent of the expenses incurred by the national authorities for the 'productive re-employment of workers' by

[245] Von der Groeben (n 64), 114.
[246] Von der Groeben (n 57), 101–02; von der Groeben (n 78), 94.
[247] See for example Marjolin (n 29), 136; see also Lindberg (n 23), 22.
[248] Müller-Armack (n 109), 324–25.
[249] This distinction is based on Levi Sandri (n 235), 2.

means of vocational retraining and resettlement allowances (Article 125(1) EEC). By contrast, measures relating more generally to the upwards levelling of social conditions tended to be worded in more vague terms. Here the Commission could generally not propose legislation, and could merely elicit cooperation among the Member States.[250] In regard to these areas, commentators diagnosed a 'lack of precision of most of the social provisions of the Treaty of Rome'.[251] However, until the early 1960s, many commentators did not generally see such ambiguity as a significant barrier to harmonization. As already discussed, the Treaty of Rome was commonly conceptualized as a 'framework treaty' that granted far-reaching harmonizing competences without significant substantive limitations, which consequently included also the area of social policy.[252] In particular, Articles 100 and 101 EEC were understood to be mostly unlimited in substantive terms, so that harmonization of social policy could be based on these provisions, a possibility also explicitly addressed by Article 117 EEC.[253] A contemporary commentator held: 'By accepting the highest standards in each country there will be a levelling upwards which will ultimately produce a series of harmonized laws providing an unparalleled social welfare system'.[254] Another argued that the Commission could elicit a 'dynamic social policy by adopting an extensive interpretation of the Treaty'.[255]

The Commission understood its mandate under the social policy provisions broadly, and engaged in numerous projects aimed at harmonization in the field of social policy, either through Community legislation or through studies and conferences that were supposed to initiate increased cooperation among the Member States. An overview of planned or implemented harmonization measures from 1966 indicates the considerable number of 31 measures concerned with social policy, as compared to 90 dealing with competition, 60 with agriculture, 40 with the freedom of establishment and services, 21 with customs, 15 with transport, two with the free movement of workers and two with the free movement of capital.[256] According to Amitai Etzioni, the reason why the far-reaching coordination of social and economic policies was kept relatively vague in the Treaty was to preempt opposition, in particular as these measures had a potential redistributive element.[257] However, the vague character of the social policy provisions was not

[250] ibid, 6.

[251] K Lewin, 'The Free Movement of Workers' (1965) 2 *Common Market Law Review* 300.

[252] See for example Kapteyn and verLoren van Themaat (n 58), 47.

[253] Lell (n 65), 24.

[254] Thompson (n 223), 311; see however Lell (n 65), 28.

[255] E Brown, 'Recent Developments in the Social Policy of the European Economic Community' (1966) 3 *Common Market Law Review* 184, 186.

[256] William Palk, 'Harmonization of the Laws of the European Common Market Countries' (1966) 2 *Manitoba Law Journal* 173, fn 1.

[257] According to Etzioni, polities were more likely to accept redistributive measures once a common sense of community was established, whereas such measures would likely encourage opposition as long as such understanding did not exist. Amitai Etzioni, 'European Unification: A Strategy of Change' (1963) 16 *World Politics* 32, 44.

understood as a significant impediment to harmonization: Etzioni expected an upwards levelling of social and economic policy essentially to take place within the transitional period.[258] As already discussed, the Commission's initial activism was dampened by increasing resistance towards continued integration by some Member States, as exemplified by the Luxembourg compromise. This resistance also manifested itself in the field of social policy,[259] so that, by 1966, the expectations for significant harmonization in the social field were considerably reduced.[260] However, this stalling in the field of social policy was a political development, and cannot be held to reflect the regulatory logic of the Treaty of Rome. This is also indicated by later developments: from the first oil crisis onwards, the Community became increasingly active in the social field, indicated by the adoption of the first 'Social Policy Action Programme' of 1974 and a number of Directives on labour market-related issues.[261] Consequently, the period between 1974 and 1985 was characterized by Mosley as a period of 'social activism' at the European level.[262] In today's literature it is sometimes claimed—often employing a dichotomic distinction between 'social' and 'economic' policies—that the Treaty was not concerned with social objectives, and/or provided only limited regulatory competences in that field.[263] Such a view must be rejected. As we saw, the raising of living standards and the upwards levelling of working conditions were explicit objectives of the Treaty. Moreover, the distinction between 'social' and 'economic' objectives has no relevance for the definition of the Community's competences: harmonization in any regulatory field was deemed possible if necessary for the functioning of the common market and for normalizing competitive conditions. The fact that the Community initially engaged in such legal harmonization process only to a limited extent must be assumed to have political, not legal causes.

Regional and Industrial Policy and the European Investment Bank (EIB)

The Messina resolution aimed at the creation of a 'European investment fund', which 'would be used for the common development of Europe's inherent economic potentialities and, in particular for the development of the less favoured regions of the participating countries'.[264] In the preamble to the Treaty of Rome,

[258] ibid, 39–40.
[259] Levi Sandri (n 235), 1–2.
[260] See ibid, passim.
[261] Floris De Witte, 'The Architecture of a "Social Market Economy"' LSE Law, Society and Economy Working Papers 13/2015, 8.
[262] Hugh Mosley, 'The social dimension of Europe integration' (1990) 129 *International Labour Review* 147, 149.
[263] See most notably Stefano Giubboni, *Social Rights and Market Freedom in the European Constitution* (Cambridge University Press, 2006), 16.
[264] *Resolution adopted by the Ministers of Foreign Affairs of the Member States of the ECSC at their meeting at Messina*, I, C; on the discussion during the negotiations see Küsters (n 50), 182–84; see also von der Groeben (n 57), 102.

The Common Agricultural Policy (CAP)

A Common Agricultural Policy (CAP) was to be developed immediately after the Treaty of Rome had entered into force (Article 43(1)–(2) EEC). It will be shown that the CAP implemented in important aspects what we have defined as the dual strategy of the Treaty of Rome, namely the establishment of a common market within normalized competitive conditions. The CAP thus follows the same regulatory approach as the remainder of the Treaty, though this fact may easily be overlooked unless the CAP is analysed within the economic and political environment of the 1950s. Without such contextualization, the CAP is liable to become a projection plane for contemporary views and narratives. I will briefly address three common assumptions that obscure a correct understanding of the CAP before we move on to the discussion of the policy itself. First, our view of the CAP tends to be shaped by a contemporary evaluation, which is often a negative one. Certainly the CAP is one of the more obviously dysfunctional European policies of the recent decades.[278] It is still one of the most protectionist policies of the Union and hurts developing countries;[279] is built on a non-transparent funding system captured by special interests;[280] and, until quite recently, it created perverse incentives to produce excessive amounts of food at above world market price levels. While these problems can, with the benefit of hindsight, certainly be traced back to structures created in the CAP's earliest days, it should not be ignored how different the original CAP's economic and political context was from today's. This context must be taken into account in an analysis of the historical CAP. Second, the CAP is frequently conceptualized as an exception to the general logic of the Treaty along the lines of the two-spheres fallacy discussed in the introduction of this book. The common view of the CAP emphasizes its protectionist and interventionist dimension, against which the remainder of the common market system is delineated.[281] This establishes a representation that is problematic if read in normative terms (e.g. if it is assumed that the logic of the Treaty is normatively biased against the regulation of market activities). As this section and the book in general aims to show, however, market-making and regulation are understood to be intrinsically connected in the European economic constitution, which speaks against such dichotomic representation. The fact that market-making in the agricultural sector required an extensive regulatory framework and subsidy system and was visibly protectionist towards third countries does not allow the conclusion that the industrial sector functioned on a qualitatively different basis. No different than the agricultural

[278] See for example the critique in Majone (n 9), 222–24.

[279] Nicola Cantore, Sheila Page and Dirk Willem teVelde, *Making the EU's Common Agricultural Policy coherent with development goals* (ODI Briefing Paper 69, 2011).

[280] See for example the Commission report cited by Majone (n 9), 215 which held that 'the richest 20 per cent of European landowners and agribusiness companies received 80 per cent of EU farm aid'.

[281] See for example Majone, who argues: 'At any rate, even the Treaty of Rome, although more "neo-liberal" than the ECSC and Euratom Treaties, contains a number of interventionist features, most strikingly in the articles dealing with the CAP'. Majone (n 9), 159.

sector, industrial production was protected by tariffs against third countries, state aid and various kinds of regulation. The fact that vested interests in the Member States were able to block the Commission's subsequent attempts—most notably the Mansholt Plan—to develop agriculture into a commercially more viable sector cannot be employed as an indicator that the historical CAP was intrinsically interventionist and protectionist in a way that the remainder of the economic sectors were not. The conceptualization of the CAP as a fundamentally exceptional policy within the Treaty of Rome must therefore be considered as mainly ideological in nature. Third, in an interesting contortion of historical facts, it is today sometimes claimed that the CAP, its protectionist structure and its subsidy system was a concession by Germany to France in exchange for the liberalization of trade in industrial products.[282] The correct part of the claim is that France, being more productive than Germany in the agricultural sector, was more interested in the liberalization of trade in agricultural products than Germany was, which was mainly focused on the liberalization of trade in industrial products.[283] Neither France nor Germany was keen on a global trade liberalization in agricultural products; both aimed at keeping prices at levels above world market level, as a form of income subsidy for their farmers, paid for by the consumers. However, it was Germany, not France, which was the more protectionist actor of the two in the agricultural sector;[284] ultimately, Germany managed to fix the common prices for agricultural products close to its higher domestic price level, rather than at the lower French one. According to Hu, the level of common prices agreed upon in 1964 was 18 per cent above the EEC average, and a full 30 per cent above the French level.[285] In the following years, Germany was able to defend the CAP structure against reform attempts pursued by the Commission and supported by less protectionist Member States, such as the Netherlands.[286] Ultimately the breakdown of the Bretton-Woods system and the establishment of a complex adjustment system necessary to

[282] See eg Majone (n 9), 305: 'In the case of the EEC the principal derogation from the principle of market liberalization was, of course, the CAP, written into the Treaty of Rome at French insistence.' See also David Marsh, *The Euro: the politics of the new global currency* (Yale University Press, 2009) 33; for a critique from a historical scholar, see N Piers Ludlow, 'The making of the CAP: towards a historical analysis of the EU's first major policy' (2005) 14 *Contemporary European History* 347, 351.

[283] See eg Lambert (n 176), 196; Pinder held: 'French industry was weak in relation to German industry, but French agriculture, based on very favourable natural conditions, was in a strong competitive position, with excellent prospects for the future. Economically, the European Community has been for France a bargain in which a risk was taken for French industry in exchange for a great and certain gain for French agriculture.' Pinder (n 10), 100. It was not only France but also the Netherlands that strongly pushed for the establishment of the CAP; Ludlow (n 282), 354.

[284] See eg Stefan Riesenfeld, 'Common Market for Agricultural Products and Common Agricultural Policy in the European Economic Community' (1965) *University of Illinois Law Review* 658, 662; on Germany's resistance against lowering the target and intervention prices in grain as agreed upon in Regulation 19 see ibid, 670; Ludlow speaks of 'Bonn's ... tendency towards agricultural protectionism". Ludlow (n 282), 362.

[285] Yao-Su Hu, 'German agricultural power: the impact on France and Britain' (1979) 35 *The World Today* 453, 460.

[286] See for example Parfitt's account of the difference in German and Dutch positions on an aspect of the Mansholt Plan that aimed at establishing farm structures that would produce a minimum

make the CAP workable under a regime of floating currencies in the 1970s allowed Germany to return to its protectionist policies.[287] Today's misrepresentation of the agricultural policies pursued by France and Germany in the early decades of the Community feeds into an ideological reading of the Community's history, in which Germany allegedly pursued market-based integration, whereas states like France had to reluctantly give up their protectionist and interventionist ways. In fact, both Germany and France pushed for liberalization in sectors where they saw benefits, but attempted to retain protectionist or interventionist approaches if it was in the interest of important national constituencies.

We will now look at the CAP within its historical context, and show that the CAP implemented the dual regulatory strategy of market-making within a framework of normalized competitive conditions.[288] Under the Treaty of Rome, the agricultural sectors of the Member States were to be reorganized as a common market on the European level. Unless the Treaty provided for an exception, the common market rules applied fully to agricultural products (Article 38(1)–(2) EEC). It is interesting to notice that the inclusion of agricultural products in the liberalization project of the Treaty of Rome was initially not uncontroversial; some Member States had floated alternative ideas that would have kept agricultural products out of the Treaty,[289] and the EFTA as the competing integration project presumably based on free trade ideas did not cover agricultural products at all.[290] While the Treaty envisaged the establishment of a common market for agricultural products, at the same time it aimed at the normalization of competitive conditions.[291] After the war, Member States had established complex systems to support agricultural incomes and to foster investment in the agricultural sector. A market in agricultural products that was undistorted of regulatory differences thus required the harmonization of these support systems. VerLoren van Themaat later commented that 'the common agricultural policy of the EEC is an inevitable consequence of the fact that without a common agricultural policy the free movement of goods in this sector would have to make do without corrections of the market mechanism that are generally considered to be necessary'.[292] There were at least

income. The plan proposed that the minimum viability threshold should be set at $10,000–12,500. Whereas Germany rejected the threshold level as too high, arguing that most Bavarian farms would have to be abandoned as a result, the Netherlands argued that it would be too low. Trevor Parfitt, 'The EEC: Mansholt in Transition' (1970) 26 *The World Today* 344, 349.

287 This is extensively described by Hu (n 285).

288 Palk (n 256), 180; see also Marjolin (n 29), 132. On the need for a common agricultural policy within the common market see von der Groeben (n 78), 97–99.

289 France, for example, initially favoured guaranteed long-term export contracts that would ensure protected demand for its agricultural surpluses instead. Milward (n 61), 273–74; see on the discussion on the agricultural chapter during the negotiations also Küsters (n 50), 173–74.

290 McLachlan and Swann (n 106), 3; see also Marjolin (n 29), 138–39.

291 See von der Groeben (n 78), 99.

292 Pieter verLoren van Themaat, *The changing structure of international economic law: a contribution of legal history, of comparative law and of general legal theory to the debate on a new international economic order* (Nijhoff, 1981) 227 and 362.

two reasons why such extensive protectionist systems were deemed necessary, one economic and the other political. From an economic perspective, public subsidies were deemed necessary to enable the modernization and industrialization of the agricultural sector. Agricultural production in many European regions was locked in a backward, pre-industrial structure, and lacked capital to finance investment. It was thus generally assumed that the modernization of agricultural production would require significant public stimulus.[293] As a consequence of public policies the agricultural sector experienced substantial productivity gains in the 1950s. Milward commented that '[i]mprovements in agricultural technology, reflected in remarkable increases in yields, were not extraneous or fortuitous; they were the consequence of government policies which financed their introduction into an area of production where the majority of enterprises were unable to afford such innovations out of their earnings'.[294]

Increasing agricultural incomes was also deemed to be of high political importance, as for example the Commission argued.[295] Partly as a consequence of the structural deficits of the agricultural sector, the growth of agricultural income had consistently lagged behind that of industrial income since the nineteenth century.[296] Even in the Dutch and the Danish agriculture, which were the most advanced in terms of investment, industrialization, specialization and export-orientation, agricultural incomes grew slower than industrial income.[297] The Conference of Stresa, which convened in July 1958 in accordance with Article 43 EEC, identified a 'comparative deterioration in agricultural incomes despite the increase in productivity'.[298] The reasons for this growth gap were multiple, and have been discussed elsewhere.[299] As the number of people engaged in the agricultural sector was still high, the growth gap posed significant political dangers.[300] Fascist and authoritarian movements in countries like Germany, Italy, Austria or Hungary had drawn

[293] EC, 'First General Report on the Activities of the Community (January 1958 to September 1958)', 72; see also von der Groeben's extensive discussion of the possibilities for public policy support to restructure the German agricultural sector: Hans von der Groeben, 'Deutschland, Europäische Gemeinschaft, Atlantische Partnerschaft' in Hans von der Groeben (ed), *Europa—Plan und Wirklichkeit* (Nomos, 1967), 56–57; Hans von der Groeben argued: 'Nur zögernd … wurde anerkannt, daß dem säkularen Umstrukturierungsprozeß, der mit der vollen Ausbildung der modernen Industriegesellschaft verbunden ist, nicht allein durch Markt- und Preispolitik für landwirtschaftliche Erzeugnisse, sondern nur durch eine Kombination dieser Politik mit einer aktiven Regionalpolitik und Agrarstrukturpolitik entsprochen werden muß, die nur im Rahmen einer allgemeinen Wirtschaftspolitik erfolgversprechend ist.' Von der Groeben (n 78), 101.

[294] Milward (n 61), 206; see also the discussion of possible efficiency gains by the Commission in the 'Memorandum of the Commission on the action programme of the community for the second stage', 33ff.

[295] EC, 'First General Report on the Activities of the Community (January 1958 to September 1958)', 69.

[296] Milward (n 61), 198; see also EC, 'First General Report on the Activities of the Community (January 1958 to September 1958)', 67.

[297] Milward (n 61), 198.

[298] Conference of Stresa, 3–11 July 1958, Resolution, reproduced in EC, 'First General Report on the Activities of the Community (January 1958 to September 1958)', 74.

[299] See for example Milward (n 61), 198ff.

[300] ibid, 198–99.

of macroeconomic processes, which Zijlstra called 'global planning'.[315] The ability of states to fully control macroeconomic developments had limits, however. States were susceptible to regional and global imbalances, a phenomenon that was believed to be exacerbated by economic integration.[316] As the European economies opened towards each other, Jelle Zijlstra argued, purely national instruments became less effective.[317] The international coordination of national macroeconomic policies thus became of ever-greater importance for the national governments.[318] Consequently, issues related to economic stability—such as trade flows, currency exchange rates or inflation, all of which were often discussed under the umbrella theme of balance-of-payments in the 1950s and 1960s[319]—were a central concern to the European policymakers.[320] Competition commissioner Hans von der Groeben, for example, wrote in 1965:

> [T]he effectiveness of competition as an instrument of integration and guidance in the Common Market depends primarily on the equilibrium of the overall balance of payments of each individual Member State. This equilibrium does not come about automatically. On the contrary, inflation can only be controlled and economic stability maintained if the Member States and the Community jointly make use of the resources of economic, monetary, budget and fiscal policy.[321]

Coordinated macroeconomic policies was assumed by many to constitute a precondition for the common market as envisaged by the Treaty.[322] The Commission argued in the first General Report, for example, that the free movement of capital required coordinated monetary policies, as otherwise discrepancies between the national regulations would lead to a diversion of capital flows.[323] The Treaty aimed at a significant degree of coordination of macroeconomic policies among the Six. Article 6(1) EEC called, in general terms, for the coordination of the economic policies of the Member States. And Article 6(2) EEC held that '[t]he institutions of the Community shall take care not to prejudice the internal and external financial stability of the Member States.' The stable development of the Member States' economies, in particular in regard to balance-of-payment issues, thereby became an obligation of the European institutions. Title II described measures

[315] Jelle Zijlstra, *Möglichkeiten und Grenzen der Konjunkturpolitik* (Universität Kiel, 1962) 6; Zijlstra (n 7), 55.

[316] Von der Groeben (n 6), 139–40; Carsten-Michael Klisch, *Die Konjunkturpolitik in der Europäischen Wirtschaftsgemeinschaft* (Nomos, 1974) 13–14; Zijlstra argued that the means of governments in open economies to fully control the conjunctural cycle were restricted. Zijlstra (n 315), 16.

[317] Zijlstra (n 7), 41–44.

[318] ibid, 42.

[319] See for example Marjolin (n 29), 136.

[320] On the need for conjunctural planning on a European level see Müller-Armack (n 109), 331–49; on economic planning in the EEC see generally Dennis Swann and Donald McLachlan, 'Programming and Competition in the European Communities' (1964) 74 *Economic Journal* 85.

[321] Von der Groeben (n 6), 139.

[322] Von der Groeben (n 78), 310.

[323] EC, 'First General Report on the Activities of the Community (January 1958 to September 1958)', 58.

relating to the 'economic policy' of the EEC, and consisted of three chapters, on conjunctural policy (Article 103 EEC), on balance of payments (Articles 104–09 EEC), and on commercial policy (Articles 110–16 EEC, which we will not further discuss here). The term 'conjunctural policy' refers to the macroeconomic management of business cycles. According to Article 103(1) EEC, 'Member States shall regard their conjunctural policies as a matter of common concern'. The Council could pass 'measures' in that field based on unanimity, and Directives implementing these measures could then be enacted on the basis of a qualified majority (paras 2–3).[324] The chapter on the balance of payments reiterated that Member States were supposed to pursue economic policies necessary for balanced trade flows, as well as to maintain confidence in their currencies, a high level of employment and price stability (Article 104 EEC). The Treaty also laid down a system of exceptional measures in cases of balance of trade difficulties (Article 108–09 EEC). The Member States were supposed to coordinate their economic policies, and formed a number of coordinative committees for that purpose.[325] Whereas the committees had consultative functions only,[326] the Council had comprehensive legislative competences, in particular based on measures under Article 103(2) and (3) EEC. These competences were essentially not subject to any significant substantive limitations.[327] In principle, a far-reaching and binding European macroeconomic policy could have been established on their basis, as for example Everling or verLoren van Themaat argued.[328] The same has been said about the flexibility clause of Article 235 EEC.[329] However, in the political practice of the

[324] On Art 103(2) and (3) see Klisch (n 316), 103–219; for an overview of early measures based on Art 103 EEC see ibid, 16, fn 17.

[325] This included the Monetary Committee (Art 105 EEC), the Short-Term Economic Policy Committee dealing with the coordination of the conjunctural policies of the Member States (based on Art 103 EEC), a Budgetary Policy Committee concerned with the cooperation between the competent government departments of Member States in the field of budgetary policy (based on Arts 105 and 145 EEC) and a Medium-term Economic Policy Committee (also based on Arts 105 and 145 EEC). These committees have since then been merged into the Economic Policy Committee. On the Monetary Committee see ibid, 90–91; on the Short-Term Economic Policy Committee see Bela Balassa, 'Planning in an open economy' (1967) 2 *Intereconomics* 75, and Klisch (n 316), 94–96; on the Budgetary Policy Committee see ibid, 97–98; on the Medium-term Economic Policy Committee see Pieter verLoren van Themaat, 'Competition and Planning in the EEC and the Member States' (1970) 7 *Common Market Law Review* 311.

[326] Klisch (n 316), 101.

[327] See ibid, 138–39, with further references.

[328] Ulrich Everling, *Die Koordinierung der Wirtschaftspolitik in der Europäischen Wirtschaftsgemeinschaft als Rechtsproblem* (Mohr, 1964) 19–35, 37. Everling argued that provisions like Art 103 and Art 235 must be interpreted in a dynamic form. They could adapt to the needs of a Community that increasingly integrated, so that the limits of these provisions were shifting over time. For a more extensive argument along the same line see also Ulrich Everling, 'Die Allgemeine Ermächtigung der EG zur Zielverwirklichung nach Art 235 EWGV' [1967] Europarecht Sonderheft 2, 2–3; verLoren van Themaat (n 292), 111 and 179; For further references see Klisch (n 316), 136–39; for arguments against such expansive interpretation of Art 103 EEC see ibid, 139–62; see also von der Groeben (n 78), 89, who rejected the proposition that Art 103 EEC could have been employed for the development of a more comprehensive macroeconomic policy, though his arguments essentially relate to practical political concerns rather than the purely legal question.

[329] Von der Groeben (n 78), 311; verLoren van Themaat (n 292), 179.

EEC, issues of conjunctural policy came to be understood as the prerogatives of the Member States, so that measures under Article 103 EEC were mostly (though not exclusively) passed as non-binding recommendations.[330] On a Community level, macroeconomic coordination and planning initially remained limited to the preparation of medium-term growth projections as well as the development of policy guidelines for the Member States.[331] In the late 1970s, however, Article 235 EEC provided the legal basis for the establishment of the European Monetary System (EMS), thus testifying to the ability of the Treaty's provisions to support far-reaching measures of macroeconomic governance.[332]

In the 1962 Action Programme the Commission had advocated for increased coordination of macroeconomic policies among the Member States on the basis of medium- and long-term economic planning.[333] This triggered a debate on whether economic planning could in fact be pursued within the legal framework of the Treaty of Rome,[334] and by extension about the socio-economic orientation of the Community in general.[335] This discussion is interesting for our purposes because it reveals the different viewpoints on the socio-economic orientation of the Community that existed in the 1960s, and how they translated into the legal discourse. It will be shown that opinions about the substantive content of the Treaty diverted to such an extent that proponents of economic planning like Marjolin and Hirsch found the Treaty to accommodate their views to the same extent as liberalists did, which indicates a pluralist nature of the Treaty.[336] A few ordoliberals, like von der Groeben, supported economic planning on a European level from the beginning.[337] However, most ordoliberal scholars strongly opposed

[330] Klisch (n 316), 132–33; The political practice thus informed the normative interpretation of the provisions; see as an illustration the view of Everling (n 328), 31–35; see also von der Groeben (n 78) 88–91, 311–16.

[331] See Bela Balassa, 'Planning and programming in the European Common Market' (1973) 4 *European Economic Review* 217, 219.

[332] Council Regulation (EEC) No 3181/78 of 18 December 1978 relating to the European monetary system [1978] OJ L 379/2.

[333] EC, 'Memorandum of the Commission on the action programme of the Community for the second stage', 7; see on this Everling (n 328), 8–10.

[334] See for example von der Groeben (n 78), 30–31, 317–21; see also Josef Scherer, *Die Wirtschaftsverfassung der EWG* (Nomos, 1970), 35; Mestmäcker (n 130), 26; Everling (n 328), 10.

[335] Swann and McLachlan (n 320), 85.

[336] See for example Etienne Hirsch, 'French planning and its European application' (1962) 1 *Journal of Common Market Studies* 117, 126; Robert Marjolin, 'Summary of M Marjolin's closing address in the colloquy on "European Planning"' Rome, 30 November–2 December 1962 aei.pitt.edu/14861/1/S141.pdf.

[337] See for example von der Groeben (n 63), 35–40. While emphasizing the importance of economic regulation based on competition on markets, von der Groeben held that such market-based regulation—which already had to be structured through a regulatory order—must be complemented with an economic and monetary policy, a conjunctural policy, social, regional and structural policy. All of these policies require rational state action based on scientific analysis and prognosis. Playing to ordoliberal sensibilities, von der Groeben argued that such analysis could even prevent short-sightened interventionism.

it, arguing that it would be in conflict with the European economic constitution, and in particular with competition policy. Mestmäcker, writing in the mid-80s, acknowledged that the initial ordoliberal concern that economic planning could conflict with competition policy turned out to be unjustified.[338] While Mestmäcker presented the original rejection of economic planning by ordoliberal scholars as a mere over-cautiousness, it cannot be overlooked that the original ordoliberal claim had not been that planning was politically undesirable, but that it was legally prohibited.[339] Mestmäcker thus essentially acknowledged that one of the central ordoliberal claims about the Treaty of Rome's normative orientation was incorrect; which, however, did not keep him from employing essentially the same argument against industrial policy, the main target of ordoliberals in the 1980s and 1990s.

Before we look at the debate on the planning and on the socio-economic orientation of the European economic constitution, we briefly lay out the historical context within which it unfolded. The one side of the debate held that a pure market economy would hinder optimal investment, and thereby obstruct innovation and economic growth.[340] The other side proposed that economic planning constituted 'coercion',[341] and compared it to a Soviet-style command economy, also arguing that it would stifle innovation and economic development.[342] From today's perspective, the debate should be read with considerable scepticism. The scathing criticism of planning voiced for example by German ordoliberals, and the corresponding praises of its virtues by, inter alia, French authors, should be understood as what they were, namely polemics in a political conflict on the socio-economic orientation of the national and the European regulatory frameworks. In practice, the systems supported by the two sides were far less different than the programmatic exclamations of that time would suggest, and 'economic planning' was not a monolithic concept, but a plurality of policies, many of which were in fact adopted in all Western European countries, including Germany. Today, this (sometimes polemical and exaggerated) conflict is sometimes incorrectly understood as a factual description of two conflicting systems of economic governance, onto which current socio-economic conflicts are then projected. In reality, the rise of planning as an instrument of economic governance in and after WWII must be understood in conjunction with the development of modern discipline of macroeconomics and its sophisticated instruments of analysis, as for example

[338] Mestmäcker (n 176), 26.

[339] See ibid, 27.

[340] See for example the positions summarized by Charles Kindleberger, 'French Planning' in Max Millikan (ed), *National Economic Planning* (National Bureau of Economic Research, 1967), 287–88, 290.

[341] See for example Karl Albrecht, *Planifikateure am Werk. Wirtschaft zwischen Zwang und Freiheit* (Econ-Verlag, 1964).

[342] See for example Röpke (n 30), 196.

the 1962 UN Economic Survey of Europe stated.[343] Based on these new technical capabilities in conjunction with an increased ability to collect and process large amounts of data, a comprehensive view of the economy could be taken.[344] This led, according to the UN Economic Survey, to a 'growing preoccupation with long-term objectives'.[345] These long-term objectives could include both development goals for economies that were rebuilding after the war as well as policy goals of fully developed economies, such as a balance of payments equilibrium, monetary stability or full employment.[346] Essentially, 'planning' described the ability of a polity to track the development of its economy and to project multiple possible future developments. On the basis of this knowledge, long-term development objectives could be defined. Economic planning further implied that the instruments that were at the disposal of governments—including the public sector that had grown in importance as a result of the war economy and of nationalizations[347]—were employed in ways to further the development objectives.[348] In other words, 'economic planning' merely described the strategic use of a government's means to achieve economic objectives, informed by a rational analysis of the economy.[349] Understood in this sense, 'economic planning' does not appear as a particularly controversial instrument of economic governance. And indeed, the UN Economic Survey of 1962 reported that not only France, but also the Netherlands—often perceived as a proponent of particularly liberal economic policies[350]—had established planning instruments, alongside Belgium, Italy, the UK, Finland, Greece, Norway, Portugal, Sweden, Turkey, Cyprus, Iceland, Ireland, Malta and Spain.[351] Jelle Zijlstra defended the Dutch central planning office and its policies as follows:

> In Dutch economic policy the central planning office plays an important role. The name of the planning office may lead to misunderstandings. Its tasks are not the instruments of a planned economy. Instead, it works with a model of the Dutch economy, according to which it is possible to establish comprehensively what the possible consequences, under assumed conditions, of a specific policy will be. In other words, the central planning office makes the economic life transparent, so that alternatives, within which the government has to decide, are defined in a precise form.[352]

[343] UN, *Economic planning in Europe* (prepared by the secretariat of the Economic Commission for Europe, Geneva, 1965), 1; see also Röpke (n 30), 170; for a discussion of early economic planning see Eucken (n 67), 58–84.

[344] UN (n 343), 1.

[345] ibid, 2.

[346] ibid, 2.

[347] ibid, 1.

[348] ibid, 1–2.

[349] See Balassa (n 325), 79; see also Pierre Massé, 'The French Plan and economic theory' (1965) 33 *Econometrica* 265, 265; see, in a similar sense, Zijlstra (n 7), 63.

[350] On planning in the Netherlands see Zijlstra (n 7), 30–31; the Dutch government had the competence, for example, to limit wage growth in the general interest.

[351] UN (n 343), 1; see also Stanislaw Wellisz, 'Economic planning in the Netherlands, France, and Italy' (1960) 68 *Journal of Political Economy* 252.

[352] Zijlstra (n 315), 6, fn 1 (my translation).

As already mentioned, 'economic planning' did not describe a specific form of economic governance, but a broad set of activities that were employed to a different extent by all European governments. This is illustrated for example by a Commission report compiled by Jelle Zijlstra.[353] In the report, Zijlstra distinguished six types of planning:[354] type I describes the prognosis of future economic developments based on collected data; type II describes all kinds of macroeconomic instruments, including budgetary, fiscal and monetary policy as well as wage and price controls; type III describes the definition of quantitative economic objectives for the economy as a whole, including growth and employment targets; types IV and V are planning by means of subsidies and fiscal incentives for economic operators, either with (type V) or without (type IV) contractual obligation of the concerned company; finally, type VI describes a command economy proper, with industries acting on the basis of detailed government measures. The study showed that all the Member States employed some or all of these types of economic planning (see table below). This also includes countries like Germany, which today is often, rather uncritically, portrayed as the antagonist of France on the issue of planning in the 1960s. Germany's system of economic governance provided instruments for strategic, long-term development on the basis of economic forecasting that was qualitatively similar to those countries that explicitly embraced economic planning.[355] Prior to the establishment of common European policies, Germany employed, for example, price controls in many sectors, including transport and agriculture,[356] and a publicly determined interest rate.[357] Like France or the Netherlands, Germany had an expanding public sector, and national champions that served as a connection belt to the private market actors.[358] Germany also employed a variety of macroeconomic instruments to influence the economy. Von der Groeben argued that many national policies in fact constitute direct interventions into the economy, including transport, housing, agriculture, research, public enterprises and conjunctural policies, and Germany was of course active in all of these areas.[359] Especially from the 1960s onwards, Germany engaged more explicitly in various forms of economic planning.[360]

Ordoliberals, despite what the debate on planning might suggest, were generally opposed neither to interventionist policies connected to the stabilization of the business cycle, nor to macroeconomic analysis or to strategic planning on the basis

[353] Zijlstra (n 7), 32–36; Balassa (n 325), 75; see also Massé (n 349), 265.
[354] Zijlstra (n 7), 32–33; see also verLoren van Themaat (n 325).
[355] Kindleberger (n 340), 291, with further references.
[356] Zijlstra (n 7), 31.
[357] ibid, 31.
[358] Though Zijlstra argued that the size of the public sector was significantly larger in countries like Italy and France than in Germany and the Netherlands. Ibid, 28–29.
[359] Von der Groeben (n 63), 37.
[360] See for example Zijlstra (n 7), 30.

of economic projections.[361] What they consistently rejected, as Hans Tietmeyer remarked, was merely comprehensive quantitative planning (ie, the setting of specific growth targets for the national economy as a whole as well as for specific industrial sectors), which they believed would interfere too much with the economic freedom of enterprises, and which they claimed was part of French-style planning.[362] However, French planners vividly denied any direct binding effect of their plans on the private sector, and emphasized that private companies were subject to the plan through indirect influence only, most notably through macroeconomic policies as well as the investment activity of the government and the nationalized industries.[363] Ultimately, the difference between the German and the French practice of macroeconomic governance was probably one of degree only.[364] For example, it seems that German scholars initially preferred a shorter time horizon in conjunctural policies of two to three years, while other countries operated with longer planning periods.[365] Moreover, the countries' policies shifted over the years: whereas French planning became more relaxed, most other countries, including Germany, moved further towards a planning approach in the late 1950s and early 1960s.[366] The debate for or against planning thus constituted a polemical simplification that must be understood within its historical context, but does not provide a correct description of the actual regulatory practices of that time. In fact, most contemporary economists and policymakers were engaged in an extensive debate on the advantages and disadvantages of various types of planning instruments, without reverting to a simplistic view of either hailing or condemning planning as a whole. McLachlan and Swann, for example, underlined the importance of economic forecasting to increase coherence and rationality of government action, and Balassa, while rejecting the idea of industry-level

[361] Wolfgang Tietmeyer, 'Die Gründung des Sachverständigenrates aus der Sicht der Wirtschaftspolitik' in Sachverständigenrat (ed), *Vierzig Jahre Sachverständigenrat* (Sachverständigenrat, 2003), 23; see also Everling (n 328), 10; Zijlstra (n 7), 28. By way of example, see Müller-Armack's proposal for a European conjunctural board. Müller-Armack (n 109), 331–49.

[362] Tietmeyer (n 361), 23; see also Zijlstra, who emphasized that medium-term planning on the European level did not aim to coordinate the decisions of individual economic actors, which seems to have been one of the central concerns of ordoliberals. Zijlstra (n 7), 61.

[363] See Hirsch (n 336), 123; Massé (n 349), 266; Balassa (n 325), 78–79; Zijlstra (n 7), 28.

[364] Robert Marjolin emphasized that, on the one hand, French-type planning did not conflict with free enterprise, and that, on the other hand, other European countries pursued instruments of planning as well, though under a different denomination. Robert Marjolin, 'A Plan for Europe?' Speech at the Congress of the Confédération nationale de la Mutualité, de la Coopération et du Crédit agricoles (1962) aei.pitt.edu/14820/1/S88.pdf, 1.

[365] Von der Groeben (n 63), 37; von der Groeben speculated that this initial rejection of planning was a reaction to the four- and five-year plans employed in Nazi Germany and the USSR. Von der Groeben (n 293), 46; For a similar argument see Zijlstra (n 7), 27.

[366] See for example Kindleberger (n 340), 296; Zijlstra (n 7), 27. On this and for an overview of planning instruments employed in Germany, see Mestmäcker (n 176), 26–27.

planning, emphasized the positive impact of planning for the public and semi-public sectors.[367] Charles Kindleberger held that 'planning is to be distinguished from dirigisme which prevailed in the interwar years—the steady interference of public decisions in response to day-to-day difficulties without systematic, long-term elicited aims'.[368]

Economic Planning in the EEC and in the Member States, According to verLoren van Themaat and Based on a Commission Study by Jelle Zijlstra[369]

Planning type	**Characteristic**	**Examples of countries employing this planning type**	**Planning in the EEC**
Type I	Prognosis of future developments	All Member States, eg Netherlands Central Planning Bureau	Medium-term economic policy committee[370]
Type II	Macroeconomic policy[371]	All Member States, including Germany[372]	Arts 103 and 108 EEC
Type III	Objectives for economy as a whole, eg growth or employment targets	All Member States, including Germany since mid-60s	
Type IV	Subsidies and fiscal incentives, with no obligation on industries	Belgium, Italy	EIB, ESF
Type V	Subsidies and fiscal incentives, industries bound by planning contract	France	Possible through Arts 92, 93 EEC
Type VI	Industry obliged by detailed government measures	Specific industry branches in all Member States (agriculture, transport)	Agriculture, transport, foreign trade

[367] Balassa (n 325), 80; Swann and McLachlan (n 320), 87.
[368] Kindleberger (n 340), 287.
[369] Table aggregated from data provided by verLoren van Themaat (n 325), 313–15 and 320–22.
[370] For Hans von der Groeben, the Committee's activities were *acceptable* because its forecasts were not considered growth targets, 'but are intended simply as pointers to the possible and probable economic trend'. Von der Groeben (n 6), 146.
[371] This entry inclues 'budget policy, fiscal policy, discount-policy of the central banks, control of the credit policy of the banks, the rate of exchange and ... some form of control of wages and prices'. VerLoren van Themaat (n 325), 313.
[372] Zijlstra particularly emphasized that Germany was engaged in such planning. Zijlstra (n 7), 34–35.

Just like the Member States, the EEC was engaged in a variety of forms of economic planning (see table above). Articles 103 and 108 EEC allowed for macroeconomic interventions necessary in the management of business cycles or in case of balance of payments difficulties (type II).[373] Both the EIB and the ESF operated on the basis of incentives for private operators (type IV); and finally, the agricultural and transport sectors were steered through detailed, binding regulations,[374] thereby essentially operating partly as a command economy (type VI). For economic forecasting (type I), the Council decided unanimously in 1964 to set up a Medium-term Economic Policy Committee within the Commission.[375] The task of the committee was to create quantitative projections of the development of specific sectors as well as of the economy as a whole for a period of five years.[376] The German Competition Commissioner, Hans von der Groeben, explained this decision as follows:

> With national economies becoming increasingly open to each other, the economic policy measures of a Member State are not without repercussions on the other economies and on the Community as a whole. There is a risk that the Member States and the European institutions may take decisions without sufficient regard to their effects on the Community's economy, and that the policies of the national and common institutions may develop along divergent lines. For these reasons it is necessary to facilitate coordination of the various measures, to make them more rational, and to direct them towards common objectives.[377]

The debate on planning also manifested itself in legal discourse. In Germany, for example, a veritable academic cottage industry developed that tried to establish whether the Treaty of Rome should be understood as having a specific socio-economic orientation that constituted the Community's *Wirtschaftsverfassung* (economic constitution).[378] As already discussed in the introduction, the term 'economic constitution' was used to describe the fundamental socio-economic orientation of a polity, expressed in its institutional and regulatory framework.[379] From a legal perspective, such an 'economic constitution' would determine the meaning of the constitutional text, and serve as an interpretative guideline. Accordingly, measures that conflict with the socio-economic orientation of the polity's 'economic constitution' would be prohibited.[380] In Germany, a common view was that the Treaty of Rome had to be understood as a political choice for a specific socio-economic system, namely a market economy within a regulatory

[373] VerLoren van Themaat (n 369), 320.
[374] ibid, 321.
[375] Décision du Conseil 64/247/CEE créant un Comité de politique économique à moyen terme [1964] OJ 64/1031; see von der Groeben (n 6), 146; von der Groeben (n 78), 319.
[376] Von der Groeben (n 6), 146.
[377] ibid, 145–46.
[378] See the extensive literature overview in Scherer (n 334).
[379] For a definition of the term 'economic constitution' see ibid, 41–52.
[380] ibid, 36.

framework that restrains potential adverse effects of the activities of market forces. This system was denominated by the various authors as *gemäßigter Liberalismus* (restrained liberalism), *bedingt freie Wettbewerbswirtschaft* (conditionally free competition economy), *institutioneller Markt* (institutionalized market), *kontrollierte Marktwirtschaft* (controlled market economy) or *soziale Marktwirtschaft* (social market economy).[381] The concepts were essentially understood to be in conflict with both a 'free' market economy (characterized by an absence of a regulatory framework for the market) on the one hand, and a centrally planned economy on the other. Accordingly, the Treaty of Rome was often understood to prohibit European economic planning.[382] By contrast, other authors concluded that the Treaty of Rome constituted a political choice for a mixed economy, or a regulatory system consisting of both free market and planning characteristics.[383] Finally, a third view held that the European economic constitution could only be defined in the negative: according to this approach (which is essentially the one also taken in this book), the Treaty of Rome constituted no choice for any particular socio-economic model. Scherer, for example, argued that the European economic constitution was 'open' in the sense that it allowed the competent lawmakers and regulatory authorities to choose the appropriate socio-economic system, within certain boundaries.[384] These boundaries could be found, however, only at the extremes: according to Scherer, the Treaty of Rome would merely prohibit a 'pure market economy' (without any regulatory interference) on the one hand, and a (Soviet-style) centrally planned economy on the other.[385] Within these limits, however, Scherer identified a 'far-reaching neutrality of the Treaty of Rome in regard to economic policies'.[386] Accordingly, Scherer held, the Treaty of Rome would allow medium- and long-term planning on European level. The debate on the socio-economic orientation of the Community therefore found no unequivocal answer, but was also rendered increasingly obsolete by the fact that economic planning became considerably less controversial during the 1960s.[387] To conclude this section it can be held that the Treaty of Rome provided, in principle, far-reaching competences to coordinate macroeconomic policies, which were subject to a controversial debate in the 1950s and 1960s. While the Member States ultimately pursued this route prior to the creation of the EMS only to a limited extent, this reflects a political choice rather than the effect of a legal restriction.

[381] See ibid, 199, with further references.

[382] ibid, 199.

[383] ibid, 200; see for example Hirsch (n 336), 125–27; Marjolin (n 336); see also Swann and McLachlan (n 320), 85.

[384] Scherer (n 334), 200.

[385] ibid, 201.

[386] ibid, 205.

[387] VerLoren van Themaat argued that the German 'neoliberals' (which in this book I refer to under the term 'ordoliberals') were 'impressed by the economic, legal, political and ethical harmful effects of an extremely far-going economic dirigism'. However, he also recognized 'an increasing general conviction that there was a need for a certain measure of correction in the market mechanism, especially of a macro-economic nature … particularly after 1960'. VerLoren van Themaat (n 292), 21.

INTERMEDIATE FINDINGS

It has been shown that the Treaty of Rome has been shaped by very different socio-economic assumptions.[388] The EEC was founded within a context of a global movement towards trade liberalization, which manifested itself in the Community's commitment towards the abolition of internal trade barriers within a customs union as well as its integration in the GATT. In the integration debate of the 1950s, the benefits arising from an abolition of tariffs and quantitative restrictions were termed the 'static' effects of integration. However, the Treaty of Rome was shaped by the assumption that the beneficial effects of economic integration would in fact be mostly caused by the changes to the structure of production that would follow the integration of the national markets into one common market: this included increased competition among producers, changed investment patterns as well as the creation of economies of scale. These effects—which were discussed under the umbrella term of the 'dynamic' gains from integration—would not be triggered automatically, but required a conducive regulatory framework. These different socio-economic assumptions all influenced the Treaty of Rome, and manifested themselves in the dual regulatory approach that shaped the Treaty. This approach is best described as the establishment of a common market within a framework of policy harmonization aimed at normalizing competitive conditions. After the war, markets as a form of organizing economic processes were far from idealized. Competition was believed to have the potential to release innovative forces, but only if the economic actors would compete on a level playing field. This required the elimination of regulatory differences among the Member States which influenced the cost structure of production. Moreover, it was assumed that, while the common market had the potential to increase the general welfare, such potential could be realized only if the destabilizing effects of market integration could be properly managed. This required the coordination of macroeconomic policies of the Member States. However, the degree to which economic policies between the Member States had to be harmonized in order to unlock the beneficial effects of competition remained conflicted. It is in this sense that the Treaty of Rome must be understood as a pluralist instrument.

This claim as to the pluralist character of the Treaty of Rome is also supported by the fact that it found broad support from both the left and the right. The Treaty of Rome is clearly a brainchild of post-war socio-economic thinking, which emphasized the importance of free economic exchange, while recognizing the importance of a regulatory framework that ensured that market activities would in fact have positive effects on the general welfare.[389] Such thinking corresponded

[388] It is in this sense that verLoren van Themaat and Gormley argued that 'the Treaty does not clearly choose which economic system is the most desirable'. VerLoren van Themaat and Gormley (n 173), 580.

[389] Maurizio Ferrera, *The Boundaries of Welfare: European Integration and the New Spatial Politics of Social Protection* (Oxford University Press, 2005) 90–96; see generally John Ruggie, 'International

with Keynesian theory,[390] but was equally embraced by other approaches, including ordoliberalism.[391] As Lindberg showed, the open regulatory character of the Treaty of Rome, which was conceptualized as a 'framework treaty', allowed the representatives of different socio-economic views to assume that their respective regulatory vision could be pursued within the framework created by the Treaty. This is one of the reasons why the Treaty of Rome was supported by a broad coalition of political actors, ranging from labour unions and social democratic parties to Christian democratic and liberal parties (with the sole exception of the Communist parties).[392]

regimes, transactions, and change: embedded liberalism in the postwar economic order' (1982) 36 *International Organization* 379.

390 Kapteyn and verLoren van Themaat argued in their treatise on the EEC: 'Since Keynes we have to recognize that a free market mechanism cannot function satisfactorily without at least some amount of overall economic policy.' Kapteyn and verLoren van Themaat (n 58), 51.

391 Ordoliberals of the 1950s and 1960s assumed that the unfolding of societally beneficial market forces in the industrialized global economy would require a rational regulatory structure. See for example Eucken (n 67), 7.

392 Lindberg (n 23), passim, in particular 107–11, 287–95.

2

Interpreting the Treaty in its Historical Context II: The 1992 Project

INTRODUCTION

WHILE THE COMMISSION'S initial plan for economic union, as laid out in the 1962 action programme, had materialized only in parts, the European integration process nonetheless advanced significantly during the transitional period. Ernst-Joachim Mestmäcker concluded in 1974 that the initial goal of European integration—the creation of conditions similar to those of an internal market—had mostly been achieved.[1] Successfully implemented projects included, most notably, the customs union, the abolition of discriminatory access restrictions in national legislation, the creation of a system of European competition law, as well as the establishment of the common commercial, agricultural and transport policies. Beyond that, important initiatives for further economic integration had been taken, such as the Werner Plan for monetary and economic union. By the end of the transitional period the EEC had become an important political arena within which a broad variety of objectives were pursued. In the 1970s, the Community took up new activities in many key socio-economic areas; these included fields such as industrial, environmental, social and consumer policy, as well as the coordination of monetary policies, for all of which the Community had enacted legislative programmes by 1974. This mirrored the expansion of the same policies on the national level, often complementing regulatory efforts of the Member States relating to policy objectives that could not effectively be pursued by domestic means alone. In particular, the Member States made increasing use of the Community framework to react to adverse international developments: for example, the 'Social Policy Action Programme' of 1974 constituted a reaction to the first oil crisis, and the Werner Plan and later the EMS were created in response to the breakdown of the Bretton Woods system. The Community turned out to have a flexible regulatory framework within which the Member States could pursue evolving socio-economic objectives, sometimes complemented with multilateral agreements among the Member States.

[1] Ernst-Joachim Mestmäcker, *Europäisches Wettbewerbsrecht* (Beck'sche Verlagsbuchhandlung, 1974), 83.

It is within this context that the Member States increasingly looked for solutions on the European level when dealing with the macroeconomic instability, low growth and high unemployment that they had experienced since the 1979 crisis. The European Council meeting in Copenhagen in December 1982 defined the Community's socio-economic priorities broadly, ranging from macroeconomic goals such as 're-establishing economic stability', 'strengthening the European Monetary System' and an active growth policy consisting of a reduction of interest rates and investment support, to an 'exploration' of labour market flexibility, employment opportunities and training for the young as well as the 'strengthening the common market and intensifying action to eliminate practices and measures which restrict trade and distort competition.'[2] These measures were to be pursued both within the existing regulatory framework of the Treaty as well as in the form of multilateral cooperation among the Member States. At the same time, the possibility of a reform of primary law was increasingly discussed as well. This is illustrated already by the German-Italian 'Draft European Act' of 1981,[3] the 'Solemn Declaration on European Union' made at the European Council in Stuttgart in 1983,[4] as well as the 'Draft Treaty Establishing the European Union' that the European Parliament proposed in 1984.[5] Based on these initiatives, the Community ultimately embarked on a broad reform process from the mid-1980s onwards, which came to be termed the '1992 project', because its asserted goal was the establishment of a European Union by 1992. We will employ the term '1992 project' to describe two Treaty reforms—the Single European Act (SEA) and the Treaty of Maastricht—as well as significant legislative projects and policy initiatives, most notably of course the 'completion' of the internal market as proposed by the Commission's White Paper as well as the 'Delors II' package to increase regional redistributive payments. This chapter will attempt to assess the normative implications of the 1992 reforms regarding the Union's socio-economic orientation.

The 1992 project parallels a broader shift in the functioning of the capitalist system observable in all Western countries, and which may be described as the advent of neoliberalism.[6] The post-war political settlement had been one where—in contrast to the communist countries—private ownership over productive means was retained (though the size of nationalized industries grew during and after World War II), but workers would receive an increasing share of the national product. This was guaranteed by an institutional structure that usually included corporatist elements and strong labour unions. It ensured wage increases in line with productivity gains, an expansion of the welfare state, and sometimes even the development of instruments of democratic economic governance. As we discussed

[2] European Council, *Presidency's Conclusions* (Copenhagen 3–4 December, 1982).

[3] Draft European Act—German-Italian Initiative (*Bulletin of the European Communities* No 11, 1981), aei.pitt.edu/1800/1/draft_european_act.pdf.

[4] Solemn Declaration on European Union (*Bulletin of the European Communities* No 6, 1983).

[5] Draft Treaty establishing the European Union (*Bulletin of the European Communities* No 2, 1984).

[6] See generally Wolfgang Streeck, *Gekaufte Zeit* (Suhrkamp, 2013), in particular 148–76.

in the first chapter, the settlement was initially considered to be beneficial from the perspective of the capitalist class, because it neutralized the risk of a complete dismantlement of the capitalist system. The extent to which such a risk was perceived as real is illustrated by the pessimistic evaluation advanced by Schumpeter in his 1942 book, *Capitalism, Socialism and Democracy*, where he answered the question as to whether capitalism could survive in the negative.[7] However, as capitalism re-stabilized, the settlement unravelled over the course of the 1970s: Moravcsik held in that regard that '[t]he business-labor bargains on which corporatism and incomes policy are based were disintegrating.'[8] This disintegration went largely at the expense of labour: wage increases no longer matched productivity gains, so that the labour share in overall income fell, the welfare state contracted, and the tax burden shifted from capital to labour.[9] The increasing macroeconomic instability that the Western world had experienced since the 1970s must be understood in this context, as for example Wolfgang Streeck explained. The 1950s and 1960s had brought an expectation of continuously growing prosperity for the general population; but with a manifest unwillingness of capital to acquiesce to a falling share of national income, and a corresponding fall in private investment, this expectation could at some point no longer be met by wage increases and a tax-financed expansion of public services.[10] According to Streeck, the inflationary episodes of the 1970s, the growth of public debt in the 1980s, and the piling up of private debt facilitated by financial deregulation of the 1990s and 2000s each constituted—ultimately unsuccessful—strategies to retain the (impression of) rising popular prosperity, despite the stagnation of wages and the contraction of the welfare state.[11]

It has been argued that economic integration, both on a regional and a global level, has played an important role in the dismantling of the post-war settlement between capital and labour.[12] Multinational corporations were increasingly able to elude national regulation and to pressure labour unions into accepting wage stagnation. States faced increasing regulatory competition; and, perhaps most importantly, the liberalization of capital movements put pressure on national tax systems to shift the tax burden away from capital.[13] The 1992 project played a significant role in this process, enacting policies which initiated or facilitated such developments. This is the case, most notably, for the liberalization of capital movements, which was fully realized in the late 1980s and enshrined in primary law by the Treaty of Maastricht.[14] The same is true for the liberalization of public services,

[7] Joseph Schumpeter, *Capitalism, Socialism, and Democracy* (Harper Colophon Books, 1975) 61.
[8] Andrew Moravcsik, 'Negotiating the Single European Act: national interests and conventional statecraft in the European Community' (1991) 45 *International Organization* 19, 53.
[9] Streeck (n 6), 85, 138.
[10] ibid, 61.
[11] ibid, 15.
[12] ibid, 102.
[13] ibid, 102.
[14] ibid, 102; see also Colin Crouch, *The strange non-death of neoliberalism* (Polity, 2011) 112–13.

in which the European Union played a particularly significant role.[15] Regulatory competition was facilitated by the Court's interpretation of the free movement provisions, and European monetary union reduced the ability of Member States to engage in autonomous fiscal and monetary policies. Consequently, the 1992 project has been described as an ideologically structured project, for example by Mark Pollack.[16] While recognizing the plural objectives implemented by the SEA and the Maastricht Treaty, Pollack nonetheless contends that 'the overall thrust of the treaties remains clearly neoliberal'. Along similar lines, Fitoussi and Saraceno argue that 'The EU institutional set-up is no accident. It reflects the neoliberal doctrine that prevailed in the early 1990s.'[17] Menéndez equally speaks of the 'substantive triumph of neoliberalism in policy terms at the European level.'[18] In this context the present chapter asks whether the 1992 reforms altered the European economic constitution in such a way that the Treaty can only be interpreted according to one specific socio-economic paradigm. Referring to the distinction set up in the introduction, we ask whether neoliberal outcomes are *required* or merely *enabled* or *facilitated* by the reformed Treaty. It will be asserted that the Treaty's pluralist character was not altered by these reforms; rather, the 1992 project illustrates the plurality of socio-economic goals pursued and of instruments employed on the European level, and the complex interrelations between them. This is not to say that the 1992 reforms did not play a significant role in the unfolding of the neoliberal project on the European level: while they facilitated the implementation of neoliberal policies within the broader political and economic shifts of the 1980s and 1990s, the Treaty remained, in principle, open to alternative socio-economic projects. In this respect it is important to keep an eye the global dimension: the neoliberal turn shaped all Western countries, and not only those that were Members of the Union. In many of them, most notably the United States, the transformations took place without any significant constitutional reform, which should be taken into account in establishing the role of the 1992 project in explaining the neoliberal turn in Europe. While the 1992 project has been enacted within its context, the two should not be equated, as the present chapter will argue.

The claim that the 1992 reforms upheld the Treaty's pluralist character will be developed in five main sections. The first addresses the socio-economic context

[15] Judith Clifton, Francisco Comín and Daniel Díaz Fuentes, *Privatisation in the European Union* (Kluwer, 2003) 99–100.

[16] Mark Pollack, 'Integrating Left and Right: Studying EU Politics' (1998) 11 *ECSA Review* 2; other scholars put forward a different view. According to Miguel Poiares Maduro, for example, the Treaty of Maastricht 'has struck a further blow to the liberal concept of European integration.' Miguel Poiares Maduro, *We the Court. The European Court of Justice and the European Economic Constitution: a critical reading of Article 30 of the EC Treaty* (Hart, 1998) 160.

[17] Jean-Paul Fitoussi and Francesco Saraceno, 'European economic governance: the Berlin–Washington Consensus' (2013) 37 *Cambridge Journal of Economics* 479, 480.

[18] Augustín José Menéndez, 'The Existential Crisis of the European Union' (2013) 14 *German Law Journal* 453, 466.

within which the 1992 project was conceived. It will be shown that the Community and the Member States experienced pressure from a diverse and potentially contradictory set of dynamics, which shaped the measures that were passed in response. Recognizing the diversity of influences to which the 1992 reforms reacted helps to evade ideologically coded narratives, and to correctly conceptualize the pluralist nature of measures that were enacted in response. The second part discusses the economic assumptions that guided the 1992 reforms on the basis of the two key studies commissioned by the European Commission in the 1980s, the Cecchini Report and the Padoa-Schioppa Report. It will be argued that the socio-economic aspects of the 1992 reforms were fundamentally characterized by the dual goal of achieving economic growth and macroeconomic stability, as well as by the assumption that the two are connected in complex ways.[19] Most importantly, from the perspective of our book, a core assumption of the 1992 project was that the potential benefits of market integration could only be realized if its destabilizing effects (most notably through capital mobility and regional imbalances) could be controlled. We will see that this dual goal draws from different socio-economic paradigms. The third part discusses the reforms of primary law as enacted by the SEA and the Treaty of Maastricht. It will be argued that, though the reforms change the European regulatory landscape in important ways, they do not alter the Treaty's pluralist character. This fact is obscured, however, by a contemporary representation of European law that is prominently based on a distinction between 'economic' and 'non-economic' concerns, which we described in the introduction as the two-sphere fallacy. It will be argued that such distinction is not only an ideologically charged and factually unwarranted analytical device, but also invites incorrect normative assumptions as to the Treaty's socio-economic orientation. The fourth part deals with two key modes of socio-economic governance in Europe, mutual recognition and harmonization. Commonly defined as opposites, the two concepts lie at the core of a common, but ideologically charged narrative of the 1992 project. The section attempts to dispel the dichotomic reading of these concepts, and embed them in a more nuanced historical representation. The fifth part will address the completive measures of the 1992 project. This includes measures such as the cohesion funds, monetary union and industrial policy. It will be argued that these measures help understand the plurality of socio-economic concerns that shaped the 1992 project: the policymakers were concerned with the effects market integration would have on macroeconomic stability as well as on regional and social cohesion. This overview over some of the flanking measures gives further evidence to the plurality of socio-economic goals pursued through the 1992 reforms.

[19] In this sense Kaarlo Tuori and Klaus Tuori, *The Eurozone Crisis* (Cambridge University Press, 2014), 36–37.

THE PRESSURES TO WHICH THE 1992 PROJECT REACTED

The End of the Post-War Boom, the Oil Crises and the Unravelling of the Capital/Labour Compromise

The 1970s brought Europe's largest economic downturn since WWII, with a recession following each the 1973 and 1979 oil shocks.[20] The downturns were accompanied by growing unemployment and rising inflation. Many economists argue that the crises, while triggered by rising energy prices, hit on deeper, structural causes in the European economy that exacerbated and prolonged each downturn.[21] Barry Eichengreen, for example, held that such structural causes were indicated by the declining productivity growth in Europe.[22] According to Eichengreen, the first decades after the war were a period of 'catch-up' growth: Europe had experienced an innovation gap during WWII as compared to the United States. After the war, it could mobilize capital on a large scale to adopt technologies that had already been developed in the United States. This period of 'extensive growth' ended in the 1970s, when Europe had finally 'caught up' with the United States. It was replaced by a phase of 'intensive growth', which required innovation and increased flexibility to invest in unknown technologies.[23] This new growth phase, Eichengreen argued, required a different institutional structure: whereas the corporatist, big-industry approach was adequate for 'catch-up' growth, it failed to create a sufficient environment for an innovative industry.[24] The post-war economic boom had ended, and the old growth models no longer seemed to work.[25] Whereas Eichengreen focused on the institutional setup of the European countries, Hyman Minsky emphasized the growing instability inherent in the post-war capitalist system.[26] Minsky showed that businesses had increasingly financed their operations with credit rather than equity. This meant that economic problems in a single company or economic sector could quickly affect the whole economy, spreading through the financial system. As a response to this increasing instability,

[20] Barry Eichengreen, *The European economy since 1945. Coordinated capitalism and beyond* (Princeton University Press, 2007) 252.

[21] See for example ibid, 252ff.

[22] ibid, 252.

[23] ibid, 5–6.

[24] ibid, 5–6.

[25] Sandholtz and Zysman held: 'As unemployment rose, the old growth model built on a political settlement in each country was challenged—initially from the left by strategies of nationalization with state investment, and then from the right by strategies of deregulation with privatization.' And: 'Throughout Europe the corporatist temptation waned; that is, management of the macroeconomy by direct negotiations among social groups and the government no longer seemed to work. In many union and left circles an understanding grew that adaption to market processes would be required.' Wayne Sandholtz and John Zysman, '1992: Recasting the European Bargain' (1989) 42 *World Politics* 95, 110 and 112.

[26] Hyman Minsky, *Stabilizing an Unstable Economy* (Yale University Press, 1986) 9.

states resorted to the macroeconomic management of their economies. While this cushioned the downturns, it also allowed the financial markets to resume their previous lending practice, thereby letting instability accumulate in the system.[27] According to Minksy, the downturn of 1966 was the last one that could be fully contained by means of macroeconomic management, and from the 1970s onwards the Western economies experienced crises at an ever-growing pace. Macroeconomic instability was exacerbated by the unravelling of the Bretton Woods system in the early 1970s, which had provided relative exchange rate stability in the preceding 25 years.[28] As discussed in the previous chapter, the Member States, which all engaged in the macroeconomic management of their economies, also increasingly looked for coordination at the European level, as illustrated by the adoption of medium-term economic planning in 1966, the Werner Plan of 1970 for the establishment of economic and monetary union, and the EMS in 1978. The problem of rising unemployment also led Member States to pursue social programmes on the national level and increasingly also on the European level. The phase between 1974 and 1985 was characterized by a commentator as a period of 'social activism'.[29] This included the first 'Social Policy Action Programme' of 1974 and a number of directives on labour market-related issues. These measures might be seen as early attempts by the Member States to employ the EEC for the economic purpose of providing greater macroeconomic stability, and were further developed in the 1980s as part of the 1992 strategy.

Perceived Increase of Competition from Japan and the United States

The competitive position of Western Europe vis-à-vis the United States was a central concern for European policymakers from the very inception of the EEC. An influential book by the French journalist and politician Jean-Jacques Servan-Schreiber, *The American Challenge*, published in 1967, described the United States and Europe as being in a state of industrial war.[30] Servan-Schreiber believed that European policy should aim at the creation of a limited number of large-size companies in technologically advanced areas that could be globally competitive. In the late 1970s, competition with Japan became an additional concern.[31]

[27] ibid, 199.

[28] VerLoren van Themaat pointed out that the breakdown of the IMF, which preceded the economic crisis of 1973, must be understood to be the consequence of structural problems not caused by the crisis itself. Pieter verLoren van Themaat, *The changing structure of international economic law: a contribution of legal history, of comparative law and of general legal theory to the debate on a new international economic order* (Nijhoff, 1981) 67.

[29] H Mosley, 'The social dimension of Europe integration' (1990) 129 *International Labour Review* 147, 149.

[30] Jean-Jacques Servan-Schreiber, *Le défi américain* (Denoel, 1967); on the influence of the book on European industrial and competition policy see for example Mestmäcker (n 1), 81.

[31] See for example Sandholtz and Zysman (n 25), 95.

European policymakers and commentators were particularly worried about Europe's growing lag in technological development, above all in the IT and telecommunication sectors.[32] According to Fligstein, 'business and political leaders across Western Europe were of the opinion that the Japanese and, to a lesser degree, American corporations were more efficient and were likely to take more market share across industries.'[33] The big European businesses were especially interested in creating a home market large enough to sustain large corporations which in turn could compete with the American and Japanese companies on a global level. Fiat CEO Clemente Signoroni explained in 1989: 'The final goal of the European "dream" is to transform Europe into an integrated economic continent with its specific role, weight and responsibility on the international scenario vis-à-vis the United States and Japan.'[34] And a text published in the early 1980s by the CEO of Philips titled *Europe 1990*, which proved to be influential for the 1992 project, held:

> There is really no choice ... and the only option left for the Community is to achieve the goals laid down in the Treaty of Rome. Only in this way can industry compete globally, by exploiting economies of scale, for what will then be the biggest home market in the world today: the European Community home market.[35]

The Commission, which had essentially espoused similar views since the EEC's inception, pursued the goal of creating a European home market for large companies with increasing force in the 1970s and 1980s, often supported by the Member States.[36] This is illustrated by the Community's industrial and R&D policy, as well as in the Commission's practice in competition law.[37] However, the ambition to foster the creation of global corporations based in Europe came into potential conflict with a competition-based form of economic regulation.[38] Both ordoliberals as well as left commentators criticized the Community's industrial policy for

[32] ibid, 113.

[33] Neil Fligstein and Iona Mara-Drita, 'How to Make a Market: Reflections on the Attempt to Create a Single Market in the European Union' (1996) 102 *American Journal of Sociology* 1, 10; along the same lines, Eichengreen described the situation in the following terms: 'Europe stagnated while the United States and Japan surged ahead, the continent losing market share in automobiles, electronics, and a variety of other industries.' Eichengreen (n 20), 335.

[34] Quoted in Sandholtz and Zysman (n 25), 95.

[35] Wisse Dekker, *Europe 1990: An Agenda for Change* (1985), quoted in Sandholtz and Zysman (n 25), 117.

[36] See for example EC, 'The Community's industrial policy. Commission Memorandum to the Council' COM(70) 100; Supplement to the Bulletin 4/1970 of the European Communities. On this see Mestmäcker (n 1), 81–82.

[37] Mestmäcker (n 1), 81–82; on the influence of Servan-Schreiber's theses on the Commission's harmonization proposals in company law, see Theodore Vogelaar, 'The Approximation of the laws of Member States under the Treaty of Rome' (1975) 12 *Common Market Law Review* 211, 219.

[38] According to verLoren van Themaat, this conflict was recognizable, for example, in the growing importance of competition law in all developed countries as well as on the international plane. VerLoren van Themaat (n 28), 92–93.

facilitating concentrations, which they perceived as economically and politically undesirable.[39]

The Centrifugal Forces of Market Integration

The EEC was not only confronted with global instability, as illustrated by the collapse of the Bretton Woods system and the oil crises, but also with centrifugal forces that arose from market integration itself. One such centrifugal force was the exacerbation of regional differences: productive factors in economic unions are assumed to move where the highest return is expected. This could potentially have destabilizing consequences: the structurally strong regions might attract financial and human capital, thereby draining the structurally weak periphery. As discussed in the previous chapter, the risk of unequal regional development had already been an important topic of debate in the 1950s and 1960s.[40] The demise of the industrial base in Southern Italy after unification in the nineteenth century—both in relative and in absolute terms—served as a paradigmatic example and was frequently cited, for example in the Ohlin Report.[41] Cushioning the adverse effects of market integration on peripheral regions was believed to require counterbalancing policy interventions. Measures proposed by the Ohlin Report to alleviate the problems of peripheral regions included subsidies, capital loans from

[39] See for example Mestmäcker (n 1), 81–83; Perry Anderson and Stuart Hall, 'The Politics of the Common Market' (1961) I/10 *New Left Review* 1, 5–6.

[40] See for example Balassa, who argued: 'Greater importance [than to diverting effects] can be attributed to adverse factor movements that are connected with agglomerative tendencies. In a common market, free factor migration will be directed, in part, to those regions where the existence of social and economic overhead and other forms of agglomeration economies contributes to higher factor returns. The movement of labour and capital would then proceed from 'poor' to 'rich' countries and regions. We shall argue at a later point that, in such a case, an absolute deterioration of living standards may result at the place of emigration if skilled workers emigrate from the depressed area, the age structure deteriorates, and the per capita burden of taxation increases.' Bela Balassa, *The Theory of Economic Integration* (George Allen & Unwin Ltd, 1961), 85.

[41] '[T]he fact that well established industries tend to benefit from widening markets by fresh opportunities for further reductions in cost is likely to have undesirable effects on regions that for one reason or another have not yet been able to develop any large industries of their own. For example, the less developed areas of southern Europe would, if international trade were liberalised indiscriminately, be in serious danger of remaining unindustrialised. The undesirable effects that trade liberalisation may have on industrially less developed areas are illustrated by reference to the experience of economic integration following the unification of the Italian states in the second half of the nineteenth century. The industries existing at that time in northern Italy benefited greatly from the larger market, but the weaker industries in the south, deprived of the protection they had previously enjoyed in competition with the more developed industries of the northern states, disappeared almost completely. This experience also points to the danger that whatever capital may be available in industrially less developed areas will tend to be attracted by the much more prosperous regions where industry is already firmly established, thus enabling these areas to undertake fresh investments while depriving the poorer areas of their capital.' B Ohlin et al, 'Social Aspects of European Economic Co-operation (Ohlin-Report, Summary)' (1956) 74 *International Labour Review* 99, 101–02.

richer countries, the establishment of a European Investment Bank, infrastructure investment and incentives for large-scale investment.[42] The asymmetrical benefits of market integration were considered to be problematic from an equity perspective, which in turn was relevant in regard to the political support of the integration project itself: an unequal distribution of the gains from integration could lead to a potential corrosion of political support. Beyond that, however, unequal development could also make macroeconomic instabilities such as trade imbalances more likely, thereby undermining the very economic benefits European integration strived to realize. It was argued by James Meade in 1957 that a common market in goods and the free movement of productive factors required efficient complementary macroeconomic instruments for its proper functioning. For Meade, economic integration would ultimately need a common monetary policy, including a central bank, a common budgetary policy, and cohesion policy for Europe's 'depressed regions'.[43] Similarly, John Pinder argued in 1968 that market integration caused trade imbalances between the Member States, which required stabilizing and accompanying measures, as otherwise the economic potential of the common market could not be realized.[44] In particular, he proposed a number of policies to tackle the Community's 'problems of inter-regional balance of payments and disparities in regional growth rates', which included transfer payments in the form of infrastructure programmes or joint unemployment aid as well as fiscal and budgetary powers for the EEC, free mobility of persons and capital (though he believed that the latter also had destabilizing effects), and the coordination of national monetary, budgetary and income policies 'to ensure that member countries do not export their problems to each other.'[45] The issue of regional

[42] ibid, 102; public investment was also supported by liberalists like Heilperin; Michael Heilperin, 'Freer Trade and Social Welfare: Some Marginal Comments on the Ohlin report' (1957) 75 *International Labour Review* 173, 183; Philip, commenting on the Ohlin Report, brought forward a more fundamental critique, arguing that the agglomeration tendencies will affect not only underdeveloped regions, as the report seems to suggest. He called for measures that would go beyond merely absorbing excessive adverse effects for underdeveloped regions, instead providing a comprehensive European investment strategy that would guide capital flows. A Philip, 'Social Aspects of European Economic Co-operation' (1957) 76 *International Labour Review* 244, 253.

[43] Meade held: 'The integration approach thus involves—in addition to the formation of a common market for goods and for factors of production and the provision of much greater international liquidity for European monetary authorities—a very extensive range of powers for what would amount to a single European government. Such a government would have to be able to control central-bank monetary policy and governmental budgetary policy throughout Europe, to determine a single European commercial and exchange-rate policy vis-à-vis third countries, and to carry out an effective special-area policy for depressed regions in Europe.' James Meade, 'The Balance-of-Payments Problems of a European Free-Trade Area' (1957) 67 *Economic Journal* 379, 387–88.

[44] John Pinder, 'Positive Integration and Negative Integration: Some Problems of Economic Union in the EEC' (1968) 24 *The World Today* 88, 89 and 109; see also Balassa (n 40), 2.

[45] Pinder (n 44), 106. The measures proposed by Pinder (ibid, 108) included (1) joint aid programmes for less-developed regions; (2) development of transport facilities to aid the economic development of less-developed regions; (3) joint unemployment and retraining aids, which seem to be intended (similar to the US federal social benefits) as quasi-redistributive measures; (4) fiscal

imbalances and the ensuing balance-of-payment problems came up again in the 1980s: the Padoa-Schioppa Report, which we will discuss more extensively below, found 'serious risks of aggravated regional imbalance' through market integration.[46] This finding was supported by the fact that regional disparities in the EEC had greatly increased since the mid-1970s,[47] and unemployment differences between regions grew by a factor of 2.5 between 1975 and 1985.[48] Accordingly, the effects of the centrifugal forces of European market integration was an important theme in the 1992 strategy. Jacques Delors argued in a 1989 address that the 'dynamics [of market integration] will exert more pressure on competition, and uncover sectoral weak points, and regional differences, which are likely to lead to the polarization of trends in regions enjoying cumulative growth and those suffering decline.'[49] An increased focus on cohesion policy as well as a push towards economic and monetary coordination were pursued in reaction.

The three factors discussed on the preceding pages provide an insight in some of the central socio-economic dynamics to which the 1992 project reacted. While other factors might surely be added, the central point to be made is that the 1992 project responded to a very diverse spectrum of both global and domestic challenges and concerns, which speaks to its pluralist character. We will see in the following section that these diverse concerns find expression in the two major studies on European integration, the Cecchini and the Padoa-Schioppa Reports, and ultimately in the Treaty reforms by the SEA and the Treaty of Maastricht.

THE ECONOMIC ASSUMPTIONS BEHIND '1992'

In the last section we saw that the 1992 project was a reaction to a variety of global, European and domestic challenges. In this section we look at the main economic assumptions that guided the process. We will see that many of the discussions

and budgetary powers for the EEC; (5) facilitating of labour mobility as a macroeconomic equalizer, though here Pinder saw the severe limits posed by cultural differences; (6) free capital mobility, though Pinder also expected a potential disequilibrating effect; (7) coordination of national monetary, budgetary and incomes policies 'to ensure that member countries do not export their problems to each other.'

46 Tommaso Padoa-Schioppa, *Efficiency, Stability and Equity. A Strategy for the Evolution of the Economic System of the European Community* (Padoa-Schioppa Report) (1987), 4.

47 Manfred McDowell and William Hudson, 'Social Democrats Choose Europe: Comparing the European Policies of the British Labour and French Socialist Parties' (Biennial Conference of the European Community Studies Association, George Mason University, Fairfax, Virginia, 22–24 May 1991), 35.

48 EC, 'The Regions of the Enlarged Community, Third Periodic Report on the social and economic situation and development of the regions of the Community' (1987), aei.pitt.edu/31139/1/Third_periodic_report.pdf, Summary, 3; see also Richard Gibb and Alan Treadgold, 'Completing the internal market: implications for the regions' (1989) *Area* 75, 80.

49 Jacques Delors, 'The Commission's programme for 1989.' Address by Jacques Delors, President of the Commission, to the European Parliament and his reply to the debate (*Bulletin of the European Communities*, Supplement 2, 1989) 28.

that started in the 1950s on the occasion of the Treaty of Rome were resumed in one form or other in the 1980s. Policymakers and scholars were still concerned with the question of how the European economic environment could be restructured to achieve more growth and to stay competitive within the global context. The issue of macroeconomic stability, while already an important concern in the 1950s and 1960s, became particularly prevalent in the debates of the 1980s. The European countries had experienced more than a decade of global economic volatility; moreover, the accession of a number of poorer Member States increased the risk of economic instability within the Community. This dual concern for growth and stability is expressed in the two major reports that Delors commissioned in the 1980s. The Cecchini Report, a massive, multi-volume study of the expected impact of the completion of the internal market focused mainly on the microeconomic effects. By contrast, the Padoa-Schioppa Report concentrated on macroeconomic questions. The authors of these reports were both convinced of the economic potential of European market integration; however, they also emphasized that in order to realize this potential, the Community had to ensure macroeconomic stability as well.

Benefits from Market Integration—The Cecchini Report

The Cecchini Report was a major study on the possible economic effects of market integration, written for the Commission, and published in 1988. The report found that the potential was staggering: up to 5 per cent of the GDP one-time effect, not counting the long-term growth effects.[50] Of course such an estimate was overly optimistic,[51] and many of the desired effects were based on purely theoretical assumptions and were not really calculable in practice.[52] The report—and in particular the summary prepared by the Commission—provides a relatively clear insight into the plural economic assumptions of the policymakers of '1992'. Different types of economic benefits can be distinguished: the report expected immediate savings stemming from the removal of physical borders and connected costs, such as border formalities and delays.[53] The removal of other barriers such

[50] EC, 'Europe 1992. The overall challenge' SEC (88) 524 final. The 5% of GDP represented one-time gains; see on this Peck Merton, 'Industrial Organization and the Gains from Europe 1992' (1989) Brookings Papers on Economic Activity 277, 277.

[51] Merton (n 50), 278.

[52] The main difficulty in calculating the economic effects of integration is that there is no comparator, ie no data on how Europe would have developed without the EEC. This has been conceded, for example, by Alexander Italianer, who attempted to establish the economic benefits of integration in 1994. Whereas the growth rate in the EEC 12 was at 4.1% in 1988, it was at 0.9% in 1992 and expected to shrink in the following year. It is not clear which part of the recession can be attributed to integration, which to German unification, which to 'insufficient macroeconomic convergence', and which to the EMU project. Alexander Italianer, 'Whither the Gains from European Economic Integration?' (1994) 45 *Revue économique* 689, 690, fn 1.

[53] EC, 'Europe 1992. The overall challenge', 3.

as technical regulations played a considerable role. Apart from these 'direct cost of identifiable market barriers'[54] the report primarily promised ('indirect') gains from a reshaped market structure, which would be large enough to create both economies of scale and productive competition.[55] The benefits of integration are therefore based on the expectation that companies would adapt to the larger market in order to 'get closer to the most efficient possible scales of production.'[56] At the same time, increased competition would not only prevent monopolistic structures and therefore push down consumer prices, but also reduce inefficiencies regarding 'overhead costs, over-manning and inefficient management of inventories.'[57] Additional benefits would be accrued from the opening of government procurement to competition, and the liberalization of financial markets.[58] Finally, 'dynamic effects' such as technical innovation and business strategies 'better suited to securing a strong place in the world market competition'[59] were believed to be significant,[60] though no calculations were provided by the report.[61] The main economic themes of the report are similar to those discussed in the 1950s and 1960s: apart from the immediate benefits of abolishing frontier formalities and delays, the report was primarily concerned with long-term growth effects stemming from changes in the European economic structure.[62] These should be accrued through the exploitation of economies of scale, increased technological advances both through scale effects and increased competition, and also the better competitive position of European-sized companies on the world market.[63] New themes included public procurement and state aid.

The focus on unequal development and on increased instabilities through market integration had become stronger, not least because of the accession of comparatively poor and underdeveloped economies in the 1980s. The report expressed the hope that all countries would gain from market integration, but emphasized that the Community's cohesion funds would have to play a considerable role in realizing this goal.[64] The possibility of unequal distribution between capital and

[54] ibid, 3.

[55] Merton (n 50), 282; Alexis Jacquemin and David Wright, 'Corporate Strategies and European Challenges Post 1992' (1993) 31 *Journal of Common Market Studies* 525, 525.

[56] EC, 'Europe 1992. The overall challenge', 2.

[57] ibid, 4; we discussed this issue earlier unde the headline of 'X-efficiencies'.

[58] ibid, 5.

[59] Michael Emerson et al, *The Economics of 1992* (Oxford University Press, 1988) 7.

[60] Lord Cockfield stated in his foreword to the Cecchini Report: 'The completion of the internal market will open up: opportunities for growth, for job creation, for economies of scale, of improved productivity … in short a prospect of significant inflation-free growth and millions of new jobs.' Quoted in Richard Baldwin, 'The growth effects of 1992' (1989) NBER Working Paper No 3119, 2.

[61] Merton (n 50), 289; see however Baldwin, who believed that '1992 could permanently add between one quarter and a full percentage point to the EC growth rate.' Baldwin (n 60), 36.

[62] Scholars like Baldwin have emphasized the importance of 'dynamic' (or growth-related) effects of integration.

[63] EC, 'Europe 1992. The overall challenge', 5.

[64] ibid, 4.

labour was equally an issue of the report. It emphasized that the benefits of market integration would be accrued by consumers to a considerable extent, but also pointed out that politics and industrial relations would have to play a significant role in order to ensure that the 'distribution of gains' would be 'fair'.[65] To that effect, the report held:

> Business must respond to the challenge and seize the new opportunities on offer. Corporate management should also seek to make industrial relations less conflictual, encourage employee involvement in the life of the enterprise, and ensure that workers share in the jointly achieved productivity gains.[66]

Finally, the report acknowledged that the growth potential of market integration would be realized only if an effective macroeconomic policy were pursued. It held: 'These favorable expectations will need to be backed by a well coordinated, growth-orientated macroeconomic policy.'[67] In particular, it pointed out that the liberalization of capital movement would create additional instability, which 'must be countered by increased monetary policy co-operation through a strengthened EMS.'[68] It should be emphasized that many believed that the success of the 1992 project would depend less on automatic economic 'laws' (of comparative advantage, or economies of scale, etc), and more on the psychological effects of integration.[69] The binding and irreversible commitments of the Member States to European integration would create 'changed expectations'[70] of the European businesses, which would restructure their production (scale, location, etc) on the basis of changed long-term expectations.[71] Such changed expectations were indeed observable, for example in the 'merger wave' of the early 1990s.[72]

Market Integration, Economic Stabilization and Equitable Distribution: The Padoa-Schioppa Report

In 1986, the Commission asked Tommaso Padoa-Schioppa, deputy director of the Italian central bank (and later Italian Minister of Finance) to chair a group that

[65] ibid, 6.
[66] ibid, 6.
[67] ibid, 7.
[68] ibid, 7; For an early argument that a reduction of capital controls would lead to increasing macroeconomic instability see Alfred Müller-Armack, *Wirtschaftsordnung und Wirtschaftspolitik* (Verlag Rombach, 1966), 338.
[69] Sandholtz and Zysman (n 25), 95; on the importance of trust in the long-term existence of the Treaty commitments, see Hans von der Groeben, *Aufbaujahre der Europäischen Gemeinschaft. Das Ringen um den Gemeinsamen Markt und die Politische Union (1958–1966)* (Nomos, 1982), 124–25.
[70] Sandholtz and Zysman (n 25), 95; Jacquemin and Wright (n 55), 525.
[71] These changed expectations and behaviour by the economic actors had been observed after the signing of the Treaty of Rome as well. See Marianne Gellner, 'Relations between the Six and the Seven: A Survey of Recent Developments' (1960) 16 *The World Today* 278, 279.
[72] Jacquemin and Wright (n 55), 526.

would issue a report on the macroeconomic effects of continued European integration, in particular in the context of the Spanish and Portuguese enlargement.[73] The report, titled 'Efficiency, Stability and Equity', was issued in 1987.[74] The title expressed the view of the authors that a successful economic development of the European Community would require progress in three policy areas: the integration of the European market, increased macroeconomic stability, and an increased redistributive dimension. The report conceptualized the second and the third objectives as indispensable preconditions for the first. It held: 'Greater Community involvement in stabilization and redistribution policies is the indispensable complement of the most ambitious project of completing the internal market: this is our first and most important proposition.'[75] The Community of the 1980s was far more heterogeneous than the initial EEC, 'in terms of economic structure, living standards, social systems and policy institutions.'[76] Accordingly, 'the complete opening of the market in the enlarged Community will have distributive effects that are likely to be stronger and more disruptive than those experienced in the sixties when trade integration proceeded among less heterogeneous countries and in a context of faster economic growth.'[77] In order to achieve the 'stabilization of the economy' and an 'equitable distribution of gains' to complement market integration, measures like monetary policy coordination and 'redistributive functions performed through the budget and the lending instruments of the Community' were necessary.[78] Macroeconomic policies to ensure stability and to foster growth were seen as necessary to realize the potential benefits of market integration.[79] While the report found these policies necessary on purely economic terms, it also held that ignoring the issue of stability and inequality would undermine the political viability of market integration:

> If these interactions between policies were neglected, or if the solutions chosen for them were inadequate, what in 1985 were rightly applauded as significant steps in the construction of Europe could encounter obstacles and entail inconsistencies. These could be erroneously taken as signs that the programme was mistaken, or too ambitious. The primary objective of a fully integrated internal market in an enlarged Community would lose political support and eventually fail, thereby depriving the Community of a major source of additional economic welfare.[80]

The report emphasized the importance of equitable distribution, arguing that 'the risks of an uneven distribution of the gains from trade on the one hand and of

[73] Padoa-Schioppa (n 46), 3; other members of the group included Mervyn King (later the Governor of the Bank of England), Lucas Papademos (later Governor of the Greek central bank and Greek Prime Minister) and Fritz Scharpf.
[74] ibid.
[75] ibid, Preamble, v.
[76] ibid, Preamble, iii.
[77] ibid, Preamble, iv.
[78] ibid, Preamble, iv and v.
[79] ibid, 20.
[80] ibid, Preamble, iv.

transitional employment problems on the other are serious'.[81] While the authors were convinced of the economic potential of market integration, they believed that there would be 'no a priori certainty that the aggregate gains ... will translate into gains for all participants at the level of regions or countries.'[82] In other words, the report emphasized the fact that certain regions or whole countries could potentially lose in the integration process despite overall gains for the Community. Moreover, the Padoa-Schioppa Report did not take the growth effects of market integration for granted. Regional aid schemes to facilitate structural change in the regions and to avoid distributive inequalities as well as the use of macroeconomic instruments to support growth were deemed important.[83] Increased attention to stability and equitable distribution was necessary to ensure the viability and robustness of the integration process.[84]

To conclude this section, it can be argued that the economic and political issues considered by the Padoa-Schioppa and the Cecchini Reports illustrate the pluralist character of the 1992 project: market integration would make the realization of both 'direct' and 'indirect' gains possible, but had to be complemented with measures ensuring macroeconomic stability as well as social and regional cohesion.

THE PRIMARY LAW REFORMS OF THE 1992 PROJECT

In this section, we will look at the primary law reforms of the 1992 project, as enacted through the SEA and the Treaty of Maastricht. It will be shown that the reforms, while changing the European constitutional landscape in important ways, did not alter its pluralist socio-economic character.[85] Surely the 1992 reforms were enacted in an intellectual climate that differed significantly from that of the 1950s, which was characterized by a dominance of the neoclassical synthesis, a merger between neoclassical and Keynesian theory. As Andrew Moravcsik pointed out, the liberalization programme enshrined in the White Paper and the SEA was imprinted with neoliberal thinking.[86] The EMU, which was enacted by the Maastricht Treaty, could also be understood as implementing a specific ideological paradigm, as will be discussed later. However, as already discussed in relation with

[81] ibid, 19.
[82] ibid, 23.
[83] ibid, 5.
[84] ibid, 23.
[85] This view is not shared across the board. Bartl, for example, describes the White Paper, the SEA and the Maastricht Treaty as 'political endorsements' of 'neoliberal thought'. Marija Bartl, 'Internal Market Rationality, Private Law and the Direction of the Union: Resuscitating the Market as the Object of the Political' (2015) 21 *European Law Journal* 572, 577.
[86] Moravcsik (n 8), 50. The new Art 100a EEC provides a telling example by prescribing majority voting for harmonization measures, but excluding 'fiscal provisions', provisions 'relating to the free movement of persons' and 'those relating to the rights and interests of employed persons', which consequently are still subject to the unanimity requirement of Art 100 EEC.

Assessing the Normative Implications of the Treaty Reforms

The 1992 reforms triggered a renewed round of discussion on the socio-economic orientation of the Union. The reforms were strongly criticized for example by some German liberalists, who found the measures to undermine what they held to be the quasi-ordoliberal structure of the Community.[139] In particular, the increased engagement in industrial policy was strongly criticized, as will be discussed in a later section. For example, Streit and Mussler held that 'the non-market elements contained in the European economic constitution as well as the provisions allowing discretionary political action on behalf of the Community have been decisively strengthened already by the SEA.'[140] This was in turn recognized by commentators like Sauter or Poiares Maduro, who found that the chapters on policies like consumer and environmental concerns, monetary union and all areas related to industrial policy, including R&D, networks and cohesion policy, undermined the interpretation of the Treaty as a manifestation of an ordoliberal economic order. According to Sauter, '[t]he Single European Act of 1987 deepened the dichotomy between 'integration by regulation and integration by competition,' and strengthened the non-market elements of the original Treaty and discretionary policy making.'[141] And concerning the Treaty of Maastricht, Poiares Maduro held:

> The Treaty of Maastricht has struck a further blow to the liberal concept of European integration. Though primarily concerned with currency and monetary stability ... the Treaty on the European Union has in effect reinforced pre-existing interventionist elements and created new forms and mechanisms for public intervention. Moreover, the Treaty stresses not only economic efficiency, but also social and redistributive values. It therefore calls for a broader concept of the European Economic Constitution and its relation to political values.[142]

Such depictions require us to take a critical stance insofar as they forget about the extensive regulatory competences—also in social and redistributive affairs—the Treaty granted even prior to the 1992 reforms and because they seem to adhere to the economic/non-economic dichotomy that we have considered to be ideologically loaded. It is quite unclear, for example, how European market integration, which routinely required extensive legislative action (as for example illustrated by the bulk of secondary law necessary for the integration of the financial markets) would not be as 'interventionist' as redistributive or social policies. Similarly, it seems far-fetched to describe regulatory areas such as industrial, consumer or R&D policy as 'non-market elements' even though they are clearly aimed at shaping the

[139] Following Sauter, the new harmonization competence of Art 100a 'was seen as at odds with the principle of enumerated powers, since it did not clearly limit the scope of the new harmonization legislation for internal market purposes', Wolf Sauter, *Competition law and industrial Policy in the EU* (OUP, 1997), 52.

[140] Manfred Streit and Werner Mussler, 'The economic constitution of the European community: From Rome to Maastricht' (1994) 5 *Constitutional Political Economy* 319, 339.

[141] Sauter (n 139) 52.

[142] Poiares Maduro (n 16), 160–61.

European *economic* landscape in no different way than for example competition policy does. However, the statements accurately identify the pluralist character of the European regulatory framework in socio-economic questions. Poiares Maduro thus speaks quite appropriately of the 'open' character of the European economic constitution.[143] This 'open' character was, though grudgingly, also recognized by liberalists like Mestmäcker, who argued that '[t]he balance of diversity and unity must, of course, be considered in light of competing and frequently conflicting Community objectives and activities. To some the Social Charter is indispensible for the further development of the Community, while for others it charts the way to socialism.'[144]

At the same time, however, a new discussion erupted on the Union's socio-economic orientation, this time focusing on the new Article 3a, which held that the economic policy of the Community and the Member States should be 'conducted in accordance with the principle of an open market economy with free competition'. This was yet again understood by some liberalists as an expression of a socio-economic order to their liking. Mestmäcker, for example, argued: 'Economic policies implementing the task of establishing an economic and monetary union are to be conducted "in accordance with the principle of an open market economy with free competition" (Art 3A) … The outlined development of Community law may be interpreted as the implementation of an economic order based upon markets and undistorted competition.'[145] Like the ordoliberals of the 1950s and 1960s, Mestmäcker thus attempts to identify the Treaty with a comprehensive choice in favour of a specific socio-economic order, which he finds to be spelled out in Article 3a. But similarly to the ordoliberals of the 1950s and 1960s, the specific 'economic order' Mestmäcker could distil from the provision has no distinctive quality. While surely such definition would exclude the establishment of a centrally planned economy, any other socio-economic view held by the left or the right in the 1980s and 1990s would certainly fit: employing 'open markets' as one form among others of organizing socio-economic relations was certainly not a controversial position; the key question rather was which areas should be organized as markets, and which should not. Similarly, the claim that competitive conditions on markets should be undistorted by regulatory differences that gave undue advantages to certain market participants appears equally uncontroversial. The question, rather, is to what extent national regulation had to be harmonized

[143] ibid, 159.

[144] Ernst-Joachim Mestmäcker, 'On the Legitimacy of European law' (1994) 58 *Rabels Zeitschrift für ausländisches und internationales Privatrecht/The Rabel Journal of Comparative and International Private Law* 615, 634. At another point, Mestmäcker argued: 'The European Union is founded on the European Communities supplemented by the policies and forms of cooperation established by the Maastricht Treaty. This undertaking, obviously to the surprise of its authors, has come to be the most controversial step in the process of "creating an ever closer Union among the peoples of Europe" (art A). One of the reasons is probably the assumed legitimacy of progressive integration in the post war tradition, combined with far-reaching but rather nebulous visions of the future. The Treaty itself reflects its uncertain and partly contradictory objectives.' Ibid, 617.

[145] ibid, 633.

in order to enable 'undistorted competition'. Article 3a stays quiet on both of these questions. Accordingly, Mestmäcker's reading of Article 3a as implementing a specific economic order is either irrelevant because all existing socio-economic positions fit the definition, or manipulative because he attempts to associate Article 3a, despite its open phrasing, with a specific view to his liking. Moreover, 3a cannot be read in isolation from the more general Article 2, which proposed a broad set of regulatory objectives of the Community. Article 2 held that the Community's task was,

> by establishing a common market and an economic and monetary union and by implementing the common policies or activities ... to promote throughout the Community a harmonious and balanced development of economic activities, sustainable and non-inflationary growth respecting the environment, a high degree of convergence of economic performance, a high level of employment and of social protection, the raising of the standard of living and quality of life, and economic and social cohesion and solidarity among Member States.

Quite similar to the Treaty of Rome, then, the EC Treaty thus defines the creation of a common market on the one hand and European-level co-ordination or harmonization on the other as the means of the Community to achieve a diverse set of socio-economic goals. Given the complex, multidimensional nature of the primary law reforms enacted by the SEA and the Treaty of Maastricht as well as the plurality of regulatory goals that are expressed in Article 2 EC, Poiares Maduro's characterization of the Treaty as 'open' in socio-economic terms is far more convincing than Mestmäcker's assertion that it should be read as a manifestation of any specific socio-economic paradigm, especially if it is based on an idiosyncratic reading of an isolated article.[146]

THE REGULATORY STRATEGIES OF '1992'

Whereas the Treaty of Rome addressed tariffs and quotas as the main impediments to economic integration, the 1992 reforms identified the so-called 'non-tariff barriers' as the paradigmatic obstacle to the completion of the internal market. According to the Padoa-Schioppa Report, 'new market barriers outweighed new liberalising action' from the early 1970s on, and had considerable negative effects on growth.[147] And the 1985 White Book framed the problem as follows:

> The recession brought another problem. The Treaty specifically required not simply the abolition of customs duties as between the Member States, but also the elimination of

[146] However, this position is not uncontested. For example, Lane argued that '[t]he Treaty will therefore cease to be neutral in national economic policy; Maastricht entrenches the free market within the Community legal order and imposes upon the Member States an obligation of economic discipline significantly more burdensome than that which now obtains.' Lane (n 114), 944.

[147] Padoa-Schioppa (n 46), 5.

> quantitative restrictions and of all measures having equivalent effect. Originally it was assumed that such 'non-tariff barriers,' as they are commonly called, were of limited importance compared with actual duties. But during the recession they multiplied as each Member State endeavoured to protect what it thought was its short term interests—not only against third countries but against Member States as well.[148]

The concept of 'non-tariff barriers' is a broad one: in common usage it includes not only measures with clear trade-distorting objectives or effects, such as quantitative restrictions, non-tariff import charges, discriminatory procurement policies and export subsidies, but also regulatory standards that have the effect of restricting trade merely because they vary from country to country. The allegation of a supposed protectionist intent behind the rise of non-tariff barriers forwarded in the White Paper should be taken with a grain of salt, especially when it comes to regulatory standards. The reproach of protectionism usually has a discursive-strategic function, and can hardly serve, without extensive factual support, as a neutral analytical category. In many instances it is in fact difficult to establish whether a regulatory standard has been enacted for legitimate purposes—eg public health, safety or consumer protection—or for protectionist reasons.[149] It can generally be held that the Community's focus on the so-called 'non-tariff barriers' or 'technical barriers to trade' corresponded with a similar increase in attention on the international sphere from the late 1960s onwards.[150] Based on proposals reaching back to at least 1970, the GATT Tokyo round of 1973 and the Geneva round of 1975 were centrally concerned with non-tariff barriers.[151] The phenomenon of non-tariff barriers and the increased attention paid to it by scholars and policymakers is thus neither a European phenomenon alone, nor is it a primary consequence of the two economic downturns of the 1970s. Different reasons have been proposed to explain the perceived rise in non-tariff barriers, especially the proliferation of regulatory standards. First, with the dismantlement of tariffs by both the GATT and the EEC, non-tariff barriers would increasingly move into the focus, as for example the Commission held already in the 1960s.[152] The greater visibility of non-tariff barriers is thus, prima facie, an indication of advanced economic integration.[153] Second, modern economies relied on a sophisticated

[148] EC, 'Completing the Internal Market', White Paper from the Commission to the European Council (Milan, 28–29 June) COM(85) 310 final, 5.

[149] Jon Groetzinger, 'The New GATT Code and the International Harmonization of Products Standards' (1974) 8 *Cornell International Law Journal* 168, 169.

[150] Writing in 1974, Groetzinger held that '[u]ntil recently little attention was paid to the problems of both incompatible products standards and other types of NTB's.' ibid, 169.

[151] ibid, 168.

[152] EC, 'General program for elimination of technical barriers to trade due to disparities in national legislation' COM(68) 138 final, 2.

[153] Though it has also been argued that non-tariff barriers may be viewed as new protectionist instruments that national industries were pushing for once their protection under high tariffs had vanished. See Groetzinger (n 149), 170.

regulatory framework to a much greater extent than they had done only a few decades earlier.[154] This created challenges for multilateral economic systems based on traditional instruments of trade liberalization alone. According to verLoren van Themaat, '[I]t is characteristic of a high level of technological development that the number of technical regulations for products grows along with technological progress. The differences between national regulations on this matter lead to the so-called technical barriers to trade.'[155] VerLoren van Themaat thus conceptualized national technical regulations as an impediment to trade while acknowledging their underlying regulatory objectives. Finally, consumer pressure had led to an increased focus on product safety and public health protection, thereby increasing the number of standards.[156] These alternative explanations of the perceived 'rise of non-tariff barriers' challenge the narrative provided by the White Paper. The dichotomy of trade liberalization versus protectionism is ideologically coded along the lines of the two-sphere fallacy that we encountered already a couple of times. Against such framework, the present section aims to provide a more nuanced view of the 'non-tariff barriers', and of the instruments employed to deal with them.

The Commission assumed that the objective of reducing non-tariff barriers required regulatory strategies that differed from past practices. In particular, the Commission presented two regulatory innovations: it would make increased use of the principle of mutual recognition, and would pursue a reform of the instrument of harmonization. This reform encompassed the reduction of the unanimity requirement already discussed, but also the introduction of the so-called 'new approach' in harmonization, which aimed at reducing the level of detail necessary in European harmonizing measures. Measures created according the 'new approach' would harmonize certain core aspects only and otherwise prescribe mutual recognition, which should lead to faster decision-making processes. In the following sections, we will discuss these two modes of socio-economic governance. Both concepts feature prominently in ideologically coded narratives that address the socio-economic orientation of the '1992' project: in particular, the alleged conflict between 'regulatory' and 'de-regulatory' policies is routinely projected onto them, with the 'new approach' and mutual recognition usually being associated with the latter. The following sections provide an extensive historical contextualization of the two modes of governance, identifying important continuities with the regulatory practice of the 1960s and 1970s, which undermine such dichotomic representation. It will be argued that, in normative terms, neither mutual recognition nor the 'new approach' can be assumed to conform to any specific socio-economic paradigm.

[154] See verLoren van Themaat (n 28), 71–72; see also Groetzinger (n 149), 170.

[155] VerLoren van Themaat (n 28), 91.

[156] Groetzinger (n 149), 171; John McCarthy, 'Protectionism and Product Harmonization in the EEC' (1979) 10 *Economic and Social Review* 187, 188–89.

Mutual Recognition

The principle of mutual recognition was assigned a central role in the 1992 project. In a first step, we may distinguish between a legislative and a judicial principle of mutual recognition:[157] the former implements mutual recognition by means of secondary law, eg through Directives that establish minimum standards in all Member States in conjunction with a requirement to allow products produced according to these standards in another Member State on the domestic market. The latter, first developed in *Cassis de Dijon* and the Commission Communication on that matter, assumes that the requirement of mutual recognition follows from primary law, and can be enforced through judicial means.

The legislative principle of mutual recognition has been introduced as a tool of socio-economic governance already by the Treaty of Rome. Most notably, Article 57 EEC required the European legislator to realize the mutual recognition of professional qualifications through legislative means: the Council was to 'issue directives for the mutual recognition of diplomas, certificates and other evidence of formal qualifications.' Beyond the field of professional qualifications, mutual recognition had been of early interest in regard to the recognition of legal personality. Various national statutes provided for the recognition of foreign legal persons on the condition of reciprocity, and many bilateral agreements included such requirement as well.[158] Building on these structures, Article 220 EEC required Member States 'so far as is necessary' to 'enter into negotiations with each other with a view to securing for the benefit of their nationals ... the mutual recognition of companies or firms ... the retention of legal personality in the event of transfer of their seat from one country to another, and the possibility of mergers between companies or firms governed by the laws of different countries.' This led to the Convention on the Mutual Recognition of Companies and Legal Person, signed between the Member States in 1968.[159] Moreover, the principle of mutual recognition was also considered beyond these areas; Ivo Schwartz reported that, prior to the 1962 Action Programme, the Commission had initially considered the idea of prescribing a general mutual recognition requirement for the realization of the common market before ultimately settling on legislative harmonization on the basis of Article 100 EEC as the central regulatory strategy.[160] Finally, as we will discuss in the subsequent section, various harmonization measures of the 1960s and 1970s

[157] The distinction has been proposed by Pelkmans; Jacques Pelkmans, 'Mutual recognition in goods. On promises and disillusions' (2007) 14 *Journal of European Public Policy* 699, 702.

[158] On this see Berthold Goldman, 'The Convention Between the Member States of the European Economic Community on the Mutual Recognition of Companies and Legal Persons' (1969) 6 *Common Market Law Review* 104, 106.

[159] ibid, 104.

[160] Ivo Schwartz, '30 Jahre EG-Rechtsangleichung' in Ernst-Joachim Mestmäcker, Hans Möller and Hans-Peter Schwarz (eds), *Eine Ordnungspolitik für Europa: Festschrift für Hans von der Groeben zu seinem 80 Geburtstag* (Nomos, 1987), 353.

prescribed mutual recognition in one form or another. The proposition of judicial mutual recognition in the field of goods by the Court in *Cassis de Dijon* and the Commission in its subsequent Communication thus builds on legal concepts not novel to internal market law.[161] In the 1992 project, the principle of mutual recognition featured prominently: most notably, the White Paper assigned an important function to it. Moreover, the SEA introduced Article 100b EEC, which allowed the Council to declare mutual recognition in all fields that were not harmonized until 1992.[162]

As a principle of CJEU adjudication, mutual recognition requires that Member States allow products manufactured and marketed lawfully in another Member State to enter its domestic market. This obligation can be enforced judicially.[163] A Member State can require imported products to conform to its domestic regulations only if two conditions are fulfilled: first, the area has not been harmonized comprehensively; and second, it must be shown that the regulations of the Member State where the product was manufactured do not ensure an equivalent level of protection. From a doctrinal perspective, all national product regulations constitute a restriction of the Treaty freedoms, which can be justified on grounds of public interest only if Member States can show that they are not sufficiently protected in the country of origin.[164] The second condition, which may be termed the principle of equivalence, has been spelled out by the Court, for example in the decision *Fietje*.[165] In this judgment, the Court held that a labelling requirement was unjustifiable if the product already carried a label that gave the same information and was comprehensible to the consumer.[166] The equivalence criterion was subsequently emphasized by the Commission in its Communication:

> The principles deduced by the Court imply that a Member State may not in principle prohibit the sale in its territory of a product lawfully produced and marketed in another Member State even if the product is produced according to technical or quality requirements which differ from those imposed on its domestic products. Where a product 'suitably and satisfactorily' fulfills the legitimate objective of a Member State's own rules (public safety, protection of the consumer or the environment, etc.), the importing country cannot justify prohibiting its sale in its territory by claiming that the way it fulfills the objective is different from that imposed on domestic products.[167]

[161] See also EC, 'Communication from the Commission concerning the consequences of the judgment given by the Court of Justice in case 120/78 *(Cassis de Dijon)*' [1979] OJ C256/2.

[162] See George Bermann, 'The Single European Act: A New Constitution for the Community' (1988) 27 *Columbia Journal for Transnational Law* 529, 546.

[163] Pelkmans (n 157), 702.

[164] See for example Gordon Slynn, 'Aspects of the Law of the European Economic Community' (1985) 18 *Cornell International Law Journal* 1, 13–14.

[165] Case C-27/80, *Criminal proceedings against Anton Adriaan Fietje* [1980] ECR 3839 (hereinafter *Fietje*); on *Fietje* see Peter Oliver, 'Measures of equivalent effect: a reappraisal' (1982) 19 *Common Market Law Review* 217, 234.

[166] *Fietje*, para 15.

[167] EC, 'Communication from the Commission concerning the consequences of the judgment given by the Court of Justice in case 120/78 (*Cassis de Dijon*)'.

Peter Oliver commented on the principle of equivalence as follows:

> As the Commission pointed out in its Communication, even if a product is lawfully produced and marketed in a Member State, it may not be sold within another Member State which has higher standards than the Member State of production—provided always that those higher standards are justified as being necessary to satisfy mandatory requirements. Thus if the optimal standard for a given product is one hundred and the importing Member State requires eighty, then it may justifiably prohibit the sale of goods conforming to the standard of only seventy imposed by the producing Member State. The same applies, a fortiori, if the producing Member State imposes no minimum standards at all. But, as already explained, there is always a rebuttable presumption that the higher standard is not necessary. On the other hand, if two Member States both require a standard of eighty but lay down different means of reaching that result, then each must permit the sale of the other's product. That is what we have called the principle of equivalence.[168]

The principle of equivalence conforms to the regulatory goal of the Treaty of Rome that trade shall be enabled within conditions undistorted by regulatory differences. As von der Groeben argued already in 1967, the Treaty 'did not allow establishing the free movement of goods at the expense of the equality of competitive conditions.'[169] Claims by authors like Streit and Mussler, that the case law on mutual recognition developed on the basis of *Cassis de Dijon* 'legitimized' the 'opportunities to choose between institutional systems', thus constitute a significant misunderstanding, insofar as they insinuate a normative 'legitimization' of regulatory competition, thereby ignoring the equivalence requirement.[170] From a doctrinal perspective, a common misunderstanding is to read the principle of mutual recognition as a conflict-of-laws measure, in which only the rules of the country of origin apply. Rather, the principle of equivalence requires Member States to actively take into account requirements fulfilled by products in their state of origin, but does not force them to accept products made on the basis of substantively lower regulatory standards. The principle of mutual recognition is thus best understood as a procedural standard that Member States must comply with before imposing their own standards on imported products, rather than a conflict-of-laws rule. In essence, it requires Member States to make an effort to ensure that imported goods are not subjected to double regulation, if such burden is not justified on plausible grounds.[171]

Nicolaïdis and Schmidt advance a similar view in regard to the provision of services. They argue that mutual recognition in the EU has historically been

[168] Oliver (n 165), 235.

[169] Hans von der Groeben, 'Zur Politik der Rechtsangleichung in der Europäischen Wirtschaftsgemeinschaft' (1967) 8 *Zeitschrift für Rechtsvergleichung* 129, 129, quoted in Schwartz (n 160), 352–53.

[170] Streit and Mussler (n 140), 329, 332.

[171] See in this regard Slynn (n 164), 14; see also Oliver (n 165), 235: 'It will not always be clear whether two standards are in fact equivalent. It is submitted that Member States are under a duty to take active steps to establish whether this is so.'

applied in a form that they call 'managed' mutual recognition. The nature of mutual recognition as applied by the CJEU becomes clear when contrasted with the country-of-origin principle that was proposed in the first draft of the Services Directive ('Bolkestein Directive'). The Bolkestein Directive had proposed a country-of-origin principle that excluded the equivalence requirement, which had characterized the Court's case law. Drijber described the difference between mutual recognition and country-of-origin principle in a parliamentary hearing on the draft Directive as follows:

> Under the Court's rulings, the law of the host state must be 'disapplied' to incoming services in so far as its application would give rise to an unjustified restriction of free trade. In other words, mutual recognition is a conditional obligation because the host state may always try to justify a restrictive means. By contrast, the country-of-origin principle works like a rule of conflict. It sets aside the law of the host state, including rules that are compatible with the Treaty. Mutual recognition becomes an unconditional obligation. The [Bolkestein] Directive therefore goes much further than the case law.[172]

In the final version of the Services Directive the country-of-origin principle was retracted. According to Nicolaïdis and Schmidt 'the final compromise succeeded precisely because it recovers the spirit of managed mutual recognition.'[173] They argue that mutual recognition had always been 'a conditional process and did not have the either-or character of the country-of-origin principle.'[174]

Any attempt to read mutual recognition as a normative requirement of regulatory competition, as for example proposed by Streit and Mussler, is incorrect. However, a factual tendency towards the lowering of regulatory standards, as feared by some, cannot be excluded. In particular, two doctrinal features have been frequently found to support such tendency: first, mutual recognition inverts the burden of proof, as it is for the Member States to demonstrate that the regulations of the country of manufacture do not ensure a level of protection equivalent to its own standards. Depending on the strictness of evidentiary standards applied, such proof can be difficult, which could create a bias towards lower standards in practice.[175] Second, the level of protection that the country of reception applies is open to scrutiny in the proportionality test. Depending on the standards applied by the court, a high level of protection may be found to be disproportionate, which may facilitate a regulatory race to the bottom. However, this is not a

[172] Berend Drijber, 'The country of origin principle', hearing before the Committee Internal Market and Consumer Protection on the Proposed Directive on Services in the Internal Market (2004), europarl.europa.eu/hearings/20041111/imco/contributions_en.htm, 3–4; see also Kalypso Nicolaïdis and Susanne Schmidt, 'Mutual recognition "on trial": the long road to services liberalization' (2007) 14 *Journal of European Public Policy* 717, 729.

[173] Nicolaïdis and Schmidt (n 172), 717.

[174] ibid, 729.

[175] See eg Noreen Burrows, 'Harmonisation of technical standards: reculer pour mieux sauter?' (1990) 53 *Modern Law Review* 597, 597–98.

necessary consequence: the normative setup of the principle of mutual recognition also allows for very different outcomes. Courts may decide that the desired level of protection of the country of reception is justified on grounds of the public interest, that the regulations of the country of origin do not ensure the same level of protection, or apply looser evidentiary standards. The principle of mutual recognition is therefore normatively open towards different interpretations of the Treaty freedoms in the light of competing socio-economic paradigms. Mutual recognition *can* be interpreted in a way that facilitates a 'race to the bottom', but does not *need* to be interpreted that way. As has been shown, a 'race to the bottom' is one possible consequence in an integrated market with a non-centralized governance structure, a 'race to the top' another. The latter may occur, for example, when an economically important region sets the standards that become de facto universal because they are adopted by producers, as was the case for example with car emission standards set by California.[176] Other factors were believed to have a potentially similar effect: for example, Burrows argued that the strict liability standard laid down in the Product Liability Directive would motivate producers and importers to follow the highest national standards.[177] In the light of the Court's practice, scholars like Pelkmans and Schmidt argue that the principle of mutual recognition does not per se lead to a 'race to the bottom'.[178] Schmidt holds that 'few examples of downward spirals have actually become known',[179] though she concedes that 'this does not mean that mutual recognition does not have dynamic implications'.[180] Jacques Pelkmans rejects the assumption that the normative setup of the principle of mutual recognition leads to a deregulatory bias in practice. According to Pelkmans, the effectiveness of judicial mutual recognition as a tool of individual businesses to combat regulation in the country of reception is considerably limited for a number of practical reasons.[181] First, for many companies it is difficult to assess whether their products could benefit from mutual recognition; and second, enforcing mutual recognition in face of national authorities that insist on compliance with local technical requirements may turn out to be a costly and protracted process.[182] Pelkmans therefore argues:

> [Mutual recognition, MR] in the EU goods market is thus characterized by multiple and substantial benefits and a number of costs which, for business, tend to accumulate to possibly deterrent levels. There are also costs for national authorities, but only when they

[176] See the discussion of the so-called 'California effect' in Fritz Scharpf, 'Introduction: the problem-solving capacity of multi-level governance' (1997) 4 *Journal of European Public Policy* 520, 522–23.

[177] Burrows (n 175), 600.

[178] Pelkmans (n 157) 700; Susanne Schmidt, 'Mutual recognition as a new mode of governance' (2007) 14 *Journal of European Public Policy* 667, 677.

[179] Schmidt (n 178), 677.

[180] ibid, 677.

[181] Pelkmans (n 157), 708ff.

[182] For a similar argument see already Burrows (n 175), 598.

Third, the Commission introduced what it called the 'new approach' in harmonization.[193] According to this 'new approach', a harmonization measure is supposed to lay down in general terms only the most important public regulatory interests, most notably health, environmental and safety concerns.[194] Technical specifications, on the other hand, are not decided upon in a legislative act, but in European harmonized standards. These standards are mandated by the Commission to one of the three European standards organizations, and then published in the EU's *Official Journal*.[195] The standardization organizations thus became something like a 'European standards institute', an idea floated by the Commission at least since the late 1970s.[196] The harmonized standards are detailed technical solutions to the general requirements laid down in the harmonization legislation, quite like standards produced by national or international standardization bodies (such as the Deutsches Institut für Normung, DIN, or the International Organization for Standardization, ISO). Products that comply with these standards are presumed to be in conformity with the requirements laid down in the EU's harmonized acts. However, the European standards were voluntary: manufacturers may opt for a different solution to fulfil the standards required by the European harmonization measure. Moreover, the Commission attempted to propose regulatory solutions for general regulatory areas, and no longer for specific categories of products. A fourth and final innovation that should be mentioned in relation to the 1992 project was Directive EEC/83/189, which required Member States to notify the Commission of any new regulation, and built upon an agreement among the Member States and the Commission dating back to the 1960s.[197] Implementation was subject to a standstill clause, and the Commission could oppose them under certain conditions. The Directive has been described by Pelkmans as the most significant measure in practice ensuring the continued functioning of the internal market.[198]

The reforms of the 1992 process were thus liable to change the dynamics in the regulatory process to a considerable extent. The partial removal of the unanimity requirement reduced the ability of individual Member States to stall regulatory processes. The judicial principle of mutual recognition facilitated, at least in

[193] See Council Resolution on a new approach to technical harmonisation and standards [1985] OJ C136/1. See also Andrew McGee and Stephen Weatherill, 'The Evolution of the Single Market—Harmonisation or Liberalisation' (1990) 53 *Modern Law Review* 578, 582–87; Jacques Pelkmans, 'The new approach to technical harmonization and standardization' (1987) 25 *Journal of Common Market Studies* 249.

[194] EC, *Completing the Internal Market*, 19, para 65; see also Schwartz (n 160), 354–55.

[195] The three organisations are: the European Committee for Standardization (CEN), the European Committee for Electrotechnical Standardization (CENELEC) and the European Telecommunications Standards Institute (ETSI).

[196] See for example EC, *The removal of technical barriers to trade* (Office for Official Publications of the European Communities, 1979), 7.

[197] Council Directive 83/189/EEC laying down a procedure for the provision of information in the field of technical standards and regulations [1983] OJ L 109/8; on this see for example Burrows (n 175), 601.

[198] Pelkmans (n 157), 705–07.

principle, trade even in absence of harmonization, which altered the incentives of stalling harmonization. And finally, the 'new approach' in harmonization reduced the number of issues on which the Member States had to agree on in order to pass legislation: Fritz Scharpf reported that 'The more abstract formulation of safety principles has made it easier to reach agreement in the Council of Ministers.'[199]

The Distinction Between the 'New' and an Alleged 'Old' Approach—An Ideologically Coded Dichotomy

These changes to the instrument of harmonization were discussed controversially in the 1980s. The debate was shaped by a strong analytical focus on the alleged dichotomy between (re-)regulation and de-regulation. For commentators like Scharpf, who believed that the ability of Member States to shape their own socio-economic development was strongly reduced as a consequence of the integration process, the 1992 process only imperfectly re-constituted efficient regulatory means on the European plane.[200] Weatherill and McGee argued that the 'new approach', which relied heavily on standardization by non-state parties, was, for financial reasons and because consumer interests were badly organized in some countries, likely to be captured by industry interests.[201] The altered practice of harmonization was thus held to strengthen what they saw as de-regulatory tendencies. On the other hand it was argued that the 1992 reforms in fact increased the Community's re-regulatory abilities: most notably, the majority requirement certainly made re-regulation on the European level easier than before.[202] Moreover, Article 100a EEC was held to provide an, at least potentially, unrestricted legal basis for harmonization, as for example Petersmann argued with reference to the Court's *Titanium Dioxide* decision.[203] In granting considerable discretion to the European legislators, the Court significantly facilitated re-regulation on the European level, as Weatherill and McGee observed. Directives concerning air pollution by motor vehicle emissions, for example, were adopted on the basis of Article 100a and its majority requirement, instead of the unanimity requirement necessary for environmental legislation under Article 133.[204] Some liberalist

[199] Fritz Scharpf, 'Community and autonomy: multi-level policy-making in the European Union' (1994) 1 *Journal of European Public Policy* 219, 14.

[200] According to Scharpf, central impediments to the re-regulation on the European level were the ability of individual Member States to stall progress, the muddled nature of compromises that were achievable on the European level, the limited autonomous force of the Commission, differences in political culture, as well as the lack of legitimacy of European democracy. Accordingly, Scharpf advocated for improvements in 'the policy-making capacities of the European Union.' At the same time, he held it to be 'equally important to defend or win back the problem-solving capacity of member states.' ibid, 3–5; see also McGee and Weatherill (n 193) 586, who speak of a 'regulatory gap'.

[201] McGee and Weatherill (n 193), 585.

[202] See on this ibid, 592–94.

[203] Ernst-Ulrich Petersmann, 'Grundprobleme der Wirtschaftsverfassung der EG' (1994) 48 *Aussenwirtschaft* 389, 412; Lane (n 114), 972–73, explains: 'If a proposal has an internal market component which is more than merely ancillary it may, in the light of the judgment of the Court of Justice in *Titanium Dioxide* require a Treaty basis not in Article 130s at all, but in Article 100a.'

[204] McGee and Weatherill (n 193), 594.

commentators were highly critical of such facilitation of harmonization. Streit and Mussler criticized the extensive potential scope of harmonization, and also complained that Article 100a would undermine the possibility of regulatory competition among the Member States.[205] In conjunction with a tendency of the Court to interpret the provision broadly, this created, from their perspective, an unwanted bias towards harmonization.[206]

The (re-)regulation/de-regulation dichotomy shaped the discussion on the 1992 process to a significant extent, and contemporary EU law scholarship routinely replicates this dichotomic understanding in some form. While the concept is helpful to address the factual ability or inability to regulate situations on the European level if regulation on the national level is no longer possible for legal or factual reasons, it should not be uncritically imported into legal discourse. Here the dichotomy is problematic because it employs a misleading quantity-based metaphor in relation to regulation; however, from a legal perspective, a situation cannot be 'more' or 'less' regulated. A situation in which producers have to adhere to few product requirements is not regulated 'less', but *different* than a situation where they have to adhere to many. It is a choice in favour of few or low standards, as opposed to many, but a choice for a specific regulatory setup nonetheless. In fact, liberalized markets often require considerably more complex regulation than, for example, public monopolies. The concept of 'de-regulation' insinuates that a specific regulatory setup is somehow the neutral default situation of markets (a market free of regulation), whereas others are a deviation from that position. This, however, is an ideologically charged position. Analysing the 1992 reforms to harmonization along these lines is thus liable to project a specific socio-economic worldview onto them. This overshadows the complex process of change and reforms that the Community's harmonization strategy went through, and thereby creates an incorrect and ideologically charged representation of the *normative* implications of the reforms. This is particularly prevalent in regard to the alleged antagonism between the 'new approach' on the one hand and the regulatory practice that preceded it on the other. In the literature, the 'new approach' is routinely developed, directly or indirectly, against an alleged 'old approach' in the 1960s and 1970s, which is presumably characterized by zealous, excessively detailed regulation.[207] Such dichotomy manifestly draws from the conceptual distinction between de-regulation and re-regulation. However, such representation has little factual support. Rather than breaking with some dysfunctional 'old'

[205] Streit and Mussler (n 140), 337.

[206] ibid, 337.

[207] See for example Majone (n 124), 244–45: 'From the early 1960s to about 1973—the date of the first enlargement of the Community—the Commission's approach to harmonization was characterized by a distinct preference for detailed measures designed to regulate exhaustively the problems under consideration, to the exclusion of previously existing national laws and regulations—the approach known as "total harmonization" … By the mid-1970s, however, the limitations of this approach had become clear; while mounting opposition to what many member states considered excessive centralization convinced the Commission that harmonization had to be used so as not to interfere too much with the regulatory autonomy of the national governments.'

regulatory strategy, the 'new approach' builds in many ways on regulatory innovations already developed in the 1960s and 1970s. It should thus be understood as a reform step within a long process of learning by the regulators and the legislators, and of adaption to new regulatory challenges. The proclamation of a 'new' approach mainly served a strategic-discursive function for the Commission, rallying support and deflecting criticism of its harmonization program. Not incidentally, the Commission had, for the same purpose, proclaimed a 'new' approach to harmonization already twice before, once in the late 1960s and once in the 1970s. This indicates that any attempt to charge the 'new approach' of the 1980s with a specific normative meaning is thus liable to misrepresent the complex development of the Community's regulatory strategy (that we will look at in the next section), and mistake a rhetorical device for a factual legal development.

The Commission's Three 'New Approaches': Continuities and Change in the Community's Harmonization Strategy

The Commission started to focus on the problem of differences in technical standards as trade barriers on a systematic level in the late 1960s. As already discussed, the heightened attention for the adverse effects on trade of regulatory differences between technical standards in the Community corresponded to an increased interest on the international plane in the same issue.[208] The Commission argued that, with the successful elimination of tariffs, the restrictive effects of regulatory differences between the Member States became more pressing.[209] In 1968 it submitted the General Programme on the 'Elimination of technical obstacles to trade'.[210] The programme proposed around 150 harmonization measures that the Commission wished to see implemented by the end of the year 1970.[211] In these programmes, the Commission proclaimed what it called its 'new approach to harmonization', thereby announcing the first of a total of at least three 'new approaches': The 'new approach' of the 1960s consisted, first, in the proposition of 'homogenous sets' of directives, in which a general directive provided the generally applicable rules in a certain sector, with more detailed directives providing further specifications if necessary. Second, the harmonization measures were intended to provide common solutions to the specific regulatory concerns that characterized the targeted sector alone (eg consumer safety in regard to electrical equipment).[212] Third, the harmonization of these core concerns would then allow for the mutual

[208] Craig Mathews, 'Non-Tariff Import Barriers and the Kennedy Round' (1965) 2 *Common Market Law Review* 403.

[209] EC, 'General programme for elimination of technical barriers to trade due to disparities in national legislation', 2.

[210] ibid.

[211] See EC, 'Elimination des entraves techniques aux échanges dans la CEE: Le point de la situation' (Information Memo, 1972), 3.

[212] EC, 'First General Report on the Activities of the Communities 1967' (1968), 197.

recognition of controls, thereby realizing the free movement of goods. With the emphasis on horizontal harmonization measures, the focus on core regulatory concerns and the mutual recognition of controls, the harmonization strategies proposed in the 1968 programme already anticipated the 1992 reforms in important ways.[213] In particular, the Commission argued that, depending on the regulatory area in question, different forms of harmonization were appropriate.[214] The five possible forms of harmonization proposed by the Commission ranged from 'total' harmonization (Solution I), 'optional' harmonization (Solution II) and the harmonization of core standards (Solution III), to the conditional and the automatic mutual recognition of controls (Solution IV and V). Total harmonization describes the complete substitution of national rules by a European measure. In optional harmonization, European standards must be implemented alongside the national product standards: products that are produced according to the former may be sold across the EEC, while Member States may uphold their national standards for domestic production. Solution III proposed that the harmonization measure would define general safety requirements alone, which would be further fleshed out by standards drawn up by international standardization institutes. According to the Commission, this would allow a quick and flexible adaption of technical standards to changing technical conditions. Solutions II, III, IV and V seem to anticipate the 'new approach' of the 1980s in important aspects. The Commission also proposed an agreement among the Member States to notify any planned reforms to national standards to the Commission, which was passed as a Council Resolution and, as acknowledged by the White Paper, constitutes a precursor to Directive EEC/83/189 discussed above. A second Council resolution proposed the mutual recognition of controls in areas where production requirements were harmonized.[215] Finally, the general programme also proposed a simplified procedure in which the Commission and a Committee of Member State representatives was granted power to adapt Directives to the 'technical progress'.[216] The contemporary depiction of the pre-1980s practice of harmonization as preoccupied with 'total' harmonization alone has thus little to do with the nuanced and multi-faceted approach that was in fact pursued by the Commission since the 1960s. For example, the 1967 Commission proposal for the harmonization of pharmaceutical products is based on the principle of the automatic mutual

[213] The Commission considered two central concerns that required caution in the harmonization process: first, national regulation often served important public objectives, which should not be compromised; and second, European harmonization made it more difficult to adapt regulation to the 'technical progress'. EC, 'General programme for elimination of technical barriers to trade due to disparities in national legislation', 3.

[214] ibid, 28–31.

[215] Council Resolution on a new approach to technical harmonisation and standards [1985] OJ C136/1.

[216] EC, 'General programme for elimination of technical barriers to trade due to disparities in national legislation', 21–23.

recognition of permits issued by other Member States.[217] Most harmonization measures relating to the free movement of goods, for example the various Directives on motor vehicles, constituted 'optional' harmonization.[218]

The Commission's initial legislative plan that it had laid out in the General Programme, which had aimed for the adoption of the 150 harmonization measures within a period of a little more than one and a half years, proved to be too optimistic. Impediments to the harmonization process acknowledged by the Commission by 1972 included the complexity of national responsibilities for the harmonization of standards, the resistance of dominant enterprises, and the difficulties related to find common solutions, eg regarding methods of analysis and testing among experts socialized in different national technical cultures.[219] Finally, the accession of Denmark, the UK and Ireland was also cause for delay of the Commission's initial programme. Prior to their accession, a consultation mechanism had been introduced[220] which allowed these countries to participate in the legislative process even prior to accession, but also made harmonization more onerous.[221] The aspects of the Commission's harmonization project that seem to have gathered the most negative attention, most notably in the UK, were those concerning processed food.[222] An example was the proposed Directive on beer, which was held to prescribe uniform production standards derided as 'Eurobeer'. It illustrates the extent to which the rhetoric on the Commission's alleged regulatory zealousness simply misrepresents the legal facts. Far from imposing uniform production standards, the measure in fact aimed at opening the European markets for beer produced according to the various production techniques and ingredients employed in the Member States.[223] The central target of the proposed Directive was the German market, where production standards required the use of malted barley or wheat-malt. By contrast, the other Member States allowed the use of other cereal products also, as well as certain additives. The measure further provided for standardized rules on packaging and labelling, as well as revoking certain subsidies for raw materials used in the brewing process. All of this aimed at facilitating trade and enabling undistorted competition *without* imposing a uniform production standard: the effect of the measure, had it been implemented,

[217] M Seidel, 'The Harmonization of Laws Relating to Pharmaceuticals in the EEC' (1969) 6 *Common Market Law Review* 309, 316–17.

[218] Finn Gundelach, 'Closing speech for the European Symposium on Trends in the Regulations concerning motor vehicle design' (1975), 2.

[219] EC, 'Elimination des entraves techniques aux échanges dans la CEE: Le point de la situation', 3.

[220] 'Etude du Comité économique et social sur les problemes concernant le rapprochement des législations relatives aux entraves techniques', 7.

[221] The Commission also noted the delays caused by translation difficulties, particularly into Danish. See EC, 'Etat d'avancement des travaux relatifs au programme général pour l'élimination des entraves techniques aux échanges dans le domaine industriel' (1973).

[222] See for example the discussion of the issue in George Thomson, 'Address to the Birmingham Chamber of Commerce and Industry' (Birmingham, 5 November 1974), 4–5.

[223] For a description and extensive defence of the measure see EC, 'Harmonization of legislation pertaining to beer' (Newsletter on the common agricultural policy No 6, 1970).

would have been that beer produced according to the various production standards could have been sold across the EEC. The portrayal of the measure in political discourse as imposing a uniform type of 'Eurobeer' has thus little resemblance with its factual content.[224]

But as the Commission was losing the public relations battle over this and other proposals, it decided to scrap it in 1973, together with a number of other proposed measures.[225] This formed part of a broader overhaul of the Commission's harmonization strategy, which was announced by the new Danish Commissioner Finn Gundelach in a speech at the European Parliament in 1974 as the 'new approach to the approximation of legislation'; thereby proclaiming the Community's second 'new approach'. Gundelach held that 'the concept "harmonization" is no longer a relevant description of the Commission's efforts to promote the free movement of goods and services',[226] and argued: 'To the extent that such approximation is an indispensable necessity for the maintenance and development of a free market for goods and only when this objective cannot be attained through other means. Approximation or harmonization is not sought for the mere sake of harmonization.'[227] Gundelach proposed an increased use of harmonization strategies other than 'total harmonization', not unlike the Commission had already done in 1968: this included reliance on mutual recognition (possibly paired with certain minimum standards), 'optional harmonization' in which Community-wide standards allowing the import and export of products were introduced alongside national standards, and horizontal harmonization. A year later, the Commission explained that

> the method of harmonisation of legislation used is never more than strictly necessary. The so-called 'optional' method is usually employed—by which the national standards remain intact, and the Community specifications need only be followed by a producer who wishes to sell throughout the Community as a whole. The 'total' method, by which the national rules are replaced by the Community system is only used where required for reasons of public health or safety, or protection of the environment.[228]

[224] The factual beneficiaries of the withdrawal of the proposal on beer were German brewers, who retained their market protection. See Martin Sherwood, 'Eurobeer' *New Scientist* (21 February 1974) 494.

[225] See for example Commissioner Gundelach's speech to the European Parliament in February 1974, reported in EC, 'A new approach to the approximation of legislation' (Information Interior Market, 1974), 3; *The Economist* reported in the same month that 'one genuine triumph of British entry has been to see the harmonizing habit put to flight in Brussels'; quoted in Vogelaar (n 37), 222; a suprisingly self-ironic recognition by the Commission of the bad reputation of its harmonization projects can be found in a press release from 1986: 'Eurobread, Eurobeer and now Eurotelevision. Nothing, it seems, is safe from the meddling of the Eurocrats in Brussels. But the European Commission has a duty to help create a common market not only for television sets but also the programmes they receive, as it made clear a year ago with its Green Paper "Television Without Frontiers".' EC, 'Television and Broadcasting' (Background Note, 1986).

[226] EC, 'A new approach to the approximation of legislation', 5.

[227] ibid, 1.

[228] EC, 'Abolition of technical barriers to trade in industrial products during 1974: the present situation' (Information Memo P-7/75, 1975), 1.

In a similar vein, the British Commissioner George Thomson argued in a speech in 1976:

> [T]here has grown up a new and more pragmatic approach to the problems of harmonisation—seeking the minimum essential for the development of the Community or for public health and safety, and making the arrangements optional wherever possible.[229]

The 'new approach' of the 1970s thus followed similar ambitions as the 'new approach' of both the 1960s and the 1980s.[230] The unfinished harmonization proposals were picked up in late 1973 in the Community's Action Programme 'in the field of technological and industrial policy',[231] with which the Commission hoped to create a renewed dynamic in the Council to adopt the remainder of the measures by 1977.[232] The regulatory techniques developed by the Commission to evade the need for comprehensive harmonization, such as 'optional' harmonization, a focus on core regulatory concerns such as health and safety, the mutual recognition of controls, the use of non-legislative technical standards and simplified amendment procedures, were implemented in a variety of measures proposed under the 'new approach' of the 1960s as well as that of the 1970s. An example for a measure that defined safety requirements in a very general form, and otherwise relied on standards drawn up by standardization bodies was Directive 73/23/EEC 'on the harmonization of the laws of Member States relating to electrical equipment designed for use within certain voltage limits'.[233] The Directive had, with some exceptions, general application to all electrical equipment (Article 1). It laid down only essential safety requirements (Annex I): the annex listed 11 requirements of a very general nature, for example (2.d): 'Measures of a technical nature should be prescribed … in order to ensure: … d) that the insulation must be suitable for foreseeable conditions.' Article 3 required Member States to ensure that the free movement of products complying with the safety standards 'shall not be

[229] George Thomson, 'Address to the Pharmaceutical Society of Great Britain' (Dundee, 15 September 1976). The whole passage reads: 'One of the big changes that has taken place within the Community over recent years is the reaction against any idea of harmonisation for harmonisation's sake. Back in 1969, and again in 1972, the European Commission put forward ambitious proposals for the imposition of an identical professional statute for pharmacists within the then Community. Even within the six founding members with their long experience of the Community, this ran into serious difficulties. And when the three new members arrived, the task was given up as politically impossible. Since then, there has grown up a new and more pragmatic approach to the problems of harmonisation—seeking the minimum essential for the development of the Community or for public health and safety, and making the arrangements optional wherever possible.'

[230] Roth identified significant changes in harmonization strategy by the mid-70s: harmonization was to be restricted to the 'absolute minimum necessary", and harmonization proposals in fringe areas were scrapped. A proposal that was supposedly retracted was on the harmonization of so-called correspondence courses. Roth (n 192), 39.

[231] EC, 'Programme of action in the field of technological and industrial policy' SEC (73) 3824 final.

[232] ibid, 1; while this in fact led to a number of measures being adopted by the Council, the Commission also expressed reservations concerning the issuance of too many new proposals (ibid, 2).

[233] Council Directive 73/23/EEC on the harmonization of the laws of Member States relating to electrical equipment designed for use within certain voltage limits [1973] OJ L 77/29.

impeded for reasons of safety'. In particular, Member States were obliged to ensure that products complying with 'harmonized standards' could be put on their markets (Article 5(1)). Harmonized standards were established by agreement among national standardization bodies, and published in the OJ (Articles 5(2)–(3)). In the absence of such harmonized standards, Member States had to ensure that equipment produced according to the safety provisions of another Member State could be put on their market 'if it ensures a safety level equivalent to that required in their own territory' (Article 7). The provision thus proscribed a mutual recognition requirement. Producers could opt for an alternative proof of conformity with the Directive's safety standards (Article 8(2)). Article 10 prescribes a presumption of conformity of product marks and certificates issued by a national body. It should be quite obvious that the Directive bears a close resemblance to the model again forwarded by the Commission under the 'new approach' of the 1980s. Of course, a considerable amount of harmonization measures—regardless of whether they followed the 'optional' or the 'total' approach—were in fact far more comprehensive and detailed. This is true, for example, of the harmonization of tractor type approval, which required 21 Council Directives between 1974 and 1983, according to a Commission overview.[234] The standards laid down in these measures are considerably more detailed than those of the Directive on electrical equipment.[235] At the same time, however, these measures still implemented a variety of the innovative elements proposed in the general programme: this included, most notably, the establishment of a simplified procedure that allowed for adaptation of the standards by a 'Committee on the Adaptation to Technical Progress'[236] and the recognition of approval decisions by the authorities of another Member State.[237] The harmonization measures on motor vehicles equally provided for the 'mutual recognition of vehicle authorizations', which made it 'possible to use and market equipment dealt with in special proposed directives without repeating the tests.'[238] Additionally, they frequently drew from international standards, where available.[239]

[234] See ec.europa.eu/enterprise/sectors/automotive/documents/directives/tractors/index_en.htm.

[235] See for example the Annexes of Council Directive 74/151/EEC on the approximation of the laws of the Member States relating to certain parts and characteristics of wheeled agricultural or forestry tractors [1974] OJ L 84/25; and Council Directive 74/152/EEC on the approximation of the laws of the Member States relating to the maximum design speed of and load platforms for wheeled agricultural or forestry tractors [1974] OJ L 84/33.

[236] See eg Arts 11–13 of Council Directive 74/150/EEC on the approximation of the laws of the Member States relating to the type-approval of wheeled agricultural or forestry tractors [1974] OJ L 84/10.

[237] See eg Art 7 of the Directive.

[238] EC, 'First General Report on the Activities of the Communities 1967', 199.

[239] See as an example Council Directive 70/157/EEC on the approximation of the laws of the Member States relating to the permissible sound level and the exhaust system of motor vehicles [1970] OJ L 42/16, Annex, I.2: 'The noise emitted by vehicles shall be measured by means of a sound-level meter of the type described in Publications 179, 1st edition (1965), of the International Electrotechnical Commission.' See also McCarthy (n 156), 204–05.

The 'new approach' of the 1980s constitutes not only a break, but also a continuation of the Commission's earlier harmonization strategies. This can be illustrated, for example, by a comparison of the Commission's 1979 proposal on 'simple pressure vessels' on the one hand, to be read in conjunction with the general Directive 76/767/EEC on pressure vessels, and the measure on 'simple pressure vessels' ultimately adopted in 1987 on the other.[240] Illustrating the increased reliance on non-legislative standards, the annex, which specified technical standards as well as the testing procedure, shrank from 31 pages in the original proposal to six in the new measure, thus seemingly illustrating the impact of the 'new approach.' A closer look shows, however, that the picture is more complex: the 1979 proposal itself already made use of international standards (ISO and Euronorm) at many points, thereby anticipating the later Directive in important ways. Furthermore, the general Directive 76/767/EEC had already implemented many of the strategies the Commission employed instead of 'total' harmonization: first, the Directive was an example of 'optional' harmonization, ie, Member States had to allow the marketing of pressure vessels that complied with the relevant requirements (Article 3), but could uphold alternative national standards applicable to national production. Secondly, it only defined minimum standards for the national inspection bodies (Article 12), and otherwise provided for the 'mutual recognition of inspection procedures by the Member States'. Thirdly, it provided for the simplified procedure already discussed in which the requirements of the Directive can be adapted to the 'technical progress' (Articles 18–20). A closer scrutiny thus reveals that Directive 76/767/EEC anticipates the reforms that are now associated with the 'new approach' of the 1980s in many ways. While the 1987 measure removed the technical specifications from the annex and relied on non-legislative harmonized standards instead, it also built on essential characteristics of the earlier harmonization strategies.

This brief overview shows that the Commission already pursued a differentiated approach to harmonization in the 1960s and 1970s, which in many aspects anticipated the 'new approach' of the 1980s. As we have seen, it introduced a variety of innovative harmonization strategies, including optional harmonization, reliance on non-legislative standards, simplified adaptation procedures, mutual recognition, horizontal harmonization and a notification and standstill requirement that were picked up and further developed in the 1980s. It is thus plainly incorrect to claim that the harmonization strategy prior to the 1980s aimed at a 'total' harmonization, when in fact the Commission attempted to limit the use of the 'total' harmonization technique since the 1960s. Instead, the 'new approach' of the 1980s must be understood as a continuation of a process of learning and adaptation to new circumstances that had characterized the Community's harmonization

[240] Council Directive 78/404/EEC on the harmonization of the laws of the Member States relating to simple pressure vessels [1987] OJ L 220/48.

strategy from the 1960s onwards. While it provided the Commission with an opportunity to modify its harmonization strategy, the reform also built on and systematized previous innovations, thereby constituting a continuation as well as a break from the previous strategy. The fact that the Commission had announced a 'new approach' to harmonization twice before, in the late 1960s and again in the 1970s, indicates not only the continued process of reform, but also the communicative-strategic aspect of such announcement. In both instances the Commission had proclaimed a 'new approach' in order to rally support and to appease critics, in particular of course the UK, where criticism of the Commission's alleged regulatory over-zealousness had become a standard trope in political debate. It seems thus unwarranted to essentialize an alleged opposition between an 'old' approach on the one hand and the 'new approach' on the other, or to charge it with a normative meaning.

The preceding overview over two central instruments of socio-economic governance, mutual recognition and harmonization, have attempted to show two things: first, while both instruments certainly experience significant alterations over the course of the 1992 project, these reforms also build on previous developments in multiple ways, and thus form part of a complex process of learning and adaptation that has been ongoing since the 1960s. It is therefore problematic to conceptualize the reforms that formed part of the 1992 project as incisive to an extent that they must be assumed to alter the overall socio-economic orientation of the Treaty. Second, the common representation of the two instruments on the basis of the ideologically charged two-sphere fallacy discussed in the Introduction obscures their complex operation. In fact, neither mutual recognition nor the 'new approach' in harmonization can be properly analysed on its basis; instead, they appear to be ideologically ambivalent instruments. This supports the general claim of this book that the Treaty must be read as a pluralist regulatory framework. The subsequent sections put this in a broader context, discussing the extensive spectrum of socio-economic measures that were enacted to complement market integration.

THE COMPLETIVE MEASURES OF '1992'

The project to 'complete' market integration was conceived as a reaction to some of the economic difficulties related to the recession of the early 1980s: most notably, a fully integrated market should create an improved home position for Europe's businesses in global competition. At the same time, policymakers were aware that such intensified market integration could create new or exacerbate existing imbalances, for example in regard to regional differences or the balance of payments. A significant factor was the accession of Greece, Spain and Portugal: the EEC of the 1980s was, as the Padoa-Schioppa Report emphasized, in many respects more economically heterogeneous than the EEC of the 1950s. This made macroeconomic stability and equitable distribution of gains a much more pressing concern for the Community.[241] The report held: 'The internal market programme creates both opportunities and needs for complementary action to foster macroeconomic stability and growth of the Community.'[242] The White Paper similarly emphasized the importance of completive, (in the broadest sense) stability-oriented measures for the functioning of the internal market. This included 'the strengthening of coordination of economic policies',[243] stricter competition policies (directed against both private and public actors),[244] social and regional cohesion policy,[245] but also social and employment policy coordination.[246] Despite the Commission's optimism about the beneficial effects of market integration, it did not fail to mention that market integration might also in turn cause greater instability and inequality, for example between core and peripheral regions:

> The Commission is firmly convinced that the completion of the Internal Market will provide an indispensable base for increasing the prosperity of the community as a whole. The Commission is, however, conscious that there may be risks that, by increasing the possibilities for human, material and financial services to move without obstacle to the areas of greatest economic advantage, existing discrepancies between regions could be exacerbated and therefore the objective of convergence jeopardized.[247]

The 1992 project should thus be understood to have two interconnected regulatory objectives: first, the project of market integration; and second, the adoption of a macroeconomic framework that would absorb imbalances expected to arise as a consequence of further market integration.[248] Ultimately, the trade measures on the one hand and the accompanying policies on the other were conceptualized as intrinsically connected: stability- and equity-oriented measures were a precondition that the potential benefits of market integration would be realized in practice. However, the degree to which flanking policies were necessary, and, if yes, how they should be designed, was a considerably conflicted issue. In the following, we will look at some of the most important completive policies, discuss their relation to the project of market integration, and look at some of the different perspectives on the respective policy. It will be argued that these flanking measures indicate the pluralist and often conflicting nature of the policies pursued by the 1992 project.

[241] Padoa-Schioppa (n 46), Preamble, iv.
[242] ibid, 3.
[243] EC, 'Completing the Internal Market', 8, para 19.
[244] ibid, 8, para 19.
[245] ibid, 8, para 21.
[246] ibid, 8, para 20.
[247] ibid, 8, para 21.
[248] Robert Howse argued that the GATT system, including its exceptions and emergency provisions, was also designed to achieve these two goals—trade and macroeconomic stability—which were understood to be intrinsically connected. Robert Howse, 'From Politics to Technocracy—and Back Again: The Fate of the Multilateral Trading Regime' (2002) 96 *American Journal of International Law* 94, 95.

The Economic and Social Cohesion Funds

We already saw that regional imbalances had been seen as a potential problem in the Community from the very beginning. Capital and labour may move to the location where they achieve the highest return, which may well be from the periphery towards the centre.[249] We have seen that already the Ohlin Report discussed this possibility at length. The Werner Plan from 1970 similarly addressed the issue, proposing that monetary integration was threatened by economic imbalances:

> [T]he realization of global economic equilibrium may be dangerously threatened by differences of structure. Cooperation between the partners in the Community in the matter of structural and regional policies will help to surmount these difficulties, just as it will make it possible to eliminate the distortions of competition. The solution of the big problems in this field will be facilitated by financial measures of compensation. In an economic and monetary union, structural and regional policies will not be exclusively a matter for national budgets.[250]

The issue was again emphasized by the 1987 Padoa-Schioppa Report, which held that '[t]here are serious risks of aggravated regional imbalance in the course of market liberalisation.'[251] The report went on to argue that market integration would create increased opportunities for convergence among the regions, but also strengthen economic forces that pushed towards divergence.

The first cohesion fund, which was included in the Treaty of Rome, was the European Social Fund (ESF), which we discussed in the previous chapter. The European Agricultural Guidance and Guarantee Fund (EAGGF) was set up in 1962 as part of the CAP;[252] finally, the European Regional Development Fund (ERDF) came into being in 1975. Initially, the policies of the cohesion funds closely followed national interests.[253] The allocation of funds was negotiated between the states with an eye on offsetting budgetary imbalances arising from other Community policies. The Member States individually decided which regions

[249] This is a common argument that accompanied the development of the internal market since the very beginning. See for example Hans von der Groeben, 'Mitbestimmung in the Europäischen Aktiengesellschaft—der Vorschlag der Kommission der EG' in Hans von der Groeben, Heinz Vetter and Otto Friedrich (eds), *Europäische Aktiengesellschaft: Beitrag zur sozialen Integration?* (Europa Union Verlag, 1972) 10–12.

[250] Pierre Werner, 'Realisation by Stages of Economic and Monetary Union in the Community—Werner-Report' (*Bulletin of the European Communities*, Supplement 11/1970) 11; see also Gian Paolo Manzella and Carlos Mendez, 'The turning points of EU Cohesion policy' (2009) Working Paper, ec.europa.eu/regional_policy/archive/policy/future/pdf/8_manzella_final-formatted.pdf, 8.

[251] Padoa-Schioppa (n 46), 4.

[252] Council Regulation (EEC) No 25 on the financing of the common agricultural policy [1962] OJ 30/991.

[253] The development of a regional development policy in the 1970s was supported by an alliance of Italy with the new Member States, UK and Ireland. Patrick Ziltener, *Strukturwandel der europäischen Integration: die Europäische Union und die Veränderung der Staatlichkeit* (Westfälisches Dampfboot, 1999) 127–29; see also Dennis Swann, *The Economics of the Common Market* (Penguin Books, 1992), 81; Manzella and Mendez (n 250), 8.

and which projects would be supported, with no overarching European-wide strategy.[254] Starting in the 1980s, the Commission set out to transform the system of intergovernmental budgetary transfer to one based on development objectives coordinated on a European level.[255] The Commission defined economic and social cohesion as one of six priority issues for the completion of the internal market.[256] Delors explained in 1985:

> The underdeveloped regions on the periphery of the industrial heart of Europe have been joined by a number of old industrial regions whose traditional economic base is in structural decline. But the two are fundamentally different. The Community's structural Funds should—provided, of course, that they have sufficient resources—make it possible for the Community to support structural conversion and adjustment projects in regions in difficulty. The Commission aims to reverse the trend towards treating these Funds as mere redistribution mechanisms.[257]

The SEA introduced the title of Economic and Social Cohesion (Articles 130a–130e).[258] According to Article 130a, 'the Community shall aim at reducing disparities between the various regions and the backwardness of the least-favored regions.' Article 130b held that the Community's structural funds should be employed to reach this objective. After the adoption of the SEA, the Commission started to work on the reform of the structural funds ('paquet Delors', or 'Delors II'). According to George Ross, the Commission considered this reform to be at least as crucial for the functioning of the '1992' project as the SEA itself.[259] Manzella held that 'the strengthening of cohesion was presented by the Commission as the *sine qua non* of this ambitious integration drive in recognition of the potentially damaging effects of the 1992 Programme on the more fragile economies of the Union.'[260] And Leibfried and Pierson argued that '[t]he rebuilding of the two Structural Funds into a second leg of the 1992 process symbolizes that horizontal fiscal equity (revenue sharing) and social redistribution between member states have become important bargaining chips between center and periphery in the process of market integration.'[261] Both the Padoa-Schioppa and the Cecchini Reports emphasized the need to substantially increase the volume of the structural funds, and to orient their efforts towards disadvantaged and peripheral regions in

[254] Manzella and Mendez (n 250), 10.

[255] ibid, 12.

[256] EC, 'The Single Act: A New Frontier for Europe. Communication from the Commission to the Council' COM(87) 100 final, 15 February 1987 (*Bulletin of the European Communities*, Supplement 1/87); see on this Lane (n 114), 961.

[257] EC, 'Programme of the Commission for 1985.' Statement by Jacques Delors, President of the Commission, to the European Parliament and His Reply to the Ensuring Debate (Strasbourg, 12 March 1985, *Bulletin of the European Communities*, Supplement 4/85), 15; see also Manzella and Mendez (n 250), 13.

[258] Manzella and Mendez (n 250), 14.

[259] George Ross, *Jacques Delors and European Integration* (Polity Press, 1995) 40–42.

[260] Manzella and Mendez (n 250), 13.

[261] Stephan Leibfried and Paul Pierson, *Prospects for Social Europe* (Center for European Studies, Harvard University, 1992) 15.

order to facilitate the structural reform of their industries.[262] The economic and social cohesion policy would require a substantial financial transfer on the basis of solidarity considerations.[263] Moreover, the cohesion policy was also believed to have an important macroeconomic function. Lane held that

> Cohesion becomes all the more imperative as a necessary corollary of a principal objective of the EC Treaty, economic and monetary union. First, it will be necessary in order to ensure the high degree of sustainable convergence required for entry into the third stage of EMU; and second, since EMU means a surrender of fiscal and monetary control, it is the price of agreement of the less prosperous and weaker currency Member States which are to be deprived of these tools—what in a federation would be called regional equalization payments.[264]

The cohesion funds were supposed to operate as a stabilizing mechanism within an open European market, following Mundell's concept of the optimum currency area.[265] As the European budget was small, the cohesion funds were one of the relatively few mechanisms to ensure stabilizing money flows on the European level.[266] Scholars disagree on the success of these funds;[267] it was often argued that the funds ultimately remained too small to perform their assigned functions.[268] Nonetheless, it is clear that social and regional cohesion were perceived as central objectives to offset adverse effects of market integration, and thereby as decisive for the functioning of the 1992 project in general.

European Monetary Union (EMU)

A managed system of currency exchange rates has been a key policy flanking the internal market since the creation of the EEC. In the Community's early days, this task was performed by the Bretton Woods system. When the Bretton Woods system

[262] Padoa-Schioppa (n 46), 10.

[263] Ross (n 259), 42.

[264] Lane (n 114), 961.

[265] This is further discussed in the following section.

[266] Padoa-Schioppa (n 46), 4.

[267] For example, Martin and Tyler argued that the EU's structural policy has created about one million jobs in Objective 1 regions. By contrast, Rodríguez-Pose and Fratesi doubted that the structural funds had the capacity to foster growth and reduce the gap between core and peripheral regions. Ron Martin and Peter Tyler, 'Evaluating the impact of the structural funds on objective 1 regions: An exploratory discussion' (2006) 40 *Regional Studies* 201, 209; Andrés Rodríguez-Pose and Ugo Fratesi, 'Between Development and Social Policies: The Impact of European Structural Funds in Objective 1 Regions' (2004) 38 *Regional Studies* 97, 109–10. For an overview of scholarship, see Manzella and Mendez (n 250), 2–3; see also Nick Robinson, 'The European Investment Bank: The EU's Neglected Institution' (2009) 47 *Journal of Common Market Studies* 651, 659ff.

[268] Scharpf held that the funds were 'ridiculously under-financed in relation to the problems they are supposed to attack'. Fritz Scharpf, 'The Joint-Decision Trap: Lessons From German Federalism and European Integration' (1988) 66 *Public Administration* 239, 241; Leibfried and Pierson, on the other hand, argued in 1992: 'But as a percentage of GNP in the peripheral countries, Structural Fund expenditures are quite significant: 3.8% for Portugal, 2.6% for Ireland and 1.6% in Greece. Structural Fund expenditures account for 15% of Portugal's and 10% of Greece's gross investments.' Leibfried and Pierson (n 261), 14.

faltered in the late 1960s, the European Member States sought to replace it with a European instrument: the Werner Plan of 1970 aimed to complete 'economic and monetary union' by 1980. However, for a number of reasons only a limited aspect of the Werner Plan, a system of currency coordination called the 'snake', was enacted. This aimed at keeping the participating currencies within a certain band, with the goal of reducing exchange rate fluctuations. As a consequence of the economic turmoil of the early 1970s, a number of currencies soon had to leave the 'snake', with the Deutschmark and some smaller currencies that followed German policy remaining inside. The European Monetary System (EMS) of 1978 constituted a new attempt of monetary integration, building on the 'snake'. Finally, in the context of the 1992 project, the Member States decided to pursue European Monetary Union (EMU), aimed at the creation of a common European currency.

The present section provides an overview of the EMU within its historical context. It aims to show that the EMU conforms to what we have identified as the dual objective of the '1992' project of furthering market integration while aiming to manage the adverse effects of economic integration. Confronted with high inflation, rising unemployment and macroeconomic instability on both the national and the international planes, Member States opted to re-establish a form of currency coordination among themselves, rather than letting currencies float freely. A central concern was that, with wildly fluctuating exchange rates, the CAP would no longer be functional, and the potential benefits of the common market would remain unrealized. In many ways, monetary union was thus assumed to safeguard previous integrative steps as much as it would constitute a further movement towards European integration. At the same time, the form such currency coordination should take, and the institutional, legal, political and economic preconditions for it to function, were heavily contested among economists and policymakers alike. The present section provides an insight into the plurality of socio-economic assumptions that informed the project of monetary integration as well as the contradictions inscribed into it. One key contradiction—characterizing post-war monetary integration on both the European and the global levels—is that between capital mobility and currency pegs. Bretton Woods was embellished with extensive capital controls to prevent speculation against the pegged currencies. The liberalization of capital flows on both a global and on the European level increased speculation, and ultimately undermined limited forms of currency pegs such as the EMS. The choices for full monetary union must be understood against this background.

Economists came down on both sides of the debate, though with those having a critical outlook on European monetary integration possibly being in the majority. Today, it may be assumed that the pursuit of monetary integration based on such a contested economic case may be overtly risky. It is in this context that for example Majone has argued that the project of monetary union was driven by a federalist vision, which—characterized by a 'political culture of total optimism'[269]—did not

[269] Majone (n 124), 58–62.

take doubts about the viability of the EMU sufficiently seriously.[270] While such criticism is undoubtedly plausible, it does not fully represent the context within which policymakers opted for monetary integration. An implicit assumption in such an argument is that the system of floating currencies was the baseline (ie, the common way of organizing monetary relations), from which monetary integration would then have to be assumed to be a deviation in need of justification. However, the situation may have been, counterintuitively from today's perspective, the opposite: from the late nineteenth century and its pound sterling-based gold standard, to the break-up of the Bretton Woods system, some form of monetary coordination was in fact the rule, and currencies were usually allowed to float only in certain crisis situations. As recently as 1970 a system of coordinated currency rates would be considered the conservative, prudent choice, whereas flexible currency rates were conceptualized as an 'untried' model.[271] The EEC had been developed on the basis of the Bretton Woods system, and either its policies (most notably the CAP) directly relied on stable exchange rates, or its function (most notably market integration based on economies of scale) was believed to depend on it.[272] Retaining coordinated exchange rates was thus frequently seen as protecting the status quo of European political *and* economic integration. Moreover, the 1970s, when a system of freely floating currencies was implemented essentially for the first time,[273] were characterized by an unstable global macroeconomic environment, with increasing inflation and unemployment in the domestic realm. Against such a background, the contrasting relative economic stability of the 1950s and 1960s under the Bretton Woods system appeared in sharp relief, so that a system of currency coordination appeared desirable to many. A common European currency was certainly an important objective of European federalists; however, monetary integration could also mobilize important economic arguments in its favour. At the same time, even proponents of monetary integration disagreed in important respects, most notably as regards the extent of the institutional framework

[270] In 2008, the Commission gave the following representation of the state of debate before and after the creation of the EMU: 'Before it was created there was a lively academic and political debate on the viability or desirability of a monetary union for Europe. There was a very broad spectrum of views on the subject: some predicted a bumpy start or even collapse, while others were more sanguine. However, many tended towards a pessimistic view and this may have adversely affected perceptions of the euro area's performance in its early years. The assessments were coloured also by the global economic downturn in the early 2000s and the depreciation of the euro against the US dollar in the period 1999–2002, both roughly coinciding with the run-up to and introduction of euro coins and notes in 2002. This is in contrast with the assessment in Part I of this Report, from which emerges a predominantly favourable picture of the first ten years of the euro—even if weaknesses, shortcomings and unfinished business are also highlighted.' EC, 'EMU@10. Successes and challenges after ten years of Economic and Monetary Union' (2008) 2 *European Economy* 17.

[271] Anthony Lanyi, *The case for floating exchange rates reconsidered* (Princeton University, Essays in International Finance No 72, 1969), 34.

[272] See Loukas Tsoukalis, 'Is the re-launching of economic and monetary union a feasible proposal?' (1976) 15 *Journal of Common Market Studies* 231, 244.

[273] Canada, which allowed its currency to float in the 1950s, constitutes the only exception. Ronald McKinnon, 'Mundell, the Euro, and Optimum Currency Areas' in Thomas Courchene (ed), *Money, Markets, and Mobility* (McGill, 2001), 44.

necessary on the European level to complement monetary union. The disagreement found expression in the ambivalent legal architecture of the EMU, which kept many significant regulatory choices undecided. Majone argued in that regard:

> The 1992 Maastricht Treaty provided a legal framework for monetary union, but left many basic institutional and political questions unresolved. Thus, nothing was said about what to do to contain and resolve systemic crises ... Another unsettled issue was the design of the external monetary policymaking machinery ... This ambiguity, like the other ambiguities and omissions of the Treaty, was not the result of bad drafting, but rather of unresolved disagreements among the member states about key aspects of monetary union. Because of such disagreements, the only way to move ahead was to produce a treaty article open to all interpretations ... At Maastricht, governance issues and all remaining open questions were left to be settled in the future.[274]

Some Economic Observations About Monetary Union

Between countries, three paradigmatic forms of exchange rate management can be distinguished: first, countries may engage in an irrevocable currency union, as in federal states (eg the United States). Second, currencies may have an adjustable peg (such as Bretton Woods, which we will discuss below), or may float within a certain band (such as the EMS, also discussed below). Third, currencies may float freely against each other on a currency market, though central banks seek to influence the exchange rate.[275] (A fourth possibility is that currencies are non-exchangeable, as was the case in post-war Europe before the introduction of the EPU, when cross-border exchanges essentially took the form of barter trade through bilateral agreements.) The key argument in favour of freely floating exchange rates, which are established in a decentralized way through trades on a currency market, is that such market-based mechanism can best establish the respective value of currencies.[276] By contrast, a central argument for the management of exchange rates, as opposed to freely floating currencies, is that in practice exchange rates tend to fluctuate more widely than the underlying fundamentals would justify.[277] The reason for this is, according to the influential thesis of economist Rudi Dornbusch, that financial markets on the one side and labour or commodity markets on the other adjust at different speeds, leading to high volatility in the former.[278] Rapid changes in exchange rates may in turn have significant adverse effects on other economic sectors, and may also negatively affect

[274] Majone (n 124), 28; see also ibid 60, 204.

[275] See for example Barry Eichengreen, James Tobin and Charles Wyplosz, 'Two cases for sand in the wheels of international finance' (1995) 105 *Economic Journal* 162, 163.

[276] Milton Friedman, 'The Case for Flexible Exchange Rates' in Milton Friedman (ed), *Essays in Positive Economics* (University of Chicago Press, 1953).

[277] Eichengreen, Tobin and Wyplosz (n 275), 162.

[278] Rudiger Dornbusch, 'Expectations and exchange rate dynamics' (1976) 84 *Journal of Political Economy* 1161; see also Eichengreen, Tobin and Wyplosz (n 275), 162.

the political support for trade liberalization in general.[279] In such an environment, investors are not orienting themselves at longer-term fundamental economic data, but at speculations about what 'the market' will do.[280] This supports the case for exchange rate management, either in the form of a system where a currency is kept within a specific band to another currency or a basket of currencies, or a fixed exchange rate (such a system is sometimes termed a currency peg). The short-term management of exchange rates is performed through the monetary instruments available to central banks, such as changes to the interest rate, the manipulation of the market through acquisition and sale of the domestic currency in exchange for foreign currency reserves as well as a guaranteed exchange rate.

Retaining a specific exchange rate over the long run requires either capital controls or a conducive macroeconomic environment, which includes, most notably, monetary and fiscal policy. The dependency of a currency peg on capital controls or on conducive macroeconomic conditions is commonly expressed in the economic literature in the form of a trilemma: of the three regulatory goals of pegged exchange rates, capital mobility and national autonomy in economic policies, only two can be upheld at the same time.[281] For example, with free capital mobility, lower interest rates implemented in one country to stimulate investment would be followed by capital flight to countries with higher interest rates. A country would therefore either have to adjust the exchange rate, restrict capital mobility, or give up its autonomous monetary and fiscal policy.[282] The trilemma implies that the relationship between market integration and monetary integration is a complex one, as we will discuss in this section. European integration aimed at enabling capital mobility to realize the full economic benefits of a common market. Yet, at the same time, exchange rate volatility following from liberalized capital movements was perceived as a barrier to exactly such integration, as currency revaluations were assumed to make European-size production unprofitable so that the risk of currency fluctuations could thus prevent investment that would realize economies of scale. However, a currency peg would either require limits on capital mobility, or reduce the autonomy of the Member States in setting their respective economic policies.

Short Historical Overview of European Monetary Integration

The Bretton Woods system was established after WWII as part of a global economic system to facilitate trade and enhance macroeconomic stability. It was a

[279] Eichengreen, Tobin and Wyplosz provide the following example: 'For example, the appreciation of the US dollar against the Japanese yen in the early 1980s nearly destroyed the American automotive industry and jeopardised support for multilateral trade liberalisation in the United States.' Eichengreen, Tobin and Wyplosz (n 275), 163.

[280] ibid, 165; Paul De Grauwe, *Economics of Monetary Union* (OUP, 2012) 49.

[281] See for example Eichengreen, Tobin and Wyplosz (n 275), 162.

[282] Eichengreen, Tobin and Wyplosz (n 275), 162, argue that 'In today's world of high capital mobility, even the minor exercise of policy autonomy can produce major exchange market pressures.'

system of fixed exchange rates between the major global currencies. The national currencies were pegged to the dollar, with adjustable exchange rates that were set by the IMF.[283] The peg was upheld by the central banks, which bought or sold currencies if necessary. The dollar was, in turn, pegged to gold. The Bretton Woods system was based in parts on a draft plan by Keynes during the war; Keynes pitched the proposed model as a modern version of the gold standard (when the pound sterling was pegged to gold), which had provided for exchange rate stability before WWI (as well as during parts of the interwar period).[284] The post-war global economic system had the United States as its undisputed political and economic centre, which facilitated policy coordination. The United States was economically and politically powerful to an extent that its currency was inviolable and thus guaranteed a high degree of stability.[285] The Bretton Woods system was backed up by capital controls, which aimed to prevent speculative capital flows.[286] This allowed—corresponding to the trilemma just discussed—the individual states a certain degree of autonomy in their national monetary and fiscal policies, while upholding the currency peg. A central criticism of Keynes of the gold standard had been that the non-adjustability of the exchange rate required countries to deflate out of trade imbalances, with depression and unemployment as the consequence.[287] With capital controls, exchange rates were adjustable in the event of changes in the macroeconomic fundamentals of a country. The EEC was founded in the context of this system of stabilized exchange rates.[288] Mestmäcker argued, for example, that exchange rate coordination was 'presupposed, if not normatively required' by the Treaty of Rome.[289] This is particularly the case for the CAP, as we will discuss further below.

The Bretton Woods system was rocked by occasional currency crises, in particular in the late 1960s: the United States had built up a significant trade deficit, whereas countries like Japan and Germany featured persistent trade surpluses. These trade imbalances constituted a significant source of instability, as they fuelled currency speculation, which was facilitated by the increasing liberalization of capital movements. Moreover, the power of the dollar as the predominant global currency put inflationary pressure on the European countries: US banks offered dollar-denominated accounts and credit in Europe (the so-called 'Eurodollars'); if, as Mundell explained, European central banks tried to tighten money in order to

[283] On the Bretton Woods system, from a European perspective, see for example Larry Neal, *The Economics of Europe and the European Union* (Cambridge University Press, 2007) 95.

[284] John Maynard Keynes, 'Proposals for an International Currency (or Clearing) Union [February 11, 1942]' in Keith Horsefield (ed), *The International Monetary Fund 1945–1965, Vol III: Documents* (IMF, 1969), 9, 17–18.

[285] Eichengreen, Tobin and Wyplosz (n 275), 163.

[286] ibid, 162–63.

[287] John Maynard Keynes, *The General Theory of Employment, Interest, and Money* (First Harvest/ Harcourt, 1964) 382–83.

[288] See for example von der Groeben (n 69), 89.

[289] Mestmäcker (n 160) 10 (my translation).

curb inflation, economic actors would switch to Eurodollars, thereby undermining the attempt.[290] The adverse influence of the dollar on the European currencies was one of the reasons why scholars and policymakers considered a European currency system as an alternative. Looking back at the breakdown of the Bretton Woods system, the Padoa-Schioppa Report argued a decade later that '[t]he period as a whole supports the proposition that it is not possible to have free trade, freedom from capital restrictions, pegged exchange rates and autonomous macroeconomic policies. Such a system will not work, because it allows inconsistent policies to develop.'[291] This, of course, is a version of the trilemma that we discussed a little earlier. The Bretton Woods system collapsed between the late 1960s and the early 1970s, and eventually all major currencies were floating freely.[292]

A common European monetary system had been discussed since the early 1960s.[293] The immediate cause for such considerations were increased pressure for currency revaluations, which led to the Deutschmark appreciation of 1961.[294] It was proposed by Marjolin, for example, that pooled foreign exchange reserves could have prevented these upheavals.[295] As early as the 1962 Action Programme the Commission floated plans for monetary union.[296] As the goal of the EEC was to create and protect conditions similar to an internal market, a monetary union, or at least stable exchange rates, were deemed to be necessary.[297] In particular, stabilized exchange rates were believed to help prevent 'disturbances in competition'.[298] The Action Programme held in that regard:

> [M]onetary policy is of vital importance to the Common Market … From the end of the transition period on, if not even sooner economic union will involve fixed rates of exchange between Member States with very narrow limits on the variations allowed. Any

[290] Robert Mundell, 'A Plan for a European Currency' (Paper Prepared for Discussion at the American Management Association Conference on Future of the International Monetary System, New York, 10–12 December 1969) 8. According to Mundell, the dominance of the dollar had other drawbacks as well for the European countries; most notably, they would not gain the seignorage (ibid, 22).

[291] Padoa-Schioppa (n 46), 27.

[292] Neal (n 283), 96.

[293] See for example Hans von der Groeben, 'Die Bedeutung der EWG für Europa' in Hans von der Groeben (ed), *Europa—Plan und Wirklichkeit* (Nomos, 1967), 65; In the article von der Groeben supports a common currency, but acknowledges that this is not an uncontroversial goal. See also Hans von der Groeben, 'Die nächsten zehn Jahre', in Hans von der Groeben (ed), *Europa—Plan und Wirklichkeit* (Nomos, 1967) 159–60; On the early discussion on monetary integration see also David Marsh, *The Euro: the politics of the new global currency* (Yale University Press, 2009) 38–41.

[294] Marsh (n 293), 48.

[295] ibid, 48.

[296] EC, 'Memorandum of the Commission on the action programme of the Community for the second stage', paras 127–38; see on this Barry Eichengreen, 'European monetary unification' (1993) 31 *Journal of Economic Literature* 1321, 1323.

[297] Von der Groeben, 'Vier Jahre Gemeinsamer Markt' in Hans von der Groeben (ed), *Europa—Plan und Wirklichkeit* (Nomos, 1967), 111. Changing exchange rates may alter the competitive situation of a country in a common market abruptly, so that market actors will not rely on the longevity of market conditions, and will consequently treat the other Member States just like other third countries. See von der Groeben, 'Die nächsten zehn Jahre' (n 293), 160, and von der Groeben (n 249), 9.

[298] Von der Groeben, (n 297), 111.

> major modification would so much upset the trade of countries no longer protected by any customs barrier, and, because of the guaranteed Community intervention price for grain and other basic agricultural products, would cause such sudden changes in prices of farm products and therefore in farm incomes also, that the Common Market itself could be imperilled.[299]

In his texts from the 1960s and the early 70s, Commissioner von der Groeben appears confident about a relatively speedy establishment of a monetary union.[300]

Calls for European monetary coordination became stronger in the late 1960s, when instabilities became more pronounced: most notably, trade imbalances between France and West Germany required considerable readjustments in 1969.[301] Writing in 1969, Mundell argued that 'The money markets of Europe have not been as disturbed as they have over the past three years since the chaotic periods of 1930s.'[302] These instabilities led the Member States to assign Luxembourg prime minister Pierre Werner the task of proposing a plan for European monetary union. The Werner Plan, presented in 1970, proposed a three-stage programme to complete economic and monetary union by 1980.[303] It aimed at irrevocably fixed exchange rates, in conjunction with fully liberalized capital movements, the harmonization of tax systems and a far-reaching Europeanization of economic policies.[304] The reasons why the Member States agreed to such an ambitious project were diverse, as for example Tsoukalis pointed out:

> It appears that interest in EMU was born as a result of a convergence of widely different interests, ranging from the German need for a 'Westpolitik' to a concern about the survival of the customs union and the CAP, from the safeguarding of fixed exchange rates to the protection of the Community from British entry and the possibility of its dilution into a free trade area, and from the need to adopt a common policy vis-a-vis the United States. This convergence of interests did not last for very long.[305]

By 1973 at the latest the Werner Plan for economic and monetary union was no longer being pursued on a serious basis. The necessary steps—essentially the establishment of supranational economic and monetary governance—required a transfer of sovereignty, which the Member States had conditionally committed to, but did not want to realize in practice.[306] Only the exchange rate coordination of the first stage was implemented in the form of what was often termed

[299] EC, 'Memorandum of the Commission on the action programme of the Community for the second stage', para 128.

[300] Von der Groeben (n 249), 12.

[301] Neal (n 283), 96; George Zis, 'The European Monetary System 1979–84: An Assessment' (1984) 23 *Journal of Common Market Studies* 45, 50.

[302] Mundell (n 290), 4.

[303] Werner (n 250); on the Werner Report see Neal (n 283), 97; Zis (n 301), 48.

[304] Werner (n 250), 9–14; see on this also James Ingram, *The case for European monetary integration* (Princeton University, Essays in International Finance No 89, 1973), 1.

[305] Tsoukalis (n 272), 243.

[306] Ian Davidson, 'Prospects for Monetary Reform' (1972) 28 *The World Today* 377, 384.

the 'snake', where exchange rate movements between the participating currencies were limited to a certain band. The oil shock of October 1973 compromised the snake; with countries being affected asymmetrically by the shock, some countries appreciated their currencies while others depreciated, others leaving the system altogether.[307] The remaining snake was dominated by the Deutschmark, which became the European anchor currency until the formation of the EMU.[308] This, however, created problems for the peripheral countries, as for example McKinnon argued: as the Deutschmark was the central money in which cross-border trade and transactions were recorded, the exchange risks to the other European currencies found expression in higher interest rates for the latter.[309] The issue was described by McKinnon as follows:

> In the pre-euro regime, the D-mark was king—the central or safe-haven European currency for the group. In effect, Europe was on a common monetary standard based on a key currency where other European countries tried, with some uncertainty, to maintain exchange rate stability against the mark. Thus, private corporations in European countries on Germany's financial periphery—such as Italy, Portugal and Spain, which mainly issued bonds in lire, escudos and pesetas respectively—suffered currency risk relative to German issuers of mark-denominated bonds. The resulting risk premia, i.e. higher interest rates particularly longer term in these club-med countries kept finance short term and largely bank based. For example, in the early to mid-1990s, interest rates on Italian lire-denominated bonds were as much as 5 percentage points higher than those on German mark-denominated bonds.[310]

Fluctuations of exchange rates proved to be particularly poisonous in regard to the CAP,[311] where they made administratively highly complex compensation mechanisms necessary:[312] with floating exchange rates, the national price of an agricultural product fluctuated in regard to the common price level, which then had to be revalued. These administrative actions made the system prone to constant interventionism and in particular allowed Germany, which had had one of the most protectionist agricultural policies in the EEC prior to the establishment of the CAP, to return to former practices.[313] Moreover, the complexity of the CAP within a system of floating exchange rates led to rampant smuggling by

[307] Eichengreen (n 296), 1323.

[308] Tsoukalis (n 272), 244; Ronald McKinnon, 'Optimum Currency Areas and Key Currencies: Mundell I versus Mundell II' (2004) 42 *Journal of Common Market Studies* 689, 697.

[309] McKinnon (n 308), 698–99.

[310] ibid, 706.

[311] Zis (n 301), 50; see also 'Wir sind ein junges, entschlossenes Land' *Der Spiegel* (1/1979), 46; 'Helm fester' *Der Spiegel* (2/1979), 68–69.

[312] Padoa-Schioppa (n 46), 37.

[313] Y-S Hu, 'German agricultural power: the impact on France and Britain' (1979) 35 *The World Today* 453, 455–60.

producers, which in turn necessitated increased border controls.[314] Another problematic issue related to flexible exchange rates was that of 'exchange dumping':[315] the depreciation of a currency could quickly improve the competitive position of the exporters in one country, and worsen that of producers in others.[316] It was assumed that under such circumstances producers would not invest in European-scale production. The re-establishment of a stable currency exchange system thus became in many ways necessary to protect previous integrative steps: according to De Grauwe, European monetary integration was 'a reaction to the large exchange rate variability of community currencies during the 1970s, which was seen as endangering the integration process in Europe.'[317]

Moreover, as already mentioned, global trade had developed on the basis of coordinated exchange rates since the nineteenth century. It is such context that led for example Anthony Lanyi to explain in 1969 that an arrangement of floating currencies was an 'untried system'.[318] To some extent, the project of European monetary union must thus be viewed as a choice to continue a version of the existing system with all its shortcomings, rather than adopting a new, untried model, with unpredictable risks. In the 1960s and early 1970s, economists disagreed on whether a system of floating currencies was superior to a pegged currency regime. Even Lanyi, who was in favour a system of floating currencies, had to concede: 'There is no cut-and-dried answer to the question of whether, on economic grounds, floating exchange rates are superior to fixed rates. The answer will differ among countries, and perhaps even among periods in the same country's history.'[319] Exchange rates were initially allowed to float only as a temporary measure in the economic turmoil of the early 1970s, suspending the requirement of states to intervene to sustain the currency peg, and thus relaxing speculative money flows.[320] Only by the mid-1970s was it considered to be a functional regulatory choice.[321]

In 1978, the European Monetary System (EMS) was conceived, a further attempt to establish a system whereby European currencies could float against each other within certain margins (the mechanism was termed 'Exchange Rate Mechanism' (ERM), and the basket of all currencies was the ECU).[322] When a currency reached

[314] Richard Pomfret, 'What is the Secret of the EMS's Longevity?' (1991) 29 *Journal of Common Market Studies* 623, 630.

[315] Eichengreen (n 296), 1329–30.

[316] The depreciation of the pound after the exit from the ERM in 1992 led to a number of production relocations from the continent to the UK, which were strongly criticized. See on this ibid, 1329.

[317] Paul De Grauwe, 'What Have we Learnt about Monetary Integration since the Maastricht Treaty?' (2006) 44 *Journal of Common Market Studies*, 106, with further references.

[318] Lanyi (n 271), 34.

[319] ibid, 17.

[320] Otmar Emminger, *The D-Mark in the conflict between internal and external equilibrium, 1948–75* (Princeton University, Essays in International Finance No 122, 1977), 53.

[321] See ibid, 53–54, with further references.

[322] Stephen Overturf, 'The Economics of the Renewed Integration Movement' (1994) *Annals of the American Academy of Political and Social Science* 84, 86.

the margins, central banks would either intervene to keep it within the band, or revalue it.[323] The EMS should create, according to the European Council, a 'zone of monetary stability'.[324] It held that '[a] system of closer monetary cooperation will only be successful if participating countries pursue policies conducive to greater stability at home—and abroad; this applies to deficit and surplus countries alike.'[325] This points towards the need to coordinate macroeconomic policies within a monetary union. However, the EMS was less ambitious than the Werner Plan, insofar as it did not aim at the development of a common monetary and economic policy, nor at the expansion of the EEC budget.[326]

With capital mobility, adjustable pegs are open to speculative attacks, if speculators assume that the monetary authorities will devalue under pressure.[327] It may be costly for a government to uphold a certain exchange rate, as the central bank may be forced to deplete its currency reserves to buy up its own currency, or to raise interest rates.[328] Because of the existence of capital controls, the Member States retained some, albeit limited, ability of running different monetary and fiscal policies in the EMS, which constituted a central difference to the later EMU.[329] The EMS aimed to prevent recurring currency crises by making frequent and small currency revaluations, rather than the few and massive ones that had characterized earlier decades. Eichengreen described the EMS as follows:

> The EMS was a hybrid of pegged and adjustable exchange rate regimes. Extended periods of exchange rate stability delivered many of the benefits of fixed rates, while periodic realignments redressed serious competitiveness problems. But periods of exchange rate stability punctuated by occasional realignments were possible only because capital controls protected central banks' reserves against speculative attacks motivated by anticipations of realignment.[330]

The EMS remained functional throughout the 1980s.[331] At the same time, monetary integration created new economic and political problems, as Paul Taylor described:

> It was widely thought that the EMS proposed by the West Germans and the French, as with the 'snake', would be more in the interest of the heartland countries than of the

[323] De Grauwe (n 317), 106.

[324] 'Conclusions of the Presidency of the European Council on 6 and 7 July' (*Bulletin of the European Communities* No 6, 1978), 18; see also Zis (n 301), 46; Overturf (n 322), 85; 'Vielleicht eine Chance' *Der Spiegel* (6/1978), 23; David Currie, 'European Monetary Union: Institutional structure and economic performance' (1992) 102 *Economic Journal* 248, 248.

[325] *Annex to the Conclusions of the Presidency of the European Council* (Bremen, 6 and 7 July, 1978), para 5; see also Horst Ungerer, 'The European monetary system and the international monetary system' (1989) 27 *Journal of Common Market Studies* 231, 233.

[326] Eichengreen (n 296), 1323–24.

[327] Eichengreen, Tobin and Wyplosz (n 275), 163, 166.

[328] ibid, 162.

[329] Eichengreen (n 296), 1324.

[330] ibid, 1328.

[331] Ungerer (n 325), 231.

> periphery and that this advantage had to be offset by a significant transfer of resources from the richer to the poorer. West Germany would establish a more stable currency regime in Western Europe and would thus lay the basis for a further expansion of trade with her more important trading partners: she would, in effect, 'internalize' the market by eliminating the exchange rate risk; she would avoid the problem faced through the 1960s of either importing inflation from 'weaker' partners, or of revaluing the D-mark and thus weakening the competitive position of her products; she would reduce the chances that the declining dollar would increase pressure unequally upon the various European currencies, tending to push the stronger currencies upwards in relation to the weaker; and she would increase pressures upon the governments of the poorer countries to pursue stability-inducing policies, rather than risking more inflationary 'growth' policies. The weaker countries would also lose the weapon of devaluation traditionally used to improve the competitive position of their products. It was to offset these advantages, which threatened to accelerate the transfer of wealth from the weaker to the stronger countries, thus exacerbating existing inequalities, that it was argued there was a need for redistributive measures, and for 'the needs of the weaker areas to be tackled much more vigorously than at the present'.[332]

The Hanover Summit in 1988 called for the development of a European Monetary Union (EMU).[333] Jacques Delors was appointed to head a committee evaluating the possibilities of European monetary integration, which presented a report on economic and monetary union in 1989.[334] The report framed most of the subsequent debate and provided the blueprint for the EMU adopted in 1992.[335] A central difference in the functioning between the EMS and the proposed EMU was the complete absence of capital controls in the latter, following the full liberalization of capital movements that formed part of the 1992 programme.[336] Under such conditions a limited system like the EMS became increasingly open to speculative attack, and thus no longer appeared as a viable option of currency management. Instead, the Member States had to choose between a full, irrevocable monetary union, or a system of freely floating currencies. It is in this regard that the Commission argued that, in regard to monetary integration, 'the alternative to progress is regress, rather than the status quo'.[337] In the same year as the Maastricht Treaty was signed, currency speculators put overvalued European currencies under massive pressure, so that the UK and Italy had to devalue and withdraw

[332] Paul Taylor, 'Interdependence and autonomy in the European Communities: the case of the European monetary system' (1980) 18 *Journal of Common Market Studies* 370, 377. The quote in the last sentence is by Commission president Roy Jenkins.

[333] 'Hanover European Council, Conclusions of the Presidency' (*Bulletin of the European Communities* No 6, 1988) 165–66.

[334] Jacques Delors, *Report on economic and monetary union in the European Community (Delors Report)* (1989).

[335] Michael Artis, 'The Maastricht Road to Monetary Union' (1992) 30 *Journal of Common Market Studies* 299, 299.

[336] Eichengreen (n 296), 1328–29.

[337] EC, 'One Market, One Money' (*European Economy* No 44), 18.

from the Exchange Rate Mechanism.[338] As speculators turned against the franc, the ERM band was widened to +/– 15% in reaction, thereby effectively ending the EMS.[339] The exchange rate crisis of 1992–93 was, as Marsh reports, an important factor influencing policymakers to become more supportive of monetary union as a more durable solution.[340]

The Case for and Against Monetary Union

The Werner Report had been accompanied by an intensive debate among economists as to the risks and merits of European monetary integration.[341] The debate drew from an academic discussion on the respective benefits of the Bretton Woods currency peg on the one hand, and a system of floating currencies on the other, that had been ongoing at least since the 1950s. Looking first at the downsides of monetary integration identified in that debate, it can be argued that the main cost of monetary union was considered to be the loss of monetary autonomy; as the members of a currency union could no longer set interest rates autonomously or revalue the exchange rate, monetary policy could not cater to the specific needs of the individual country.[342] This point was often illustrated by reference to the Phillips curve, which suggested a trade-off between unemployment and inflation: lower unemployment would correspond to higher inflation, and vice versa. It was claimed that countries would, depending on their political preferences, pursue a different 'policy mix', but that this was no longer possible within a monetary union: countries had to accept inflation and unemployment rates that were sub-optimal from a perspective of their own policy preferences. By contrast, it was assumed that a system of floating exchange rates would grant states more leeway in defining their domestic economic policy.[343] This would include the ability of countries to pursue the objective of full employment rather than targeting a low inflation rate and accepting a correspondingly higher unemployment rate. It was later commented by McKinnon that such thinking corresponded to the then-dominant macroeconomic belief that the economy could be fine-tuned through national monetary and fiscal policies, and flexible exchange rates were assumed to provide a buffer between the different national policies (in a later chapter we will encounter this view under the description 'bastard Keynesianism', which Joan Robinson employed to distinguish the 'fine tuners' of the neoclassical synthesis from what she believed was the

[338] On the EMS crisis see for example Paul De Grauwe, Sérgio Rebelo and Jürgen Von Hagen, 'Towards European Monetary Union without the EMS' (1994) 9 *Economic Policy* 149, 153.
[339] Marsh (n 293), 175.
[340] ibid, 184–85; for a similar argument see De Grauwe (n 317), 715.
[341] For an example of a negative evaluation see Warner Corden, *Monetary Integration* (Princeton University, Essays in International Finance, No 93, 1972); for a positive outlook see Ingram (n 304).
[342] See for example Corden (n 341), 8–9.
[343] Lanyi (n 271), 12–13.

proper Keynesian position, which held that such fine-tuning was impossible, given the uncertain nature of future developments).[344] Monetarists like Milton Friedman equally embraced the idea of flexible exchange rates, which they believed would shield domestic price stability better from global inflationary tendencies.[345] Beyond such considerations relating to the autonomy of national policy choices, it was argued for example that a system of pegged currencies constituted a de facto subsidy for foreign trade and investment.[346] If exchange rate uncertainty constitutes a cost on business, then government activity to prevent exchange rate fluctuation (eg through costly interventions by the central banks) corresponds to a subsidy for those engaged in cross-border economic activities.

Turning to the arguments made in favour of monetary union, a central claim was that it would eliminate the various problems associated with exchange rate fluctuations. Most notably, Mundell argued that currency areas constituted a form of risk-sharing: a shock that asymmetrically hits one country is absorbed by the monetary union as a whole.[347] Especially in the final years of Bretton Woods, exchange rate fluctuations were believed to be a greatly destabilizing factor. For example, in countries where a currency appreciation was expected, the interest rates were low, while they were high in those countries whose currencies were expected to fall.[348] In this regard, Mundell held: 'The expectations of exchange rate changes greatly unsettle the money markets, make planning difficult, and, in the long run, weaken the control a government has over economic policy.'[349] Moreover, it was argued that monetary union would be a necessary correlate to the common market in which common prices for goods had developed. According to Ingram, 'These common prices serve as signals for the allocation of resources and for the determination of comparative-advantage positions in the several member nations.'[350] Monetary integration was thus necessary to realize the potential benefits arising from allocative efficiency in a common market. It was also argued that stable exchange rates were necessary to realize economies of scale: only with predictable exchange rates would producers adapt production to the common market, rather than to the domestic market alone. Finally, monetary union would allow the full liberalization of capital movements while protecting previous integrative steps, most notably the CAP: with pegged but alterable exchange rates, capital movements had to remain restricted to limit currency speculation; by contrast, exchange rate flexibility would allow the liberalization of capital movements,

[344] McKinnon (n 308), 691.

[345] Milton Friedman, 'The Case for Flexible Exchange Rates' in Milton Friedman (ed), *Essays in Positive Economics* (University of Chicago Press 1953).

[346] Lanyi (n 271), 6.

[347] Robert Mundell, 'Uncommon arguments for common currencies' in Harry Johnson and Alexander Swoboda (eds), *The Economics of Common Currencies* (1973) 115; see on this also McKinnon (n 308), 695.

[348] Mundell (n 290), 4.

[349] ibid, 4.

[350] Ingram (n 304), 3.

but undermine the common price system developed by the CAP.[351] In this sense Ingram argued:

> The choice Europe faces is between (a) further steps toward economic integration, including monetary union, and (b) a retreat from economic integration and toward the separation of national economies, through either exchange-rate flexibility or restrictions on trade and payments.[352]

While the costs of monetary union as discussed above were acknowledged, scholars argued that, under certain conditions, these costs were greatly reduced. Such arguments were often based on the theory of the optimum currency area (OCA), today associated in particular with Robert Mundell: in his 1961 article, Mundell proposed that OCAs are regions within which a high degree of labour and capital mobility exists that would outbalance asymmetrical shocks.[353] Mundell describes the hypothesis of his paper as holding that 'the fixed-exchange-rate system is better within areas where factors are mobile and the flexible-exchange-rate system is better for areas between which factors are immobile.'[354] We will look at a more detailed version of Mundell's theory further below. The OCA theory was later often employed by critics of European monetary integration who argued that the Community did not constitute an OCA, so that monetary union would lead to sub-optimal results.[355] Mundell himself, however, was highly in favour of monetary integration in Europe, and laid out a 'plan for a European currency' in 1969.[356] According to Mundell, 'Europe possess[es] enough of the characteristics of an optimum currency area to move toward narrower, rather than wider fluctuations in exchange rates.'[357] This could be further strengthened by increasing labour and capital mobility, following the US example. McKinnon argued in 1963 that the optimality of a currency area could not be evaluated 'ex ante' alone, ie, on the basis of whether factor mobility was already present prior to the establishment of a common currency. Rather, 'the currency arrangements themselves would affect factor mobility, so the extent of factor mobility has to be considered ex post'.[358] This argument has some resemblance with the 'endogeneity' thesis that we will discuss a little later.

[351] ibid, 4–5.

[352] ibid, 5.

[353] Robert Mundell, 'A Theory of Optimum Currency Areas' (1961) 51 *American Economic Review* 657, 661–62.

[354] ibid, 664, fn 8.

[355] See McKinnon (n 308), 692; while the OCA theory was thus often recruited in defence of flexible exchange rates, Mundell had proposed in his article only that a system of flexible currency rates may be efficient under the condition that the currency areas actually are OCAs. However, he argued that national currency areas may not necessarily be OCAs because they comprise different regions with only limited factor mobility between them. Thus, a system of floating *national* currencies did not necessarily find support in Mundell's OCA theory, unless national boundaries corresponded to *regional* boundaries. See Mundell (n 290), 659–60.

[356] Mundell (n 290).

[357] ibid, 5.

[358] Ronald McKinnon, 'Optimum currency areas' (1963) 53 *American Economic Review* 717, 724.

It was also argued that the effectiveness of monetary instruments was already much reduced for countries that were well-integrated in the global economy. McKinnon argued in 1963 that 'if we move across the spectrum from closed to open economies, flexible exchange rates become both less effective as a control device for external balance and more damaging to internal price-level stability.'[359] In particular, McKinnon questioned (as Mundell had already done in his 1961 article) the efficiency of currency devaluations as a tool to regain competitiveness in open economies.[360] Currency devaluations were assumed to re-establish competitiveness of an economy after wage increases, because a devaluation would push down the real wage while leaving the nominal wage unaffected (ie, workers receive the same amount of money, but can afford less imported goods after the devaluation, thereby experiencing a real wage loss).[361] However, McKinnon argued that the more open an economy is, the less workers will likely accept such cuts in real wages: unions will subsequently demand a new round of wage increases to make up for the lost buying power, thereby neutralizing the effect of the currency devaluation.[362] With monetary policy being inefficient in practice, the adverse effects of entering a monetary union were thus assumed to be limited. It was also argued, for example by Ingram, that the factual ability of states to set autonomous monetary policies had in fact already been greatly limited within the Bretton Woods system. With considerable capital mobility that followed the liberalization of capital movements in the 1950s and 1960s, the monetary policy of one Member State could no longer appreciably deviate from those of the others. Under conditions of fixed exchange rates, a low interest or a high inflation rate would lead to capital flight.[363] Even under flexible exchange rates, Member States were limited in their monetary policy; for example, an expansionary policy would lead to currency depreciations.[364] Thus, Ingram essentially argued that the economic autonomy available to the Member States after monetary integration would not be less than the restrictions they had already faced under the Bretton Woods system.[365] Based on such considerations, Robert Mundell declared in 1969 that 'the economic case for a European money is a very strong one.'[366]

Disagreement characterized not only the case for or against monetary union itself, but also—once monetary and economic union was agreed upon—the steps necessary within the transition process. The literature of the late 1960s and early 1970s sometimes distinguished between two competing perspectives, described as the 'economist' view on the one side and the 'monetarist' view on the other

[359] ibid, 719.
[360] ibid, 723–24.
[361] This had been criticized by Mundell (n 308), 663.
[362] McKinnon (n 358); see the discussion in Corden (n 341), 12 and 17–18.
[363] Ingram (n 304), 3.
[364] ibid, 8.
[365] ibid, 8.
[366] Mundell (n 290), 10.

(the use of this terminology is confusing, because the term 'monetarist' is today commonly employed to describe a variant of neoclassical theory associated with Milton Friedman).[367] France supported monetary union (most notably in the interest of retaining common prices under the CAP), but essentially opposed the transfer of sovereignty to supranational institutions.[368] This position, informed by the long-standing French preference for intergovernmental coordination as opposed to supranational integration, found support in the assumption that monetary union would force the Member States to coordinate their economic policies, thereby ultimately leading to their convergence.[369] By contrast, the German (as well as Dutch and Italian) position was that economic convergence should precede monetary union, and should be pursued by the harmonization of national policies and ultimately a common economic policy executed on the European level in conjunction with a common European institutional framework.[370]

In many ways this discussion on the risks and benefits of monetary integration of the 1960s and 1970s was resumed in the debate on the EMU. Jacques Delors argued in 1994:

> Trade rules alone can no longer ensure that commerce develops smoothly if other imbalances emerge elsewhere. Today, the biggest threat to trade development appears to be the failure of international monetary relations. The extreme instability of currencies in the last fifteen years has been largely responsible for the slowdown in the growth of world trade from eight percent in the 1960s to four percent in the 1980s. As we approach the end of the 1990s, the uncontrolled expansion of the financial sector is distorting the relation between real changes in economies and those which merely reflect fluctuations in interest and exchange rates. We should neither be surprised by this development nor resign ourselves to it.[371]

The Delors Report predicted increased macroeconomic stability as well as gains in European trade as a consequence of monetary integration. According to the report, a single currency area 'would add to the potential benefits of an enlarged economic area' for the following reasons: (1) it would reduce transactions costs;[372] (2) it would 'reduce the susceptibility of the Community to external shocks';[373] (3) and it would reduce exchange-rate uncertainties[374] and thereby generally

[367] For contemporary discussions of the debate see for example Ingram (n 304) 9; Corden (n 341), 7.

[368] Davidson (n 306), 384.

[369] Tsoukalis (n 272), 232.

[370] ibid, 232.

[371] Jacques Delors, 'The Future of Free Trade in Europe and the World' (1994) 18 *Fordham International Law Journal* 715, 716.

[372] Delors (n 334), 17; though economists like Eichengreen doubted that these effects would in fact bee significant. Barry Eichengreen, *Should the Maastricht Treaty be Saved?* (Princeton University, Studies in International Finance No 74, 1992), 4.

[373] Delors (n 334), 17.

[374] ibid, 17; see also Daniel Gros and Niels Thygesen, 'The institutional approach to monetary union in Europe' (1990) 100 *Economic Journal* 925, 926.

promote market integration and growth.[375] Overall, the Commission estimated the yearly benefits at 0.25–0.5 per cent of the European GDP.[376] At the same time, the report emphasized repeatedly that monetary integration—conceived to fend off global imbalances—could itself be a cause of increased instabilities within the Community, and could intensify the destabilizing effects of market integration. In particular, monetary union would eliminate exchange rate readjustment as a policy tool to counter instabilities:[377]

> [E]xchange rate adjustments would no longer be available as an instrument to correct economic imbalances within the Community. Such imbalances might arise because the process of adjustment and restructuring set in motion by the removal of physical, technical and fiscal barriers is unlikely to have an even impact on different regions or always produce satisfactory results within reasonable periods of time. Imbalances might also emanate from labour and other cost developments, external shocks with differing repercussions on individual economies, or divergent economic policies pursued at national level.[378]

The abolition of capital controls was another important factor that the report assumed would be likely to intensify instabilities.[379] The Padoa-Schioppa Report equally emphasized that an EMS system without capital controls would be unstable and crisis-prone, which made further monetary integration an attractive alternative.[380] The Delors Report discussed at length the necessary policies to counter the instabilities that they suspected to be the likely consequence of monetary union in conjunction with the liberalization of capital movements. An important objective would be macroeconomic policy coordination, including binding budgetary rules.[381]

Despite these considerations, the Commission was ultimately very optimistic about the chances of monetary integration, even without a far-reaching budgetary and political integration to accompany it. This becomes particularly clear in its 1990 report 'One Market, One Money', in which it laid out the economic case for monetary integration.[382] At the same time, the comprehensive engagement

375 Eichengreen (n 372), 7; these 'dynamic effects' were deemed more speculative, for example by Gros and Thygesen (n 374), 926; however, liberalist scholars like Roland Vaubel doubted the beneficial effect of montary integration on market integration altogether, arguing that competition among currencies would be more beneficial. Roland Vaubel, 'Currency Competition and European Monetary Integration' (1990) 100 *Economic Journal* 936.

376 EC, 'One Market, One Money'; on this see De Grauwe (n 280), 54–71.

377 Retaining the instrument of exchange rate readjustment was considered to be relevant by those who believed that the European countries continued to face asymmetrical shocks; see Gros and Thygesen, 928. By contrast, Feldstein doubted this effect. Martin Feldstein, 'The political economy of the European economic and monetary union: political sources of an economic liability' (1998) NBER Working Paper No 6150, 34.

378 Delors (n 334), 17.

379 ibid, 11; Eichengreen (n 20), 347; see also Overturf (n 322), 89.

380 Padoa-Schioppa (n 46), 8–9; see also Eichengreen (n 20), 347; EC, 'One Market, One Money', 9.

381 Delors (n 334), 16; Padoa-Schioppa (n 46), 4.

382 EC, 'One Market, One Money'.

of the Commission with the potential benefits and risks of monetary integration points to the widespread scepticism about the feasibility of monetary integration among economists. Economists were in disagreement about the possible benefits and adverse effects of monetary integration just as they were in the 1960s and 1970s.[383] One group, which was sceptical, based its thinking on Robert Mundell's theory of optimal currency areas (OCA), which we encountered above. OCA theory makes claims about the conditions under which monetary union is beneficial for countries. In contemporary scholarship, these conditions are usually described as follows: 1) symmetry of shocks and business cycles, 2) flexibility of labour markets, 3) integration of trade, and 4) the presence of a system of fiscal transfers.[384] If the economies in a monetary union are sufficiently similar, shocks may affect them in an equal way, which allows monetary responses that benefit all countries. If, however, shocks hit economies in different ways, then no such response is possible. Flexibility of labour markets is also considered to be necessary to outbalance asymmetric shocks:[385] if some regions thrive while others falter, wages in sufficiently flexible labour markets will adapt accordingly, and workers will move to the prosperous regions, thereby creating a counterbalancing flow. If the member states of a monetary union have well integrated trade relations, the benefits of monetary union may outbalance the (macroeconomic) costs.[386] Finally, transfer systems (eg a federal system of unemployment insurance) may outbalance asymmetrical shocks. The benefits in these four areas must outweigh the macroeconomic costs of giving up the exchange rate as an instrument of macroeconomic policy.[387] Given these conditions, many economists concluded that the EC was *not* an OCA, so that the adverse effects of monetary integration would outweigh the benefits.

The counter-thesis—laid out for example by Robert Mundell in a 1969 text that we encountered earlier—assumed that the ability of a country to influence its currency's exchange rate may have lost its macroeconomic benefits, not least because of freely moving capital. The exchange rate no longer functions as a stabilizing instrument, and instead becomes a source of instability when it is targeted by currency speculators.[388] Moreover, only in a monetary union can the financial market become fully integrated, such that it is supposed to function like an insurance system against asymmetrical shocks.[389] In this view, monetary unions protect

[383] De Grauwe (n 317), 711–12.

[384] Jeffrey Frankel and Andrew Rose, 'The endogenity of the optimum currency area criteria' (1998) 108 *Economic Journal* 1009, 1011.

[385] De Grauwe (n 317), 712.

[386] ibid, 712–14.

[387] Eichengreen argued, for example, that under certain circumstances an autonomous exchange rate may be a useful tool to lower domestic prices to a level consistent with full employment; Eichengreen (n 296), 1331.

[388] De Grauwe (n 317), 714.

[389] ibid, 715.

member countries from instabilities created by international capital flows.[390] Another argument was that asymmetrical shocks were supposedly less likely in the European Union: as trade between developed states was between largely similar products, demand shocks (ie, when a certain product finds less buyers) would affect the different Member States in the same way. These arguments were forwarded by the Commission in its 1990 report 'One Market, One Money'.[391] According to the Commission, the benefits of an independently controlled exchange rate among the European countries was very limited, or even inexistent.[392] Furthermore, the Commission assumed that integrated financial markets will smoothe out shocks,[393] and flexible labour costs would serve the same function. The Commission expected country-specific shocks to become less likely as a consequence of integration.[394]

Because both theories were based on texts by Robert Mundell (which we discussed above), they have been termed Mundell I and Mundell II in the academic literature. De Grauwe points out that they must be understood in their specific intellectual background: as we mentioned, Mundell I is based on the neoclassical synthesis, 'stressing that in a world of price and wage rigidities monetary policies, including exchange rate policies, can be used effectively to stabilize the economy.'[395] By contrast, Mundell II had monetarist roots, a view that

> stressed that activist monetary policies become sources of instability and that central banks should focus on their core business, which is to maintain price stability. The logical consequence of monetarism was the view that central banks do not lose their capacity to stabilize their national economies when entering a monetary union, since they did not have such a capacity in the first place. In this monetarist vision ... the costs of a monetary union are small.[396]

Whereas Mundell I was commonly interpreted as being critical of European monetary integration, given the differences between the European economies and the limited degree of labour mobility, Mundell II was optimistic about it. It is this view that featured prominently in the Commission report 'One Market, one Money';[397] and it also prevailed in the formation of the EMU. McKinnon, for example, interpreted European monetary integration as a 'triumph' of Mundell II over Mundell I.[398] De Grauwe held: 'Since the early 1980s the "monetarist" view has gained adherents, and has changed the view many economists have about the desirability of a monetary union. The popularity of monetarism helps to explain why EMU became a reality in the 1990s.'[399]

390 ibid, 715.
391 EC, 'One Market, One Money', 11; on this see De Grauwe (n 280), 23–27.
392 EC, 'One Market, One Money', 24.
393 ibid, 24.
394 ibid, 24.
395 De Grauwe (n 317), 715.
396 ibid, 715.
397 EC, 'One Market, One Money'; on this see De Grauwe (n 280), 72.
398 McKinnon (n 308), 695.
399 De Grauwe (n 280), 74.

The different perspectives provided by Mundell I and Mundell I illustrate that the economic case for or against monetary integration in Europe had remained deeply conflicted. Disagreement extended also to the questions which policies and what kind of institutional framework on the European level was necessary for monetary union to function, and to which degree a transfer of competences from the Member States to the Union was necessary. The Commission report strongly emphasized that full political integration was not necessary for the functioning of the monetary union. It argued that, while a common European monetary policy was useful, 'the case for centralized powers over budgetary policy is much weaker.'[400] Such view found economic support in Frankel and Rose's theory of the 'endogeneity of the optimum currency area criteria'. The authors argued that '[t]he suitability of European countries for EMU cannot be judged on the basis of historical data since the structure of these economies is likely to change dramatically as a result of EMU.'[401] According to their study, trade integration would lead to more closely correlated business cycles; as monetary union would likely increase trade and thereby lead to increasingly synchronized cycles, it could, over time, turn the Community into an OCA:

> [S]ome countries may appear, on the basis of historical data, to be poor candidates for EMU entry. But EMU entry per se, for whatever reason, may provide a substantial impetus for trade expansion; this in turn may result in more highly correlated business cycles. That is, a country is more likely to satisfy the criteria for entry into a currency union ex post than ex ante.[402]

Convergence among the Member States may thus be the consequence of monetary union and of increased economic integration that goes along with it. According to such view, the need for an extensive regulatory and institutional structure on the European level and for a substantial transfer of competences would indeed be limited. However, the endogeneity thesis was contested; economists like Eichengreen or Krugman argued that a monetary union may in fact become less of an OCA over time: within a common market the various regions may not diversify but specialize, which would mean that asymmetrical shocks could become more likely.[403] While the Commission considered the limited institutional setup of the EMU to be sufficient, the Commission nonetheless assumed that more competences would be required on the European level over time. The competences as granted in 1992 were, according to the Commission, 'basically evolutionary in nature'.[404]

[400] EC, 'One Market, One Money', 13.
[401] Frankel and Rose (n 384), 1011.
[402] ibid, 1024.
[403] See in particular Paul Krugman, 'Lessons of Massachusetts for EMU' in Francisco Torres and Francesco Giavazzi (eds), *Adjustment and growth in the European Monetary Union* (CUP, 1993); Eichengreen (n 372), 14–16.
[404] EC, 'One Market, One Money', 17.

To conclude this section, it can be held that the project of European monetary union initiated in the 1980s constituted an intensification of the integration process as much as a continuation of previous attempts to stabilize the exchange rate which had complemented the EEC since the 1950s. European monetary integration as initiated in the 1970s was understood by its proponents as a necessary means to protect past integration steps, most notably the CAP. However, monetary integration was always a controversial objective, and economists came down on both sides of the debate. The EMU, as developed in the 1990s, relied on a limited European institutional framework, which was, however, conceptualized by the Commission as evolutionary in nature. The assumption that monetary union could nonetheless function on such foundation rested on a growingly dominant current in economic theory which emphasized the automatic stabilization abilities of markets, and dismissed the idea that governments were able to satisfactorily manage the economy through monetary and fiscal policy. This is illustrated by the trust scholars like Mundell or McKinnon put in an integrated European financial market, their rejection of what they dismissed as 'big government', as well as Frankel and Rose's 'endogeneity' thesis. We will return to this discussion when we look at the macroeconomic governance measures enacted in the wake of the 2008 crisis.[405]

Industrial Policy

The concept of industrial policy describes measures aimed at shaping the economic structure of a polity. In a narrower sense, it includes measures that support domestic industries, for example through R&D grants, investment support, export subsidies and the like. The concept is equally assumed to encompass measures that strategically employ public resources to achieve socio-economic policies such as the development of certain industries or regions, for example the construction of transport or communication infrastructure. More generally speaking, however, any regulatory activity, ranging from tax and social policy to trade policy can be employed strategically to further the socio-economic goals of a polity, and thus as an instrument of industrial policy. Industrial policy has been an important concern of the Community since its inception. The Treaty of Rome established the EIB as a vehicle to finance investment projects, and the ESF to facilitate the restructuring process of the European industrial landscape that was expected to follow economic integration. It was already mentioned that the position of the European industries vis-à-vis the American (and later the Japanese) competitors became an important trope of policy debate in the 1960s, as illustrated by Jacques Servan-

[405] A report by the United States International Trade Commission cited monetary instability as one of the causes for delays in the implementation of the 1992 measures; USITC, *Implementing the European Community Single Market: Sixth Followup Report* (USITC Publication, 1994) ix.

Schreiber's influential book *The American Challenge*. The EC's 1967 General Report declared that 'One of the Community's fundamental tasks at the present time is to work out a coherent industrial policy.'[406] The goals of the Community's industrial policy were defined to include the 'further improvement of overall productivity, the maintenance of a high level of employment and the strengthening of the competitiveness of community firms vis-à-vis those of non-member countries.'[407] The Colonna Report of 1970 on 'Industrial Policy in the Community' proposed 'five basic lines of action' to form part of the Community's industrial policy: 'the achievement of a single market; the unification of the legal, fiscal and financial framework; the reorganisation of industrial structures; adjustment to change; greater Community solidarity in relations with third countries.'[408] The list indicates the broad understanding of 'industrial policy' employed by the Commission, which is equally identifiable in the 1973 'Programme of Action in the Fields of Technological and Industrial Policy'.[409] Regarding industrial policy in a narrower sense, the programme announced measures relating to 'the European-scale promotion of competitive advanced-technology undertakings' as well as the 'conversion and modernization of industrial branches in a state of crisis'. Beyond that, the programme proposed measures relating to issues such as the removal of technical barriers to trade as well as corporate law reforms aimed at facilitating cross-border mergers in order to foster the establishment of large-scale companies. Such promotion of cross-border mergers brought industrial policy in potential conflict with the Community's goal of strengthening competition, as the programme acknowledged.[410]

Even though industrial policy was thus a central concern of the Community from early on, its role became even more prominent in the 1992 project.[411] As discussed, a title dealing specifically with industrial policy was introduced into the Treaty, alongside provisions on R&D and Trans-European networks, which are also closely related to industrial policy. The cohesion funds must similarly viewed as an important aspect of the Union's industrial policy. As Lane argued, by the 1990s the Community's 'leitmotif' had become that of industrial competitiveness, and it entered the Treaty in its new Article 130 EC, paragraph 1 of which held: 'The Community and the Member States shall ensure that the conditions necessary for the competitiveness of the Community's industry exist.' The Community was supposed to further competitiveness through all of its policies (paragraph 3), which illustrates the broad understanding of industrial policy applied. The White Paper emphasized the necessity of industrial policy to accompany market integration

[406] EC, 'First General Report on the Activities of the Communities 1967', 192.
[407] ibid, 192.
[408] EC, *Industrial Policy in the Community* (Colonna Report) (Brussels, 1970) 17.
[409] EC, 'Programme of action in the field of technological and industrial policy'.
[410] ibid, 4.
[411] See EC, 'Growth, competitiveness, employment. The challenges and ways forward into the 21st century' (White paper) COM(93) 700.

so that companies could benefit from the increased potentials, and regions could adapt to the changed circumstances. It held:

> In order to facilitate the key role which the internal market can play in the policy for the recovery of industrial structures, the suspension of internal borders must be accompanied by actions which strengthen research and the technological base of the Community's industry. Such actions will allow firms to benefit from the size of the single market. It is within this context that the present work of strengthening the Community's technological base should be seen.[412]

Far from expecting that the benefits of the integrated market would accrue automatically, the Commission emphasized the necessity of industrial policy in the process of market integration. Industrial policy would help European companies to restructure relatively quickly to the new environment, and to enhance their ability to benefit from the scale effects of the enlarged market. Moreover, a European investment policy was also assumed to have beneficial macroeconomic stability effects, as the Padoa-Schioppa Report pointed out.[413] The report argued that the dynamics of market integration and the recent accession of relatively poor and structurally underdeveloped countries would create imbalances that would require, inter alia, countervailing interventions in the form of industrial policy. Moreover, 'new trends in industrial technologies' made a European investment policy the more desirable.[414]

The strong commitment of the 1992 project to industrial policy is illustrated, for example, by the Union's policy in the telecommunication sector. In the 1980s the telecom sector underwent significant technological change, as the Commission made clear in its 1987 Green Paper on Telecommunications. This included increased digitalization of services and the development of 'optical cables, computer networks, cell phones, satellites, etc.'[415] The innovative pressure from American and Japanese companies was strong, and the European policymakers feared that the telecommunication sector could meet the same fate as the European IT sector, which had been successful in the 1970s, but accrued a significant trade deficit by 1980.[416] The EEC industries had failed to lead the development of computers and semiconductors, and policymakers believed that the telecommunication sector faced a similar risk.[417] According to the Commission, the fragmented European markets were the reason why potential economies of scale had not been realized.[418] This fear of a 'technology gap' sparked the interest of Member States

412 EC, 'Completing the Internal Market', 7, para 18.
413 Padoa-Schioppa (n 46), Preamble, v.
414 ibid, 10.
415 'Towards a Dynamic European Community' (Green Paper on the Development of the Common Market for Telecommunications Services and Equipment) COM(87) 290 final, 1.
416 EC, '25 Years of Digital Europe', ec.europa.eu/information_society/doc/digitaleurope-historial.pdf, 3.
417 ibid, 3.
418 ibid, 3.

in enhanced European cooperation.[419] The Commission and the Member States were keen on fostering enhanced cooperation in the technology field.[420] In particular the perceived success of the state-sponsored R&D collaboration in Japan was seen as a role model.[421] R&D became an important issue at the Intergovernmental Conference, and the subsequent treaty reforms.[422] The SEA introduced an approach for Community-wide research initiatives.[423] It provided for 'framework programmes' that should plan the Community's R&D budget and its research initiatives.[424] This led Bermann to comment in 1989:

> The considerable attention given to research and technological development in the Single European Act leaves the strong impression that changes in this field, more than in any other that has now formally been brought within the Treaty framework, lie at the heart of Community reform under the Act.[425]

The Commission attempted to initiate a major innovation drive together with the big players from the industry (companies like Siemens, Philips and Olivetti formed a 'Big 12 round table'). Whereas earlier attempts of the Commission to establish transnational cooperation in R&D in the 1960s and 1970s had failed, the initiative of the 1980s turned out to be successful.[426] Peterson held that 'the Commission helped engineer an industrial consensus for new collaborative schemes, was supported by industry in urging the transfer of authority over technology policy to the EC level, and was ultimately able to convince governments to launch the ESPRIT programme in 1983.'[427] ESPRIT (European Strategic Programme for Research and Development in Information Technologies) started in 1984, and RACE (Research and Development in Advanced Communications Technologies) in 1988. ESPRIT focused primarily on computers (microchips, software, etc), whereas RACE was focused on telecommunications. Innovative projects funded under the Community's research budget included DSL broadband, optical fibres, the GSM standard, 3G, DVB, MPEG4 and IPTV, to list some of the more well-known technological innovations. Thus, many high-tech developments in Europe since the 1980s were based on R&D investment from the Community, additionally to that of the national research programmes. The development of the telecommunication sector since the 1980s in Europe is therefore closely related to the industrial policy pursued by the Community and the Member States.[428]

[419] Juliet Lodge, 'The Single European Act: Towards a New Euro-Dynamism?' (1986) 24 *Journal of Common Market Studies* 203, 203.

[420] ibid, 216.

[421] J Peterson, 'Technology Policy in Europe: Explaining the Framework Programme and Eureka in Theory and Practice' (1991) 29 *Journal of Common Market Studies* 269, 275–76.

[422] Lodge (n 419), 216.

[423] Bermann (n 162), 562.

[424] Art 130i SEA.

[425] Bermann (n 162), 563.

[426] Peterson (n 421), 275.

[427] ibid, 276.

[428] EC, 'Growth, competitiveness, employment. The challenges and ways forward into the 21st century' (White paper); see also Editorial, 'Growth, competitiveness and unemployment: the challenges facing the Union' (1994) 31 *Common Market Law Review* 1, 2.

In the 1980s and 1990s, industrial policy as a Union competence was hotly contested.[429] Streit/Mussler criticized the 'interventionist or planning approach to industrial policy', which they described as 'picking the winners and helping the losers'.[430] Moreover, it was argued that, as governments lacked information, industrial policy would lead to sub-optimal outcomes.[431] The policies were held to be prone to capture by strong interest groups, most notably by domestic industries. In particular Streit and Mussler criticized the heavy industry involvement in the 'Big 12 round table', because it gave large companies an undue influence over Commission policy. According to Streit and Mussler, 'Half of the European Community's financial support providing for some 240 projects during the first phase of the program (1984–88) was given to the 'Big 12', the same twelve who also developed the basic concept for ESPRIT.'[432] Framing such criticism in legal terms, Mestmäcker claimed that industry policy was diametrically opposed to the Union's objective of fostering competition.[433]

The central role played by industrial policy in the 1992 project indicate that the potential benefits from market integration were not taken for granted. It was assumed that they could be realized better within a conducive policy framework, which would mobilize public funds to speed up and cushion restructuring processes, support high-tech sectors and the adaptation of industries towards production on a European scale, and the establishment of trans-European networks. However, industrial policy was always also perceived in a broader form, describing the strategic use of a polity's general activities for the achievement of socio-economic goals. The 1992 project aimed at reshaping the regulatory landscape in a way most conducive to reaping the possible benefits of market integration, and to increasing the competitive position of European producers on the global market.

INTERMEDIATE FINDINGS

We have seen in the previous chapter that the EEC Treaty was located at the intersection of different socio-economic paradigms. Western Europe had engaged in an ambitious, US-led project of trade liberalization since the 1940s, both in the context of GATT and the OEEC. This was largely successful; in some respects, the EEC Treaty's trade liberalization was a continuation and intensification of this

[429] See for example Mestmäcker (n 160), 27–34; Mestmäcker (n 144), 634–35. One of Mestmäcker's criticisms, namely that the new policies conferred wide political discretion on the European institutions not subject to judicial control other than procedural control, mirrors a central concern of ordoliberals in the 1950s and 1960s, who emphasized that the economic framework should be general and rule-based.

[430] Streit and Mussler (n 140), 342.

[431] For a critical overview of these arguments see for example Dani Rodrik, 'Industrial policy for the twenty-first century' [2004] CEPR Discussion Paper No 4767, 36–37. Rodrik argues that there is 'more than a grain of truth' in these arguments, but emphasizes that there are strong counter-arguments as well.

[432] Streit and Mussler (n 140), 338.

[433] Mestmäcker (n 160), 27.

project. However, we have seen that orthodox, comparative advantage-oriented scholars were rather cautious because of the potential protectionist effects of regional trade integration, as compared to the ideal model of global trade liberalization. The economic motives that really captured the minds of the policymakers of the EEC Treaty were those termed the 'dynamic' effects of integration. In essence, this concept describes the positive growth effects of market integration that would move the European structure closer to the model of the United States, which economically, technologically and socially was the most advanced economy of that time. They include economies of scale, increased competition, a faster rate of technological change, changes in the terms of trade, and changes in investment patterns. The EEC Treaty was thus shaped by different—sometimes conflicting—socio-economic paradigms.

This changed little over the following decades. The 1992 project again pursued an agenda that followed not a single, but different socio-economic paradigms. One of the most important concerns of the 1992 project was to make European companies powerful enough to compete on a global scale: this required, most importantly, a home market large enough to support companies of a similar size to those of US and Japanese competitors, and an industrial policy to help European companies to quickly benefit from the increased returns to scale, most notably in the field of R&D. At the same time, Europe faced increased pressures of macroeconomic instability, which stemmed both from the new, more volatile global situation that followed the breakdown of Bretton Woods, and from the macroeconomic imbalances that were the consequence of prior market integration of the EEC as well as the accession of poorer countries. The policymakers expected that the 1992 project—most notably the abolition of capital controls—would further increase economic volatility. They therefore conceived a number of accompanying policies that should strengthen macroeconomic stability, including the massively boosted social and regional cohesion funds, monetary union, and industrial policy (most notably in the field of R&D). The understanding was that the potential gains from further market integration could be realized only if the existing and projected macroeconomic instabilities could be contained. Trade, growth, integration and stability were thus seen as intrinsically connected by the policymakers of '1992.' An analysis of the Treaty freedom provisions in their historical context shows no normative preference towards any particular socio-economic view. Over the course of its history, the Treaty has been shaped by numerous socio-economic views, none of which can therefore be safely assumed to be the 'correct' reading of the Treaty freedom provisions. It is for this reason that the Treaty is best described as a pluralist instrument.

3

The Internal Market Law Provisions and the Case Law Developed on its Basis

INTRODUCTION

IN THE PREVIOUS chapters we looked at the Treaty of Rome and its reforms in the 1980s and 1990s from a bird's-eye view. The objective was to make a general statement about the Union's socio-economic orientation. In this chapter we will take a different approach, and zoom in on a specific set of provisions for a detailed doctrinal analysis. As an example case the present chapter focuses on internal market law, more specifically on the free movement of goods and services and on establishment.[1] The central question that we try to answer in this chapter is whether the Treaty freedoms and the interpretation given to them by the CJEU, for example the broad scope of the Treaty freedoms as defined in cases like *Dassonville*,[2] must be understood as an expression of a specific socio-economic paradigm that underlies the European economic constitution. We will see that the Treaty freedoms and the doctrinal system developed on its basis do not favour any specific socio-economic model, and should thus be understood as pluralist in nature. It will be argued that this pluralism finds expression in the doctrinal distinction between the formal scope of the Treaty freedoms on the one hand, and their normative substance on the other.[3] The '*Dassonville* formula' must essentially be understood as a jurisdictional rule that brings a national measure within the scope of internal market law, but does not presuppose the substantive outcome. The fact that a national measure falls within the formal scope of the Treaty

[1] Ideally, competition law should have been covered as well, given its important role in shaping the socio-economic structure of the Union. For a great treatment of the topic see Sauter, *Competition law and industrial Policy in the EU* (Clarendon Press, 1977).

[2] Case 8/74, *Procureur du Roi v Benoît and Gustave Dassonville* [1974] ECR 837 (hereinafter *Dassonville*).

[3] For a similar argument see for example Peter Oliver, *Free Movement of Goods in the EEC* (European Law Centre, 1982) 87; see also Michael Dougal, who argued: '[O]ne might begin with the observation that it has become so easy to trigger the application of the provisions on Union citizenship that the mere existence of a prima facie infringement of the Treaty has surely lost its ability to tell us anything meaningful about the balance of policy interests at stake in any given dispute.' Michael Dougan, 'The Bubble that burst: Exploring the Legitimacy of the Case Law on the Free Movement of Union Citizens' in Maurice Adams et al (eds), *Judging Europe's Judges* (Hart, 2013) 136.

freedom provisions has no bearing on the question of whether that measure is prohibited in substantive terms. The substantive question of whether a national measure is prohibited or justified is decided within the framework of the proportionality analysis, which must be understood as a pluralist instrument.

In contemporary scholarship, internal market law is usually presented in the form of a narrative that suggests an expansionary movement: the case law is arranged in a way that seems to illustrate an ever-growing reach of the Treaty freedom provisions.[4] Such expansionary narrative may be problematic if it insinuates a normative meaning: as, over time, more and more types of national regulation have been found to fall within the scope of the Treaty freedoms (and were then often held to be prohibited), it might be assumed that internal market law exhibits some form of increasing normative bias against national regulation, or against some of the regulatory objectives usually pursued through national law. This, however, is an incorrect assumption. One of the central purposes of this chapter is to show that, as regards its essential features, the doctrinal system employed in internal market law today has remained essentially unchanged since the early days of the Community. While the CJEU's case law is certainly expanding in the sense that, over the years, more types of national regulation have been challenged under the Treaty freedoms, the normative substance of the Treaty freedoms was not subject to any significant qualitative change: the Treaty freedom provisions have always been interpreted as formally broad and pluralist in substance.

In the second part of the chapter we address two specific doctrinal issues related to internal market law where formal and substantive questions are frequently, but incorrectly, mashed up, leading to faulty assumptions about the socio-economic orientation of internal market law. They concern two interpretative doctrines employed by the CJEU, the 'interpreting strictly', and the 'purely economic nature' doctrines. Both of these doctrines are routinely misunderstood to have substantive implications, either as favouring individual economic freedoms over other regulatory concerns, or prohibiting certain types of justifications. It will be shown that any substantive reading of these doctrines is incorrect, and that they must be understood in purely procedural terms. This has important implications for the analysis and application of internal market law. It has been argued by many authors, including myself, that the CJEU's case law frequently exhibits a neoliberal bias.[5] The present chapter suggests that, because internal market law doctrine itself has a pluralist character, such bias must be the consequence of other factors,

[4] For example, it is often argued that the Court moved from an interpretation of the Treaty freedoms as a prohibition of discrimination to a prohibition of (non-discriminatory) restrictions. See for example Giandomenico Majone, *Rethinking the Union of Europe Post-Crisis—Has Integration Gone Too Far?* (Cambridge University Press, 2014), 306; Fritz Scharpf, 'After the crash: A perspective on multilevel European democracy' (2015) 21 *European Law Journal* 384, 386, fn 9; however, the situation is more complex, as will be argued in this chapter. From the 1960s onwards, the Treaty freedoms were interpreted by the Commission as covering both discriminatory and certain (non-discriminatory) restrictive measures alike. The Commission's approach was essentially picked up by the Court in its earliest case law.

[5] Alexander Somek has argued for example that the Court's sweeping, obstacle-based approach is liable to produce neoliberal outcomes. Alexander Somek, 'The Argument from Transnational Effects I:

such as implicit economic or political assumptions that enter the interpretation process.

THE PLURALIST CHARACTER OF ARTICLE 34 TFEU: THE TREATY TEXT AND ITS EARLY INTERPRETATION

Article 30 EEC (now 34 TFEU) prohibited quantitative restrictions on imports (a concept also employed in the GATT)[6] and measures having an equivalent effect as quantitative restrictions (MEEs). By 1958, when the Treaty of Rome came into force, quantitative restrictions in Europe had already been greatly reduced under the auspices of the OEEC.[7] The Treaty of Rome required Member States to abolish quantitative restrictions completely by the end of the transitional period in December 1969, a goal that was successfully achieved. When Article 30 EEC became directly effective in 1970,[8] therefore, the problem of quantitative restrictions had largely been solved.[9] From relatively early on, then, restrictions other than quantitative restrictions came into the focus of the Community institutions.[10] Competition Commissioner von der Groeben explained in 1965, for example, that 'Experience shows that the dismantling of internal duties and quantitative restrictions and the building up of the common external tariff have reached a stage at which the other barriers to trade are making themselves more and more strongly felt.'[11] The prohibition of MEEs in Article 30 EEC provided the doctrinal space to go after such restrictions.

The notion of 'quantitative restrictions' describes measures that establish constraints on imports in quantitative terms, by limiting either the volume or the value of products imported.[12] The concept of 'measures having equivalent effect

Representing Outsiders through Freedom of Movement' (2010) 16 *European Law Journal* 315, 332–34; see also Lukas Oberndorfer, 'Post-neoliberale Integrationsweise der EU. Perspektivenwechsel an der Schnittstelle Politik/Ökonomie/Recht' in Barbara Blaha and Josef Weidenholzer (eds), *Freiheit Beiträge für eine demokratische Gesellschaft* (Braumüller, 2010).

[6] For an early discussion of the concept of quantitative restrictions, see Ernst Wohlfarth et al, *Die Europäische Wirtschaftsgemeinschaft: Kommentar zum Vertrag* (Vahlen, 1960), 78–79; AWH Meij and JA Winter, 'Measures having an effect equivalent to quantitative restrictions' (1976) 13 *Common Market Law Review* 79, 81, with further references; see also Walter Van Gerven, 'The recent case law of the Court of Justice concerning Articles 30 and 36 of the EEC Treaty" (1977) 14 *Common Market Law Review* 5, 8, with further references; Eric White, 'In Search of the Limits to Article 30 of the EEC Treaty' (1989) 26 *Common Market Law Review* 235, 239–41.

[7] Paul Kapteyn and Pieter verLoren van Themaat, *Introduction to the Law of the European Communities* (Sweet & Maxwell, 1973), 202.

[8] ibid, 202.

[9] This can be understood as a significant early political success of the Treaty of Rome. In this sense see Dennis Swann, *The Economics of the Common Market* (Penguin Books, 1992), 97.

[10] See for example Dennis Thompson, 'Harmonization of Laws' (1965) 3 *Journal of Common Market Studies* 302, 303; see also Alfred Müller-Armack, *Wirtschaftsordnung und Wirtschaftspolitik* (Verlag Rombach, 1966), 326.

[11] Hans von der Groeben, 'Competition Policy in the Common Market and in the Atlantic Partnership' (1965) 10 *Antitrust Bulletin* 125, 151.

[12] Wohlfarth et al (n 6), 73.

as quantitative restrictions', which remained undefined in the Treaty, essentially allows two interpretations—one narrower, the other broader. The narrow interpretation assumed that because quantitative restrictions prevented goods from physically crossing the border, the concept of MEEs was read as encompassing only measures that were equivalent in this sense. By contrast, the broader interpretation focused on the term 'effect'.[13] As quantitative restrictions limited the volume (or value) of imported goods, MEEs were such measures that had a similar effect of hindering trade. The narrow interpretation was a minority view, and has been asserted, to my knowledge, only by one author, Gerd Meier.[14] According to Meier's opinion, MEEs encompassed only such measures that 'directly' (*unmittelbar*) affected the import of goods in the sense of physically restricting the movement of goods across borders.[15] By contrast, 'indirect' restrictions, such as restrictions on sale, minimum or maximum prices, or distorting state aid, were excluded from its scope. Meier argued that even openly discriminatory measures were not prohibited under Article 30 EEC, as long as they did not prevent goods from physically crossing the border.[16]

The broader understanding of MEEs, by contrast, would include measures which, even though they did not constitute such border measures in a narrow sense, still had the practical effect of restricting imports in some form. A broader interpretation of Article 30 EEC appears to have been relatively uncontroversial in the early literature, for a number of reasons. One of them was that the GATT, which provided the regulatory background against which the EEC was designed, established a relatively far-reaching requirement of non-discrimination.[17] Article III GATT requires the signatories to ensure 'national treatment' of imported goods in areas of both a fiscal and a non-fiscal nature.[18] The non-discrimination requirement applies to measures 'affecting the internal sale, offering for sale, purchase, transportation, distribution or use of products, and internal quantitative regulations requiring the mixture, processing or use of products in specified amounts

[13] See for example Dietrich Ehle, 'Massnahmen gleicher Wirkung wie mengenmässige Beschränkungen und ihre Abschaffung im Gemeinsamen Markt' [1967] *Aussenwirtschaftsdienst des Betriebs-Beraters* 453, 455.

[14] This is indicated for example by Hans von der Groeben, Hans von Boeckh and Jochen Thiesing, *Kommentar zum EWG-Vertrag* (Nomos, 1974) 255; Eberhard Grabitz, 'Das Recht auf Zugang zum Markt nach dem EWG-Vertrag' in Rolf Stödter and Werner Thieme (eds), *Hamburg—Deutschland—Europa (Festschrift Ipsen)* (JCB Mohr (Paul Siebeck), 1977) 650.

[15] Dietrich Ehle and Gerd Meier, *EWG-Warenverkehr: Außenhandel—Zölle—Subventionen* (Schmidt, 1971) 159.

[16] ibid, 159 and 163.

[17] It has also been noted by various authors that in a number of federal systems, including the United States, Canada and Australia, the federal trade rules are interpreted in a similarly expansive form. See Meij and Winter (n 6), 82; Leslie Zines, 'The Balancing of Community and National Interests by the European Court' (1972) 5 *Federal Law Review* 171, 176.

[18] Art III GATT, para 1 holds: 'The contracting parties recognize that internal taxes and other internal charges, and laws, regulations and requirements affecting the internal sale, offering for sale, purchase, transportation, distribution or use of products, and internal quantitative regulations requiring the mixture, processing or use of products in specified amounts or proportions, should not be applied to imported or domestic products so as to afford protection to domestic production.'

or proportions', and thereby clearly reached beyond the narrow field of border measures. Whereas the prohibition of discriminatory taxation in Article III GATT had an obvious equivalent in Article 95 EEC, the Treaty of Rome held no direct equivalent as regards discriminatory non-fiscal measures. For a number of authors, this justified a broader reading of the concept of MEEs in analogy to the national treatment requirement of Article III GATT.[19] As the Treaty of Rome aimed at a considerably deeper degree of integration than the GATT, verLoren van Themaat argued, Article 30 EEC had to be interpreted as reaching at least as far as Article III GATT.[20]

The Treaty text proper supports both a narrow reading such as the one proposed by Meier, as well as a broader interpretation that encompassed all measures that had a restrictive effect on trade, even if they were not border measures in a narrow sense.[21] While most commentators employed the broader reading, the precise scope of the provision remained subject to considerable debate. Of great practical significance, of course, was the legal view of the Commission, which was assigned by Article 33(7) EEC the role of 'establishing the procedure and timetable' for abolishing MEEs. In the first General Report, issued in September 1958, the Commission held in regard to this task: 'Probably the most difficult problem is to list a string of regulations and administrative practices which vary from one state to another and whose protectionist effect is not always evident to those who operate them.'[22] The statement implies that the concept of MEEs may encompass measures that had not been enacted on the basis of protectionist intentions, and also did not visibly have such effect. It thus suggests a scope that reaches beyond openly discriminatory measures if it is assumed that the protectionist effect of openly discriminatory measures will usually be obvious. Another point of interest is that the Commission seemed to assume that restrictive effects may originate from the mere fact that regulation varies among Member States, which also points towards a relatively expansive reading of the concept of MEEs that reaches beyond a prohibition of discriminatory measures alone.

The predominant understanding of MEEs in the early years was that it entailed, as a very minimum, a prohibition of formal discrimination.[23] This is identifiable for example in Directive 66/683/EEC, which prohibited national measures that

[19] Pieter verLoren van Themaat, 'Bevat Artikel 30 van het EEG-Verdrag slechts een non-discriminatie-bedingsel ten aanzien van invoerbeperkingen?' [1967] *Sociaal Economische Wetgeving* 632, 641–42; see also René Christian Béraud, 'Les mesures d'effet équivalent au sens des articles 30 et suivants du Traité de Rome' [1968] *Revue trimestrielle de droit europeen* 265, 289.

[20] For an argument similar to that of verLoren van Themaat, see Ernst Steindorff, *Der Gleichheitssatz im Wirtschaftsrecht des Gemeinsamen Marktes* (Walter De Gruyter & Co, 1965) 29–30.

[21] This finding was not, however, shared across the board. Leslie Zines argued in relation to *International Fruit Co* that 'the Court gave the phrase "quantitative restrictions ... and ... measures having equivalent effect" a meaning that it could in normal language hardly bear.' Zines (n 17), 191.

[22] EC, 'First General Report on the Activities of the Community (January 1958 to September 1958)', 53.

[23] Steindorff (n 20), 6.

prescribed the use of domestic products.[24] However, from relatively early onwards, the Commission assumed that Article 30 EEC would, under certain conditions, reach beyond openly discriminatory measures. Such a view was, first of all, supported by the wording of Article 36 EEC: it held that restrictions on trade should not be employed as a 'disguised restriction on trade between Member States'. As directly discriminatory measures can hardly constitute a 'disguised' restriction, Article 36 EEC seems to imply that the concept of MEEs encompasses, at the very least, both directly and indirectly discriminatory measures.[25] A broad scope of Article 30 EEC was also supported by an analogous reading of Article III GATT.[26] Its paragraphs 4 and 5 suggest that both direct and indirect forms of discrimination are prohibited, and thereby establishes a relatively broad requirement of 'national treatment'. The early literature mostly embraced a broad interpretation of Article 30 EEC as encompassing both distinctly and indistinctly applicable measures, though the discussion was not very systematic in the early years. Wohlfarth et al held in 1960 that measures could constitute MEEs if they were 'influencing imports' or if they were 'restricting trade or making it impossible'.[27] CJEU judge Nicola Catalano argued in his 1962 textbook that minimum price legislation constituted MEEs, which implied that the concept of MEEs applied at least to some indistinctly applicable measures.[28]

The Commission first attempted to give a more principled definition of MEEs in 1967 in a response to a parliamentary inquiry, though it emphasized that the definition was ultimately for the CJEU to make. The Commission explained that 'the general prohibition of Article 30 defines measures solely in regard to its effect, and not its type or content. Thus, every measure, irrespective of its type or its content, may constitute a measure having equivalent effect to quantitative restrictions solely because of its effect on the free movement of goods, as long as it does not fall under the scope of another title of the Treaty.'[29] In its response to a follow-up question as to the exact definition it employed, the Commission defined MEEs as 'all laws, administrative provisions and administrative practices which hinder imports or exports which could otherwise take place, including those provisions

[24] Commission Directive 66/683/EEC eliminating all differences between the treatment of national products and that of products which, under Articles 9 and 10 of the Treaty, must be admitted for free movement, as regards laws, regulations or administrative provisions prohibiting the use of the said products and prescribing the use of national products or making such use subject to profitability [1966] OJ 220/3748; see Ehle and Meier (n 15), 165.

[25] For a similar reading see Ehle and Meier (n 15), 172; For a slightly different interpretation, but with the same outcome, see verLoren van Themaat (n 19), 638.

[26] See Steindorff (n 20), 14–15.

[27] Wohlfarth et al (n 6), 82 (my translation).

[28] Nicola Catalano, *Manuel de droit des Communautés européennes* (Dulloz et Sirey, 1962) 276; for a similar argument see Wohlfarth et al (n 6), 82.

[29] Ergänzende Antwort der Kommission der Europäischen Wirtschaftsgemeinschaft auf die schriftliche Anfrage Nr 118 von Herrn Deringer [1967] OJ 59/901 (my translation); see also the original inquiry: Schriftliche Anfrage Nr 118 von Herrn Deringer an die Kommission der Europäischen Wirtschaftsgemeinschaft [1967] OJ 9/122.

and practices which make importation or exportation more difficult or costly than the disposal of domestic production'.[30] This definition is clearly very far-reaching. While the Commission argued that 'provisions which are equally applicable to domestic and imported products do not as a rule constitute measures having an effect equivalent to quantitative restrictions', it clearly did not conceptualize the application of Article 30 EEC to indistinctly applicable measures as exceptional.[31] Cases on the application of Article 30 EEC date back to the early 1960s: among the examples provided by the Commission for national measures prohibited under Article 30 EEC were cases of indistinctly applicable measures, such as that of a Belgian regulation that increased the minimum amount of nitrate in fertilizer to a higher level than hitherto common in the rest of the Member States.[32] While the measure was indistinctly applicable, it nonetheless made importing more difficult, and the Commission successfully pressured the Belgian government to repeal the measure.[33] In another early example from the 1960s, the 'French blanket case', a French decree held that only blankets of a specific size could be sold in France. Again, the Commission successfully made the French government repeal this measure as it hindered imports, even though it was indistinctly applicable.[34]

The parliamentary inquiry triggered an increased interest among scholars in the issue of the scope of Article 30 EEC.[35] A central point of concern was that the broad definition proposed by the Commission would affect a potentially unlimited spectrum of national regulation, which raised significant competence issues.[36] Unlike some federal constitutions such as the German *Grundgesetz*, the Treaty of Rome did not draw a clear substantive delineation of competences between the national and the European sphere.[37] The discussion on the meaning

[30] Schriftliche Anfrage Nr 64 von Herrn Deringer an die Kommission der Europäischen Wirtschaftsgemeinschaft [1967] OJ 169/11 (translation in Meij and Winter (n 6), 83).

[31] The definition provided by the Commission was considered to be a relatively pragmatic description of the Commission's practice in the roughly 100 cases of MEEs that it had hitherto been confronted with. See for example Béraud (n 19), 287.

[32] The Commission argued that the industry of that Member State would surely adapt to the new limit because its main market was in that Member State. By contrast, an adaptation to these standards was not profitable for the industries in the other Member States, as only a fraction of their production was exported to that state. The Commission noted that the concerned Member States had chosen to comply with the Commission's assessment and withdrew the objected measure, instead of referring the issue to the Court. On this case as well as the 'French blankets case' see Oliver (n 3), 65–66; for further examples see also Ehle (n 13), 453.

[33] See Peter Oliver, 'Measures of equivalent effect: a reappraisal' (1982) 19 *Common Market Law Review* 217, 224.

[34] ibid, 224.

[35] Peter Ulmer, 'Zum Verbot mittelbarer Einfuhrbeschränkungen im EWG-Vertrag' [1973] *Aussenwirtschaftsdienst des Betriebs-Beraters* 349, 351.

[36] ibid, 355; Meij and Winter (n 6), 81–82, 88; see also von der Groeben, von Boeckh and Thiesing (n 14), 264.

[37] Manfred Zuleeg, 'Relationship of Community Law to National Law' (1977) 5 *International Journal of Law Libaries* 5, 5–6. Zuleeg argued that the synchronization of the European and the national legal systems required both a clarification regarding the distribution of competences, as well as 'collision rules to solve conflicts which might occur despite the distribution of competency'.

of the term MEEs takes place in this context. Much of the scholarship agreed with the Commission's assessment that Article 30 EEC should apply, at least in certain instances, to distinctly and indistinctly applicable measures alike. As we already saw, such understanding was not particularly controversial because it corresponded with a similar approach in international trade law.[38] At the same time such broad definition raised, as we just saw, potential competence issues, which made it necessary to clarify the distribution of competences and/or to define rules of conflict. The Commission's assertion that indistinctly applicable measures do not, 'as a rule', constitute MEEs is an attempt to sketch such limitation, but it was vague and obviously not operable in that form. The literature of the late 1960s and early 1970s became increasingly concerned with exploring limitations on the scope of MEEs in a form that provided greater clarity than the Commission's initial suggestion. One of them, as already discussed, was Meier's attempt to limit the definition of MEEs to measures that 'directly' affected goods crossing borders, while measures that concerned the sale or marketing of goods should remain excluded. This essentially constituted an attempt to define the scope of Article 30 EEC to include border measures, but to exclude the regulation of domestic markets. Another proposal to limit the scope of the concept of MEEs was to apply it exclusively to certain types of national regulation, such as 'trading rules'.[39] The concept of 'trading rules' was in fact later picked up by the CJEU in *Dassonville*, but has since then been dropped. Yet another proposition forwarded by some scholars was to interpret Article 30 EEC as prohibiting directly discriminatory measures only.[40]

The obvious benefit of all of these formal limitations was that they would ostensibly establish a relatively clear dividing line between national measures that would fall under the definition of MEEs, and those that would not. However, each of these limitations raised new problems of either a doctrinal or a practical-political nature. If Article 30 EEC were to be applied to directly discriminatory measures alone, Member States could effortlessly circumvent such prohibition.[41] Moreover, such definition was much less clear in practice than it appeared in theory:[42] is, for example, a measure that restricts products which are not produced domestically *directly* or *indirectly* discriminatory? Similarly, the dividing line between discriminatory measures and indistinctly applicable measures with adverse effects on trade is blurry as well, as for example Ulmer showed.[43] Other definitions merely shifted

[38] See Steindorff (n 20), 14–15; Zuleeg (n 37), 6.

[39] Meij and Winter (n 6), 104.

[40] Michael Graf, *Der Begriff 'Maßnahmen gleicher Wirkung wie mengenmäßige Einfuhrbeschränkungen' in dem EWG-Vertrag* (Heymann, 1972) 98; see however the critique of Ehle and Meier (n 15), 171–72.

[41] Von der Groeben, von Boeckh and Thiesing (n 14), 263–64; verLoren van Themaat (n 19), 633–34; Oliver (n 3), 69; Meij and Winter (n 6), 90.

[42] For a critique of this position see Ehle (n 13), 455.

[43] Ulmer (n 35), 355.

the problem of delineation to another doctrinal location. Steindorff proposed, for example, that Article 30 EEC should apply to both directly and indirectly discriminatory measures (thereby evading the difficult distinction between the two types of measures) but not to measures that merely had an incidental effect on trade.[44] However, this raises the question of when an adverse effect on trade is merely incidental. Finally, definitions that attempted to limit the scope of Article 30 EEC to measures regulating a specific subject matter such as measures that have 'direct effect' on trade or that constitute 'trade measures' in turn made circumvention possible, and raised difficulties of delineation.[45] To some extent, these problems were inversely related: a narrow definition of MEEs as encompassing only a certain type of measures would be relatively clear in its scope, but would facilitate circumvention, whereas a broad definition of MEEs caught any kind of measure, but required a further, substantive delineation.

In late 1969, the Commission issued Directive 70/50/EEC, which provided a principled definition of MEEs and clarified the Commission's position on indistinctly applicable measures.[46] Meij and Winter described the Commission's approach as establishing a 'per se prohibition for measures discriminating against foreign imports, and a more flexible approach with reference to trade measures indiscriminately applicable to national and foreign products.'[47] Oliver similarly held that while 'overtly discriminatory measures were automatically considered to be measures of equivalent effect, there was a presumption that "indistinctly applicable" measures were compatible with Article 30.'[48] According to Article 2(1) of the Directive, MEEs are 'measures, other than those applicable equally to domestic or imported products, which hinder imports which could otherwise take place, including measures which make importation more difficult or costly than the disposal of domestic production.' Article 2(3) gave a list of 20 distinctly applicable measures that had to be abolished, reaching from measures that '(a) lay down, for imported products only, minimum or maximum prices below or above which imports are prohibited, reduced or made subject to conditions liable to hinder

[44] Discussed in von der Groeben, von Boeckh and Thiesing (n 14), 264.

[45] Peter Oliver argued, for example, that the criterion whether a measure 'directly' restricts trade, which for example verLoren van Themaat or Waelbroeck had proposed instead of the discrimination criterion, would in fact be no less difficult to establish. See Oliver (n 3), 68.

[46] The Directive was based on the Commission's competence to enact implementing measures after the end of the transitional period in 1970, which was laid down in Art 33(7) EEC. See Commission Directive 70/50/EEC on the abolition of measures which have an effect equivalent to quantitative restrictions on imports and are not covered by other provisions adopted in pursuance of the EEC Treaty [1969] OJ L 013/29. On the Directive see for example Pieter verLoren van Themaat, 'E.E.G.-richtlijnen betreffende discriminerende aankoop-politiek overheidsinstellingen, discriminerende prijsvoorschriften en andere maatregeln van gelijke werking als kwantitatieve invoerbeperkingen' [1970] *Sociaal Economische Wetgeving* 258; The Commission also issued Directive 70/32/EEC, which defined indistinctly applicable measures in its Art 3(3) in the same way as Directive 70/50/EEC. Richtlinie 70/32/EWG der Kommission über die Lieferungen von Waren an den Staat, seine Gebietskörperschaften und die sonstigen juristischen Personen des öffentlichen Rechts [1969] OJ L 13/1. Overall, the Commission issued five directives on the basis of Art 33(7); see on this Oliver (n 33), 221–22, fn 24.

[47] Meij and Winter (n 6), 90.

[48] Oliver (n 33), 225.

importation' to measures that '(s) confine names which are not indicative of origin or source to domestic products only.' As regards indistinctly applicable measures, the Commission essentially shunned attempts to define strict prima facie limitations on the scope of Article 30 EEC that had been proposed by some scholars. Instead, it defined Article 30 EEC in a formally broad fashion, and established additional criteria for the substantive evaluation of measures that fell within its formal scope. Article 3 dealt with indistinctly applicable measures, and held in its first part:[49]

> This Directive also covers measures governing the marketing of products which deal, in particular, with shape, size, weight, composition, presentation, identification or putting up and which are equally applicable to domestic and imported products, where the restrictive effect of such measures on the free movement of goods exceeds the effects intrinsic to trade rules.

The Commission Directive therefore applied to 'measures governing the marketing of products', even if they were indistinctly applicable. The type of national measures that the Directive wished to target was defined in formally broad form; the accompanying list of measures ('shape, size, weight, composition, presentation, identification or putting up') had a merely indicative function ('in particular'). At the same time, however, the Directive asserted that indistinctly applicable measures were not per se prohibited, even if they happened to have adverse effects on trade. In that regard, the Commission explained in the Directive's preamble:

> [MEEs] must also be considered to include those which, at any marketing stage, grant to domestic products a preference, other than an aid, to which conditions may or may not be attached, and where such measures totally or partially preclude the disposal of imported products; ... such measures hinder imports which could otherwise take place, and thus have an effect equivalent to quantitative restrictions on imports; ... effects on the free movement of goods of measures which relate to the marketing of products and which apply equally to domestic and imported products are not as a general rule equivalent to those of quantitative restrictions, since such effects are normally inherent in the disparities between rules applied by Member States in this respect; ... however, such measures may have a restrictive effect on the free movement of goods over and above that which is intrinsic to such rules.

Indistinctly applicable measures therefore did not constitute MEEs even if they had an adverse effect on trade, if such effect was 'intrinsic to trade rules'. Whether such adverse effects on trade were 'intrinsic' was to be established, according to Article 3 of the Commission Directive, through a proportionality test:

> This is the case, in particular, where:
>
> — the restrictive effects on the free movement of goods are out of proportion to their purpose;
>
> — the same objective can be attained by other means which are less of a hindrance to trade.

[49] See also Meij and Winter (n 6), 84.

The Commission Directive proposed a system of proportionality balancing to establish whether an indistinctly applicable measure constituted an MEE.[50] Such would be the case only if they were out of proportion to their own regulatory purpose or if a less restrictive means was available. The Directive employed a conceptual split between the potential reach of Article 30 EEC on the one hand and its normative substance on the other. Whereas the formal scope of Article 30 EEC was virtually unlimited, its substance was defined only in a procedural form, so that the legality of the national measure had to be established on a case-by-case basis. The underlying reason for this approach may be found in the regulatory goals of the Treaty of Rome as discussed in an earlier chapter. The Treaty of Rome aimed at establishing a common market: accordingly, the Commission Directive defined the scope of Article 30 EEC in a formally broad way because the type of national measures that could have adverse effects on trade was not limited to a specific form, such as distinctly applicable measures, or a specific type of measures, such as 'trading rules'. At the same time, not every measure that created a restriction on trade should be prohibited: the Treaty's main ambition was not to establish a common market that was free of regulation nor one of maximized trade,[51] but one that enabled 'undistorted competition'. While regulatory differences between the Member States may create burdens on trade or increase costs, they do not necessarily distort competition in a significant way (a point that essentially also underlies the *Keck* approach).[52] An example discussed in the literature that illustrates the point is wage differences: if differences in wages between regions represent underlying structural differences (for example different levels of productivity), then they do not create unfair advantages or disadvantages that require judicial intervention. The Treaty of Rome aimed at establishing a common market free of distortions but did not wish to level all regulatory differences. Accordingly, trade restrictions such as costs and other burdens on trade that were the consequence of these differences could not per se be found to indicate a breach of Article 30 EEC. Instead, measures that created such burdens on trade were prohibited only if this adverse effect exceeded their purpose, or if the purpose could be achieved with other, less restrictive means.

To summarize this section it can be held that Article 30 EEC was interpreted in a mostly expansive fashion from the 1960s onwards, in the literature as well as by the Commission. The narrow interpretation, which focused on measures specifically regulating the crossing of borders by goods alone, did not gain traction in the

[50] According to ibid, 91, the proportionality test is essentially derived from Art 36 EEC second sentence. The proportionality test was also proposed in Directive 70/32/EEC; see also Ehle and Meier (n 15), 172.

[51] Otherwise any measure that potentially reduces demand would infringe the Treaty freedoms. As Meij and Winter (n 6), 104, observed, the reduction of demand (which may include both imported and domestic goods) may be a necessary measure of economic policy, eg 'in order to combat inflation or to correct a balance of payments disequilibrium'.

[52] See ibid, 87–88; For a similar argument see Steindorff (n 20), 35.

discussion during and after the transitional period. Instead, the Commission and the early literature interpreted MEEs in a broader sense, essentially as implying an obligation of national treatment. From early on, the Commission understood this requirement as applying to both distinctly and indistinctly applicable measures. As such definition reached deeply into what was considered the 'reserved domain' of the Member States, scholars increasingly attempted to define formal limitations to such broad definition, which, however, raised either problems of circumvention or merely shifted the problem of delineation. In its Directive 70/50/EEC, the Commission shunned such formal limitations, and instead defined a formally broad (essentially unlimited) scope of the term MEEs. However, it proposed that measures had to be subjected to an additional, substantive evaluation on the basis of a proportionality test. We can therefore identify a conceptual distinction between the formal definition of the scope of MEEs, which was extensive, and a substantive prohibition, which was laid down in procedural terms alone and required a case-by-case evaluation. As the Directive defined the national measure's own regulatory purpose as the benchmark for its evaluation, it did not aim at an evaluation on the basis of an extraneous standard. The question of whether a measure unduly restricted trade had to be analysed from a perspective of the measure's regulatory purpose. The Directive may thus be described as pluralist, as it does not prejudge which regulatory goals are legitimate and which means are acceptable to further it.

THE PLURALIST CHARACTER OF THE FREE MOVEMENT OF GOODS CASE LAW: REASSESSING *DASSONVILLE*, *CASSIS* AND *KECK*

The Commission's approach of Directive 70/50/EEC was largely adopted by the CJEU:[53] the formal scope of Article 30 EEC was defined in a very broad fashion, while the question of which national measure were actually prohibited was left unspecified in substantive terms, relegated to a case-by-case evaluation in the form of a proportionality test. This doctrinal framework established by the CJEU thereby essentially retained the pluralist character of Article 30 EEC as developed by the Directive. The Commission's proposition that indistinctly applicable measures would not constitute MEEs if they passed the proportionality requirement was picked up by the CJEU for example in *Sacchi*, which was issued some months before *Dassonville*.[54] The CJEU held:

> [M]easures governing the marketing of products where the restrictive effect exceeds the effects intrinsic to trade rules are capable of constituting measures having an effect equivalent to quantitative restrictions. Such is the case, in particular, where the restrictive

[53] Oliver (n 3) 56. However, it has been contended that a central difference between the Directive and the post-*Cassis* case law was a reversal of the presumption of legality. See for example ibid, 72.

[54] Case 155/73, *Giuseppe Sacchi* [1974] ECR 409 (hereinafter *Sacchi*), para 8.

> effects are out of proportion to their purpose, in the present case the organization, according to the law of a Member State, of television as a service in the public interest.[55]

In *Sacchi*, the CJEU employed the proportionality test as defined in Directive 70/50/EEC to establish whether the effect a measure had on trade exceeded its intrinsic effects, and thereby constituted an MEE. In *Dassonville*, the proportionality requirement was reconceptualized in the form of an obligation for national measures to be 'reasonable'. The definition of MEEs given by the CJEU in *Dassonville* has two important prongs. The first prong is commonly known as the '*Dassonville* formula': 'All trading rules enacted by Member States which are capable of hindering, directly or indirectly, actually or potentially, intra-Community trade are to be considered as measures having an effect equivalent to quantitative restrictions.'[56] The second prong of the CJEU's definition of MEEs follows in the next paragraph of the judgment:

> In the absence of a Community system guaranteeing for consumers the authenticity of a product's designation of origin, if a Member State takes measures to prevent unfair practices in this connection, it is however subject to the condition that these measures should be reasonable and that the means of proof required should not act as a hindrance to trade between Member States and should, in consequence, be accessible to all Community nationals.[57]

The CJEU thereby defined three conditions: 1) there must not be a harmonized Community system in place to achieve the regulatory goal pursued by the national measure; 2) if the national measure defines procedural requirements to be met by the traders, these must be accessible to all Community nationals, and not hinder trade; and 3) the national measure must be 'reasonable'. The last requirement is commonly termed the 'reasonable measures clause' or 'rule of reason'.[58]

The first prong, the *Dassonville* formula, defines the formal scope of Article 30 EEC: any measure with a restrictive effect on trade may constitute an MEE. The formula obviously defines the scope of Article 30 EEC in very broad terms. The second requirement, ie that the national measure 'should be reasonable', serves as a counterweight to the broad definition of MEEs in the *Dassonville* formula. The function of this 'reasonable measures clause' appears similar to the requirement defined by the Commission in Article 3 Directive 70/50/EEC that the effects of a measure on trade should not exceed 'the effects intrinsic to trade rules', ie, should be proportional to its purpose and should constitute the least restrictive means.[59]

[55] *Sacchi*, para 8.
[56] *Dassonville*, para 5.
[57] ibid, para 6.
[58] Rene Barents, 'New developments in measures having equivalent effect' (1981) 18 *Common Market Law Review* 271, 283–91; see also Pieter verLoren van Themaat and Laurence Gormley, 'Prohibiting Restriction of Free Trade within the Community: Articles 30–36 of the EEC Treaty' (1981) 3 *Northwestern Journal of International Law & Business* 577, 584–88.
[59] On the use of the proportionality principle in the early case law see Oliver (n 3), 130–33.

While the central importance assigned in the literature to *Dassonville* is usually in relation to the first prong, ie the *Dassonville* formula, the 'reasonable measures clause' is in fact as important.[60] And while the CJEU did not elaborate on the concept of 'reasonableness' in *Dassonville*, it essentially did so in cases like *Sacchi* by reference to the proportionality vocabulary as defined in Directive 70/50/EEC, and did again in cases like *Cassis*.[61] From the *Dassonville* formula it can only be inferred that no, or at least relatively few, national measures are per se excluded from the scope of Article 30 EEC, but not whether they are in fact prohibited, which depends on the question whether they are considered to be 'reasonable'. The conceptual distinction between a broad formal scope of Article 30 EEC on the one hand, and a substantive scope that remains open on the other, which we encountered in relation with Directive 70/50/EEC, thereby reappears in the *Dassonville* decision.

As already mentioned, the Treaty did not provide a clear distribution of competences between the Community and the Member States: it allowed for harmonization on the European level and prohibited restrictions through its Article 30 EEC, but it did not make explicit what impact this would have on national competences to regulate the economy in the broadest sense. A general pre-emption in all areas touching the common market was deemed implausible, and, after harmonization projects stalled from the mid-1960s onwards, also impractical.[62] Accordingly, Member States were considered to retain their competence to regulate the economy in principle, but the scope of the right was unclear, and appeared precarious in the light of a broad interpretation of Article 30 EEC.[63] Von der Groeben et al worried, for example, that a definition of MEEs as including indistinctly applicable measures would touch on national measures that 'as a rule serve legitimate goals, which, however, are not fully covered by Article 36 EEC'.[64] The concern was to ensure a space for 'legitimate' regulation in those areas where Community-wide harmonization had not or not yet fully replaced national regulation.[65] This concerned a significant number of regulatory areas, for many of which Article 36 EEC did not provide an exemption.[66] The 'reasonable measures clause' in *Dassonville* thus served as a doctrinal instrument to allow for national measures that pursued

[60] For one of the many examples of scholars ignoring the reasonable measures clause, see John Mackenzie Stuart, 'The Court of Justice of the European Communities: The Scope of its Jurisdiction and the Evolution of its Case Law under the EEC Treaty' (1981) 3 *Northwestern Journal of International Law & Business* 415, 432.

[61] See Gabriel Moens, 'Freedom of Movement of Goods in the European Community' (1989) 17 *Melbourne University Law Review* 733, 735.

[62] See generally Zuleeg (n 37), 5.

[63] Meij and Winter (n 6), 81–82.

[64] Von der Groeben, von Boeckh and Thiesing (n 14), 264 (my translation).

[65] Béraud pointed out that the harmonization competence of Article 100 EEC, unlike many other provisions in the Treaty, does not include a standstill clause. This indicated, according to him, that 'les Etats membres n'ont pas entendu renoncer à leur pouvoir d'instaurer de nouvelles réglementations jusqu'à l'harmonisation des dispositions concernées.' Béraud (n 19), 289.

[66] ibid, 290.

such 'legitimate goals.' This central implication of the 'reasonable measures clause' becomes particularly clear when set in relation to the alternative interpretations of Article 30 EEC that were floated in the 1960s and 1970s. Scholars proposed a broad variety of interpretations for Article 30 EEC, just as they did for Article 36.[67] The suggested approaches differed in important doctrinal aspects: for example, some wished to interpret Article 30 EEC to cover openly discriminatory measures only, whereas others argued that MEEs should include all distinctly and indistinctly applicable measures alike. Similar doctrinal differences existed in regard to the interpretation of Article 36 EEC: some understood the exemptions as merely indicatory, and argued that other regulatory concerns, such as consumer protection, should also be exempted from the scope of Article 30 EEC.[68] By contrast, others advocated for a narrow interpretation of Article 36 EEC, arguing that the provision would not allow for additional exemptions.[69] Even though these doctrinal solutions are widely different, they have a common denominator: they all create a space for 'legitimate' national measures that remains essentially open in substantive terms.[70] Graf, for example, proposed a narrow understanding of Article 36 EEC, but also suggested that MEEs should only cover directly discriminatory measures.[71] In effect, national governments thereby retain the ability to enact all kinds of measures, with the exception of those that are directly discriminatory and serve other regulatory goals than those listed in Article 36 EEC. By contrast, Waelbroeck preferred a much broader reading of Article 30 EEC, which would include both distinctly and indistinctly applicable measures. However, his definition of MEEs is limited by a further condition: only those indistinctly applicable measures should constitute an MEE which restrict imports 'directly'.[72] Accordingly, Member States retain the right to enact measures with a restrictive effect on imports if such effect is only 'indirect'. According to Waelbroeck, an example for measures that affect trade only indirectly are tax measures. Similar to Waelbroeck, Ulmer proposed that Article 30 EEC should apply to distinctly and indistinctly applicable measures alike. This essentially means that all measures are subject to the proportionality test.[73] However, he proposed a different rule to exempt legitimate national measures from the scope of Article 30 EEC. According to Ulmer, measures that are proportional for achieving the purported policy goal do not constitute MEEs.[74] Member States therefore retain the right to enact measures if they are indistinctly applicable and proportional. Ulmer's solution is

[67] See for example the overviews by Meij and Winter (n 6), 84–86; Ulmer (n 35), 504–07; Graf (n 40), 74–81.

[68] For an overview see Oliver (n 3), 72–76.

[69] Von der Groeben, von Boeckh and Thiesing (n 14), 264.

[70] See Béraud (n 19), 289.

[71] Graf (n 40), in particular at 63–65, 94–98, 125.

[72] Michel Waelbroeck, *Les reglementations nationales de prix et le droit communautaire* (Ed de l'Univ de Bruxelles, 1975) 34.

[73] Oliver (n 33), 227.

[74] Ulmer (n 35), 512; see also Béraud, who argues that the right of Member States to regulate commerce ends where it becomes abusive ('abus de droit'). Béraud (n 19), 290.

obviously drawing from the 'intrinsic effects clause' defined by Directive 70/50/EEC, and the 'reasonable measures clause' of the *Dassonville* judgment essentially points into a similar direction.

For conceptual reasons, we can distinguish two types of strategies proposed by the various authors to secure a space for 'legitimate' regulation by the Member States, namely the establishment of 'internal' and of 'external' limitations on the scope of MEEs. The approaches of commentators like Waelbroeck and Ulmer as well as by the Commission in Directive 70/50/EEC and the CJEU in *Dassonville* employ limitations *internal* to the definition of MEEs, ie, they restrict the scope of the concept itself with the help of some further criterion: according to these approaches, indistinctly applicable measures constitute MEEs only if they are unreasonable (*Dassonville*), restrict imports directly (Waelbroeck) or are disproportionate (Commission, Ulmer). By contrast, other commentators employed a broad reading of MEEs in combination with an extensive interpretation of Article 36 EEC, which could be understood as an *external* limitation: the national measure was held to be an MEE, but could be justified on the basis of Article 36 EEC. In his opinion in *Cassis*, AG Capotorti interpreted Article 36 EEC expansively so that it could justify measures that served regulatory goals other than those explicitly listed in the provision, such as for example consumer protection.[75] While the various commentators thus interpreted Articles 30 and 36 EEC in quite different ways, they all shared a common feature of establishing a considerable space for Member States to enact 'legitimate' regulation that remains mostly undefined in substantive terms.

The doctrinal solution developed in *Cassis* is another variation of the second approach.[76] Article 30 EEC is defined broadly as encompassing indistinctly applicable measures, and no further *internal* limitation on this definition is provided. Moreover, Article 36 EEC is interpreted narrowly, ie, exempting only national measures that serve one of the six regulatory purposes explicitly listed in that provision. However, the CJEU accepted additional grounds for justification that are employed in analogy to Article 36 EEC, namely the 'mandatory requirements':

> Obstacles to movement within the Community resulting from disparities between the national laws relating to the marketing of the products in question must be accepted in so far as those provisions may be recognized as being necessary in order to satisfy mandatory requirements relating in particular to the effectiveness of fiscal supervision, the protection of public health, the fairness of commercial transactions and the defence of the consumer.[77]

[75] Case 120/78, *Rewe-Zentral AG v Bundesmonopolverwaltung für Branntwein* [1979] ECR 649 (hereinafter *Cassis de Dijon*, or simply *Cassis*), Opinion of AG Capotorti, 672.

[76] In a 1981 article, Gormley argued that the judgment in *Cassis* (as well as other decisions like *Fietje*) 'are by no means revolutionary (for they do not substantially modify Community law)'. Laurence Gormley, 'Cassis de Dijon and the Communication from the Commission' (1981) 6 *European Law Review* 454, 454.

[77] *Cassis* (n 75), para 8.

Similar to the other interpretations just discussed, the CJEU's doctrinal solution in *Cassis* thereby retains the Member States' competence to enact 'legitimate' national measures. The CJEU defined them as measures 'necessary' to 'satisfy mandatory requirements' relating to an open-ended list of public interest considerations. The term 'necessary' can be understood, as for example Ivo Schwartz proposed, as essentially meaning the same as proportional.[78] Similar to the other approaches, the space within which Member States are allowed to enact national measures is outlined only in an abstract form, and remains undefined in substantive terms. In essence, the 'mandatory requirements' are functionally equivalent to the 'reasonable measures clause' of *Dassonville* and the 'intrinsic effect clause' of Directive 70/50/EEC. The 'reasonable measures' clause, initially understood as a limitation of the scope of MEEs (ie, an 'internal' limitation), merely moved back in the doctrinal analysis to become justificatory grounds employed in analogy with Article 36 EEC in *Cassis* (ie, an 'external' limitation).[79]

The following table presents an overview of the different doctrinal solutions presented by the various authors and institutions in the 1960s and 1970s. The first column gives the definition of MEEs used by the respective authors, whereas the second column holds additional conditions that are used to restrict its scope. The first and the second column therefore represent the definition of MEEs and their *internal* limitations. The third column lists the *external* limitations accepted by the respective author. The table shows, as discussed above, that all models create a space for Member States to enact legislation that is not significantly limited in substantive term (indicated by the shaded fields). This finding also holds true for the CJEU's judgments in *Dassonville* and in *Cassis*: while the CJEU interpreted Article 30 EEC broadly and Article 36 EEC narrowly, it either excluded 'reasonable' national regulation from the scope of Article 30 EEC (pre-*Cassis*) or found it to be justified on the basis of mandatory requirements, ie on policy grounds other than those of Article 36 EEC (post-*Cassis*). As already discussed in a previous chapter, the principle of mutual recognition, which *Cassis* touches upon, does not alter the normative openness of the doctrinal system developed by the CJEU: the principle does not force Member States to alter their regulatory goals or their standard of protection, and merely requires them to acknowledge that products may already fulfil functionally equivalent product standards of other Member States.

[78] Ivo Schwartz, '30 Jahre EG-Rechtsangleichung' in Ernst-Joachim Mestmäcker, Hans Möller and Hans-Peter Schwarz (eds), *Eine Ordnungspolitik für Europa: Festschrift für Hans von der Groeben zu seinem 80 Geburtstag* (Nomos, 1987), 356.

[79] Barents and Van Gerven made an essentially similar observation: Barents (n 58), 294–95; Van Gerven (n 6), 9 and 13. The exact relationship between the 'mandatory requirements' and Art 36 EEC was the subject of some debate in the 1980s. See for example A Evans, 'Economic Policy and the Free Movement of Goods in EEC Law' (1983) 32 *International and Comparative Law Quarterly* 577, 593–96.

Comparison of Doctrinal Approaches in Regard to the Free Movement of Goods Provisions

	MEEs are ...	With the exception of ...	Justified by ...
Directive 70/50 (1969)	all distinctly applicable (Article 2) and many indistinctly applicable measures (Article 3)	indistinctly applicable measures whose restrictive effects are proportional	Article 36 only
Ehle and Meier (1971)[80]	measures that 'directly' restrict imports		Article 36 only[81]
Graf (1972)	only discriminatory measures		Article 36 only
Ulmer (1973)	both distinctly and indistinctly applicable measures	measures that are proportional for achieving the purported policy goal[82]	Article 36 EEC only (although it no longer has an autonomous function if the proportionality requirement is applied).[83]
Dassonville (1974)	both distinctly and indistinctly applicable measures (para 5)	'reasonable' indistinctly applicable measures (para 6)	Article 36 only
Waelbroeck (1976)	both distinctly and indistinctly applicable measures	measures that affect imports only indirectly (eg no tax measures)[84]	Article 36 only, but expansively interpreted to include, for example, consumer protection[85]
AG Capotorti in *Cassis de Dijon* (1979)	both distinctly and indistinctly applicable measures		Article 36 only, but expansively interpreted to include, for example, consumer protection
Cassis de Dijon (1979)	both distinctly and indistinctly applicable measures		Article 36 as well as mandatory requirements

80 Ehle and Meier (n 15), 164–73.
81 ibid, 174–77.
82 Ulmer (n 35), 512.
83 ibid, 512.
84 Waelbroeck (n 72), 34.
85 ibid, 34.

While a version of the proportionality test had been employed by the CJEU as early as 1974 in the decision Sacchi, by the early 1980s proportionality balancing had manifestly become the central doctrinal tool to reconcile Article 30's broad formal scope with the competence of Member States to enact 'reasonable' legislation. The system was, from the very beginning, characterized by the conceptual split between a formally broad scope of MEEs that potentially covered any national measure, and a normative substance that remained open and had to be established on a case-by-case basis. In his 1982 book, Peter Oliver emphasized the distinction between the provision's formal scope and its substantive content and argued that 'the question whether a measure is compatible with Article 30 … must always be examined in two stages.'[86] According to Oliver, '[a] distinction must always be made between the question of whether a measure constitutes a measure of equivalent effect and whether it is justified.'[87] And Dauses explained in 1985:

> In each case [the CJEU] undertakes, on the basis of the principle of 'proportionality' (rule of reason), an appraisal of values and interests as between the requirements of the free movement of goods and the legitimate protective purpose of the contested national measure.[88]

Keck does not alter the open normative character of Article 30 EEC, but merely establishes a rebuttable presumption in regard to the legality of selling arrangements.[89] Selling arrangements are considered not to constitute MEEs as long as they apply indistinctly to 'all relevant traders' within the national territory, and as long as they affect imported and domestic goods 'in the same manner, in law and in fact.' *Keck* does not alter the scope or legal meaning of Article 30 EEC: selling arrangements that either discriminate against imported goods or affect imported goods in a different way than domestic goods in practice are still assumed to constitute MEEs. *Keck* essentially picks up on a proposition made by the Commission in its Directive 70/50/EEC, which held that Article 30 EEC should be interpreted as prohibiting in

[86] Oliver (n 3), 87.

[87] ibid, 87.

[88] Manfred Dauses, 'The System of the Free Movement of Goods in the European Community' (1985) 33 *American Journal of Comparative Law* 209, 222.

[89] Joined cases C-267/91 and C-268/91, *Criminal proceedings against Bernard Keck and Daniel Mithouard* [1993] ECR I-6097 (hereinafter *Keck*); Eric White conceptualized the limitations later laid down in *Keck* as a formal limitation to the scope of Art 30 EEC, that also relieved the Member States from the strict procedural requirements that the Court had defined (White (n 6), 238–39). In the light of the subsequent case law on selling arrangements such as *Lecler-Siplec*, however, it seems more plausible to understand the *Keck* formula as a rebuttable presumption. On the development of the Court's case law after *Keck*, see Takis Tridimas, *The General Principles of EU Law* (Oxford University Press, 2006) 196–209.

particular those types of indistinctly applicable measures that affect the physical character of products ('measures governing the marketing of products which deal, in particular, with shape, size, weight, composition, presentation, identification or putting up'). Conversely, rules that do not define physical characteristics such as 'selling arrangements' may generally be assumed not to constitute MEEs, unless a distinct effect in law or in fact is found. The *Keck* formula provides a rebuttable presumption, but it does not predetermine the outcome in the specific case. Not unlike other rules that create a rebuttable presumption, such as the 'purely internal effects' rule, the *Keck* formula does not alter the open normative character of the provision.[90]

It is commonly held that the CJEU has 'constitutionalized' the Treaty freedoms by assigning them supremacy over national law, by granting them direct effect and by enabling effective judicial protection by national courts and by the CJEU through the preliminary reference procedure.[91] The 'constitutionalization' of the Treaty freedom provisions assigns them a higher rank vis-à-vis national law as well as a 'trump' function in analogy to fundamental rights.[92] It could be inferred that such 'constitutionalization' also implies a hierarchy in substantive terms, where greater weight is assigned to the individual economic freedoms than to the objectives pursued by Member State regulation. However, such a hierarchy of regulatory objectives does not follow from the Treaty provisions or from the case law developed on its basis. The system developed by the CJEU requires a balancing between the individual economic freedoms on the one hand, and the regulatory concerns pursued by the Member States on the other. Similar to any other constitutionally granted right, the Treaty freedoms are not absolute.[93] Under which circumstances they trump countervailing regulatory objectives remains ambiguous. While the Treaty freedoms are thus indeed 'constitutionalized', this does not mean that they can be assumed to be weightier than regulatory objectives pursued in national law.

It can be provisionally concluded that the CJEU interpreted Article 30 EEC from the very first cases as broad in formal terms, and open in substantive terms. It was conceptualized in a formally broad way to include both distinctly and indistinctly applicable measures, and to include both trade measures in a narrow sense as well as any other national measure that had a restrictive effect on trade. Substantive openness is, to a certain extent, the necessary correlate to such formal

[90] See for example Evans (n 79), 581; see also Oliver (n 3), 84–86.

[91] Ernst-Ulrich Petersmann, 'Grundprobleme der Wirtschaftsverfassung der EG' (1994) 48 *Aussenwirtschaft* 389, 395.

[92] See for example Scharpf, who held: 'It does not follow from the Text of the Treaties of Rome or from their genesis that the European Community was meant to abolish the constitutional parity between the protection of economic freedom and market-correcting intervention. Nevertheless, as a consequence of the supremacy of European law, the four economic freedoms, and the injunctions against distortions of competition, have in fact gained constitutional force vis-à-vis the member states.' Fritz Scharpf, *Governing in Europe: effective and democratic?* (OUP, 1999) 57–58.

[93] This limitation of the Treaty freedoms by a right of Member States to enact instruments to correct 'market failures' has been recognized even by liberalist scholars like Ernst-Ulrich Petersmann (n 91), 397.

breadth.[94] As any national measure could potentially constitute an MEE, such definition would also include measures that had—to use the terminology employed by the CJEU in *Dassonville*—a 'reasonable' regulatory purpose. Just like the Commission, the CJEU did not attempt to define which measures were reasonable or unreasonable in substantive terms, and instead employed a proportionality test, which established the legality of national measures on a case-by-case basis.[95] As the Treaty freedom provisions had direct effect after the end of the transitional period, the obligation of Article 30 EEC could now also take the form of an individual right: individuals had a right to engage in economic activities free of any (distinctly or indistinctly applicable) restrictions, unless these restrictions were justified on objective grounds and executed in a proportional form. Some authors attempted to clarify the substantive scope of Article 30 EEC by arguing that the provision granted not only a (negative) right of defence (*Abwehrrecht*) that prohibited Member States from applying illegal measures, but also a (positive) right to a performance (*Leistungsrecht*).[96] According to Schiller the latter included, for example, an obligation of Member States to keep border posts and examination stations open, and to assign sufficient financial means and personnel.[97] Our reading of Article 30 EEC would suggest that this is essentially correct. However, this subjective right is limited by conflicting regulatory objectives pursued by the Member States. It does *not* grant a right to sell products despite such conflicting regulatory objectives.[98] In effect, the legality of a national measure must be established in a case-by-case analysis. It is therefore plausible to speak of the doctrinal system

[94] For a comparable argument see Tridimas, who argued that 'It may be said that equality and proportionality are in an inverse relationship: the less one relies on the first, the more it has to rely on the latter in order to determine what is a permissible trestriction on trade.' Tridimas (n 89), 196.

[95] For a similar argument see Dauses, who commented in regard to the *Dassonville* formula: 'That is a remarkably wide definition. In particular, the concept of actual or potential hindrance is capable of including virtually every national measure of a legal or factual nature. It has been clear from the outset that the Court's abstract definition can be understood only in conjunction with the individual circumstances of each case.' (Dauses (n 88), 219.) And: 'In each case [the Court] undertakes, on the basis of the principle of "proportionality" (rule of reason), an appraisal of values and interests as between the requirements of the free movement of goods and the legitimate protective purpose of the contested national measure.' (Ibid, 222).

[96] K-Volker Schiller, 'Gewährt Art. 30 des EWG-Vertrages dem Gemeinschaftsbürger neben einem subjektiven Abwehrrecht auch ein subjektives Leistungsrecht?' [1980] *Recht der internationalen Wirtschaft* 569.

[97] ibid, 571; see on this regard also Oliver (n 33), 223–24. Oliver lists a number of examples where the Court identified the Treaty freedoms to hold a positive obligation of the states: 'Subsequent judgments have revealed a further respect in which the concept of measures of equivalent effect under Article 30 is far-reaching: in some instances Member States are not only required to refrain from imposing restrictions on imports, but are under an obligation to take active steps. Thus, in *De Peijper* the Court ruled that Member States were under a positive duty to cooperate with one another so as to ensure that registration formalities with respect to parallel imports of pharmaceuticals could be reduced to a minimum; and in *Denkavit Futtermittel v Minister of Agriculture* found a similar duty to cooperate with respect to veterinary checks on animal feed. Similarly, Member States are required to provide reasonable customs for instance in keeping customs posts open during reasonable hours and in providing adequate staff and equipment to carry out veterinary and public health checks with due speed.'

[98] This is how Oliver interprets Schiller's argument; in that sense he is right that it must be rejected; Oliver (n 33), 241. See similarly Roth, who argues: 'The establishment of conditions resembling those of an internal market means that the provision of services across borders encounters no greater

developed by the CJEU on the basis of Articles 30 and 36 EEC as a pluralist framework: its function is to handle conflicts within a field characterized by overlapping regulatory competences by the Community and the Member States, but it does not enforce a specific socio-economic model. Before we take a closer look at the proportionality analysis employed by the CJEU, we turn to Articles 52 and 59 EEC to show that the provisions on services and establishment and the case law developed on its basis mirror the pluralist normative character of Article 34 TFEU.

THE PLURALIST CHARACTER OF ARTICLES 49 AND 56 TFEU AND THE DOCTRINAL SYSTEM DEVELOPED ON ITS BASIS

Articles 52 and 59 EEC (now Articles 49 and 56 TFEU) required the abolition of 'restrictions' on the freedom of establishment and the freedom to provide services. In a more narrow interpretation, the obligation to abolish 'restrictions' could be understood as a mere requirement to establish formal equal treatment.[99] In such a reading, Member States merely had to abolish formal discriminations and had to apply the same set of rules to citizens from other Member States that they applied to their own citizens. However, they would not have to adapt their national regulations to the specific needs of the former, as for example von der Groeben et al emphasized.[100] By contrast, a broader reading of Articles 52 and 59 EEC would require Member States to ensure not only formal, but also some form of substantive equal treatment. A narrow reading of the provisions was supported, as for example von der Groeben et al emphasized, by the second part of Article 52: it established the 'right to take up and pursue activities as self-employed persons and to set up and manage undertakings', but only 'under the conditions laid down for its own nationals by the law of the country where such establishment is effected.' Commentators pointed out, however, that an interpretation of the free movement provisions as prohibiting formal discrimination alone would leave some of the most important restrictions untouched that self-employed persons faced.[101] Chesné for example held in 1962:

> The abolition of discriminatory barriers will not necessarily bring similar conditions of establishment for nationals from the other Member States, or the enjoyment of exactly

obstacles than in a purely domestic market: thus, all those specific burdens and obstacles are to be removed which stem from the fact that interstate provision of services is regulated on the level of the Member States and not on the Community level. It is not, therefore, a matter of advancing commercial freedom but merely of the removal of specific obstacles resulting from the decentralised decision-making authority of the Member States.' Wulf-Henning Roth, 'The European Economic Community's Law on Services: Harmonisation' (1988) 25 *Common Market Law Review* 35, 53.

[99] Grabitz (n 14), 660; Ulrich Everling, *The Right of Establishment in the Common Market* (Commerce Clearing House, 1964) 47–48.

[100] Von der Groeben, von Boeckh and Thiesing (n 14), 465–67; Everling (n 99), 48.

[101] See for example NN, 'Die bisherigen Massnahmen der Gemeinschaft zur Verwirklichung der Niederlassungsfreiheit und des freien Dienstleistungsverkehrs im Gemeinsamen Markt' [1967] *Aussenwirtschaftsdienst des Betriebs-Beraters* 437; see also Jean-Pierre De Crayencour, 'Propos sur le Droit

> the same rights. The differences between national legislations will remain an obstacle. Even if foreigners are treated as nationals, the imposed conditions may entail a *de facto* discrimination. Under the cover of legality, Member States may revive obstacles to the right of establishment.[102]

A narrow interpretation of the free movement provisions was easy to circumvent, as Member States could re-establish restrictive measures under the guise of formal equal treatment.[103] Moreover, a narrow reading left restrictions arising from regulatory differences between the Member States unaffected.[104]

The Treaty text was ambivalent, and did not unequivocally support either a narrow or a broad reading of the free movement provisions.[105] Von der Groeben et al acknowledged, for example, that the term 'restrictions' employed in Article 52 EEC was broader than that of 'discriminations' used in Article 7 EEC, and thereby pointed towards a more comprehensive reading of the term.[106] Such broader interpretation was also supported by a number of other Treaty provisions, most notably Article 57 EEC. In order to 'make it easier for persons to take up and pursue activities as self-employed persons', the provision called for the Member States to pass legislation 'for the mutual recognition of diplomas, certificates and other evidence of formal qualifications' as well as for the 'co-ordination of the provisions … the taking up and pursuit of activities as self-employed persons'. Article 57 EEC targeted measures which are not discriminatory per se, but create 'double burdens'[107] on self-employed persons from other Member States by subjecting them to requirements that they potentially had, though maybe not in the exact same form, already fulfilled in another Member State.[108] While the provision did not have direct effect by itself, commentators argued that it had to be understood as specifying the meaning of Article 52 EEC. Another example indicating that the Treaty presupposed a broader reading of Article 52 EEC is the case of legal entities. As Everling observed, the Treaty did not explicitly provide for the mutual recognition of company forms.[109] Under a narrow interpretation of Article 52 EEC, Member States would have to grant rights related to the legal status of the

d'Établissement dans le Traité de Rome' [1968] *Cahiers de Droit Europeén* 420, 421; Yvon Loussouarn, 'L'harmonisation du droit d'établissement' [1969] *Revue trimestrielle de droit europeen* 275, 276.

102 Guy Chesné, *L'Établissement des Étrangers en France et la Communauté Économique Européenne* (R Pichon et R Durand-Auzias, 1962) 333.

103 ibid, 333.

104 ibid, 333.

105 See however Art 60 EEC, which suggests that an interpretation of Art 52 EEC as prohibiting formal discrimination alone would be too narrow: 'Without prejudice to the provisions of the Chapter relating to the right of establishment, the person providing a service may, in order to do so, temporarily pursue his activity in the State where the service is provided, under the same conditions as are imposed by that State on its own nationals.'

106 Von der Groeben, von Boeckh and Thiesing (n 14), 466; arguing that the prohibition of restrictions encompassed both direct and indirect discriminations: Wohlfarth et al (n 6), 172.

107 Von der Groeben, von Boeckh and Thiesing (n 14), 491 (my translation).

108 ibid, 491.

109 Everling (n 99), 70.

company—most notably standing in courts and the acquisition of property—only under the same conditions as they applied to domestic companies. However, such reading would have severely restricted the economic activities of legal persons. It was thus rejected by the General Programmes for the abolition of restrictions on the freedom of establishment and the freedom to provide services enacted in 1961, which held that these rights must be extended to companies from other countries.[110] This made a narrow reading of the provision implausible.[111] The General Programmes themselves targeted both formal discrimination as well as some forms of indistinctly applicable measures.[112] The Programme on services held that 'any requirements imposed, pursuant to any provision laid down by law, Regulation or administrative action or in consequence of any administrative practice, in respect of the provision of services are also to be regarded as restrictions where, although applicable irrespective of nationality, their effect is exclusively or principally to hinder the provision of services by foreign nationals.'[113]

The need to target certain forms of indistinctly applicable measures was emphasized even by those authors who assumed that Articles 52 and 59 EEC essentially held an obligation to ensure formal equal treatment alone.[114] Von der Groeben, von Boeckh and Thiesing, for example, acknowledged that indistinctly applicable measures could constitute a serious impediment to the freedom of establishment and the freedom to provide services, and should therefore, under certain conditions, be considered to be prohibited by these Treaty provisions as well. Examples of measures that were indistinctly applicable and, according to the authors, nonetheless constituted a restriction in the meaning of Articles 52 and 59 EEC included, a residence condition of a number of years prior to having the right to take up a profession, or a requirement that an individual had to complete primary school in the host Member State. Von der Groeben et al proposed that indistinctly applicable measures should only fall under the term 'restriction' if they were 'arbitrary.'[115] This condition essentially requires a case-by-case evaluation, and therefore seems to fulfil a similar function as the proportionality requirement defined by the Commission in regard to Article 30 EEC.

[110] ibid, 70–71.

[111] Other provisions in the Treaty that pointed towards a broad interpretation of the term 'restrictions' were Art 54(3)(g) EEC which called for a coordination of safeguards in company law, the co-ordination of state aid in Art 54(3)(h) EEC, and the cooperation between national authorities in Art 54(3)(b) EEC.

[112] On the prohibition of indirect discriminations in the General Programmes see Kapteyn and verLoren van Themaat (n 7), 216; see also Walter van Gerven, 'Droit d'Établissement' [1965] *Cahiers de Droit Europeén* 125, 130.

[113] General Programme for the abolition of restrictions on freedom to provide services [1962] OJ 2/32, Title III, lit A, last sentence; see also General Programme for the abolition of restrictions on freedom of establishment [1962] OJ 2/36, Title III, lit B.

[114] See for example von der Groeben, von Boeckh and Thiesing (n 14), 466.

[115] ibid, 466–67. Following these authors, examples for measures that may restrict movement and yet not be arbitrary are requirements that are preconditions for all professions, such as a sufficient command of the language.

The establishment and services provisions became directly effective after the end of the transitional period,[116] and the CJEU applied a formally broad interpretation of the Treaty freedoms as encompassing distinctly and indistinctly applicable measures alike since the very first cases.[117] We will first look at the case law on services, and then turn to establishment. Already in *Van Binsbergen* (1974), a case dealing with an establishment requirement for persons to act as legal representatives before courts, the CJEU applied an interpretation of Article 59 EEC that reached beyond a mere prohibition of formal discrimination.[118] This is illustrated by the following passage:

> The restrictions to be abolished pursuant to Articles 59 and 60 include all requirements imposed on the person providing the service by reason in particular of his nationality or of the fact that he does not habitually reside in the State where the service is provided, which do not apply to persons established within the national territory or which may prevent or otherwise obstruct the activities of the person providing the service.[119]

The CJEU's finding that measures which 'prevent or otherwise obstruct the activities of the person providing the service' constitute 'restrictions' in the meaning of the Treaty nonetheless points towards a broad interpretation of Article 59 EEC, encompassing distinctly and indistinctly applicable measures alike. The concept of 'obstructing' the service providers is reminiscent of the language of 'hindering' trade as used in *Dassonville*, which was decided earlier the same year. And just as in *Dassonville*, the CJEU recognized that indistinctly applicable measures might serve reasonable regulatory goals, and would not, prima facie, constitute a breach of the Treaty freedom provisions:[120]

> [T]aking into account the particular nature of the services to be provided, specific requirements imposed on the person providing the service cannot be considered incompatible with the Treaty where they have as their purpose the application of professional rules justified by the general good—in particular rules relating to organization, qualifications, professional ethics, supervision and liability—which are binding upon any person established in the State in which the service is provided, where the person providing the service would escape from the ambit of those rules being established in another Member State.[121]

The ensuing conflict between a broadly interpreted Article 59 EEC on the one hand and national requirements 'justified by the general good' on the other is then

[116] Everling (n 99), 60.

[117] Vassilis Hatzopoulos, *Regulating Services in the European Union* (Oxford University Press, 2012) 103.

[118] See Grabitz (n 14), 660.

[119] Case 33/74, *Johannes Henricus Maria van Binsbergen v Bestuur van de Bedrijfsvereniging voor de Metaalnijverheid* [1974] ECR 1299 (hereinafter *Van Binsbergen)*, para 10.

[120] See on this for example Philippa Watson, 'Freedom of establishment and freedom to provide services: some recent developments' (1983) 20 *Common Market Law Review* 767, 789–90.

[121] *Van Binsbergen*, para 12.

solved on the basis of a necessity test similar to the one proposed by Directive 70/50/EEC:

> [T]he requirement of residence within that State constitutes a restriction which is incompatible with Articles 59 and 60 of the Treaty if the administration of justice can satisfactorily be ensured by measures which are less restrictive.[122]

The essential doctrinal structure of today's internal market case law can therefore be identified in one of the CJEU's earliest decisions on the freedom to provide services: the formal scope of Article 59 EEC was defined in a broad way, but the substantive question whether a national measure was in fact prohibited remained open and had to be answered on a case-by-case basis. Another decision that illustrates this approach is *Wesemael* (1979), which was issued a month before *Cassis*.[123] The case dealt with a Belgian measure which held that 'the operation of a fee-charging employment agency for entertainers shall be subject to the grant of a licence by the Minister responsible for employment' and that 'foreign employment agencies for entertainers may not, in the absence of a reciprocal convention between Belgium and their country, place anyone in employment in Belgium except through a fee-charging employment agency holding a licence.'[124] The CJEU ruled:

> Taking into account the particular nature of certain services to be provided, such as the placing of entertainers in employment, specific requirements imposed on persons providing services cannot be considered incompatible with the Treaty where they have as their purpose the application of professional rules, justified by the general good or by the need to ensure the protection of the entertainer, which are binding upon any person established in the said State, in so far as the person providing the service is not subject to similar requirements in the Member State in which he is established.[125]

The CJEU declared that national measures designed to serve ('justified by') the 'general good' or 'the protection of the entertainer' were not per se incompatible with the Treaty freedom provisions. The CJEU defined the additional requirement that Member States may subject service providers from other Member States to its own requirements only if they are 'not subject to similar requirements in the Member State in which he is established', which essentially mirrors the mutual recognition requirement employed in *Cassis*.

The CJEU equally interpreted the freedom of establishment provisions in a formally broad way from early onwards. According to the CJEU, Article 52 EEC covered not only formally discriminatory measures, but also indistinctly applicable measures if they had an adverse effect on mobility. In *Thieffry*, the CJEU found that the requirement to hold a French diploma to join the Bar association—a requirement that did not formally discriminate on grounds of the nationality

[122] ibid, para 16.

[123] The parallel between the cases is identified also by Watson (n 120), 823–24.

[124] Joined Cases 110 and 111/78, *Ministère public and 'Chambre syndicale des agents artistiques et impresarii de Belgique' ASBL v Willy van Wesemael and others* [1979] ECR 35 (hereinafter *Wesemael*), para 3.

[125] ibid, para 28.

of the individual concerned—constituted a restriction of the freedom of establishment.[126] At the same time, the CJEU clearly held, as it already had in *Van Binsbergen*, that national measures restricting the free movement could prevail if the national measures were justified on grounds relating to the general interest.[127] Measures justified by the public interest are not prohibited under Article 52 EEC, as the CJEU held, for example, in *Commission/Germany* (1986):

> It therefore appears that in the field in question there are imperative reasons relating to the public interest which may justify restrictions on the freedom to provide services, provided, however, that the rules of the State of establishment are not adequate in order to achieve the necessary level of protection and that the requirements of the State in which the service is provided do not exceed what is necessary in that respect.[128]

We can see that, similarly to Article 30 EEC, Articles 52 and 59 EEC were interpreted already in the earliest cases as broad in a formal sense, and open in substance. It is therefore plausible to define Articles 49 and 56 TFEU as pluralist instruments.

BALANCING IN INTERNAL MARKET LAW

Since the end of the transitional period, the Treaty freedoms have been interpreted as individual rights that could be enforced directly in national courts. The core substance of these rights has been held to be national treatment: they prohibit differential treatment on the basis of nationality, seat or origin of goods. As we have seen, however, the scope of the Treaty freedoms have been viewed as reaching beyond this core from very early onwards, granting a right of economic mobility free from restrictions. Like any legal right, however, this right is only relative. Its specific substance cannot be defined in the abstract, and must be established in relationship to the specific national law concerned. We have seen that the underlying assumption is that an interpretation of the Treaty freedoms that extends to indistinctly applicable measures is liable to come into conflict with potentially 'reasonable' national regulation, which cannot be exempted by an general formula, but must often be dealt with on a case-by-case basis.[129] The doctrinal tool to establish the substantive meaning of the Treaty freedom provisions in relation to the specific situation in question is proportionality balancing. This instrument was proposed by Directive 70/50/EEC, and was adopted by the CJEU in some of its earliest internal market law decisions. On the following pages we will look closer at proportionality balancing. We attempt to identify how the instrument of proportionality balancing relates to the pluralist character of the Treaty freedom provisions that we have identified in the previous sections. We will first look at

[126] Case 71/76, *Jean Thieffry v Conseil de l'ordre des avocats à la cour de paris* [1977] ECR 766 (hereinafter *Thieffry*).

[127] *Thieffry*, para 19.

[128] Case 205/84, *Commission/Germany* [1986] ECR 3755, para 33.

[129] See Alec Stone Sweet and Jud Mathews, 'Proportionality balancing and global constitutionalism' (2008) 47 *Columbia Journal of Transnational Law* 73, 142.

some of the theoretical scholarship. It will be shown that many commentators conceptualize balancing as a pluralist instrument, as it presupposes the existence of different, prima facie equally valid regulatory interests. We will then look at the way the CJEU employs the proportionality analysis in practice.

Proportionality Balancing as an Open-Ended Process and as Political Choice

Stone Sweet and Mathews describe proportionality balancing as 'a decision-making procedure and an "analytical structure" that judges employ to deal with tensions between two pleaded constitutional "values" or "interests".'[130] And:

> The move to balancing makes it clear: (a) that each party is pleading a constitutionally-legitimate norm or value; (b) that, a priori, the court holds each of these interests in equally high esteem; (c) that determining which value shall prevail in any given case is not a mechanical exercise, but is a difficult judicial task involving complex policy considerations; and (d) that future cases pitting the same two legal interests against one another may well be decided differently, depending on the facts.[131]

Whereas rule-based adjudication is sometimes mistakenly conceptualized as a quasi-technical endeavour whereby 'correct' solutions are deduced from general provisions,[132] proportionality balancing is more obviously based on the assumption that general rules do not presuppose a specific outcome; the result of balancing is a priori open-ended. Stone Sweet and Mathews state: 'In balancing situations, such frameworks incorporate inconsistency—that is, argumentation—to the extent that each inference step offers both a defensible argument and counter argument, from which contradictory but defensible conclusions can be reached.'[133] Some proponents of balancing, like Robert Alexy and Aharon Barak, have attempted to show that judgments based on proportionality balancing are more than arbitrary choices by the judges, as the doctrinal system of balancing requires them to engage in a highly rational form of reasoning. Alexy's 'law of balancing' is an attempt to objectify judicial choice in balancing. Alexy's rule holds: 'The greater the degree of non-satisfaction of, or detriment to, one principle, the greater must be the importance of satisfying the other.'[134] Barak aims in a similar direction: 'Some claim that [balancing] attempts to balance incommensurable

[130] ibid, 75.

[131] ibid, 88.

[132] Paulson described this as the 'formalist fallacy', which is 'to mistake a theorist's deduction for a legal effect—here, to suppose that a logically valid inference from N to n yields a legally valid individual norm n.' Stanley Paulson, 'Book review on Überlegungen zu Hans Kelsens "Allgemeine Theorie der Normen" by Kazimierz Opalek, and "Untersuchungen zur Stufenbaulehre Adolf Merkls und Hans Kelsens", by Jürgen Behrend' (1982) 27 *American Journal of Jurisprudence* 159, 161.

[133] Stone Sweet and Mathews (n 129), 89; see also Aharon Barak, 'Proportionality and Principled Balancing' (2010) 4 *Law & Ethics of Human Rights* 1, 5; Alexander Aleinikoff, 'Constitutional Law in the Age of Balancing' (1987) 96 *Yale Law Journal* 943, 960f.

[134] Robert Alexy, *A Theory of Constitutional Rights* (Oxford University Press, 2002) 102.

items. My answer is that a common base for comparison exists, namely the social marginal importance.'[135] Barak assumes that comparing 'marginal' gains and losses is a way for the court to evade grand policy choices:

> How can one compare the benefit to state security with the limitation on freedom of speech? Bearing these difficulties in mind, at the very outset it seems appropriate to make two clarifications: First, the comparison is not between the advantages gained by realizing the goal in contrast to the effect brought by limiting the right. Nor is it between security and liberty. The comparison is between the marginal benefit to security and the marginal harm to the right caused by the restricting law and as such, the comparison is concerned with the marginal and the incremental.[136]

Accordingly, Julian Rivers argued that proportionality analysis should be 'understood as a rational device for the optimization of interests.'[137]

But even if proportionality balancing may be exercised in a highly 'rational' form, any decision ultimately constitutes a choice by the judge.[138] Alexy acknowledges that his theory does not answer the question what relative importance judges attribute to the balanced principles.[139] And Barak explains that the proportionality test 'cannot eliminate value judgment in the process of balancing.'[140] This element of choice in balancing, Stone Sweet and Mathews hold, can be described as judicial law-making: 'When it comes to constitutional adjudication, balancing can never be dissociated from lawmaking: it requires judges to behave as legislators do, or to sit in judgment of a prior act of balancing performed by elected officials.'[141] According to Stone Sweet and Mathews this means that 'however inherently "judicial" one takes the procedure to be, the least restrictive means test, and balancing stages of proportionality analysis fully expose judges as lawmakers.'[142]

Of course, procedural rules that surround balancing may limit judicial discretion: rules on the burden of proof or on levels of scrutiny can significantly influence the outcome of the judgment.[143] At the same time, such procedural structures themselves frequently imply judicial choice. Most notably, this is the case with the framing of the proportionality analysis. Fried argued in this regard:

> In choosing what it considers the appropriate formulation of the conflict, the Court must decide not only against what background, in terms of what social role, the interests of the parties ought to be judged, but also what role the Court will assign to itself in this area.[144]

[135] Barak (n 133), 16.
[136] ibid, 8.
[137] Julian Rivers, 'Proportionality and Variable Intensity of Review' (2006) 65 *Cambridge Law Journal* 174, 207.
[138] See for example Bernhard Schlink, 'Proportionality in Constitutional Law: Why Everywhere but Here' (2011) 22 *Duke Journal of Comparative & International Law* 291, 299.
[139] Alexy (n 134), 100, 105.
[140] Barak (n 133), 8.
[141] Stone Sweet and Mathews (n 129), 87.
[142] ibid, 76.
[143] In this sense Schlink (n 138), 300.
[144] Charles Fried, 'Two Concepts of Interests: Some Reflections on the Supreme Courts Balancing Test' (1962) 76 *Harvard Law Review* 755, 759.

Aleinikoff provided the following example of how such framing may shape the outcome:

> Balancing opinions typically pit individual against governmental interests. This characterization, however, is arbitrary. Interests may be conceived of in both public and private terms. The individual interest in communicating one's ideas to others may also be stated as a societal interest in a diverse marketplace of ideas. Time, place, and manner limitations on expressive behavior may be based on a governmental interest in public safety or a private interest in unencumbered access to public facilities.[145]

Proportionality balancing therefore seems to be best understood as a doctrinal instrument that structures or rationalizes judicial decision-making, but does usually not presuppose its outcome, or at least leaves ample discretion. In particular, it does not reduce the element of (explicit and implicit) political choice inherent in judicial decision-making.[146] It is in this sense that proportionality analysis can be described as a potentially pluralist instrument because it frequently will not predetermine the outcome in substantive terms. In the next section, we will look at the way the CJEU employs proportionality balancing in practice.

Proportionality Balancing in Internal Market Law

We have seen in the previous sections that the CJEU adopted, from its earliest judgments onwards, the proportionality test in order to adjudicate competence conflicts between the European and the national levels. It aims to balance the Treaty freedoms with the regulatory goals pursued by the Member States. A typical formulation employed by the CJEU to describe this task can be found in the *Beer Cans* case:

> [I]n the absence of common rules relating to the marketing of the products in question, obstacles to free movement within the Community resulting from disparities between the national laws must be accepted in so far as such rules, applicable to domestic and imported products without distinction, may be recognized as being necessary in order to satisfy mandatory requirements recognized by Community law. Such rules must also be proportionate to the aim in view. If a Member State has a choice between various

[145] Aleinikoff (n 133), 981.

[146] Kumm has described balancing as an 'analytical structure', and authors like Barak or Alexy have developed complex frameworks to improve and refine the balancing test in the interest of transparency and predictability as well as the limitation of discretion. It has been emphasized by Kumm and Cohen-Eliya and Porat that judicial review on the basis of proportionality analysis can also potentially enhance legislation, as it forces legislators to justify their choices. Barak (n 133), 14; Moshe Cohen-Eliya and Iddo Porat, 'Proportionality and the Culture of Justification' (2011) 59 *American Journal of Comparative Law* 463, 466–647; Mattias Kumm, 'Institutionalising Socratic Contestation: The Rationalist Human Rights Paradigm, Legitimate Authority and the Point of Judicial Review' (2007) 1 *European Journal of Legal Studies* 2, 142; Mattias Kumm, 'Constitutional rights as principles: On the structure and domain of constitutional justice' (2004) 2 *International Journal of Constitutional Law* 574, 579.

> measures for achieving the same aim, it should choose the means which least restricts the free movement of goods.[147]

In the absence of harmonization at the European level which may pre-empt national regulation, Member States are free to enact measures to pursue regulatory goals they deem important. The precise character of the regulatory goals that Member States can pursue was subject to some debate in the 1970s and 1980s. AG Trabucchi proposed in *Kramer* (1976) that exceptions could be understood as expressions of the regulatory interests either of the Member States, or of the Community.[148] In the latter sense the Member States would essentially act as agents of the Community interests. *Kramer* dealt with a Dutch measure aimed at conserving maritime resources. As the Community had not yet regulated this field, AG Trabucchi argued, national measures could be constructed as measures enacted in lieu of Community measures:

> In such circumstances the State may be regarded as having acted as an agency of the Community and its action, reflecting the common interest, could be adopted by the Community, possibly through formal ratification by the authority which, under the Treaty, was itself empowered to adopt restrictive measures in the same field or to authorize their adoption on the part of the States.[149]

From this perspective, restrictive measures could be justified if they served Community interests.[150] While this view re-emerges from time to time (the quote from the *Beer Cans* case similarly implies such understanding), the CJEU usually seems to assume that Member States may pass regulation for any reason they seem fit, and in any area that is not pre-empted.[151] Arguing in this sense, Zuleeg held: 'The member states of the European Communities are restricted in the execution of their legislative competencies only insofar as the intended regulation contradicts Community law.'[152] This approach can be observed, for example, in the *Cinéthèque* decision:

> The reply to the questions referred to the Court is therefore that Article 30 of the EEC Treaty must be interpreted as meaning that it does not apply to national legislation which regulates the distribution of cinematographic works by imposing an interval between one mode of distributing such works and another by prohibiting their simultaneous exploitation in cinemas and in video-cassette form for a limited period, provided that the prohibition applies to domestically produced and imported cassettes alike and any barriers to intra-Community trade to which its implementation may give rise do not exceed

[147] Case 302/86, *Commission/Denmark* (beer cans) [1988] ECR 4607, para 6.

[148] Case 3/76, *Cornelis Kramer and Others* [1976] ECR 1279 (hereinafter *Kramer*).

[149] *Kramer*, Opinion of AG Trambucchi, para 1326.

[150] See also Tridimas who argues that the Court 'assesses the proportionality of a national measure not *vis-á-vis* its adverse impact on the primary Community interest (ie free movement), which is what brings the measure within the scope of Community law in the first instance, but on an incidental Community objective (ie human rights) with which the measure must conform.' Tridimas (n 89), 194.

[151] See Moens (n 61), 735, Zuleeg (n 37), 6.

[152] Zuleeg (n 37), 21.

> what is necessary for ensuring that the exploitation in cinemas of cinematographic works of all origins retains priority over other means of distribution.[153]

The passage from *Cinéthèque* shows that, as long as they apply indistinctly to domestic and imported goods alike, national measures may be based on all kinds of regulatory objectives, including more obscure goals such as that 'the exploitation in cinemas of cinematographic works of all origins retains priority over other means of distribution'. The CJEU does not subject the national measure to substantive requirements, and merely demands it to 'not exceed what is necessary' for achieving that regulatory objective.[154]

The CJEU often emphasizes that it is up to the Member States to decide on the appropriate level of protection in regard to the regulatory interests they pursue.[155] In *De Peijper*, the CJEU had argued that 'it is for the Member States, within the limits imposed by the Treaty, to decide what degree of protection they intend to assure and in particular how strict the checks to be carried out are to be.'[156] In *Läärä*, the CJEU held that 'the mere fact that a Member State has opted for a system of protection which differs from that adopted by another Member State cannot affect the assessment of the need for, and proportionality of, the provisions enacted to that end. Those provisions must be assessed solely by reference to the objectives pursued by the national authorities of the Member State concerned and the level of protection which they are intended to provide.'[157] In the current doctrinal system of internal market law the proportionality therefore serves the function to accommodate the Treaty freedoms with other regulatory goals pursued by the Member States, which they are free to set as they wish under the conditions discussed above. The abstract structure of the proportionality test is, as we have seen, potentially pluralist, as it presupposes that in a given situation a number of equally valid regulatory interests may be at stake. This seems to be the case also in internal market law: the right to free movement is, prima facie, of the same importance as, for example, goals like health or environmental protection. Within this pluralist framework, judicial decision-making constitutes an act of political choice because the legal system does not assign priority to one of the affected values over others.[158]

The clearest manifestation of proportionality analysis as a pluralist instrument within which judicial decision-making appears as an act of political choice is in the

[153] Joined Cases 60 and 61/84 *Cinéthèque SA and others v Fédération nationale des cinémas français* [1985] ECR 2605 (hereinafter *Cinéthèque*), para 24.

[154] Evans (n 79), 593.

[155] Jan Jans, 'Proportionality revisited' (2000) 27 *Legal Issues of Economic Integration* 239, 249.

[156] Case 16/74 *Centrafarm BV and Adriaan de Peijper v Winthrop BV* [1974] ECR 1183 (hereinafter *De Peijper*), para 15.

[157] Case C-124/97, *Markku Juhani Läärä, Cotswold Microsystems Ltd and Oy Transatlantic Software Ltd v Kihlakunnansyyttäjä (Jyväskylä) and Suomen valtio (Finnish State)* [1999] ECR I-6067 (hereinafter *Läärä*), para 36; see also Jans (n 155), 249.

[158] According to Tridimas, within the system of internal market law characterized by a broad scope of the Treaty freedoms and a proportionality analysis, the Court engages in 'choices of a broadly political nature'. Tridimas (n 89), 198.

exceptional cases when the CJEU explicitly employs the third step of the proportionality test, the proportionality analysis *stricto sensu*. In *B & Q Plc*, one of the UK Sunday trading cases, the CJEU held: 'Appraising the proportionality of national rules which pursue a legitimate aim under Community law involves weighing the national interest in attaining that aim against the Community interest in ensuring the free movement of goods.'[159] In this formula, the CJEU describes its task in the same way we did just now, ie, as the decision between competing regulatory interests. This decision is an active act of political choice by the CJEU, as the Treaty rules do not prima facie determine the outcome. This underlines the pluralist character of the doctrinal structure within the balancing is performed. But even in a setting where the CJEU does not explicitly engage in a weighing of the competing interests, the doctrinal structure remains pluralist: in the overwhelming part of the case law, the CJEU does not explicitly employ the third prong, restricting itself to the first and second prongs instead.[160] According to a common formula employed by the CJEU, it must be ensured 'that the provisions of national law in question must be proportionate to the objective pursued and that objective must not be capable of being achieved by measures which are less restrictive of intra-Community trade.'[161] The CJEU therefore is ostensibly not engaged in an active weighing of competing regulatory interests, and merely evaluates the national measure in its own terms, ie, whether the national measure is suitable to achieve the purported goal, and whether there are means to achieve the same purpose that are less restrictive to the free movement. Nonetheless the normative character of the proportionality analysis remains pluralist even in this form because it does not restrict the regulatory goals that a national measure can pursue or define some form of substantive limitation.[162]

As already briefly discussed at an earlier point, the CJEU's internal market law adjudication has repeatedly been criticised for its lopsided outcomes. For example, Gareth Davies has identified a bias in favour of free movement vis-à-vis other regulatory objectives.[163] Fischer-Lescano and Möller have argued that, in cases where the Treaty freedoms conflicted with social rights, the CJEU

[159] Case C-169/91, *Council of the City of Stoke-on-Trent and Norwich City Council and B & Q Plc* [1992] ECR I-6654 (hereinafter *B & Q plc*), para 15; see also Jans (n 155), 249.

[160] ibid, 249.

[161] Case C-368/95, *Familiapress v Bauer Verlag* [1997] ECR I-3709, para 19; see also Jans (n 155), 249.

[162] At the same time, the first and in particular the second prong imply political choices as well. The Court has, for example, held in *Commission/Austria* (2005) that entry examinations constitute less restrictive means to quotas indirectly based on nationality. By contrast, in *Bressol* (2010), the Court emphasized that the choice between open and restricted university access is a political choice that is for the Member States to make. It could be argued, therefore, that—whether or not proportionality *stricto sensu* is explicitly taken under consideration—the proportionality test establishes a degree of discretion for the Court. Case C-147/03, *Commission/Austria* [2005] ECR I-5969, para 61; Case C-73/08, *Nicolas Bressol and Others and Céline Chaverot and Others v Gouvernement de la Communauté française* [2010] ECR I-2735 (hereinafter *Bressol*), paras 28–29.

[163] Gaseth Davies, 'Democracy and Legitimacy in the Shadow of Purposive Competence' (2015) 21 *European Law Journal* 2, 12.

had consistently given preference to the former.[164] Höpner and Schäfer have pointed at the 'golden share' cases, the *Centros* case law on secondary establishment, and at taxation cases like *Cadbury Schweppes* as ideologically biased decisions.[165] Consumer law scholars have frequently criticized the consumer ideal that underlies the CJEU's decisions.[166] I myself argued a while ago that the CJEU's decisions in the 2007/2008 labour law cases—*Laval*, *Viking*, *Rüffert* and *Commission/Luxembourg*—exhibit a neoliberal bias.[167] I still believe that this is the case. However, the argument made in this chapter is that this bias does not follow from the Treaty provisions or the doctrinal system developed on its basis, which remains agnostic as to the weight to be assigned to the various interests concerned. This means that the bias must be located at a different point. For example, it may partly follow from the way the CJEU assigns the burden of proof, as Davies seems to suggest.[168] Or, as I argued, the bias may have entered the decision because the CJEU interprets the Treaty provisions on the basis of one-sided economic assumptions which over-estimates the beneficial effects of cross-border mobility. However, the CJEU is not required by the Treaty to assign the burden of proof the way it does, or to interpret the free movement provisions on the basis of a specific socio-economic paradigm, to the exclusion of others (as will be shown in the next chapter). Instead, these decisions must be conceptualized as political choices by the CJEU, which consequently require political justification.

To conclude, it can be held that the Treaty freedoms have been interpreted as broad in formal terms, and open in substantive terms ever since the Community's early years. This openness finds doctrinal expression in the proportionality analysis, which we identified as a potentially pluralist instrument. Surely it is possible that internal market case law or a subset thereof is biased in favour of certain interests or regulatory objectives for reasons that may range from the procedural setup of the system to hegemonic economic ideology and political preferences of the judges. The central claim of the preceding sections was that any such bias cannot be assumed to be normatively required by internal market law, which is pluralist in nature and does not give preference to any specific socio-economic paradigm or regulatory concern. Rather, such bias would then have to be conceptualized as a political choice, which of course constitutes an inherent part of judicial

[164] Andreas Fischer-Lescano and Kolja Möller, 'Soziale Rechtspolitik in Europa' Friedrich Ebert Stiftung library.fes.de/pdf-files/id/ipa/09344.pdf, 8.

[165] Martin Höpner and Armin Schäfer, 'Embeddedness and Regional Integration: Waiting for Polanyi in a Hayekian Setting' (2012) 66 *International Organization* 429, 442–45.

[166] See for example Vanessa Mak, 'Standards of Protection: In Search of the "Average Consumer" of EU Law in the Proposal for a Consumer Rights Directive' (2010) 19 *European Review of Private Law* 25.

[167] Clemens Kaupa, 'Maybe not activist enough? On the Court's alleged neoliberal bias in its recent labor cases' in Bruno De Witte, Mark Dawson and Elise Muir (eds), *Judicial Activism at the European Court of Justice: Causes, Responses and Solutions* (Edward Elgar, 2013).

[168] Davies (n 163), 12.

decision-making. While the Treaty freedoms have thus been 'constitutionalized', this can ultimately be understood only as the imposition of certain procedural requirements.

TWO STUDIES OF DOCTRINES IN INTERNAL MARKET LAW ADJUDICATION

The CJEU employs a number of interpretative doctrines in internal market law that are sometimes assumed to have substantive implications. In this section, we will look at two important examples: the 'interpreting strictly' doctrine and the 'reasons of a purely economic nature' doctrine. These doctrines are sometimes misunderstood to have a substantive implication in the light of competing socio-economic paradigms. It will be shown, however, that both doctrines are of a purely procedural nature, and cannot be read in substantive terms.

The 'Interpreting Strictly' Doctrine

The CJEU routinely holds that exceptions in EU law should be 'interpreted strictly' or 'narrowly'. One field of application of this doctrine is internal market law, where the CJEU rules that the Treaty-based exceptions (such as Article 36 TFEU) are to be interpreted 'strictly' or 'narrowly'.[169] As I will show, the CJEU's case law is extremely clear and consistent on the meaning of this interpretative doctrine: if a provision constitutes an exception to a rule, no expansive (but also no reductionist) understanding of this provision should be adopted. Ultimately, the 'interpreted strictly' doctrine is nothing but a restatement of the general hermeneutic requirement that provisions should be interpreted according to their textual meaning and their regulatory function.

Despite the CJEU's clear and consistent case law, the doctrine can give rise to considerable misunderstandings in the field of internal market law. These misunderstandings are based on what could be called a 'metaphorical understanding' of the doctrine: according to this view, the 'interpreting strictly' doctrine would be read as a mandate for the CJEU to accord more weight to the rights based on the Treaty freedoms than to other regulatory interests. Understood metaphorically, the scale would lean toward the Treaty freedoms so that the competing interests would have to be of exceptional weight in order to trump the Treaty freedoms. However, such an understanding of the 'interpreting strictly' doctrine is incorrect. First, the CJEU has always used the doctrine solely in regard to the express Treaty derogations, and not in regard to mandatory requirements/overriding interests. It employed the doctrine not to whittle down the exceptions, but to restrict the reasons that can be invoked under Article 36 TFEU, which is relevant mainly in regard

[169] The CJEU employs the two phrases interchangeably. For reasons of clarity I will exclusively use the form of 'interpreting strictly' from here onwards.

The 'Interpreting Strictly' Doctrine in Internal Market Law

In internal market law, the CJEU held that the Treaty exceptions—such as Article 36 TFEU—are to be interpreted 'strictly' because they constitute exceptions from the fundamental principle of free movement.[184] An early case where the doctrine was discussed in the context of internal market law was *Salgoil.*[185] The case dealt with the question whether a company had a subjective right under Article 31 EEC to take action against a refusal of an import licence by the Italian authorities. In that case it was also pointed out by AG Gand—and confirmed by the CJEU—that provisions such as Articles 36, 224 and 226 EEC 'are provisions authorizing exceptions, which should be interpreted strictly, and which cannot be invoked to deny the existence of rights created by other provisions of the Treaty.'[186] In *SAIL* (1972), AG Roemer further explained how the 'interpreting strictly' doctrine should be understood. The case dealt with an Italian milk-selling monopoly, where the right to sell milk was granted exclusively to 'milk centres':

> [I]t appears above all that because it is a derogating provision Article 36 must be interpreted strictly. Unquestionably, it is not enough that the words used by the national legislature show that the measure in question was adopted on the grounds of the protection of health; independently of the manner in which the legislature has described it, it is necessary on the contrary to consider whether this measure is necessary and suitable for the purpose described.[187]

AG Roemer defined the 'interpreted strictly' requirement essentially in procedural terms: determining whether the measure was in fact 'necessary' and 'suitable' to achieve the purported goals. The CJEU followed the AG, and held that the monopoly was not necessary in the sense that the current technical conditions and the rules to which milk was subject were 'in themselves sufficient to ensure hygiene and public health.'[188] Today, both criteria—suitability and necessity—are routinely applied as part of the proportionality test.

established by means of interpretation. Provisions that appear connected in such way may in fact be 'an independent component of the obligation system' (AG Kokott in *SPCM*, para 42). See, as an example, discussions on the question whether the Treaty's transport chapter constitutes merely an exception to the services chapter: Case 167/73, *Commission/France* [1974] ECR 359, Opinion of AG Reischl, p 378; Case C-251/04, *Commission/Greece* [2007] ECR I-67, Opinion of AG Sharpston, para 28; see also Case C-558/07, *The Queen, on the application of SPCM SA, CH Erbslöh KG, Lake Chemicals and Minerals Ltd and Hercules Inc v Secretary of State for the Environment, Food and Rural Affairs* [2009] ECR I-5783 (hereinafter *SPCM*), Opinion of AG Kokott, para 42.

[184] Case 29/72, *SpA Marimex v Italian Finance Administration* [1972] ECR 1309; Case 34/79, *Regina v Maurice Donald Henn and John Frederick Ernest Darby* [1979] ECR 3795, Opinion of AG Warner, p 3825.

[185] Case 13/68, *SpA Salgoil v Italian Ministry of Foreign Trade, Rome* [1968] ECR 661 (hereinafter *Salgoil*).

[186] *Salgoil*, Opinion of AG Gand, p 459.

[187] Case 82/71, *Ministère public de la Italian Republic v Società agricola industria latte (SAIL)* [1972] ECR 119, Opinion of AG Roemer, p 145 (hereinafter *SAIL*).

[188] *SAIL*, 133.

The way the CJEU has applied the 'interpreting strictly' doctrine since its first decisions is mainly procedural. By this I mean that the CJEU requires national measures to be consistent with the goal they purport to pursue, and that no less restrictive a measure is conceivable that would lead to the same outcome. I call this approach 'procedural' because the CJEU does not rule on whether the measure is reasonable in substantive terms. Instead, it merely scrutinizes the consistency of the Member State's own contention. Other decisions add to the picture that the CJEU applies a mainly procedural framework when it demands exceptions to the Treaty freedoms to be interpreted 'strictly'. In *Denkavit* (1979), for example, the CJEU held that it is up to the Member States that rely on Article 36 EEC to prove that their measures actually satisfy the criteria of that provision.[189] The CJEU would review a Member State's measure without actually questioning or disputing its political considerations, but merely the consistency of the measure.

This system—with the CJEU expressively deferring to the Member State's regulatory choices, while reviewing the consistency of the measure—has been most clearly expounded in the CJEU's review of Treaty-based restrictions on the free movement of persons. The classic formulation of this approach can be found in *van Duyn*:

> The concept of public policy in the context of the Community and where, in particular, it is used as a justification for derogating from a fundamental principle of Community law, must be *interpreted strictly*, so that its scope cannot be determined unilaterally by each Member State without being subject to control by the institutions of the Community. Nevertheless, the particular circumstances justifying recourse to the concept of public policy may vary from one country to another and from one period to another, and it is therefore necessary in this matter to allow the competent national authorities an area of discretion within the limits imposed by the Treaty.[190]

The CJEU acknowledged the political choices of the Member States in regard to their security, public policy and health concerns, while at the same time reviewing the consistency of these choices in the light of their Treaty obligations. This approach was pursued in other 1970s mobility cases such as *Bonsignore, Rutili* and *Bouchereau*, and in countless other cases since.[191]

The tight limitations that the CJEU enforced on the Member States' ability to invoke the public policy/security/health exceptions should not be misunderstood as a substantive choice by the CJEU. It would be wrong to take these cases as evidence that the CJEU generally assigned a greater weight to mobility rights than to the Member States' security interests. Instead, the CJEU enforced the Member

[189] Case 251/78, *Firma Denkavit Futtermittel GmbH v Minister für Ernähung, Landwirtschaft und Forsten des Landes Nordrhein-Westfalen* [1979] ECR 3369 (hereinafter *Denkavit*), para 24.

[190] Case 41/74, *Yvonne van Duyn v Home Office* [1974] ECR 1337 (hereinafter *van Duyn*), para 18, emphasis added.

[191] Case 67/74, *Carmelo Angelo Bonsignore v Oberstadtdirektor der Stadt Köln* [1975] ECR 297 (hereinafter *Bonsignore*); Case 36/75, *Roland Rutili v Ministre de l'intérieur* [1975] ECR 1219 (hereinafter *Rutili*); Case 30/77, *Régina v Pierre Bouchereau* [1977] ECR 1999 (hereinafter *van Bouchereau*).

States' own legislative choices, as expressed in Directive 64/221/EEC.[192] Most limitations on the discretion of Member States that today are associated with CJEU case law have in fact been adopted in this Directive. These include the following rules: measures must be based exclusively on the individual's personal conduct (Article 3(1)); previous criminal convictions do not in themselves constitute sufficient grounds for measures like expulsion (Article 3(2)); expiry of documents does not justify expulsion (Article 3(3)); the application of due process rights (Article 8), etc. Clearly the CJEU has since then played an important role in fortifying these strong limitations on Member States' discretion. Nonetheless, the Member States themselves defined this level at the outset. This is expressed, for example, in AG Mayras' opinion in *Bonsignore*:

> In order to begin my consideration of these questions, I consider it necessary to refer to the Court's important judgment in the van Duyn case. In that decision you confirmed, first, that Article 48 of the Treaty is directly applicable, while maintaining that, as regards the principle of free movement and the right of residence of migrant workers, the third paragraph of this article subjects them to limitations justified on grounds of public policy and, in particular, public security. However, this limitation, which constitutes an exception to the right conferred by Article 48 on EEC nationals, must be *strictly construed in the light of Council Directive No 64/221/EEC.*[193]

The Treaty-based exceptions were therefore interpreted according to the regulatory goal of the European legislators.[194] In this sense, interpreting the exceptions 'strictly' means allowing little discretion to move away from the limits set by the text and the purpose of the provision. This is expressed, for example in the decision in *Sotgiu* (1974), where an Italian postal worker in Germany received a smaller 'separation allowance' for living away from home than German workers.[195] The CJEU refused the application of the public service provision of Article 48(4) EEC, arguing that it allowed restricting admission to certain activities, but not discrimination of workers once they have been admitted to public service. The CJEU reasoned: 'Taking account of the fundamental nature, in the scheme of the Treaty, of the principles of freedom of movement and equality of treatment of workers within the Community, the exceptions made by Article 48(4) cannot have a scope going beyond the aim in view of which this derogation was

[192] Council Directive 64/221/EEC on the coordination of special measures concerning the movement and residence of foreign nationals which are justified on grounds of public policy, public security or public health [1964] OJ 56/850.

[193] *Bonsignore*, Opinion of AG Mayras, p 310, emphasis added.

[194] Today, the Court sometimes interprets the Treaty provisions not in the light of the secondary law specifications, but against them, eg in *Grzelczyk* and *Bidar*. Case C-184/99, *Rudy Grzelczyk v Centre public d'aide sociale d'Ottignies-Louvain-la-Neuve* [2001] ECR I-6193 (hereinafter *Grzelczyk*); Case C-209/03, *The Queen, on the application of Dany Bidar v London Borough of Ealing and Secretary of State for Education and Skills* [2005] ECR I-2199 (hereinafter *Bidar*).

[195] Case 152/73, *Giovanni Maria Sotgiu v Deutsche Bundespost* [1974] ECR 153 (hereinafter *Sotgiu*).

included.'[196] The CJEU's argument is not based on a substantive evaluation of what does and what does not count as public service; instead, the CJEU applied a procedural, consistency-oriented test: 'The very fact that they have been admitted shows indeed that those interests which justify the exceptions to the principle of non-discrimination permitted by Article 48(4) are not at issue.'[197] A 'strict' interpretation of the public-service exception therefore essentially means taking the regulatory choices of the European legislators seriously. If they explicitly allowed for differential treatment in regard to the access to public employment, then this exception is to be accepted. Apart from that, however, the general rule of equal treatment of workers—to which Article 48(4) EEC constituted an exception—prevents an expansive interpretation of the public-service provision that is not covered by the text and purpose of the provision.

After *Cassis de Dijon*, the 'interpreting strictly' doctrine received an additional function. As new grounds—such as consumer protection—could now be invoked to justify restrictions of Article 30 EEC (Article 34 TFEU), the doctrine now helped the CJEU to differentiate between grounds that could justify directly discriminatory measures (those of Article 36 TFEU), and those that could not (the mandatory requirements).[198] The CJEU refused to let Member States invoke grounds other than those of Article 36 TFEU to justify directly discriminatory measures. It bolstered the position with the argument that Article 36 TFEU is to be interpreted 'strictly', so that no other grounds could be granted a similar effect.[199] While the CJEU employed the 'interpreting strictly' doctrine to differentiate between these two types of justifications, it virtually never held that mandatory requirements themselves should be 'interpreted strictly', though a few exceptions can be found.[200] This makes a substantive understanding of the doctrine implausible,

[196] *Sotgiu*, para 4.

[197] *Sotgiu*, para 4.

[198] See for example Case C-312/98, *Schutzverband gegen Unwesen in der Wirtschaft eV v Warsteiner Brauerei Haus Cramer GmbH & Co KG* [2000] ECR I-9187, Opinion of AG Jacobs, para 55: 'Although the Court appeared to accept that the need to protect producers against unfair competition and consumers against deception regarding the origin of products could constitute justification on grounds of public policy under Article 36, subsequent case-law has made it clear that, since Article 36 derogates from a fundamental rule of the Treaty enshrined in Article 30, it must be interpreted strictly and cannot be extended to objectives—such as protection against unfair competition and consumer protection—which are not expressly mentioned therein. Justification on the grounds of consumer protection for the national legislation at issue must accordingly be sought elsewhere.'

[199] Eg Case 113/80, *Commission/Ireland (Irish Souvenirs)* [1981] ECR 1625, paras 7–10.

[200] For a rare example where it might be argued that the Court has done that, see Case C-199/84, *Procuratore della repubblica v Tiziano Migliorini and Tibor Tiburzio Fischl* [1985] ECR 3317, para 14: 'In order to reply to the question put to the Court it must be pointed out in the first place that the Court has already stated on numerous occasions that the abolition of restrictions on trade between Member States constitutes a fundamental principle of the common market applicable to all goods, with the result that exceptions, which in any event must be strictly construed, must be clearly laid down (see the judgment of 20 April 1978 in Joined Cases 80 and 81/77 *Société Les Commissionnaires Réunis SARL v Receveur des Douanes* [1978] ECR 927 and the cases referred to therein).'

according to which the Treaty freedoms should weigh stronger in a metaphorical balancing exercise. The reason why the CJEU never saw a necessity to extend the doctrine to non-Treaty justifications is likely explained by the fact that the CJEU had from early on applied them in conjunction with a necessity or proportionality test. As we have seen, the CJEU applied the 'interpreting strictly' doctrine routinely by employing tests (such as suitability or necessity) that form part of today's standard proportionality test. In *Commission/Germany*, for example, the CJEU held that invoking the public health exception—which is 'to be interpreted strictly'—required the national authorities 'to show in each case, in the light of national nutritional habits and in the light of the results of international scientific research, that their rules are necessary to give effective protection to the interests referred to in that provision and, in particular, that the marketing of the products in question poses a real risk to public health.'[201]

To conclude, it can be held that the 'interpreted strictly' doctrine is a general rule of interpretation in EU law, and is not particular to the CJEU's internal market jurisprudence. It defines a two-fold interpretative standard: 1) if a provision constitutes an exception to a general rule, then it should not be assumed that other, additional exceptions exist, or that the provision should otherwise be interpreted expansively; 2) at the same time, the general rule cannot be interpreted in a way to erode the exemption altogether. In internal market law, the CJEU has routinely framed the requirement to interpret exceptions 'strictly' in procedural terms. In particular, the CJEU scrutinized national measures as to whether they were suitable and necessary to achieve their stated objective. These requirements are mostly analogous to the tests performed in the proportionality test the CJEU employs today. After *Cassis*, the main function of the doctrine was to restrict the number of grounds that could justify directly discriminatory national measures. A substantive understanding of the doctrine, which would hold that claims based on the Treaty freedoms would be 'weightier' than countervailing interests, is incorrect.

The 'Reasons of a Purely Economic Nature' Doctrine

According to a standard formula employed by the CJEU, 'reasons of a purely economic nature cannot constitute overriding reasons in the public interest justifying a restriction of a fundamental freedom guaranteed by the Treaty.'[202] The formula exists in two other variations as well: the CJEU routinely holds that 'budgetary considerations' as well as the goal of preventing a 'reduction in tax revenue' cannot justify restrictive measures. At first sight, the doctrine might be understood as

[201] Case C-387/99, *Commission/Germany* [2004] ECR I-3751, para 72.
[202] Case C-384/08, *Attanasio Group Srl v Comune di Carbognano* [2010] ECR I-2055, para 55.

defining a substantive requirement:[203] it might be held to establish a dichotomy whereby the exercise of the rights granted by the Treaty freedoms is considered to be 'economic' in nature, whereas concerns related to the public interest are reduced to 'non-economic' goals. We have seen in a previous chapter that such dichotomic framework is an ideologically charged concept. For observers unfamiliar with the CJEU's actual practice, the doctrine could create the impression that the Treaty freedoms should be interpreted along specific ideological lines. This, however, is an incorrect understanding of the case law. The CJEU refers frequently to the 'purely economic nature' doctrine, but in fact there is not a single case where it fulfils an autonomous function. It will be shown that the formula merely constitutes a restatement of the formal requirement that national measures that restrict the Treaty freedoms must be justifiable on objective grounds and be proportional.

'Economic' Justifications Accepted by the CJEU Despite the 'Purely Economic Nature' Doctrine

It has been repeatedly observed that the postulated distinction between 'economic' and 'non-economic' reasons cannot be very strict, as the CJEU has routinely accepted justifications that must rationally be considered to be of an 'economic' nature.[204] This is already confirmed by a look at Article 36 TFEU, which holds that measures protecting industrial and commercial property may justify derogating from Article 30 TFEU. This goal undoubtedly constitutes an 'economic' objective in any meaningful use of the term. Similarly, the grounds for justification that the CJEU proposed in *Cassis de Dijon*—measures relating to the effectiveness of fiscal supervision, the fairness of commercial transactions and the defence of the consumer—equally are of an 'economic' nature.[205] A quick overview of the case law reveals numerous additional regulatory goals that are clearly 'economic', and yet have been accepted by the CJEU.[206] This includes the following justifications:

— guaranteeing the quality of skilled trade work and of protecting those who have commissioned such work (*Corsten*);[207]
— professional rules for the protection of the recipient of services (*Wesemael*);[208]

[203] For an early example of such misunderstanding see Meij and Winter (n 6), 90.
[204] See for example Catherine Barnard, 'Derogations, Justifications and the Four Freedoms: Is State Interest Really Protected?' in Catherine Barnard and Okeoghene Odudu (eds), *The Outer Limits of European Union Law* (Hart, 2009) 280; see also Barents (n 58), 278.
[205] *Cassis de Dijon*, para 8.
[206] The following list has in parts been compiled from two sources: Case C-288/89, *Stichting Collectieve Antennevoorziening Gouda/Commissariaat voor de Media* [1991] ECR I-4007 (hereinafter *Gouda*), para 14; and Barnard (n 204), 277.
[207] Case C-58/98, *Josef Corsten* [2000] ECR I-7919 (hereinafter *Corsten*), para 38.
[208] *Wesemael*, para 28.

— protection of workers (*Webb*);[209]
— prevention of social dumping (*Commission/Germany*);[210]
— prevention of unfair competition (*Wolff & Müller*);[211]
— prevention of an abuse of the freedom to provide services (*Rush Portuguesa*);[212]
— avoiding disturbances on the labour market (*Rush Portuguesa*);[213]
— combating concealed employment (*Commission/France*);[214]
— cohesion of the tax system (*Bachmann*);[215]
— effectiveness of fiscal controls (*Bachmann*);[216]
— the need to ensure the effective collection of income tax (*Scorpio*);[217]
— prevention of wholly artificial arrangements aimed at circumventing the application of the legislation of the Member State concerned (*Cadbury Schweppes*);[218]
— protection from the risk of seriously undermining the financial balance of the social security system (*Kohll*).[219]

A number of these justificatory grounds are concerned with the protection of different types of market participants, including service recipients, employees and consumers. While the term 'economic' in common usage is often primarily associated with the activities of businesses, it should be obvious that service recipients, employees and consumers are in fact active on the market in the same way that businesses are. The protection of their interests is therefore clearly an 'economic' goal. The fact that the CJEU has accepted these concerns as justificatory grounds completely undermines the plausibility of a substantive reading of the 'purely economic nature' doctrine. Other justificatory grounds deal with issues of market organization (eg concerning the labour market), which are 'economic' concerns as well. Finally, a number of justifications concern the field of taxation (eg the effectiveness of fiscal supervision and the coherence of taxation schemes). Of course goals like effective fiscal supervision serves equity- and rule-of-law-related

[209] Case 279/80, *Criminal proceedings against Alfred John Webb* [1981] ECR 3305 (hereinafter *Webb*), para 19.

[210] Case 244/04, *Commission/Germany* [2006] ECR I-885, para 61.

[211] Case 60/03, *Wolff & Müller GmbH & Co KG v José Filipe Pereira Félix* [2004] ECR I-9553 (hereinafter *Wolff & Müller*), para 41.

[212] Case C-113/89, *Rush Portuguesa Ldª v Office national d'immigration* [1990] ECR I-1417, para 17 (hereinafter *Rush Portuguesa*).

[213] *Rush Portuguesa*, para 13.

[214] Case 255/04, *Commission/France* [2006] ECR I-5251, para 52.

[215] Case C-204/90, *Hanns-Martin Bachmann v Belgian State* [1992] CRI I-249, para 28 (hereinafter *Bachmann*).

[216] *Bachmann*, para 18.

[217] Case C-290/04, *FKP Scorpio Konzertproduktionen GmbH v Finanzamt Hamburg-Eimsbüttel* [2006] ECR I-9461 (hereinafter *Scorpio*), para 35.

[218] Case C-196/04, *Cadbury Schweppes plc and Cadbury Schweppes Overseas Ltd v Commissioners of Inland Revenue* [2006] ECR I-7995 (hereinafter *Cadbury Schweppes*), para 51.

[219] Case C-158/96, *Raymond Kohll v Union des caisses de maladie* [1998] ECR I-1931, para 41 (hereinafter *Kohll*).

interests, but ultimately governments levy taxes primarily for the reason to raise revenue. This makes the assertion rather implausible that justifications based on the goal of preventing a 'reduction in tax revenue' are inadmissible. The list shows that the CJEU routinely accepts grounds of justification that must be considered to be 'economic' in any meaningful use of the term. In the light of these examples, the 'purely economic nature' doctrine insinuates a meaning that in fact does not correspond to the CJEU's practice. Different to what the doctrine states, 'economic' grounds can clearly be invoked to justify restrictive measures.

On the Origins of the Doctrine

The 'purely economic nature' doctrine has its origins in the early 1960s.[220] CJEU decision 7/61 (*Commission/Italy*), where the doctrine first appeared, dealt with the following situation: Italy had reintroduced measures to limit imports of pork products because the 'market in pig meat was encountering serious and persistent difficulties'.[221] The sector had already been liberalized, so that pork products were covered by the standstill obligation of Article 31 EEC. Italy tried to justify the measures on the basis of both Article 36 and Article 226 EEC.[222] The latter provision granted temporal protection in situations where the internal market rules created economic difficulties during the transitional period. The second paragraph of the provision held that Member States had to request the Commission to authorize safeguard measures, and could not apply them unilaterally. In a first step the CJEU declared that Italy had failed to follow the procedure of Article 226(2) EEC, which, however, was a necessary precondition for claiming the exception. In the second step the CJEU turned to Article 36 EEC. It gave the following explanation on the delineation of Articles 226 and 36 EEC:

> Article 36, as distinct from Article 226, is directed to *eventualities of a noneconomic kind* which are not liable to prejudice the principles laid down by Articles 30 to 34, as the last sentence of the article confirms. In particular, it does not establish a generic protective clause additional to that provided by Article 226 and allowing Member States to derogate by unilateral action from the procedure and the guarantees laid down by that article.[223]

Article 226 EEC granted Member States the right to temporarily reintroduce protectionist measures during the transitional period, but required them to follow the adequate procedural steps. By contrast, Article 36 EEC was not supposed to

[220] Case 7/61, *Commission/Italy* [1961] ECR 319 (hereinafter *Commission/Italy—protective measures*).
[221] *Commission/Italy—protective measures*, p 323.
[222] Art 226(1) EEC held: 'In the course of the transitional period, where there are serious difficulties which are likely to persist in any sector of economic activity or difficulties which may seriously impair the economic situation in any region, a Member State may ask for authorisation to take measures of safeguard in order to restore the situation and adapt the sector concerned to the Common Market economy.'
[223] *Commission/Italy—protective measures*, p 329, emphasis added.

justify protectionist measures. The CJEU employed the doctrine to fend off an understanding of Article 36 EEC as a further protective clause against negative effects of market integration.[224] The statement that Article 36 EEC 'is directed to eventualities of a noneconomic kind' therefore initially served solely as a delineation from Article 226 EEC. As Article 226 EEC could be invoked only during the transitional period the doctrine lost its initial function after 1970. The doctrine was picked up by Directive 64/221/EEC, which laid down conditions and limitations for national measures that aimed at restricting movement and residence rights of citizens from other Member States on grounds of public policy, public security or public health. In Article 2(2), the Directive held that '[s]uch grounds *shall not be invoked to service economic ends*'.[225] Today, a nearly identical version of this provision is to be found in Article 27(1) of the Residence Directive 2004/38. Paragraph 2 of Directive 64/221/EEC should be understood in a similar sense as CJEU decision 7/61: Article 36 EEC was not intended to justify protectionist measures, ie national measures that undermine the obligations of market integration that Member States have agreed to.

From the 1980s onwards, the doctrine started to appear regularly in the case law. In *Commission/Italy*, for example, the CJEU held that 'Article 36 refers to matters of a non-economic nature.'[226] In *Duphar* the CJEU broadened the concept with the generalizing appraisal that Article 36 EEC 'cannot … justify a measure whose *primary objective is budgetary*'.[227] Since about the late 1990s onwards, the CJEU has employed the doctrine no longer solely in relation to the Treaty-based exceptions (such as Article 36 TFEU) alone, but also in connection with the mandatory requirements and overriding reasons in the public interest. However, the CJEU made an important modification by adding the term 'purely', thereby defining a far-reaching limitation.

Case Groups

In this section we will analyse some of the CJEU's case law where the 'purely economic nature' doctrine is employed. We will substantiate the claim that the doctrine serves no autonomous purpose: all decisions where the CJEU refers to the 'purely economic nature' doctrine can in fact be explained perfectly well on the basis of the general objectivity and proportionality requirement alone. Because the case law is extensive, a few examples must suffice.[228]

224 For a similar reading see Evans (n 79), 594; Barents (n 58), 278f.
225 Emphasis added.
226 Case 95/81, *Commission/Italy* [1982] ECR 2187, para 27.
227 Case 238/82, *Duphar BV and others v The Netherlands State* [1984] ECR 523, para 23 (hereinafter *Duphar*), emphasis added.
228 The full results of this study may be published elsewhere at some point.

Case Group 1: Budgetary Considerations

The CJEU regularly holds that 'budgetary considerations' cannot justify discriminatory measures. In other words, differential treatment is not justifiable solely because equal treatment would be too costly. The CJEU has ruled in this sense in cases that concern discrimination against women (eg *Roks*),[229] part-time workers (eg *Zentralbetriebsrat der Landeskrankenhäuser Tirols*)[230] and of workers in transnational situations (e.g. *Kranemann*).[231]

The *Kranemann* decision dealt with a German measure according to which trainee lawyers posted in a city other than their hometown would be reimbursed for their travel expenses by the government, but only if that city was located in Germany. Mr Kranemann, who was employed in London, was reimbursed only for travel costs equal to a train ride to the German border. The CJEU found the measure to constitute a restriction of the free movement of workers. According to the German government, the measure was justified on the ground that trips abroad would be too costly, and a limitation of travel expenses was necessary because of budgetary constraints. The CJEU accepted in principle that limitations on public expenditure were necessary, but held that the measure in question was arbitrary in this regard: journeys to distant cities within Germany were not necessarily cheaper than to cities in other countries located in close proximity to the border.[232] A general cap on reimbursements, which would apply to trips to domestic and non-domestic locations alike, would serve the same purpose, and would at the same time apply indiscriminately to trips to locations within and outside Germany.[233] In its judgment, the CJEU referred to the 'purely economic nature' doctrine, arguing that 'aims of a purely economic nature cannot constitute pressing reasons of public interest justifying a restriction of a fundamental freedom.'[234] However, the doctrine obscures rather than illuminates the decision, which is based on an otherwise perfectly clear application of the requirement that differential treatment must be justified on objective grounds. As there is no objective reason to differentiate between trips to domestic and to non-domestic locations, and as there is a

[229] Case C-343/92, *MA De Weerd, née Roks, and others v Bestuur van de Bedrijfsvereniging voor de Gezondheid, Geestelijke en Maatschappelijke Belangen and others* [1994] ECR I-571, para 35 (hereinafter *Roks*); Case C-196/02, *Vasiliki Nikoloudi v Organismos Tilepikoinonion Ellados AE* [2005] ECR I-1789, para 53; Joined Cases C-4/02 and C-5/02, *Hilde Schönheit v Stadt Frankfurt am Main and Silvia Becker v Land Hessen* [2003] ECR I-125/75, para 85; Case C-77/02, *Erika Steinicke v Bundesanstalt für Arbeit* [2003] ECR I-9027, para 66; Case C-243/95, *Kathleen Hill and Ann Stapleton v The Revenue Commissioners and Department of Finance* [1998] ECR I-3739, para 40.

[230] Case C-486/08, *Zentralbetriebsrat der Landeskrankenhäuser Tirols v Land Tirol* [2010] ECR I-3527, para 46 (hereinafter *Zentralbetriebsrat der Landeskrankenhäuser Tirols*), para 46.

[231] Case C-109/04, *Karl Robert Kranemann v Land Nordrhein-Westfalen* [2005] ECR I-2421, para 34 (hereinafter *Kranemann*).

[232] *Kranemann*, para 35; *Kranemann*, Opinion of AG Geelhoed, para 19.

[233] *Kranemann*, para 32.

[234] ibid, para 34.

less restrictive means available to achieve the objective of limiting public expenses, differential treatment is unjustified.

The CJEU's reference to the 'purely economic nature' doctrine creates the impression that national measures somehow cannot take budgetary concerns into account, when in fact the opposite is the case: the CJEU fully accepts that budgetary constraints can require Member States to establish limitations on benefits. The German government can limit the subsidy to whatever level it deems right, but must do so in a way that does not put workers employed in other Member States at a disadvantage, unless it is justified on objective grounds.

A comparable decision is *Roks*, where the CJEU decided that 'budgetary considerations' could not justify indirect discrimination on the grounds of gender.[235] The national measure in question restricted entitlements to benefits for incapacity for work to persons whose prior income had been above a certain threshold. The CJEU found that this measure constituted indirect discrimination on the grounds of gender because the income requirement affected primarily women.[236] It further held that the measure was not justifiable if the sole justificatory ground were budgetary constraints, and explained: '[A]lthough budgetary considerations may influence a Member State' s choice of social policy and affect the nature or scope of the social protection measures it wishes to adopt, they cannot themselves constitute the aim pursued by that policy and cannot, therefore, justify discrimination against one of the sexes.'[237] As in *Kranemann*, the CJEU quashed the measure not because it restricted entitlements on grounds of budgetary considerations, but because it unjustly differentiated on the ground of gender. In order to justify differential treatment of men and women it must be shown that the 'measure is based on objectively justified factors unrelated to any discrimination on grounds of sex'.[238] This has purely logical reasons: the existence of budgetary constraints does not explain why expense cuts should be realized to the detriment of women alone; differential treatment must be justified on objective grounds unrelated to the incriminated distinction. A simple example will illustrate this proposition: if parents give two pieces of candy to their son and none to their daughter, then this choice cannot be justified with the argument that the parents do not have two additional pieces for the daughter. She will want to know why the candy is not split *evenly*. Unless the parents have a good reason for their decision, the daughter will likely be upset. As in *Kranemann*, the outcome in *Roks* can be explained as an application of the objectivity and proportionality requirements alone. It can be seen that the 'purely economic nature' doctrine served no autonomous function, and obfuscates otherwise perfectly clear decisions.

[235] *Roks*, para 35.
[236] ibid, para 33.
[237] ibid, para 35.
[238] ibid, para 33.

Case Group 2: Special Rights for Companies

The CJEU has regularly ruled that special rights for specific companies cannot be justified if they are motivated by 'economic' considerations alone. This was first held in *Campus Oil*. An Irish law held that importers of petroleum products had to obtain a certain percentage from the state-owned INCP, which ran the Whitegate refinery in Cork. The law ensured a reasonable sales volume for the refinery, which was the only oil refinery located in Ireland. In the light of the supply shortfalls Europe had experienced as a consequence of the oil crises in the 1970s, the Irish government saw this as a crucial factor in ensuring security of energy supplies. The CJEU qualified the measure as a measure falling under Article 30 TFEU. As concerned possible justifications, the plaintiffs argued that the law aimed at ensuring that the refinery would not run at a loss; as this was essentially an economic consideration, the measure could not be justified under the public policy or security exception of Article 36 TFEU.[239] The CJEU tentatively agreed, and stated that 'Article 36 refers to matters of a non-economic nature. A Member State cannot be allowed to avoid the effects of measures provided for in the Treaty by pleading the economic difficulties caused by the elimination of barriers to intra-Community trade.'[240] The CJEU then decided, however, that ensuring a minimum supply of petroleum products constituted an objective that was covered by the concept of public security, as 'the aim of ensuring a minimum supply of petroleum products at all times is to be regarded as transcending purely economic considerations and thus as capable of constituting an objective covered by the concept of public security.'[241] The reference to the 'purely economic nature' doctrine again introduces a deeply confusing element into an otherwise perfectly plausible decision, which can be summarized as follows: the obligation to buy from the state-owned refinery clearly constitutes a restriction of the free movement of goods. The purpose of the measure was to ensure the profitability of the refinery, and thereby its long-term existence. This is undoubtedly an economic measure, which, however, is justified on grounds of public security. It is completely unclear how the 'purely economic nature' doctrine contributes in any form to that outcome. It creates the impression that 'economic' strategies to pursue public security goals are somehow problematic, when in fact the opposite is the case: such a measure is completely acceptable as long as it is justified on objective grounds such as public security.

A similar decision is *Evans Medical* (1995), which dealt with an exclusive right to produce a certain opiate for pain treatment that the UK had granted to a company, and had otherwise prohibited its import. The government argued that importation 'threatens the viability of the sole licensed manufacturer in the first State and jeopardizes reliability of supply of diamorphine for medical purposes'.[242]

[239] Case C-72/83, *Campus Oil Limited and others v Minister for Industry and Energy and others* [1984] ECR 2727 (hereinafter *Campus Oil*), para 24.

[240] ibid, para 35.

[241] ibid, para 35.

[242] Case C-324/93, *The Queen v Secretary of State for Home Department, ex parte Evans Medical Ltd and Macfarlan Smith Ltd* [1995] ECR I-563 (hereinafter *Evans Medical*), para 34.

The CJEU declared that the objective of maintaining the viability of a company could not be justified under Article 36 TFEU, as the provision refers to non-economic matters only. However, ensuring reliable supplies of medication 'for essential medical purposes' could fall under Article 36 TFEU's objective to protect the health and life of humans, provided that the measure would not fail the proportionality test. In effect, the 'purely economic nature' doctrine again suggests an outcome that turns out to be the opposite of what the judgment in fact holds. Measures that grant special rights to a company to ensure its economic viability are perfectly legitimate if they are justified on objective grounds, such has public health.

In some decisions the CJEU has held that the 'protection of a particular economic sector' constitutes an 'economic aim' that is not justifiable. The phrasing of the 'purely economic nature' doctrine in these cases is conceptually close to the way it was originally applied in Decision 7/61, which we discussed at the beginning of the chapter: Member States cannot justify measures that aim at protecting a domestic sector or industry from the effects of market integration. However, it stands to reason that the objectivity and proportionality requirements are perfectly capable of dealing with protectionist measures. The 'purely economic nature' doctrine therefore serves no additional function and, if taken at face value, is deeply misleading, as for example the *STTG* decision (1997) shows.[243] It dealt with a Greek measure according to which tourist guides who worked and resided in Greece would automatically be in an employment relationship with the contracting entity, eg the domestic or foreign travel agency or the owners of cruise ships. Although the measure did not apply to non-resident tourist guides who did not have a domestic diploma or licence and who merely accompanied tour groups to Greece,[244] the CJEU nonetheless found the measure to conflict with the freedom to provide services. The CJEU argued that foreign tour guides could have an interest in acquiring a diploma and yet remain self-employed.[245] The Greek government responded that the measure had been a compromise to resolve a long-lasting conflict between tour guides and travel agencies. The measure thereby aimed to 'prevent any adverse effects on tourism, and consequently on the country's economy … the rules at issue were adopted in order to ensure the proper functioning of the national economy',[246] as tourism was a crucial economic sector in Greece.[247] The CJEU held that this constituted an 'economic aim':

> [M]aintaining industrial peace as a means of bringing a collective labour dispute to an end and thereby preventing any adverse effects on an economic sector, and consequently

[243] Case C-398/95, *Syndesmos ton en Elladi Touristikon kai Taxidiotikon Grafeion v Ypourgos Ergasias* [1997] ECR I-3091 (hereinafter *STTG*).

[244] *STTG*, para 10; *STTG*, Opinion of AG Lenz, para 27.

[245] *STTG*, para 12.

[246] ibid, para 22.

[247] ibid, Opinion of AG Lenz, para 55.

> on the economy of the State, must be regarded as an economic aim which cannot constitute a reason relating to the general interest that justifies a restriction of a fundamental freedom guaranteed by the Treaty.[248]

However, the CJEU subsequently moved on to the proportionality test, and argued that it had not been shown that the measure was 'necessary' to maintain industrial peace.[249] The national measure thereby constituted a restriction of the Treaty freedoms because it did not pass the proportionality test. This outcome appears to be a reasonable application of the proportionality requirement: fostering industrial peace is a plausible regulatory objective that all Member States pursue in one form or another. However, a measure that automatically subjects all tour guides to an employment contract goes beyond what is necessary to achieve this objective. The 'purely economic nature' doctrine adds nothing to this finding. Even more troublesome is that the implications of the 'purely economic nature' doctrine in this case are untenable if taken at face value. It is completely implausible to argue that the objective of 'maintaining industrial peace' can under no circumstances constitute a public interest capable of justifying restrictive national measures because it is 'economic' in nature. The objective is far too broad and far too general to be excluded in an outright fashion. Moreover, as we have seen in a previous section the CJEU's own case law suggests that considerations relating to 'industrial peace', such as the protection of workers or the avoidance of disturbances on the labour market, may very well justify restrictive measures. Finally, primary and secondary EU law protects instruments of industrial relations, most notably Article 12 (freedom of assembly and association) and Article 28 (right of collective bargaining and action) of the Charter of Fundamental Rights. Taken at face value, the 'purely economic nature' doctrine therefore produces completely untenable results.

In the three cases, the reference to the 'purely economic nature' doctrine seems to serve two goals: first, it seems to suggest that Member States are not allowed to enact measures that put domestic companies or industries at an unfair advantage. However, this goal is merely a restatement of the prohibition of direct and indirect discrimination, and does not serve an additional function. Second, it seems to be employed to describe the fact that Article 36 TFEU cannot be interpreted as including more grounds of justifications than are explicitly listed in the provision. However, this is nothing but an extremely confusing way of saying that the exceptions of Article 36 TFEU should be interpreted strictly.

[248] ibid, para 23.
[249] ibid, para 24.

Case Group 3: The Taxation Cases—'Reduction of Tax Revenue'

The CJEU regularly asserts that the objective of forestalling a 'reduction of tax revenue' does not in itself justify restrictive national measures.[250] The CJEU held for example in *X and Y*:

> It must be borne in mind that the reduction in tax revenue ... is not one of the grounds listed in Article 46 EC and cannot be regarded as a matter of overriding general interest which can be relied upon in order to justify unequal treatment that is, in principle, incompatible with Article 43 EC ... *Such an objective is purely economic and cannot*, therefore, according to settled case-law, *constitute an overriding reason in the general interest.*[251]

Cases like *X and Y* essentially constitute the revenue-side version of our first case group: just like budgetary constraints do not justify differential treatment unless there are objective reasons to do so, Member States cannot tax similar situations differently unless there is a good reason to differentiate between the two (to reformulate our earlier example: if the parents want to eat candy, and their two children have two pieces of candy each, it would probably cause significant discontent if they took both pieces of candy from one child and none from the other. The first child would want to know why the parents did not take one piece of candy from each child.)

The CJEU employed the 'purely economic nature' doctrine in regard to tax cases for the first time in *Svensson and Gustavsson.*[252] Two Swedish nationals residing in Luxembourg had taken out the loan with a Belgian bank. They applied for an interest rate subsidy for the construction of an apartment in Luxembourg.[253] The Luxembourg authorities denied the application, as such subsidy was granted only if the loan was taken out with a bank established in Luxembourg. The government argued that the subsidy was very costly, amounting to 1 per cent of the whole national budget. More than half of the costs were retrieved, however, through a tax on earnings of banks established in Luxembourg. Consequently, Luxembourg argued, the subsidy could be upheld in its current form only with the help of revenue levied through this tax. As the subsidy was therefore intrinsically connected to the tax, differential treatment was justified. In particular, Luxembourg referred to a justification first accepted by the CJEU in the *Bachmann* decision, where the

[250] Case C-484/93, *Peter Svensson and Lena Gustavsson v Ministre du Logement et de l'Urbanisme* [1995] ECR I-3955, para 15 (hereinafter *Svensson and Gustavsson*); Case 264/96, *Imperial Chemical Industries plc (ICI) v Kenneth Hall Colmer (Her Majesty's Inspector of Taxes)* [1998] ECR I-4695, para 28; Joined Cases C-397/98 and C-410/98, *Metallgesellschaft Ltd and Others, Hoechst AG and Hoechst (UK) Ltd v Commissioners of Inland Revenue and HM Attorney General* [2001] ECR I-1727, para 59; Case C-307/97, *Compagnie de Saint-Gobain, Zweigniederlassung Deutschland v Finanzamt Aachen-Innenstadt* [1999] ECR I-6161, para 51; Case C-35/98, *Staatssecretaris van Financiën v BGM Verkooijen* [2000] ECR I-4071, para 59; Case C-436/00, *X and Y v Riksskatteverket* [2002] ECR I-10829, para 50 (hereinafter *X and Y*).

[251] *X and Y*, para 50, emphasis added.

[252] *Svensson and Gustavsson*, para 15.

[253] *Svensson and Gustavsson*, para 2.

CJEU held that a discriminatory tax measure could be justified if it is necessary to preserve the cohesion of the tax system.[254] In that case Belgium had granted a tax exemption on payments to a life insurance if the payments received from the same insurance were also taxable in Belgium. Conversely, payments from the life insurance could be exempted if the contributions had already been taxed before. The tax exemption simply aimed to ensure that the same situation (ie, contributions to and payments from a life insurance) was not taxed twice. Whereas individuals residing in Belgium could choose whether they wanted to have their contributions taxed but later receive tax-free payments or have it the other way around, this choice was not available for individuals residing outside of Belgium. In their situation, Belgium unilaterally decided that the contributions would be taxed and the payments would go tax-free because otherwise Belgium could not tax the transaction at all. The right to have contributions be tax-exempt was therefore the correlate to the fact that payments from the life insurance would be subject to taxation. The fact that such tax-exemption was not available to individuals resident outside Belgium constituted formally different treatment, but in essence was only part of a system that ensured that everybody was taxed neither more or less than once. In *Svensson and Gustavsson*, Luxembourg invoked the same exception, but the CJEU rejected the claim. It found that the tax on banks and the loan subsidy were not related closely enough:

> In those cases there was a direct link between the deductibility of the contributions and the tax on the sums payable by the insurers under death and old-age insurance policies, a link which had to be preserved in order to preserve the integrity of the relevant fiscal regime, whereas there is no direct link whatsoever in this case between the grant of the interest rate subsidy to borrowers on the one hand and its financing by means of the profit tax on financial establishments on the other.[255]

Differential treatment in *Bachmann* had been justified on objective grounds: it ensured that Belgium could tax the situation once, but also allowed it to prevent double taxation of the same situation. By contrast, no such objective grounds backed up the discriminatory measure in *Svensson and Gustavsson*: the central question to be answered was why the differential treatment of banks based on their location would be justified. However, the Luxembourg government provided no objective explanation. Tax liability depends, according to the principle of territoriality, on the seat of the bank. Banks do not pay taxes in Luxembourg if they have their seat in another country. Trying to justify unequal treatment by reference to tax liability is an attempt to justify unequal treatment on the basis of the location of the seat. This, however, does not constitute an objective justification, because it attempts to justify the discrimination by reference to a further discriminatory distinction, and must fail for that reason. The government's arguments thus fail

[254] *Bachmann*, para 27.
[255] *Svensson and Gustavsson*, para 17.

4

A Purposive Interpretation of the Treaty: The Pursuit of the Union's Diverse Socio-Economic Objectives, and Economics as Contested Knowledge

INTRODUCTION

THE REGULATORY OBJECTIVES of the Union are relevant for the interpretation of European law, which is routinely read in a purposive form.[1] The central source to establish the Union's goals is Article 3 TEU. The provision defines the Union's objectives, which encompass the promotion of 'peace, its values and the well-being of its peoples' (paragraph 1), the establishment of an 'area of freedom, security and justice' (paragraph 2), the creation of an 'economic and monetary union' (paragraph 4) and the contribution 'to peace, security … sustainable development of the Earth, solidarity and mutual respect among peoples, free and fair trade, eradication of poverty and the protection of human rights' on the international plane (paragraph 5). Of most direct relevance for our purposes is paragraph 3, which addresses the socio-economic objectives of the Union. Article 3(3) TEU holds:

> The Union shall establish an internal market. It shall work for the sustainable development of Europe based on balanced economic growth and price stability, a highly competitive social market economy, aiming at full employment and social progress, and a high level of protection and improvement of the quality of the environment. It shall promote scientific and technological advance. It shall combat social exclusion and discrimination, and shall promote social justice and protection, equality between women and men, solidarity between generations and protection of the rights of the child. It shall promote economic, social and territorial cohesion, and solidarity among Member States. It shall respect its rich cultural and linguistic diversity, and shall ensure that Europe's cultural heritage is safeguarded and enhanced.

[1] The Court explained in *CILFIT* that 'every provision of Community law must be placed in its context and interpreted in the light of the provisions of Community law as a whole, regard being had to the objectives thereof and to its state of evolution at the date on which the provision in question is to be applied.' Case 283/81, *CILFIT v Ministry of Health* [1982] ECR 3417, para 20.

The provision indicates a broad understanding of the Union's regulatory objectives in the socio-economic realm. The internal market that is to be maintained shall be characterized by a multitude of macroeconomic and societal objectives, ranging from issues such as price stability, full employment, environmental protection to social justice and territorial cohesion. Quite obviously Article 3(3) TEU does not subscribe to any specific socio-economic worldview, and instead covers a variety of objectives that can be held to have very different historical and political pedigrees. Whereas issues such as 'price stability' and the 'highly competitive social market economy' tend to be seen as important political goals mainly by conservative and liberal scholars and policymakers, objectives such as 'balanced economic growth' or the 'protection … of the environment' seem to relate well to green political and economic thought. Finally, 'full employment and social progress' and 'social justice' appear to be consistent with a social democratic or Christian democratic worldview.[2] These different political pedigrees hint at the fact that the Union's regulatory objectives will not always complement each other harmoniously, and indeed may often be in conflict. Poiares Maduro argued that, while in certain questions the Treaties may provide guidance as to how these goals should be rated in regard to each other,[3] most often there are multiple possibilities of how these goals—if they conflict—could be balanced.[4] In this sense Poiares Maduro identified, as we already discussed, an 'open character of the European Economic Constitution'.[5] The diverging nature of the EU's socio-economic goals, as exemplified in Article 3(3) TEU, gives an idea of the severe difficulties that a purposive interpretation of the Treaty freedoms faces. If the Union's socio-economic goals conflict—and, given their diverse nature, this will often be the case—a purposive interpretation of the Treaty freedoms will often remain ambiguous.[6]

This ambiguity is further increased by the fact that for none of these regulatory objectives does an uncontroversial strategy exist as to how to achieve them.[7]

[2] See also Armin Hatje, 'Wirtschaftsverfassung im Binnenmarkt' in Armin von Bogdandy and Jürgen Bast (eds), *Europäisches Verfassungsrecht. Theoretische und dogmatische Grundzüge* (Springer, 2009) 801ff.

[3] Miguel Poiares Maduro, *We the Court. The European Court of Justice and the European Economic Constitution: a critical reading of Article 30 of the EC Treaty* (Hart, 1998), 151.

[4] ibid, 151 and 153.

[5] ibid, 159; A similar argument has been made by Robert Howse in regard to the WTO; Robert Howse, 'From Politics to Technocracy—and Back Again: The Fate of the Multilateral Trading Regime' (2002) 96 *American Journal of International Law* 94, 110.

[6] See however Mestmäcker, who claims that the interpretation of the Treaty must be primarily economic-functional, and thus seems to assume that such interpretation will deliver sufficiently unambiguous results. Ernst-Joachim Mestmäcker, *Europäisches Wettbewerbsrecht*, 29.

[7] This argument has found expression in scholarship that employs the so-called 'Varieties of Capitalism' (VoC) concept to analyse the European Union. The premise of VoC is that there is not one, but various versions of capitalist regimes. Instead of conceptualizing the differences between Member States as deviations from an ideal version of capitalist organization, VoC attempts to describe different economic regimes as potentially equally efficient solutions (a typical distinction is between Anglo-Saxon, Nordic and continental versions of capitalism). VoC understands non-market (eg welfare) institutions as preconditions for the functioning of markets. See most notably Peter Hall and David Soskice, 'An Introduction to Varieties of Capitalism' in Peter Hall and David Soskice (eds), *Varieties of*

In our discussion of the socio-economic debates that accompanied the signature of the Treaty of Rome we encountered a number of controversies as regards the optimal strategy to achieve the Community's objectives. For example, the question as to what extent adverse effects of market integration on peripheral regions might be counteracted with regulatory interventions found a variety of different answers among economists and policymakers. An equally controversial issue was the Community's objective of the upwards-oriented levelling of living standards: as we saw, there was no agreement whether it could be assumed that this would automatically follow market integration, or whether this required the harmonization of social and labour regulation. The situation is no different in regard to the objectives of the Union today, as we will discuss in this chapter: for example, the question how goals such as balanced economic growth, technological progress or regional cohesion are to be achieved finds wildly conflicting answers, depending on which economist or policymaker is asked. Given such fundamental disagreement as to how the Union's objectives are best achieved, any purposive interpretation of European law must remain deeply ambiguous: even if we accept that Union law must be interpreted in the light of the Union's objectives such as fostering growth and regional cohesion, this provides no unambiguous outcome if there is disagreement on how these objectives are to be achieved.

This problem is by no means specific to European Union law; in fact, many bodies of national and international economic law, including private law or competition law, are characterized by the same ambiguity. In legal interpretation, such impasse may often be sidestepped by an explicit or (more often) implicit choice for a specific socio-economic paradigm as the supposedly superior scientific approach. For example, Robert Bork's interpretation of US antitrust law along the lines of his preferred approach in neoclassical economic theory was based on the claim that this approach constituted the state-of-the-art of economic theory.[8] More common than such active choice for any specific socio-economic paradigm is the tacit acceptance of a dominant paradigm as the correct one. Legal interpretation often accepts what Galbraith once called the 'conventional wisdom' in the socio-economic realm as the basis for a purposive interpretation.[9] But while such practice may be common and potentially understandable (if it is accepted that legal

Capitalism The Institutional Foundations of Comparative Advantage (Oxford University Press, 2001); for a recent application on the internal market see for example Martin Höpner and Armin Schäfer, 'A New Phase of European Integration: Organised Capitalisms in Post-Ricardian Europe' (2010) 33 *West European Politics* 344. From a VoC perspective, secondary EU law or CJEU decisions can be criticized for not sufficiently taking the role of non-market institutions for the functioning of capitalist regimes into account, or for employing a certain variant as the standard. See for example ibid, 361–64.

[8] Bork held: 'All of this means that the judge, legislator, or lawyer cannot simply take the word of an economist in dealing with antitrust, for the economists will certainly disagree. Unless we would be driven to a sterile agnosticism, therefore, we must work through the arguments and make up our own minds. And we will find that on most subjects there is a better view which we ought to accept until fresh analysis provides yet a superior position.' Robert Bork, *The Antitrust Paradox* (Basic Books, 1978) 117–18.

[9] See John Kenneth Galbraith, *The Affluent Society* (Houghton Mifflin Company 1998), 6–17.

scholars and judges cannot be legitimately expected to know of the intradisciplinary disagreements in economics), this can hardly serve as a *principled* justification for basing a purposive interpretation of economic law on the dominant paradigm. Moreover, I doubt that in the past decades any socio-economic paradigm could have been found to be dominant to an extent that all alternative approaches could have safely been dismissed. But even if we provisionally accept that at some point in the past there was such overwhelming consensus for a specific socio-economic paradigm, this is certainly no longer the case as of the outbreak of the economic crisis of 2008.[10] At least since that moment it became obvious for non-economists that the discipline of economics is characterized by various, strongly dissenting approaches, none of which has any superior claim to truth.[11] A purposive interpretation of European law on the basis of the Union's regulatory objectives must therefore not only take the broad and conflicting character of these objectives into account, but also the conflicted nature of economic knowledge as such.

The chapter lays out the extent to which economic knowledge, on which a purposive interpretation of EU economic law must necessarily be based, is contested. It will be shown that, depending on the socio-economic paradigm they subscribe to, economists and policymakers will give widely diverging answers as to how the Union's regulatory objectives are best achieved. Given our previous discussion of the Union's history, it seems implausible to assume that any specific socio-economic paradigm could be picked as the basis for a purposive interpretation. Rather, the existence of economic dissent itself must be accounted for in a purposive interpretation of EU economic law. In certain areas, recognition of dissent in economic knowledge has already found its way into (EU) law scholarship: most notably, the insight that the neoclassical conceptualization of humans as rational maximizers of utility may provide an incomplete understanding of real-world behaviour has been picked up and put into operation in legal discourse by scholars of behavioural law and economics. The main argument in this chapter is that dissent in economics is not limited to specific questions but is in fact ubiquitous, so that economics can generally not be held to provide an unambiguous answer to most questions central for European economic law. In interpreting European law, courts face the following problem: on the one hand, European economic law—especially primary law—is often textually broad, which means that a purposive interpretation is indispensable. On the other hand, there is often no

[10] In this sense Kaarlo Tuori and Klaus Tuori, *The Eurozone Crisis* (Cambridge University Press, 2014), 8.

[11] It appears deeply problematic to base a purposive interpretation of EU law on any specific existing socio-economic paradigm without taking the well-known fact into account that each of these paradigms hold true only on the basis of specific moral and political assumptions about the human nature and of society, none of which can be legitimately held to be uncontroversial. See on this John Kenneth Galbraith, *American Capitalism. The Concept of Countervailing Power* (Hamish Hamilton, 1952), Foreword, xi; see similarly Zijlstra, who argued: 'The vision that people have of the optimal economic order ultimately finds its roots in considerations that are no longer economic in nature' (my translation). Jelle Zijlstra, *Economische politiek en concurrentieproblematiek in de EEG en de lid-staten* (Staatsdrukkerij- en Uitgeversbedrijf, 1966) 46.

that followed the Great Depression. Against this background, authors like Keynes developed the idea that markets may not be able to achieve optimal outcomes by themselves at all times; in fact, the development could stall at various sub-optimal states of equilibrium, and thus require collective intervention in some situations. Stiglitz sums up the Keynesian revolution in the wake of the Great Depression as follows:

> Prior to Keynes, there was, among classical economists the general belief that markets worked well, that they were stable and efficient. Indeed, so strongly were these beliefs held that in the midst of the Great Depression, a majority of American economists supported the notion that government should do nothing. Markets would self-correct. (These economists did not, of course, explain why matters had gone so disastrously.) Keynes provided an answer—a theoretical model, or perhaps more accurately, a set of theoretical models, with clear policy implications, the central tenets of which were: (a) markets were not self-correcting, at least in the relevant time span—unemployment could persist; (b) in deep downturns, monetary policy was ineffective; and (c) fiscal policy—government spending—could stimulate the economy, by a multiple of the amount that was spent.[15]

A central methodical difference between pre- and post-Keynesian economics is that the latter tends to see an important difference between individual transactions on the one hand and aggregate developments of the economy as a whole on the other. Forces that structure the interaction of economic actors on the individual plane may not translate into harmonious developments on the aggregate level; for example, behaviour that is rational from an individual perspective may still lead to sub-optimal or unstable results for the general economy. Pre-crisis economics was criticized for ignoring that difference, for example by the ordoliberalist scholars Franz Böhm and Walter Eucken.[16] The methodical consequence of its recognition is the separation of microeconomics and macroeconomics.

After WWII, the Keynesian position was reintegrated into the neoclassical stream, leading to the so-called neoclassical synthesis, which proved to be dominant until around the 1970s. Neoclassical synthesis attempted to merge the neoclassical axioms with Keynesian analysis of imperfect markets.[17] It essentially retained the equilibrium and efficiency thesis of neoclassical theory for the long run, while acknowledging that the short run could be 'contaminated' with certain market imperfections, which could justify governmental intervention.[18]

[15] Stiglitz (n 12), 3.

[16] Franz Böhm, Walter Eucken and Hans Grossmann-Doerth, 'Unsere Aufgabe' in Franz Böhm (ed), *Die Ordnung der Wirtschaft als geschichtliche Aufgabe und rechtsschöpferische Leistung, 1* (Kohlhammer, 1937) viii.

[17] An often-cited text that initiated such reintegration is John Hicks, 'Mr Keynes and the "Classics"; A Suggested Interpretation' (1937) 5 *Econometrica* 147; For an overview of critical positions about the neoclassical synthesis see Paul Davidson, *Money and the real world* (Macmillan, 1978) 1–2.

[18] Joan Robinson described the issue as follows: 'A new orthodoxy was soon established by a simple device. A substitute for Say's law was provided by the assumption that a well-managed Keynesian policy keeps investment running at the level which absorbs the saving forthcoming at full employment. The rest of the doctrine of the neoclassics could then be revived.' Joan Robinson, *Economic heresies* (Basic Books, 1971), x. And Stiglitz argued: '[U]sing Keynesian interventions to ensure that

The 1960s and 1970s also brought a strong opposing movement from the centre-left, where for example Cambridge economist Joan Robinson charged the neoclassical synthesis with being 'bastard Keynesians'.[19] According to Robinson, they ignored Keynes' central insight that the present economic system is fundamentally unstable; the reason for this instability is that investment in a capitalist economy depends on individual, profit-oriented decisions made under conditions of uncertainty.[20] Robinson criticized the underlying belief of the neoclassical synthesis in the stability and optimality of market outcomes in the long run, as this supported the assumption that sub-optimal outcomes could be eliminated through macroeconomic fine-tuning by the state. Such criticism of the neoclassical synthesis constitutes the precursor to present-day Keynesian positions, which are, confusingly for non-economists, termed 'Post-Keynesian'.[21] Even more confusingly, the neoclassical synthesis is often termed 'new Keynesian'.

From the 1970s onwards, economists on the right developed a paradigmatic approach—today termed 'new classical theory'—in delineation from the neoclassical synthesis, which rejected the existence of market imperfections. The new classical school (eg Robert Lucas) essentially believed in market forces creating optimal outcomes without any requirement of macroeconomic coordination in the short or the long run. Instabilities were assumed to be the consequence of external shocks (ie, developments outside the economic sphere proper), such as policy interventions. By contrast, the second dominant line in the contemporary economic mainstream—the 'new Keynesians'—retained the main points of the neoclassical synthesis and believe in the equilibrium forces of the market in the long run, but see a certain limited role for fiscal and monetary coordination in the short run. The 'new classical' and the 'new Keynesian' views form, in the words of Stiglitz, the two 'churches' of present-day mainstream theory.[22] Additionally to these two strands of mainstream thinking, numerous alternative approaches exist (often termed 'heterodox', to delineate them from mainstream or 'orthodox' theory). These include, as already mentioned, post-Keynesianism and, for example, institutional, feminist and Marxist economics, as well as the so-called Austrian school, which is influential on the US libertarian right.

the economy remained at full employment, and once that was done, the standard neoclassical propositions would once again be true.' Joseph Stiglitz, 'Information and the Change in the Paradigm of Economics' Prize Lecture, 8 December 2001, nobelprize.org/nobel_prizes/economics/laureates/2001/stiglitz-lecture.pdf, 477.

[19] See for example Joan Robinson, 'Review of Money, Trade and Economic Growth by HG Johnson' (1962) 72 *Economic Journal* 690, 691, where she writes: 'But the bastard-Keynesian model is not only silly. It is seriously defective in logic.'

[20] See also Minsky, who argued that '[c]onventional theory is not hospitable to the thought that market capitalism left to its own devices will, from time to time, experience financial crises that can lead to bone-crunching depressions.' Hyman Minsky, *Stabilizing an unstable economy* (Yale University Press, 1986), 39.

[21] Minsky described post-Keynesianism as a 'rather unfortunate label'. Hyman Minsky, 'The Financial Instability Hypothesis: A Restatement' in Hyman Minsky (ed), *Can 'it' happen again? Essays on Instability and Finance* (ME Sharpe, 1982) 93.

[22] Stiglitz (n 12), 4.

Can the Economy be 'Left Alone', and What Happens if it is? The Issue of Equilibrium and Disequilibrium, and the Need for Macroeconomic Regulation

A central and century-old debate is to what extent the economy can achieve coherent results if it is, to use a simplistic yet influential phrase, 'left alone'.[23] If this is the case, many or all non-market forms of coordination such as macroeconomic governance and institutional structures may be either superfluous or actually harmful. If it is not the case, non-market forms of coordination may be necessary to achieve optimal outcomes. In economics, the debate on 'laissez-faire' finds expression in the question whether the economy can be analysed as being in or moving towards an 'equilibrium' position. We will first look at the 'equilibrium' thesis as an analytical tool in economics, and then briefly discuss its implications for economic law and regulatory practice.

The equilibrium position describes a situation where all resources are put to use, ie, full employment. The essential idea is that at a certain price there is a buyer for every product.[24] 'Partial equilibrium' describes an equilibrium position on a specific market, whereas 'general equilibrium' means that the whole economy finds such position. The equilibrium thesis presupposes a static perspective: assuming a given quantity of products, they will all find a buyer for a certain price, which 'clears the market'. Dynamic processes are conceptualized as a sequence of static equilibrium states, comparable to a round-based computer game: in each round, products appear on the market, which then find buyers at a certain price.[25] A central implication of the equilibrium thesis is that excess supply (eg overproduction as an excess supply of a certain good, or unemployment as an excess supply of labour) is impossible if prices are allowed to adapt. As we will see a little later, this proposition has relevant implications for example in labour market regulation. A common version of the equilibrium thesis is the claim that 'supply creates its own demand', sometimes termed 'Say's law' after the French economist Jean-Baptiste Say.[26] The idea is that income received for the production of a product automatically goes back to the market as demand, so that, in the aggregate, supply

[23] Since the eighteenth century, 'laissez-faire, laissez-passer' was a common call against what was considered undue public involvement in economic activities.

[24] The view is criticized because it essentially conceptualizes the modern economy in analogy to a barter trade society, where goods are traded against goods. Money enters only subsequently as a facilitator to barter trade. However, economists like Keynes or Minsky emphasized that in a modern economy with 'sophisticated financial institutions' the financial sphere is not neutral, but has its own dynamics, which are the cause for fluctuations, booms and busts. See for example Mark Hayes, *The Economics of Keynes* (Elgar, 2006) 3; Hyman Minsky, 'The financial instability hypothesis' (1992) Jerome Levy Economics Institute Working Paper No 74, 61–62.

[25] The concept of the general equilibrium is attributed to Léon Walras. The classical modern formulation of the general equilibrium stems from Kenneth Arrow and Gerard Debreu, 'Existence of an Equilibrium for a Competitive Economy' (1954) 22 *Econometrica* 265 and Lionel McKenzie, 'On the Existence of General Equilibrium for a Competitive Market' (1959) 27 *Econometrica* 54.

[26] Screpanti and Zamagni (n 14), 85–87; for a critical analysis of Say's law see Galbraith (n 11), 14, 22 and 73–75; Robinson (n 18), viii–ix.

cannot exceed demand. This proposition is important for example in the management of economic crises, as we will discuss in a bit. As a theoretical assumption, the equilibrium thesis is supposed to show that, at least in principle, coherent results are possible as the outcome of market interactions even in the absence of non-market coordination.[27] In more political terms, the equilibrium concept defines a relative autonomy of the economic system vis-à-vis non-market forms of coordination; it postulates the system's ability to produce coherent outcomes despite the fact that nobody consciously manages the big picture, though the significance of legal and political institutions may be acknowledged to a greater or lesser degree.

Many economists have either relativized the equilibrium thesis as being analytically of little use, or of limited relevance in the description of real-world economic processes, or have discarded it altogether.[28] Gunnar Myrdal argued that the equilibrium thesis was based on the incorrect assumption 'that a change will regularly call forth a reaction in the system in the form of changes which on the whole go in the opposite direction to the first change.' Myrdal believed that

> in the normal case there is no such tendency towards automatic self-stabilisation in the social system. The system is by itself not moving towards any sort of balance between forces, but is constantly on the move away from such situation. In the normal case a change does not call forth countervailing changes but, instead, supporting changes, which move the system in the same direction as the first change but much further.[29]

Along similar lines Nicholas Kaldor argued that equilibrium-based economics is 'barren and irrelevant as an apparatus of thought to deal with the manner of operation of economic forces, or as an instrument for non-trivial predictions concerning the effects of economic changes, whether induced by political action or by other causes.'[30] He criticized that the equilibrium thesis is not grounded in empirically derived hypotheses, arguing that it describes only *logical* relations on the basis of its very own assumptions, but does not provide *scientific* explanations.[31] Most notably, Kaldor argued, conceptualizing the economy in the static form of the equilibrium is unhelpful to understanding processes of economic change, such as economic growth.[32] Keynes equally emphasized the limitations of the equilibrium thesis:[33] he accepted the equilibrium concept for economic short-term analysis of situations in which uncertainty about future developments

[27] Minsky (n 20), 116.

[28] See for example János Kornai, *Anti-Equilibrium. On economic systems theory and the task of research* (North-Holland, 1971).

[29] Gunnar Myrdal, *Economic theory and under-developed regions* (Duckworth, 1957), 13.

[30] Nicholas Kaldor, 'The Irrelevance of Equilibrium Economics' (1972) 82 *Economic Journal* 1237, 1237.

[31] ibid, 1237.

[32] ibid, 1244; see also Allyn Young, 'Increasing Returns and Economic Progress' (1928) 38 *Economic Journal* 527, 528.

[33] Hayes (n 24), 10.

'It is strange, in fact, that macroeconomic theories focusing on wage and price rigidities became so fashionable, when in the Great Depression, wages and prices fell so deeply and rapidly. Would things have been better if they fell even faster?'[47] The example of labour markets show how different views on the equilibrium thesis supports radically different outlooks on labour market regulation and economic policies in general.

Conceptualizing the economy in a state of equilibrium or, alternatively, of disequilibrium clearly has important policy consequences in regard to European economic law, for example internal market law. According to a strong equilibrium thesis, government interventions are bad for stability, pushing the economy into disequilibrium, whereas left alone, the economy would gravitate towards equilibrium. According to a weaker equilibrium thesis that understands equilibrium as a long-term state or as a merely theoretical quality of markets, but acknowledges short-term or real-life disequilibria caused by market failures, there are certain government tasks that are welfare-enhancing. Finally, according to the *dis*equilibrium thesis, equilibrium is no property of market forces at all, so that economic stability is partly or mainly dependent on other factors like institutions or policy. Depending on which of these views underlie the decision-making process, EU law may be interpreted in very different ways. For example, a judge who believes in the equilibrating potential of market forces will likely evaluate justifications for restrictive national measures in internal market law in a different way than one who is convinced of the opposite.

What is the 'Optimal' Outcome? Does the Market Reach the Optimal Outcome? And How do we Know it Did? The Criterion of 'Pareto Efficiency'

The question of whether markets arrive at 'optimal' outcomes usually appears in conjunction with the discussion whether and what extent non-market forms of coordination (eg government or cooperative coordination) are necessary in organizing the socio-economic realm, an issue that we will discuss in a later section. At first sight, it may be assumed that the answer to this question will depend on what the regulatory objective is, ie, which outcomes we think are 'optimal': depending on the societal ends, the means to achieve them will likely differ. For example, the answer to the question whether markets reach 'optimal' outcomes in absence of non-market coordination is probably different for the goal of a zero-carbon-emission society than for one that aims at the maximization of aggregate wealth as expressed in the GDP as currently calculated. The 'optimality' of the outcome may thus be assumed to depend on the regulatory objective, the latter being a political choice. This means that the (political) question of what is considered

[47] ibid, 9.

to be an 'optimal' outcome must be answered before it can be assessed whether markets or non-market forms of coordination achieve it better.[48]

Some strands of scholarship are based on explicit assumptions about what society's main regulatory objectives are or should be. Richard Posner's version of the economic analysis of law, for example, postulates that the creation of the most wealth—which probably must be understood as the maximization of GDP as currently measured—constitutes an undisputed regulatory goal that should form the foundation of socio-economic regulation.[49] From this basis, Posner develops his normative vision of law, which tends to assume that market-based regulation is better in maximizing wealth than non-market forms of organizing economic interaction. However, in the light of some of the central socio-economic problems of our time, most notably the climate crisis and inequality, it appears highly questionable whether wealth maximization based on the current way of measuring the GDP should really be seen as the central regulatory objective of contemporary societies.[50] But even if such an objective is accepted, there is still wild disagreement about the means necessary to achieve it. As we will see in a later section, a hotly disputed question among economists and policymakers is to what extent non-market coordination, such as macroeconomic management, must accompany the activities of markets in order to maximize growth. A variant of Posner's approach is the concept of 'productive efficiency', which describes the maximization of output with a given input. The critique raised against Posner's approach applies here as well: while the maximization of output is surely a relevant objective, there is no reason to assume that it should be the only one. Beyond that, it is open to contest which form of societal organization of production is actually more successful in this regard.

However, much of orthodox economic literature provides a different answer to the question of what exactly markets are good at. The key claim is that markets are characterized by 'allocative efficiency', which describes the ability to allocate products to those who can make the greatest use of them. The most common definition of 'allocative efficiency' is that of Pareto, which describes a situation where nobody can be made better off without somebody being made worse off.[51] Classical economists had assumed that products had some kind of objective or real value: the price of a product represented the costs of the resources that went into its production.[52] On this basis it could be argued that a 'better' economic system is one that creates greater aggregate value. Nineteenth-century scholars like

[48] A structurally similar argument is made by Arthur Okun, *Equality and Efficiency: The Big Tradeoff* (The Brookings Institution, 1975), 61.

[49] Richard Posner, *Economic Analysis of Law* (Aspen Publishers, 2007) 10–15.

[50] For a critical view see Joseph Stiglitz, Amartya Sen and Jean-Paul Fitoussi, 'Report by the Commission on the Measurement of Economic Performance and Social Progress' (2009) stiglitz-sen-fitoussi.fr/documents/rapport_anglais.pdf.

[51] Screpanti and Zamagni (n 14), 226.

[52] See ibid, 20.

Jeremy Bentham and John Stuart Mill replaced the 'objective' value criterion with the 'subjective' concept of 'utility',[53] which Bentham defined as 'the greatest happiness of the greatest number'.[54] The better economic system is thus the one that creates more aggregate utility. This concept was adopted and later reformed by the neoclassical economists, who replaced the function of aggregate utility with a system of individual preferences that defied any attempt at aggregation. The subjective well-being of individuals, it was held, cannot be compared between persons, or aggregated. Persons have a unique ordering of preferences: a person may prefer a car over public kindergartens, or spare time over income, etc. Under such an assumption, the question of whether an economic system produced optimal outcomes could no longer be established on the basis of aggregated value or 'utility'.[55] The preferences of an individual are expressed by their actions alone, most notably by their choices to buy or sell products on markets (Samuelson speaks of 'revealed preferences'[56]).[57] Based on these assumptions, only markets fulfil the requirement of 'Pareto efficiency': individuals can freely engage in all transactions that will better their situation; if they do not engage in certain deals, it must be assumed that this is because it would make them worse off.[58] By contrast, non-market (eg government) allocation is per se inefficient: if an intended outcome was Pareto efficient, market actors would already have reached it by themselves; but if they haven't done so, then the intended outcome cannot be assumed to be Pareto efficient.

The concept of Pareto efficiency does not provide an objective standard on the basis of which different forms of socio-economic regulation can be *empirically* evaluated. Rather, it describes a quality of markets that is based on *logical* deductions from a set of axioms. These axioms include, most notably, the assumption that individuals have an unambiguous, hierarchical order of preferences (Volvo over Audi over spare time over kindergarten etc) that is unchangeable over time,

[53] See ibid, 42.

[54] Jeremy Bentham, *A Fragment on Goverment* (Eighteenth Century Collections Online 1776), Preface, i.

[55] See Screpanti and Zamagni (n 14), 224–25.

[56] Paul Samuelson, 'A Note on the Pure Theory of Consumer's Behaviour' (1938) 5 *Economica* 61; see however Amartya Sen, 'Rational fools: A critique of the behavioral foundations of economic theory' (1977) *Philosophy & Public Affairs* 317, 322–24.

[57] See for example Gregory Mankiw, 'Defending the one percent' (2013) 27 *Journal of Economic Perspectives* 21, 12. Mankiw argues: 'One classic problem is the interpersonal comparability of utility. We can infer an individual's utility function from the choices that individual makes when facing varying prices and levels of income. But from this revealed-preference perspective, utility is not inherently measurable, and it is impossible to compare utilities across people. Perhaps advances in neuroscience will someday lead to an objective measure of happiness, but as of now, there is no scientific way to establish whether the marginal dollar consumed by one person produces more or less utility than the marginal dollar consumed by a neighbor.' See also Okun (n 48), 2: 'In relying on the verdicts of consumers as indications of what they want, I, like other economists, accept people's choices as reasonably rational expressions of what makes them better off.'

[58] Mankiw (n 57), 1: 'The transaction is a voluntary exchange, so it must make both the buyer and the seller better off.'

and which remains unaffected by any collective form of will-building (ie, no public debate can convince an individual that the construction of kindergartens is more important than to get a car). Pareto efficiency is best understood as a thought experiment showing that, under certain conditions, market participants will achieve a coherent allocation of a given set and given distribution of resources through decentralized market interactions without the need for non-market allocation of resources.

Criticism of the proposition that markets are 'efficient' or that the concept is of analytical relevance can be voiced from within or from outside the language of orthodox theory.[59] Orthodox theory generally acknowledges that real-life market outcomes may not necessarily be 'efficient', either in its definition as 'productive efficiency', ie, the maximization of output, or as Pareto efficiency. These deviations are conceptualized as 'market failures', ie typified situations when market outcomes fail to be 'efficient'. Generally recognized market failures include: externalities,[60] information asymmetries between the market participants, public goods and principal–agent problems. Orthodox economists disagree in regard to the extent they recognize the existence of market failures, and in how far they believe these can be alleviated by government action. Joseph Stiglitz, for example, accepting the concept of Pareto efficiency in principle, argued that markets virtually never reach this position in practice.[61]

A common criticism of the usefulness of Pareto efficiency as an analytical concept is that it ignores the existing distribution of resources.[62] A situation in which a single, immensely wealthy individual buys up all available resources for their own enjoyment while the mass of people starves of hunger would be Pareto efficient; by contrast, a redistribution from this individual to the hungry mass

[59] Many scholars have rejected the practical relevance of Pareto efficiency. Guido Calabresi, for example, has declared Pareto efficiency to be a plainly absurd criterion: 'Unfortunately, the set of Pareto superior changes which would make no one worse off and at least one person better off must ex ante be a void set. For if strict or fanatical Pareto is the criterion, why wouldn't any change that belonged in the set have already been made? Since, by definition, no one would in any way be hurt by the change, why would anyone object? The existence of ex ante objectors itself must mean that there are some people who—rightly or wrongly—believe that they will lose something from the change. Putting it another way: if Pareto optimality means a place where no improvement can be made without ex ante creating the possibility that there will be some losers, then we are always there.' Guido Calabresi, 'The Pointlessness of Pareto: Carrying Coase Further' (1991) 100 *Yale Law Journal* 1211, 1216.

[60] The concept of externalities describes the situation when market actors do not benefit or pay for the full amount of good or damage they have caused society. Positive externalities include research and development, which is beneficial to all of society, but the benefit may not be fully acquired by the company; pollution is an example of a negative externality, the costs of which are not fully paid for by the polluter.

[61] Stiglitz (n 18), 486; According to Stiglitz, the imperfect information paradigm 'has some important implications: privately profitable transactions may not be socially desirable. The banks may have incentives to engage in contracts with each other that make, for instance, the economic system more unstable (which is exactly what they did). There are important (pecuniary) externalities associated with individuals' actions that matter and which individuals do not take into account. Price changes have not just distributive consequences, but also shift incentive compatibility, self-selection, and collateral constraints.' Stiglitz (n 12), 8.

[62] Minsky (n 20), 104.

on the assumption that the different factors of production—essentially labour and capital,[66] though the argument is also applied in regard to the different subsections of the labour force—are each rewarded in accordance with their contribution to production. Wage and profit each represent the remuneration of their respective marginal productivity.[67] According to Gregory Mankiw, for example, 'people should receive compensation congruent with their contributions.'[68] In his article 'Defending the one Percent', Mankiw argues: 'My own reading of the evidence is that most of the very wealthy get that way by making substantial economic contributions, not by gaming the system or taking advantage of some market failure or the political process.'[69] From such perspective the cause of rising inequality is to be found in increasing differences in the contributions to society. Concerning the income differences within the labour force, a common argument is that growing inequality may be explained by technological progress. In particular the expansion of the IT sector created a significant divide between the high-skilled labour force and less qualified workers.[70] As regards the falling labour share in total income, it has been held that the cause may be found in globalization: as low-skilled workers increasingly entered the global labour market, they lowered the average marginal productivity of labour, and thereby pushed down the labour share.[71] As the overall economic effect of technological progress and of globalization is seen as positive, however, increasing inequality is assumed to be a tolerable side-effect.

Some argue that inequality is not only fair, but also economically beneficial: if high income and high return on capital constitutes fair remuneration for contributions to society, redistributive measures like income taxation may reduce the incentives to perform or to invest capital.[72] The proposition is commonly expressed as a trade-off between equity and efficiency,[73] and is commonly illustrated in one of three metaphorical forms: Arthur Okun provided the figure of the leaky bucket: redistributive measures detract from the efficient functioning of the market (Okun defines 'efficiency' as 'productive efficiency', ie, 'getting the most out of a given input'[74]). The 'cake' metaphor holds that a functioning market system

[66] Robinson (n 18), 25: 'Social income is, so to say, divided vertically into receipts from separate commodities. When employment for wages becomes the main form of production, the division is horizontal, between income from work and income from property. Profit as a distinct category of income is a characteristic of industrial capitalism.'

[67] Mankiw (n 57), 17: 'In the standard competitive labor market, a person's earnings equal the value of his or her marginal productivity.' See on this Francesco Saraceno, 'High Inequality and its Impact on the Economy: Issues and Solutions' (Paper presented at workshop *Réformer l'Europe*, Paris, 9 January 2014) 1–2.

[68] Mankiw (n 57), 21.

[69] ibid, 17.

[70] See Mankiw (n 57), 4, with further references.

[71] See on this Saraceno (n 67), 2.

[72] See for example Okun (n 48), 1: 'The contrasts among American families in living standards and in material wealth reflect a system of rewards and penalties that is intended to encourage effort and channel it into socially productive activity.'

[73] ibid, 1.

[74] ibid, 2.

lets the overall output grow, whereas redistributive measures merely change the composition of the way it is distributed. Finally, the tide metaphor holds that market outcomes create a 'tide that lifts all boats', implying that a system that creates *relative* inequality may still be more beneficial for all groups in *absolute* terms.[75]

Both propositions—that inequality may be fair because it represents remuneration for the contributions to society, and that inequality may be economically beneficial—have found numerous challengers in economics. For example, in his Nobel prize acceptance speech, Robert Solow stated: 'there is something intrinsically ideological about the notion that profits on "capital" represents the return to a factor of production as imputed by the market.'[76] Classical economists like Smith, Ricardo and Marx assumed that the surplus created in the production process can, in principle, be appropriated either by labour or by capital.[77] The question of how the surplus is distributed in practice depends on the relative political and economic strength of the various groups.[78] Scholars like Stiglitz or Galbraith have argued that neither globalization nor technological progress can explain growing inequality, which is instead attributed to 'the rise of predatory behavior'.[79] In particular, the increasingly deregulated financial market has led to a disconnect between the labour share and marginal productivity.[80] From this perspective, market outcomes cannot be considered to represent remuneration for the relative contributions to society because they depend on the power of the respective actors

[75] In the 1950s Gunnar Myrdal criticized 'the idea that everything will come out to the satisfaction of all if the natural forces of the market are left their free play', which had the side-effect 'that it is more permissible to forget about the equality postulate.' Myrdal (n 29), 131. The focus on distribution was rejected by Robert Lucas in the following way: 'Of the tendencies that are harmful to sound economics, the most seductive, and in my opinion the most poisonous, is to focus on questions of distribution.' Robert Lucas, 'The Industrial Revolution: Past and Future' 2003 Annual Report Essay, Federal Reserve Bank of Minneapolis.

[76] Robert Solow, 'Growth theory and after' (1988) 78 *American Economic Review* 307, 313; Solow added: 'John Bates Clark may have thought, a century ago, that distribution according to marginal products was "just" but no modem economist, no modern "bourgeois" economist, would accept that reasoning.' In the light of for example Gregory Mankiw's position discussed in this section, this judgment turned out to be premature.

[77] According to Myrdal, Ricardo 'stressed … the interest conflict between the different economic classes: none of them could have an increased share of the social product except at the expense of one or both of the other classes'. Myrdal (n 29), 116; see also Engels in the Foreword to Karl Marx, *Das Kapital*, vol II (Dietz Verlag, 1963) 17–18, with further references to Smith and Ricardo.

[78] This is also true for authors important in post-Keynesian theory, such as Michal Kalecki. Stockhammer explained: 'For Kalecki the profit share, and inversely the wage share, is given by the degree of monopoly, which in turn is determined by the degree of competition, the extent of non-price competition and the organizational strength of labor. Hence the real or relative income distribution is determined by structural factors, that are fixed in the short run.' Engelbert Stockhammer, 'Robinsonian and Kaleckian growth. An update on post-Keynesian growth theories' (1999) WU Working Paper No 67 October, 6.

[79] See Saraceno (n 67), 3, with further references; See also Joseph Stiglitz, *The Price of Inequality* (Norton, 2013); James Galbraith, *Inequality and instability: a study of the world economy just before the Great Crisis* (OUP, 2013).

[80] Saraceno (n 67), 3.

to appropriate the gains created by society as a whole. Aiming into a similar direction, it has often been emphasized that market processes should not be conceptualized as governed by quasi-natural laws; instead, markets are structured through law and through institutions, which consequently shape the outcome. This is frequently described as the 'pre-distributive' effect of the market setup. Robert Wade explained in this regard:

> [T]o focus on lowering the concentration of income by tax and spending measures is to miss more than half the picture. One has to examine the whole array of state laws, regulations and policies for their effects on the distribution of market income, before taxes, particularly to show how, in high-inequality developed countries, many parts of the array (including corporate governance law, trade union law, patent law, monetary policy, exchange rate policy, and more) have the effect of sluicing market incomes upwards.[81]

Many scholars have also rejected the proposition that inequality may be economically beneficial. James Meade has famously argued that, with great inequality, the price system is no longer able to serve as an efficient coordination tool.[82] Stiglitz recently held that '[d]istribution matters. If one is concerned about social justice, then this is obvious. But distribution matters even if one is just concerned about economic performance.'[83] From a Keynesian perspective, for example, unequal distribution may be sub-optimal because individuals with a lower income have a higher propensity to consume than wealthy individuals. This means that most of their income is directed towards consumption, which keeps the economic system running:[84] income spent on consumption by one person constitutes income for another person, which will again be spent mostly on consumption and so forth. An amount spent on consumption may therefore trigger an increase in national income that goes beyond this amount, which is called the multiplier effect. By contrast, wealthy individuals save most of their income, ie, they put it into financial instruments (which in turn may fuel economic crises) or capital investment.[85] A falling income share of the lower and the middle class will lead to a fall in aggregate demand and thus to low growth.[86] Equality and growth are thus assumed to be positively related, and redistributive measures may in fact have positive economic

[81] Robert Wade, 'Capitalism and Democracy at Cross-Purposes' (2013) 56 *Challenges* 1, 19.

[82] James Meade, *Planning and the price mechanism: the liberal-socialist solution* (Allen & Unwin, 1948) 35.

[83] Stiglitz (n 12), 5.

[84] Stiglitz explained: 'It matters, in particular, if the marginal propensity to consume differs significantly for at the top and those at the bottom. While there is overwhelming evidence that that is the case—reinforced by recent work focusing on consumption behavior in this recession—there are still those who believe to the contrary, citing Milton Friedman's classic work. But Friedman ignored the importance of credit constraints; those alone explain why those at the bottom might have a higher marginal propensity to consume than those at the top.' Ibid, 6.

[85] Keynes wrote that 'up to the point where full employment prevails, the growth of capital depends not at all on a low propensity to consume but is, on the contrary, held back by it; and only in conditions of full employment is a low propensity to consume conducive to the growth of capital.' Keynes (n 12), 372–73.

[86] Saraceno (n 67), 4

effects.[87] This view has also found empirical confirmation: IMF researchers Berg and Ostry held that 'when growth is looked at over the long term, the trade-off between efficiency and equality may not exist. In fact equality appears to be an important ingredient in promoting and sustaining growth.'[88] Along the same lines, Robert Wade argued that '[o]verall there is no evidence that more unequal countries are more prosperous, even by the standard income measures.'[89]

Since the 1970s, inequality has increased significantly (both in advanced and developing economies), as has been acknowledged by institutions like the IMF and the OECD.[90] It is argued that growing inequality has been a significant contributing factor to the increasing number of economic crises that the world has experienced in the past decades. Saraceno commented that 'Precisely because the elites have been appropriating more than a fair share of national wealth, increasing inequality has been hampering well-being and distorting the economy.'[91] Saraceno highlighted the connection between rising inequality, a deregulated financial market and the recent crisis:

> At the outset of the crisis, in the summer of 2007, the world economy was in a situation of structural weakness, caused by the progressive accumulation of external imbalances. Some countries, most notably the United States and peripheral European countries had an excess of demand over domestic production, shown by increasingly important trade deficits. This deficit was financed by the excess savings that, with different causes, characterized other regions like East Asia, oil producing countries, and last but not least core European countries. These opposite imbalances compensated each other for almost two decades, resulting in an overall balance that the crisis showed to be fragile. Excessive debt of the deficit countries, be it public or private, suddenly became a burden that triggered a race to deleveraging and a generalized drop in spending. Inequality has a large role to play in explaining the accumulation of debt. The transfer of resources from the poor and the middle class to the wealthiest, i.e. from those who consume almost all of their income to those who have a high propensity to save, caused a reduction in the average propensity to consume, and increased the global mass of savings. This had two effects, that played a role in the current crisis. The first is a huge mass of liquidity that fuelled a series of speculative bubbles. High returns in finance, and its increasing weight in GDP triggered a vicious loop by which no real sector investment could compete with the yields offered by the financial sector. Resources were therefore diverted from productive uses of savings

87 See eg Keynes (n 12), 373–74.

88 Andy Berg and Jonathan Ostry, 'Equality and Efficiency' (2011) 48 *Finance & Development* 12, 13; see also Jonathan Ostry, Andrew Berg and Charalambos Tsangarides, 'Redistribution, inequality, and growth' IMF Staff Discussion Note, February 2014.

89 Wade (n 81), 12.

90 IMF, *World Economic Outlook. Globalization and Inequality* (2007); OECD, *Divided we stand: why inequality keeps rising* (OECD Publishing, 2011); Recently the issue has found wide recognition through the works of scholars like Thomas Piketty and Emmanuel Saez; see for example Anthony Atkinson, Thomas Piketty and Emmanuel Saez, 'Top incomes in the long run of history' (2009) NBER Working Paper No 15408; Thomas Piketty and Emmanuel Saez, 'Top incomes and the great recession: Recent evolutions and policy implications' (2013) 61 *IMF Economic Review* 456; Thomas Piketty, *Capital in the twenty-first century* (The Belknap Press of Harvard University Press, 2014).

91 Saraceno (n 67), 3.

Eucken assumed a universal disposition towards the formation of monopolies.[102] Ordoliberals emphasized that economic power allowed market participants to set prices unilaterally, thereby being able to exploit other market participants. For example, Franz Böhm wrote:

> If necessary goods are factually or legally concentrated in the hands of certain privileged individuals, then they are able to decide unilaterally on the scope of the reward for which they are willing to cease the good to somebody else. This power finds its objective limits only in the factual exploitability of the other.[103]

For this reason, ordoliberals like Böhm emphasized the importance of a competition policy that prevented market participants from acquiring market power: the dynamic forces of competition would then provide a counterbalance to economic power, which would often render further-reaching public intervention unnecessary. However, according to Böhm there were important exceptions, such as public goods or markets characterized by natural monopolies. In such situations, Böhm held, more extensive regulatory interventions are necessary, which may include public oversight, a legal obligation on monopolists to contract, price controls, or even nationalization.[104]

Criticism of 'perfect competition' as a foundational hypothesis of economic analysis has been systematized, inter alia, by the scholarship on 'monopolistic competition.' Under the impression of a market structure characterized by monopolies and oligopolies, as well as trusts and cartels,[105] theorists of the 1930s like Joan Robinson argued that the economy should be analysed under the paradigms of 'monopolistic' or 'imperfect competition.'[106] They assumed that an economic analysis shaped by the premise that markets are, in principle, perfectly competitive, ignores the market reality, and thereby fails to grasp central phenomena of modern capitalist economies. This can be illustrated by the example of product differentiation, a central concept of the scholarship on monopolistic competition. Products are often not readily substitutable: they may differ in quality and function, in geographical accessibility, or in branding created by

so ist von vornherein darauf verzichtet, die reale Konkurrenz, wie sie in der wirtschaftlichen Wirklichkeit existiert, zu bezeichnen.'

[102] ibid, 30–31; see also Robinson (n 18), 102.

[103] Franz Böhm, *Die Ordnung der Wirtschaft als geschichtliche Aufgabe und rechtsschöpferische Leistung* (Kohlhammer, 1937) 30 (my translation); the original reads: 'Wenn nämlich gewisse lebensnotwendige Güter in der Hand tatsächlich oder rechtlich bevorzugter Einzelner vereinigt sind, dann sind diese Bevorzugten in der Lage, das Ausmaß der Gegenleistung einseitig zu bestimmen, für die sie bereit sind, das betreffende Gut anderen zu überlassen. Und diese Macht findet ihre objektive Grenze einzig in der tatsächlichen Ausbeutungsfähigkeit der Gegenseite.'

[104] ibid, 33.

[105] See for example Galbraith (n 11), 35–36.

[106] Joan Robinson, *The Economics of Imperfect Competition* (Macmillan, 1969); Edward Chamberlin, *The Theory of monopolistic competition* (Harvard University Press, 1935); Robert Triffin, *Monopolistic Competition and General Equilibrium Theory* (Harvard University Press, 1949); for a discussion of this strand of theory see for example Galbraith (n 11), 43–46; see also Eucken (n 94), 40–43.

advertisement. Moreover, consumers can be locked in after the initial acquisition of a product, as a subsequent change may be restricted by adaptation costs. In situations where products are differentiated, companies are quasi-monopolists for their products and can unilaterally set the prices, even though they may be functionally similar to other products on the market.[107] The prevalence of imperfect information similarly allows companies to charge monopolistic rather than competitive prices.[108] Scholars of monopolistic competition also observed that large companies may benefit from size, thus experiencing increasing returns to scale.[109] This contradicted the orthodox assumption of constant or diminishing returns to scale, which implied that large companies could be under-priced by smaller, more efficient competitors. The theory of monopolistic competition essentially holds that the organization of firms and industries (their size, structure, location, etc) can play an important role in their economic success.[110] Maybe most importantly, the financial power of large enterprises allows them, as Joan Robinson held, 'to follow their own devices, manipulating not only the market economy but also national and international policy'. This 'destroys the basis of the doctrine that the pursuit of profit allocates resources between alternative uses to the benefit of society as a whole.'[111] The findings of the scholarship on monopolistic competition thus, as Schumpeter put it, made many of the orthodox propositions based on the assumption of perfect competition—most notably the equilibrium and the full employment hypotheses—inapplicable, or at least difficult to operate.[112] Galbraith similarly proposed in the 1950s that the concept of competition was an incorrect description of the real economic processes. Based on the model of monopolistic competition, he argued that modern corporations are—and, to achieve their functions, have to be—big, and thus powerful. They are held in check not by a competition that forces a price onto them, but by other economic actors of similar size, which create a 'countervailing power'. Such counterweights could be other companies, but also labour unions: as individual workers are confronted with employers of massive size and force, they need to organize in order to outbalance such concentration of power. Zijlstra emphasized that such countervailing powers would not necessarily develop by themselves,[113] so that policy was assumed to have a potentially important role to play.[114]

[107] See for example Zijlstra (n 11), 51.

[108] See for example George Akerlof, 'The market for "lemons": Quality uncertainty and the market mechanism' (1970) *Quarterly Journal of Economics* 488.

[109] Galbraith (n 11), 37; see also Robinson (n 26), 97–98.

[110] Much of the economic reality does simply not resemble perfect competition: production, for example, cannot flexibly adapt to demand changes because fixed costs lead to non-competitive pricing. On this point see Michael Spence, 'Product Selection, Fixed Costs, and Monopolistic Competition' (1976) 43 *Review of Economic Studies* 217; see also Robinson (n 18), 54.

[111] Robinson (n 18), 103.

[112] Schumpeter (n 38), 79.

[113] Zijlstra (n 11), 53.

[114] Myrdal emphasized the epistemological difficulty related to the attempt of employing the theory of perfect competition as a guidance for policy: 'Generally it is not even possible to decide whether a

Depending on whether one holds perfect or imperfect competition for the standard, the assumptions about firm behaviour and the functioning of the economy will vary widely, which in turn has important consequences for policy and legal decision-making. If market imperfections are perceived as exceptions to an otherwise functional institution, then judges, regulators and lawmakers will act differently than when they believe that those problems are inherent to the existing form of market organization. In competition law, for example, a theory that works on the background of perfect competition sees less reason for intervention by competition authorities, as the assumption is that the market will tend to self-correct malfunctioning monopolies.[115] By contrast, a competition policy that presumes that markets are frequently characterized by imperfect competition will likely pursue a less lenient approach.

Which Non-Market Preconditions do the Markets Require to Function? The Role of Institutions

Over the past century, many economics schools have addressed the institutional preconditions of market activities. These include Max Weber's historical school of economics, Commons' and Veblen's institutional school, Keynesianism and ordo-liberalism as well as, more recently, Nobel prize laureate Elinor Ostrom's school of new institutional economics.[116] The relevance of institutions has also been an increasing focus of development economics.[117] The concept of 'institutions' should be understood broadly, including not only the institutions of the state, but also the legal framework, the monetary system, habits of thought and behaviour, power relations on the market, the impact of technology, society's (economic and other) culture, etc.[118] Ostrom defined 'institutions' as 'the prescriptions that humans use to organize all forms of repetitive and structured interactions including those within families, neighborhoods, markets, forms, sports leagues, churches, private associations, and governments at all scales.'[119] Many scholars have laid out in detail how the legal system defines and structures socio-economic processes.[120]

particular policy measure in a particular country would bring us nearer to, or take us further away from, the purely fictitious state of free competition.' Myrdal (n 29), 141.

115 See on this for example Herbert Hovenkamp, 'Antitrust policy after Chicago' (1985) 84 *Michigan Law Review* 213, 226–29.

116 See for example John Commons, *Legal Foundations of Capitalism* (University of Wisconsin Press, 1968); John Commons, *Institutional economics* (University of Wisconsin Press, 1959); see also Veblen (n 64).

117 See for example Dani Rodrik, Arvind Subramaninan and Francesco Trebbi, 'Institutions Rule: The Primacy of Institutions over Geography and Integration in Economic Development' (2002) NBER Working Paper No 9305.

118 Veblen (n 64), 626.

119 Elinor Ostrom, *Understanding institutional diversity* (Princeton University Press, 2005) 3.

120 Scholars like Robert Hale, John Commons or Morton Horwitz were interested in how legal institutions shape economic processes. They showed that the institutional framework of modern

Institutionalists criticized orthodox economics for assuming abstract, eternally valid economic laws, and emphasized the importance of an empirically founded, historically contingent and path-dependent analysis. Market dynamics, perceived by orthodox scholarship as something close to natural forces, are in reality, as for example Veblen observed, 'human conduct [that] takes place under institutional norms and only under stimuli that have an institutional bearing'.[121] Hyman Minsky, a post-Keynesian, similarly argued:

> Economic systems are not natural systems. An economy is a social organization created either through legislation or by an evolutionary process of invention or innovation. Policy can change both the details and the overall character of the economy, and the shaping of economic policy involves both a definition of goals and an awareness that actual economic processes depend on economic and social institutions … An appeal to an abstract market mechanism … is not permissible; what exists are specific, historical market mechanisms.[122]

Already Adam Smith had emphasized the role of institutions such as moral and legal rules in the functioning of the economy.[123] Schumpeter similarly held that the market economy would require an intricate set of social institutions to function.[124] The importance of an institutional framework for the functioning of markets was also strongly emphasized by ordoliberalist scholars. For example, Walter Eucken ridiculed the idea that an economy could be conceptualized in absence of a regulating and enforcing state (*staatsfreie Wirtschaft*). He emphasized that even the 'laissez-faire' economic system of the nineteenth century required a sophisticated regulatory framework to function, which included for example a system of property law, contract law and of patent law.[125] As noted in a previous chapter, ordoliberals conceptualized markets and public institutions as intrinsically connected.[126] Franz Böhm, for example, argued that the liberal revolution of the nineteenth century aimed not at one-sided (economic and political) liberation, but at the realization of 'order in freedom'.[127] The unleashing of economic and creative

capitalism, like the modern contract and property regime, has a decisive influence on the structure and functioning of the economy. See Morton Horwitz, *The Tranformation of American Law, 1780–1860* (Harvard University Press, 1977); Morton Horwitz, *The Transformation of American Law 1870–1960. The Crisis of Legal Orthodoxy* (Oxford University Press, 1992); Commons, *Legal Foundations of Capitalism* (n 116); Robert Hale, 'Coercion and Distribution in a Supposedly Non-Coercive State' (1923) 38 *Political Science Quarterly* 470; Robert Hale, 'Force and the State: A Comparison of "Political" and "Economic" Compulsion' (1935) 35 *Columbia Law Review* 149; Robert Hale, 'Bargaining, Duress and Economic Liberty' (1943) 43 *Columbia Law Review* 603.

[121] Veblen (n 64), 629.
[122] Minsky (n 20), 7–8, 105–06.
[123] See Screpanti and Zamagni (n 14), 77.
[124] Schumpeter (n 38), 139–42.
[125] Eucken (n 94), 26.
[126] Eucken, for example, conceptualized the role of policy as creating a regulatory regime that would ensure not only nominal, but factual freedom of all individuals, and thereby enabling the unfolding of the potential beneficial effects of markets. ibid, 48–55.
[127] Böhm (n 103), 4.

corresponding tariff increases by other countries, so that in the absence of binding international agreements a spiral of increasing trade restrictions will follow.[142] Accordingly, the benefits of a system of free trade can accrue only if it is, as Tibor Scitovsky held, 'imposed and enforced',[143] ie, if it is embedded within an institutional framework that can ensure compliance.[144] Similarly, Röpke argued that the benefits of trade arising from the division of labour involved a growing degree of interdependence.[145] Individuals will enter such relations only if their claims are formally and materially protected, and if they feel secure enough to continue to engage in the risks related to international trade. Such security in turn requires a 'moral-legal-institutional framework'.[146] It can be argued in general terms that the realization of the expected benefits from trade and from economic integration

(Allen & Unwin, 1958) 100; Rodrik emphasized, however, that trade protection does not necessarily support the development and modernization of industries, as it indiscriminately makes outdated and modern production more profitable. Dani Rodrik, 'Industrial policy for the twenty-first century' [2004] CEPR Discussion Paper No 4767, 14.

142 Scitovsky (n 141), 100–02.

143 ibid, 109.

144 Moreover, Scitovsky argued, if it is recognized that the regulatory objectives of states go beyond the maximization of trade, and instead include a broad spectrum of economic goals such as full employment as well as enhancing a state's position on the world market (eg by establishing highly developed industries) which are not in perfect agreement with the workings of free trade, then a global free trade architecture must be complemented with other forms of international cooperation. ibid, 110.

145 Wilhelm Röpke, 'Wirtschaftssystem und internationale Ordnung Prolegomena' (1951) 4 *ORDO: Jahrbuch für die Ordnung von Wirtschaft und Gesellschaft* 261, 270; for a similar argument see Zijlstra (n 11), 40.

146 ibid, 270; according to Röpke, 'the economic integration … always presupposes a 'social' integration' (ibid, 271). Here the term 'social' does not refer to social institutions in a narrow sense, but to a broader societal framework. According to Röpke, 'the difficulty is to find a legal-institutional framework for international trade that gets even remotely close to that applying for intra-national trade.' However, Röpke claims that the international economic system of the nineteenth century, which he celebrates as a 'universal-liberal solution', allegedly constituted a 'minimum framework' (ibid, 275), in particular without governing bodies and treaties (ibid, 273–74), and argues that it was 'depoliticized' and had developed according to 'objective economic laws' (ibid, 274). In the light of the imperialist and colonialist structure within which international trade and the monetary system of the gold standard unfolded in the nineteenth century, it appears implausible to conceptualize the prevailing international economic system as being free of governing bodies, as 'universal' or 'depoliticized.' His treatment of the subject in few sentences (ibid, 276–77) is thus clearly insufficient. Röpke also ignores the fact that developing economies like the US, Germany and France each turned to protectionist measures to develop their own national industries in the late nineteenth century (on this see for example verLoren van Themaat (n 139), 21). In fact, many scholars understand the allegedly 'universal-liberal solution' of the nineteenth century as one that was dominated by the UK, and shaped according to its interests (see for example ibid, 5; Robinson (n 18), vii). Even Petersmann argues, for example, that the 'liberal' international economic order that existed between 1860 and 1914 relied on 'state guarantees (eg stable exchange rates, currency convertibility to gold) and bilateral international trade, establishment, friendship and shipping treaties' (Ernst-Ulrich Petersmann, 'Grundprobleme der Wirtschaftsverfassung der EG' (1994) 48 *Aussenwirtschaft* 389, 406, my translation). While Röpke thus recognizes the importance of an institutional framework for the functioning of international trade in principle, he fails to identify the factual institutional and political structure of the international economic order of the nineteenth century. Röpke's 'universal-liberal solution' must thus be understood as an ideological figure projected onto the past, rather than a historically accurate depiction.

will arise to a full extent only if the economic actors trust that the international economic order will remain open in the long run, and thus adapt life decisions and investments accordingly. An institutional framework binding states to such a commitment constitutes an important guarantee for such trust.[147] The need for an institutional framework for international trade even arises if one assumes that a country could realize the benefits of free trade by unilateral trade liberalization; this was also acknowledged by those authors who, like Wilhelm Röpke and, a few decades later, Ernst-Ulrich Petersmann, believed that non-state international private law orderings among economic actors could, or should, in principle appear 'spontaneously'.[148] The reason why this has not happened in modern times was, according to Petersmann, the existence of a 'protectionist trap', in which the general interests of consumers and taxpayers has no strong representation, in contrast to well-organized national industries. The opposition of the latter to free trade can be overcome only if reciprocal rights to market entry are secured for the exporting industry.[149] States are thus willing to enter a non-discriminatory international trading system only within a regulatory framework that ensures reciprocity.[150] The success of the post-war global international order must thus be explained as a result of the institutions created on a global level (most notably GATT, IMF and World Bank).[151] According to Petersmann, this applies even more for the EU: '[I]t is in particular the unlimited duration of EU law that creates incentives to cooperate, follow the rules and the focus on the common, long-term general interest.'[152] Thus, even in the accounts of liberalist scholars like Röpke or Petersmann, the potential benefits of international trade can be realized only within an institutional framework.

However, in orthodox economic theory as well as in neoliberal political thinking, the role of institutions remains ambiguous. On the one hand it is obvious that the activities of market actors rely on a certain institutional setting, which in common representations includes at the very minimum a system of private property, the freedom to contract, the necessary judicial and executive enforcement structure, as well as, as ordoliberals emphasized, a system of competition law to control economic power.[153] Moreover, as Friedman held, a system must be in

[147] In this sense Zijlstra (n 11), 40.

[148] This is based on Hayek, who argued that such orderings constituted spontaneous structures, which he termed in an obscurist fashion the 'catallaxy.' Friedrich Hayek, *Law, Legislation and Liberty*, vol II: The Mirage of Social Justice (Routledge, 1976) 107–09; such belief was based on a perhaps too romanticized and somewhat unrealistic view of the 'golden ages' of trade, such as the medieval Hanseatic and Italian city states, or the liberal/gold-standard period of the nineteenth century. As an example of such a view, see Petersmann (n 146), 393–94.

[149] See Petersmann (n 146), 393–94.

[150] ibid, 393.

[151] ibid, 402.

[152] ibid, 402.

[153] See for example Manfred Streit and Werner Mussler, 'The economic constitution of the European community: From Rome to Maastricht' (1994) 5 *Constitutional Political Economy* 319, 323–24.

place 'for the maintenance of law and order to prevent coercion of one individual by another, the enforcement of contracts voluntarily entered into, the definition of the meaning of property rights, the interpretation and enforcement of such rights.'[154] Beyond that, a monetary framework must be provided.[155] It is only within such an institutional framework that the beneficial effects of market forces can unfold. On the other hand, however, it has been a central assumption that the institutional setup necessary for the functioning of market economies involves quasi-natural phenomena, and that an institutional setup that goes beyond a setup as just defined does not improve, but possibly disrupts the functioning of markets. Thus, a central assumption of orthodox theory is, according to Stiglitz, 'that institutions did not matter—markets could see through them, and equilibrium was simply determined by the laws of supply and demand'.[156] The research agenda of orthodox scholars was often to show how market forces could achieve optimal results without the need of institutions. For example, Milton Friedman argued in the 1960s that the central functionality of markets was unaffected by institutional issues that featured prominently in contemporary economic research, most notably industrial organization and monetary policy: 'Despite the importance of enterprises and money in our actual economy, and despite the numerous and complex problems they raise, the central characteristic of the market technique of achieving coordination is fully displayed in the simple exchange economy that contains neither enterprises nor money.'[157] In other words, the central principles of market interaction would apply regardless of the institutional framework, and would shape the barter trade between two individuals on a metaphorical island the same way it would structure complex financial transactions between multinational corporations. The core institutions acknowledged as necessary by orthodox scholars, such as a system of contract and property law enforced by public force, have been understood as meta-historical, deriving from reason or as the effect of long-running processes. Hayek, for example, defended them as the result of some long-lasting evolutionary process that preceded modern-day legislation.[158] The ambivalent perspective on institutions leads to the view that institutions are necessary, and must, in our current legal-political system, be implemented through political means, while at the same time being essentially not up for negotiation, in the sense that only a specific regulatory form is the 'correct' one.[159]

[154] Milton Friedman, *Capitalism and Freedom* (University of Chicago Press, 1982) 27.

[155] ibid, 27, 44–51.

[156] Stiglitz (n 18), 483.

[157] Friedman (n 154), 14.

[158] Hayek argued that 'law is older than legislation'; Friedrich Hayek, *Law, Legislation and Liberty*, vol I: Rules and Order (Routledge, 1973) 72.

[159] The ambivalence of the orthodox as well as the neoliberal position on institutions finds expression in the contradictory, yet common, argument that public policy should be exercised in 'conformity … to the market system.' However, if certain structures or outcomes are not autonomously produced by the 'market system' but must be imposed by public policy, then it would seem that they are quite automatically *not* in 'conformity' with it. For an example of the argument see Streit and Mussler (n 153), 320, fn 3.

Institutionalists see successful market economies as the result of an intricate interaction of market activities with governmental as well as non-governmental institutions. Orthodox scholars, on the other hand, tend to see economic success more as a function of the interaction of market forces alone. From a perspective of European economic law, for example internal market law, this leads to important differences in the evaluation of national structures: orthodox theory perceives institutional variety in Europe (eg different labour market systems, different economic cultures, different concepts of social protection) mostly as potential restrictions on the market forces and therefore welfare-reducing. Institutionalists, on the other hand, might find that these institutions play an important role in the economic system of a region, so that they are welfare-enhancing.[160]

Does Policy Matter? The Role of Non-Market Coordination

Different economic schools think very differently about the role of non-market coordination in achieving optimal socio-economic outcomes. For many economists, public or other non-market forms of coordination have an important role to play for the functioning of markets. We have seen, for example, that orthodox theory usually does not claim that markets work perfectly in real life. Depending on the strength of the belief in the self-correcting powers and equilibrium forces of the market, orthodox scholars acknowledge a narrow or broad range of market failures, for example information failures and externalities. Numerous scholars thus assume a role for non-market coordination to further the general interest. Arthur Pigou, for example, proposed taxation as a tool of internalizing negative externalities (eg, if polluters do not suffer from the effects of pollution, they have no incentive to adapt a less polluting production technique. A pollution tax internalizes the societal costs caused, creating an incentive for polluters to eliminate or restrict polluting production processes.)[161] In his 1960 text 'The Problem of Social Cost', Ronald Coase argued that under the assumption of zero transaction costs the problem of externalities could be efficiently solved between the parties alone: if the aggregate benefits of a polluting activity outweighed the aggregate costs, it could be pursued after the polluter compensates those harmed for the damage incurred.[162] In such a situation, government action is not required to achieve the optimal solution. However, as Coase himself argued, the assumption of zero transaction costs is 'very unrealistic'.[163] If transaction costs routinely prevent market

[160] This issue is addressed, as already discussed, by the 'Varieties of Capitalism' approach, and has been adapted to European economic law for example by Höpner and Schäfer, 'Embeddedness and Regional Integration: Waiting for Polanyi in a Hayekian Setting' (2012) 66 *International Organization* 429; Höpner and Schäfer (n 7).

[161] On Pigou, see Screpanti and Zamagni (n 14), 203–05.

[162] Ronald Coase, 'The Problem of Social Cost' (1960) 3 *Journal of Law and Economics* 1; see also Calabresi (n 59), 1213.

[163] Coase (n 162), 15.

Unlike left-leaning orthodox scholars such as Stiglitz, or (post-)Keynesians such as Minsky, more right-wing scholars question the ability of non-market forms of coordination to achieve optimal outcomes. Drawing from Hayek, Streit and Mussler argued, for example, that public policy is unable to handle the complexity of society, which only a decentralized market system can achieve.[175] But beyond that, not only do they claim that non-market is inferior to market coordination, they also argue that the former directly inhibits the self-coordinating forces of the latter: '[R]ule-setting by the political system can reduce the problem-solving capacity of the economic system.'[176] Streit and Mussler thus assume that the dynamics of the market forces arise only in the very absence of collectively defined goals. The underlying implication is that non-market orderings are *per definitionem* sub-optimal, as they interfere with the essentially automatic self-coordinating processes in markets.[177] Similarly, authors like Kenneth Arrow have questioned the very ability of democratic, non-market coordination to achieve optimal outcomes. Assuming fixed individual preference orders, which we discussed in a previous section, compromises among individuals through the political system always constitute deviations from these individual preferences.[178] The main implication is that a market ordering is always more successful in getting people what they want, than public ordering organized through democratic processes. This mistrust in democratic processes has been picked up by public choice theory, which understands politics as being routinely hijacked by special interests.[179]

However, for many authors the relevant point is not only whether market- or non-market-based forms of coordination are superior in achieving specific results, but rather which results are in fact considered to be desirable. The very choice of what is considered a superior socio-economic outcome must be open to rational decision-making. Depending on the goals chosen, different sets of market- or government-based, or non-market and non-government based regulatory structures may be preferable. Ordoliberal scholar[180] Alexander Rüstow has argued, for

[175] Streit and Mussler (n 153), 322.

[176] ibid, 325.

[177] Myrdal has argued, however, that prices in modern states are influenced by rule-making as well as the activities of quasi-public institutions and private businesses which are strong enough to influence prices: 'Prices are manipulated. They are not the outcome only of the forces in the market; they are in a sense "political prices", depending also on the regulating activity of the state, of quasi-public and private organisations and of private businesses. The state interferences in the price system are, in a sense, the ultimate ones as, under the direction of the political process in a democracy, they are framed to regulate, offset or support the non-state interferences in order to make the total outcome correspond to the valuations and objectives which emege from the democratic political process. Within this institutional framework the price system functions, and apparently quite satisfactorily.' Myrdal (n 29), 49.

[178] Kenneth Arrow, 'A difficulty in the concept of social welfare' (1950) 58 *Journal of Political Economy* 328, 330.

[179] See for example James Buchanan and Gordon Tullock, *The calculus of consent: logical foundations of constitutional democracy* (University of Michigan Press, 1965) 283–95; Mancur Olson, *The Logic of Collective Action* (Harvard University Press, 1965) 1–3. However, scholars like Robert Howse have criticized such a position for its masked liberalist and elitist bias; Howse (n 5), 100–01.

[180] Rüstow described himself as 'neoliberal', though he employed the term in opposition to what he called 'paleo-liberalism' or laissez-faire liberalism, which is closer to the current understanding of the

example, that the choice for different regulatory solutions puts societies on different development trajectories, thus making any claim impossible that one solution is inferior or superior to the other.[181] As an example, Rüstow argued that research within a structure of big corporations will likely lead to different innovations than one that is pursued, for example, within an economy characterized by smaller economic units.[182] This, in turn, may alter the political, social and economic structure of the society as a whole.

It should be clear that the different perspectives on the role of policy, non-market coordination and democratic governance have significant implications on European economic law, for example on internal market law adjudication. Judges who believe that non-market orderings tend to be inferior to market-based outcomes will be more critical of European and of national regulation than judges who believe that non-market orderings may in fact lead to superior outcomes. Along the same lines, judges who believe that democratic policy choices are bound to deliver sub-optimal results will likely make different evaluations than those who assume that the choice between a market- and a non-market form of organizing a specific area should be open to democratic choice.

This short overview illustrates the claim of this chapter that dissent is ubiquitous in economics, and that it takes place not only at the margins of the discipline, but also at its core. The pervasiveness of dissent in economics has important repercussions for European economic law, which necessarily operates on the basis of economic assumptions. It was briefly sketched how the different economic positions would translate into European economic law. In the next sections we turn from general economic theory to two specific questions that are of particular interest for European economic law: trade theory and growth theory.

INTERNATIONAL TRADE

Paul Samuelson postulated in his 1939 article 'The Gains from International Trade' what is essentially the core assumption of trade economics: '[S]ome trade is better than no trade.'[183] More specifically, it is the hypothesis that trade has the potential to raise the global aggregate welfare that lies at the heart of everything that deals

term 'neoliberal'. For this reason, I believe it is clearer to describe his scholarship as part of ordoliberalism, a term that I employ in this book to describe the specific tradition of German liberal thinking after WWII.

[181] Alexander Rüstow, 'Kritik des technischen Fortschritts' (1951) 4 *ORDO: Jahrbuch für die Ordnung von Wirtschaft und Gesellschaft* 373, 393–96.

[182] Rüstow emphasized that non-market orderings do not necessarily need to take the form of government activities: for example, research can be pursued not only by private companies or public institutions, but also by autonomous, non-profit research institutions.

[183] Paul Samuelson, 'The Gains from International Trade' (1939) 5 *The Canadian Journal of Economics and Political Science/Revue canadienne d'Economique et de Science politique* 195, 195.

with international economic relations.[184] This assumption is, prima facie, uncontested by economists of all persuasions, at least if we conceptualize the proposition in broad terms to describe any form of international economic cooperation, and not merely a specific trade regime. What is contested, however, are the conditions under which trade is beneficial, and for whom.[185] In this section, we will look first at some different theoretical perspectives on trade, and then address two specific areas characterized by significant theoretical disagreement, namely under which conditions trade is beneficial, and whether trade leads to a convergence among the participating regions.

Competing Views on Trade: Classical, Neoclassical and New Trade Theory

Classical trade theory developed in the eighteenth century.[186] It was conceived as a refutation of mercantilist theory and policy, which had been the dominant conceptual framework in the preceding centuries.[187] The central argument of classical trade theory was that countries could benefit from measures liberalizing trade even in the absence of liberalization commitments by their trading partners.[188] Most benefits would be accrued under conditions of fully free trade. The classical case for free trade coincided, as many economists argue, with the economic interests of the UK as the economically, politically and militarily most advanced nation of the 1700 and 1800s.[189] Adam Smith conceptualized gains from trade in terms of 'absolute advantage': countries benefit if they specialize in what they do best and then trade.[190] If England was more efficient in producing cloth than Portugal, and Portugal was more efficient in producing wine than England, under conditions of perfectly free trade and no transportation or other transaction costs, England would produce all the cloth and Portugal all the wine.[191] Thus, Smith assumed that under free trade, products are produced where production

[184] Helpman showed, for example, that since the beginning of the industrial revolution the expansion of trade correlates with higher growth of the world economy. Elhanan Helpman, *The Mystery of Economic Growth* (Harvard University Press, 2010), 56.

[185] Bertil Ohlin put the issue as follows: 'The immediate cause of trade is always that goods can be bought cheaper from outside in terms of money than they can be produced at home, and vice versa. It remains to be shown why some goods can be more cheaply produced in one region than in another.' Bertil Ohlin, *Interregional and International Trade* (Harvard University Press, 1967), 7.

[186] The most important proponents include Adam Smith and David Ricardo. Adam Smith, *Wealth of Nations* (Prometheus Books, 1991); David Ricardo, *Principles of Political Economy and Taxation* (Prometheus Books, 1996).

[187] See for example Smith (n 186) 126, 328; see also Screpanti and Zamagni (n 14), 55.

[188] Howse (n 5), 94.

[189] See for example Robinson (n 18), vii; Myrdal (n 29), 145–45; see also verLoren van Themaat (n 139), 5.

[190] Smith (n 186), 342.

[191] Paul Samuelson, 'A Ricardo-Sraffa Paradigm Comparing Gains from Trade in Inputs and Finished Goods' (2001) 39 *Journal of Economic Literature* 1204, 1205.

costs are lowest.[192] Low production costs are the result of the division of labour.[193] The bigger the market, the more specialized and thus cheaper production can become.[194] Smith advocated against trade restrictions both within countries and between countries: he argued against rules limiting competition and mobility of workers and goods such as seen in guild rules;[195] against exclusive privileges of the East India trading companies of the various nations;[196] against import[197] and export restrictions; and against export subsidies.[198] These trade instruments, Smith argued, had been conceived by and in the interest of producers, but function to the detriment of consumers.[199] Authors like Smith or David Hume argued that international trade was able to reach a relatively balanced and stable position that did not necessitate regulatory fine-tuning the way it had been done under mercantilist trade policy. Hume, for example, attacked the mercantilist notion that the in- and outflows of money had to be closely managed.[200] He attempted to show that the balance of payments was secured by market forces alone. Classical trade theorists were convinced that an economic equilibrium existed on the international level.[201]

In 1817, David Ricardo brought forward the 'comparative' (or relative) advantage model. This shows how trade is beneficial even if there are countries that have no absolute advantage in regard to any product. In his famous example, Portugal has absolute advantage in the production of both wine and cloth, but produces wine more efficiently than cloth. England has no absolute advantage in the production of any product. However, with trade, both countries may benefit nonetheless: England producing cloth allows Portugal to specialize on wine production where it can produce more goods in total with the same input of labour. In effect, trade raises the aggregate income. Whereas absolute advantage is about comparing productivity of one good in two countries, relative advantage is about comparing the productivity of two products within one country with the productivity relationship of the same products in another country. While Smith's model explains how trade is beneficial in situations where each trading country has an absolute advantage in a certain industry, Ricardo's model explains how trade is beneficial even in cases where countries have no absolute advantage in any industry. Even today, Ricardo's theory provides the backbone to virtually everything that is said

192 Joseph Schumpeter, *History of Economic Analysis* (OUP, 1996) 607.
193 Smith (n 186), 9.
194 ibid, 24.
195 ibid, 126–52.
196 ibid, 344–45.
197 ibid, 348–69.
198 ibid, 392–06.
199 ibid, 445.
200 See Screpanti and Zamagni (n 14), 40.
201 Myrdal argued that the free trade doctrine is interlocked with the equilibrium thesis: 'It is a more specific corollary of the assumption of harmony of interests and expresses that assumption's inherent anti-state and anti-organisation bias.' Myrdal (n 29), 141.

about trade; current trade models are essentially formulated as either refinements or critiques of Ricardo's theory.[202]

Neoclassical theory started to develop into a consistent body of thought in the late nineteenth century. The key concept of neoclassical theory is marginalism, as briefly discussed above. In classical theory, exchange value was explained in terms of absolute value encapsulated in a product. The classical theorists such as Smith, Ricardo, Mill and Marx employed a labour theory of value: the value of a product was defined by the amount of labour that went into the production of the good.[203] Accordingly, they explained the advantages of trade in terms of labour value: with the same input of labour, more output is created. Neoclassical theory, however, saw prices solely as a function of supply and demand, and not as an expression of some intrinsic value. Therefore comparative advantage models came under attack for using the labour value approach to determine the exchange value, which had been perceived as outdated by neoclassical theory.[204] Scholars like Gottfried Haberler or Bertil Ohlin attempted to reinterpret the theory of comparative advantage from a neoclassical perspective.[205] Most notably, the Ricardo model—based on the input of one factor, namely labour—was reworked into a two- or multifactor model.[206] The most famous of them is the Heckscher-Ohlin (-Samuelson) model of trade. This held, according to Samuelson, that countries 'will tend to specialize (either partially or wholly) in the production of the commodity using much of its most abundant factor.'[207] In Heckscher-Ohlin, the 'geographical distribution of productive factors'[208] (which are not fully mobile) is the decisive precondition of trade: 'It is true that some of the factors are, under certain conditions, freely mobile, but some are not, and all those placed in the group

[202] See for example Paul Krugman, 'The Increasing Returns Revolution in Trade and Geography' (2009) 99 *American Economic Review* 561, 569–70.

[203] Jacob Viner, 'Professor Taussig's Contribution to the Theory of International Trade' in Jacob Viner (ed), *International Economics* (The Free Press, 1951), 154.

[204] See for example Ohlin (n 185), 31–32: 'There is one aspect of the interregional division of production that has always attracted much attention and been the subject of much intricate analysis, although it is in fact only one of a large class of phenomena, and easily explainable as such. According to the classical theory of value the possibility that a country may import certain goods, although they could have been produced with less labor at home than in the exporting country, has naturally been considered as an extremely important, even as the fundamental, problem of international trade. Viewed from a consistent equilibrium theory of prices it is not so.' The Heckscher-Ohlin model must be understood as a systematic move away from the classical model, as Ohlin explained: 'Both Heckscher and Taussig regard their discussion as a modification and addendum to the classical theory. Heckscher, for instance, looks upon his paper as an analysis of "the antecedents of the law of comparative costs". I cannot share this view. As a matter of fact, I do not think that it can be fitted into the classical labor cost theory at all.' ibid, 22.

[205] Robert Baldwin, 'Gottfried Haberler's Contributions to International Trade Theory and Policy' (1982) 97 *Quarterly Journal of Economics* 141, 141; Samuelson (n 183), 195; Myrdal (n 29), 148.

[206] Samuelson (n 191), 1209.

[207] Paul Samuelson, 'International Trade and the Equalisation of Factor Prices' (1948) 58 *Economic Journal* 163, 165. See also Ohlin (n 185), 7.

[208] Ohlin (n 185), 2.

called "nature" are completely immobile.'[209] Factor endowment of regions is taken as given. Ohlin: 'One region may have plenty of iron and coal but little land for wheat-growing, while another has plenty of wheat-land but a scanty supply of mineral resources.'[210] The reason for trade in the classical models is the difference in labour productivity. In contrast, Heckscher describes the neoclassical approach as follows: 'The prerequisites of initiating trade may thus be summarized as different relative scarcity, ie, different relative prices of the factors of production in the exchanging countries, as well as different proportions between the factors of production in different commodities.'[211] Despite their age, the Heckscher-Ohlin model and in particular the Ricardo model continue to be popular to illustrate the advantages of trade over autarky.

While these models seem to have an intuitive charm, scholars have found important faults in these theories. For example, a central problem is that the factual historical development of economies does not seem to conform to the development proposed by comparative advantage model. For example, the underlying logic of that model is one of increasing specialization;[212] However, Imbs and Wacziarg have shown that countries that develop actually diversify their production, thereby specializing less.[213] Only relatively highly developed countries again show a trend towards specialization; this creates a U-shaped curve for sectoral concentration. Another significant problem is that the factual structure of global trade, which is dominated by trade between industrialized countries as well as intra-industry trade, remains unexplained by both the Ricardo and the Heckscher-Ohlin models.[214] The industrialized countries of the world do not differ radically in either productivity levels (which is the key factor for trade in the Ricardo model) or factor endowment (which is decisive in Heckscher-Ohlin). But without these differences, how could the fact be explained that the dominant share of international trade was not between developing and developed world countries (which indeed differ in both productivity and factor endowment), but among developed nations? This critique was systematized in the so-called 'New Trade Theory' (NTT) advanced by scholars like Paul Krugman and Elhanan Helpman.[215]

[209] ibid, 2.

[210] ibid, 6.

[211] Eli Heckscher, 'The Effect of Foreign Trade an the Distribution of Income' in William Allen (ed), *International trade theory Hume to Ohlin* (Random House, 1967) 28.

[212] Dani Rodrik, 'Industrial policy for the twenty-first century' (2004) CEPR Discussion Paper No 4767, 6.

[213] Jean Imbs and Romain Wacziarg, 'Stages of diversification' (2003) 93 *American Economic Review* 63.

[214] See for example Elhanan Helpman, 'Imperfect competition and international trade: Evidence from fourteen industrial countries' (1987) 1 *Journal of the Japanese and International Economies* 62, 63; see, however, the critique of the 'intra-industry trade' assumption for example by Donald Davis and David Weinstein, 'What role for empirics in international trade?' (2001) NBER Working Paper No 8543, 9–14.

[215] Elhanan Helpman and Paul Krugman, *Market structure and foreign trade* (Harvester Wheatsheaf, 1985).

Helpman argued that 'The factor proportions theory [ie, Heckscher-Ohlin] contributes very little to our understanding of the determination of the volume of trade in the world economy, or the volume of trade within groups of countries. The Ricardian view of comparative advantage is also of little help in this respect.'[216] NTT mostly remained within the framework of orthodox theory, but with a few important differences: orthodox theory assumed constant (the output rises in the same proportion as the input) or diminishing returns to scale. NTT scholars, however, argued that the reality of international trade disproves this assumption: not only is it dominated by large multinational corporations, but also industries tend to cluster together in certain regions (eg Hollywood for movies, Silicon Valley for computers, Basel for pharmaceuticals, or the City of London for banking).[217] Both phenomena of international trade are inexplicable from an orthodox perspective, as the assumption of constant or diminishing returns to scale (which is necessary to uphold the assumption of perfect competition) allows for no benefit from size.[218] Similarly, orthodox theory had, apart from differences in factor prices, no explanation for regional specialization: if there are only constant returns to scale, there is no reason for companies to establish themselves in proximity of similar firms. NTT scholars argued that there are economic explanations for both phenomena, based on the concept of increasing returns to scale, which assumes that additional input may lead to disproportionately higher output. Increasing returns to scale may be either intra-company (the bigger the company, the higher the productivity) or intra-industry (the bigger the industry cluster, the higher the productivity). Different to the Ricardo and Heckscher-Ohlin models, the NTT models held that the reason for trade lies in the structure of the industries, not factor endowment or general labour productivity.[219] A specific industrial organization (of a company or of an industry) creates specialization and network effects and reduces transportation costs, which cause increasing returns to scale. Beneficial factors include, inter alia, geographic proximity: if all specialists, skilled workers and companies of a certain industry are located in one region, this region will both be better at producing these things, and will remain better because no other region can catch up. NTT therefore held that network effects and specialization, rather than productivity differences and factor endowment, explain trade between industrialized countries.[220] The Padoa-Schioppa report (which we discussed in

[216] Helpman (n 214), 63.

[217] See also Baldwin (n 205), 18ff.

[218] Helpman and Krugman (n 215), 3; see also Elhanan Helpman, 'A Simple Theory of International Trade with Multinational Corporations' (1984) 92 *Journal of Political Economy* 451, 452.

[219] Helpman and Krugman (n 215), 1.

[220] In principle, the importance of large-scale economies, specialization and path-dependence has been recognized by some neoclassical scholars. However, they have not made it part of their models; see, for example, Ohlin (n 185), 92.

a previous chapter) argued in 1987 that trade in the European Community was largely of the kind described by NTT.[221]

The orthodox model and NTT are not necessarily mutually exclusive; instead, they may be understood as describing different aspects of trade, and different forms of trade relations.[222] This plurality of views on trade and the unclear relation between these models indicate that no single, coherent theoretical framework exists that may guide decision-making. We will see in the next section that these different views on how trade works lead to very different policy recommendations for how trade can be made socially beneficial.

Dissent in Trade Theory

Dissent is as sharp and fundamental in trade theory as it is in economic theory in general. The conflicts are: is trade unconditionally beneficial? If not, then under which conditions is it beneficial? And does trade lead to regional convergence? I will discuss the conflicts in trade theory along these lines and try to sketch how these differences affect policy-making and judicial decision-making in trade law. A general critique brought forward against trade theory was and continues to be that it is not grounded in empirical research. In the 1950s, Myrdal found a 'strange isolation of the theory of international trade from the facts of economic life'.[223] And a half-century later, Davis and Weinstein held: 'Our summary judgment is that, at a deep level, the field has a quite limited empirical understanding of international trade patterns. We can say little about the relative importance of distinct fundamental determinants of trade.'[224]

Is Trade Always Beneficial?

Not even in classical and neoclassical trade theory is everyone a winner. Following the classical/neoclassical trade models, trade generates net benefits on an aggregate level, but it may be shared unequally between the trading countries. It is indeed possible that the benefits of trade are all accrued by one country.[225] Moreover, the

[221] Tommaso Padoa-Schioppa, 'Efficiency, Stability and Equity. A Strategy for the Evolution of the Economic System of the European Community' (Padoa-Schioppa Report) (1987), 33–34.

[222] See Paul Krugman, 'The new Economic Geography, now Middle-Aged' Presentation to the Association of American Geographers (2010), princeton.edu/~pkrugman/aag.pdf, 2 and 13; Krugman (n 202), 569–70.

[223] Myrdal (n 29), 151.

[224] Davis and Weinstein (n 214), 3.

[225] See Schumpeter (n 192), 614; Commenting on the political dimension of trade theory, Schumpeter argued: 'Since advocacy of free-trade policy was the main practical purpose the "classical" writers had in mind when they developed their theory of international values, they were naturally much interested in displaying the "gains" that accrue to a nation from foreign trade. We have noticed elsewhere the bias which this imparted to their argument and their tendency to underestimate the possibilities of unilateral gain from protection.' Ibid, 609–10.

gains from trade within a country are not generated across the board. Because trade creates a bigger market and thus leads to a reallocation of resources to more efficient uses (which explains the net welfare gains of trade), there will inevitably be losers in this process. While trade is seen as beneficial in regard to the total welfare creation, it can have disadvantageous distributive effects for certain groups within a country, as explained, for example, by Paul Samuelson: 'Trade theory is not a guarantee of Santa Claus gains for all. Its classical and neoclassical versions do preclude losses for all. Still, the winds of economic history can warm some and freeze others with no regard for distributive justice.'[226] More recently, this argument was advanced by Nobel prize laureate and former World Bank chief economist, Joseph Stiglitz. In *Globalization and its Discontents*, Stiglitz argued that although globalization may be beneficial in absolute terms, it often has negative effects for the most vulnerable parts of the population.[227] An even more fundamental critique of the neoclassical trade model comes from development economics. Myrdal emphasized in the 1950s the contradiction between theory and reality:

> We thus see the strange thing that in recent decades, while international economic inequalities have been growing and recently also become of more and more pressing practical concern in international politics, the theory of international trade has developed in the direction of stressing more and more the idea that trade initiates a tendency towards a gradual equalisation of factor prices and incomes as between different countries.[228]

And John Williams held that 'while since 1914 the world has been in a state of profound and virtually, continuous disturbance, formal international trade theory has continued to emphasise equilibrating tendencies.'[229] According to Myrdal, the data suggested that free trade did not lead to an equalization, but to a greater difference between more and less developed countries, both in the period before 1914 and after 1945.[230] More specifically, it was held that free trade tends to be biased in favour of the more advanced countries. In the 1950s and 1960s, UNCTAD Secretary-General Raúl Prebisch argued that exporters of primary products faced deteriorating terms of trade.[231] While Prebisch held that free trade could be positive for developing countries in principle, he argued that this was true only if it allowed them to catch up with the most industrialized nations and to diversify their production. If, on the other hand, developing countries were locked in a sub-optimal trading position, they had to pursue a potentially protectionist

226 Samuelson (n 191), 1209.

227 Joseph Stiglitz, *Globalization and its Discontents* (Norton, 2002).

228 Myrdal (n 29), 149.

229 John Williams, *Economic stability in a changing world* (OUP, 1953) 24, quoted in Myrdal (n 29), 152.

230 Myrdal (n 29), 149.

231 'Terms of trade' describes the relationship between how much imported goods a country can get for its exported goods. 'Deteriorating terms of trade' occur when the exporting country receives less imports for the same amount of exported goods. See Raúl Prebisch, 'Commercial Policy in the Underdeveloped Countries' (1959) 49 *American Economic Review* 251.

industrialization programme to ensure their development. Prebisch believed that the correction of asymmetries between the core and the periphery would ultimately have positive effects on trade for all trading countries.[232] More recently, Cambridge economist Ha-Joon Chang argued that all advanced nations initially protected their industries against competition.[233] If the most advanced nations today oppose strategic protection in less developed countries, they hinder developing nations from following the same strategy, thereby 'kicking away the ladder' (as the suggestive title of his book went). Chang suggests that different regions in different stages of development require different trade policies. This rejection of a one-size-fits-all approach has since taken hold of development economics in general.[234] Today, the economic success of the East Asian countries, for example, is often explained with reference to the strong state involvement, the countries' highly developed institutional frameworks, and the temporary strategic protection of key industries in these countries.[235]

Thus, many economists question the assumption that trade is beneficial under all circumstances.[236] In 2000, Francisco Rodríguez and Dani Rodrik argued in a much-discussed article that no robust proof had been presented that free trade in fact has positive growth effects at all: 'Our bottom line is that the nature of the relationship between trade policy and economic growth remains very much an open question. The issue is far from having been settled on empirical grounds. We are in fact skeptical that there is a general, unambiguous relationship between trade openness and growth waiting to be discovered.'[237] Rodríguez and Rodrik's article can be summarized in three propositions that are important from our perspective. First, free trade may potentially have either positive or negative net welfare effects. But second, even more importantly for our purposes, we cannot be sure about the causality between trade policy and welfare effects. In fact, the question whether trade actually causes growth (or whether growing economies attract more trade), and whether trade policy has any influence on this has been discussed very controversially in the economic literature.[238] Finally, for Rodríguez and Rodrik, as for many other economists, the question whether trade is beneficial mostly depends on the circumstances. In particular, the institutional and regulatory setup is held to be of high importance. Von der Groeben, for example, was convinced that

[232] See Mario Cimoli and Gabriel Porcile, 'Global growth and international cooperation: a structuralist perspective' (2011) 35 *Cambridge Journal of Economics* 383, 385; see also Dani Rodrik, 'Globalisation, Social Conflict and Economic Growth' (1998) 21 *World Economy* 143.

[233] Ha-Joon Chang, *Kicking away the ladder* (Anthem Press, 2007).

[234] See for example Dani Rodrik, *One economics, many recipes* (Princeton University Press, 2007).

[235] ibid, 238–39.

[236] Robert Howse argued that '[o]ne can remain true to this goal [of opposing protectionism] without having to believe in noble lies that trade is *always* advantageous and benign.' Howse (n 5), 109 (italics in the original).

[237] Francisco Rodríguez and Dani Rodrik, 'Trade Policy and Economic Growth: A Skeptic's Guide to the Cross-National Evidence' (2000) 15 *NBER Macroeconomics Annual* 261, 266.

[238] For example Frankel and Romer come to a different conclusion than Rodríguez and Rodrik. Jeffrey Frankel and David Romer, 'Does trade cause growth?' (1999) 89 *American Economic Review* 379.

international trade would require a beneficial institutional framework to function to the advantage of the trading countries.[239] Regulatory standards, often attacked by neoclassical theorists for their alleged protectionist potential, can in fact have positive implications: trade scholars like Robert Howse showed that the welfare effects of (non-discriminatory) environmental and labour regulation could well be positive.[240] Whether trade had negative or positive welfare effects can simply not be established in abstract terms.

A closer look at the trade literature thus reveals that economists disagree to a considerable extent regarding the conditions under which trade is beneficial. This disagreement has important policy implications, for example in internal market law. If the effects of trade are assumed to be positive regardless of the institutional and regulatory framework, any restriction traders face will be considered to be disadvantageous. If, on the other hand, the positive effects of trade are believed to depend on the institutional framework or on the economic position of the country, policy-makers and judges will be more circumspect in squashing national rules. In case of doubt, judges will decide in favour of traders when they follow a neoclassical model, but they might be more inclined to consider the institutional and economic particularities of a country if they follow an alternative view on trade.

Does Trade Lead to Regional Convergence?

According to orthodox trade theory, trade may eventually lead to convergence across regions.[241] Convergence firstly describes a convergence in factor prices. This, secondly, implies a convergence of the overall economic conditions. Convergence in orthodox theory is facilitated by three mechanisms: 1) diminishing returns to capital; 2) international factor movement; and 3) trade.[242] Orthodox theory assumes that factors of production may exhibit diminishing returns: for

[239] Hans von der Groeben, 'Deutschland, Europäische Gemeinschaft, Atlantische Partnerschaft' in Hans von der Groeben, (ed), *Europa—Plan und Wirklichkeit* (Nomos, 1967), 49–50.

[240] Howse (n 5) 103, with further references.

[241] This holds true in regard to factor prices and capital-labour ratios. See Ohlin (n 185), 24; Samuelson (n 207), 163. Robert Lucas described the standard neoclassical model as follows: 'The egalitarian predictions of the simplest neoclassical models of trade and growth are well known and easy to explain, as they follow from entirely standard assumptions on technology alone. Consider two countries producing the same good with the same constant returns to scale production function, relating output to homogeneous capital and labor inputs. If production per worker differs between these two countries, it must be because they have different levels of capital per worker: I have just ruled everything else out! Then the Law of Diminishing Returns implies that the marginal product of capital is higher in the less productive (ie, in the poorer) economy. If so, then if trade in capital good is free and competitive, new investment will occur only in the poorer economy, and this will continue to be true until capital-labor ratios, and hence wages and capital returns, are equalized.' Robert Lucas, 'Why Doesn't Capital Flow from Rich to Poor Countries?' (1990) 80 *American Economic Review* 92.

[242] Dimitris Kallioras and George Petrakos, 'Industrial growth, economic integration and structural change: evidence from the EU new member-states regions' (2010) 45 *Annals of Regional Science* 667, 669.

each additional unit there is less output. Factors of production will therefore migrate to different regions with better returns, where they push factor prices up, so that these will eventually converge. The export of goods has an equivalent effect to the migration of factors.[243] However, certain causes may block full convergence, as for example Ohlin explained:

> The observation that the tendency of trade is to equalize factor prices internationally must be qualified in several respects. The difference in quality between productive factors in different countries, the possibility of using entirely different technical processes, the economies of large-scale production, and differences in economic stability and taxation not only blur the outlines of the previous analysis but make it uncertain to what extent international trade as a whole actually tends to equalize factor prices.[244]

Despite these reservations, Heckscher-Ohlin models the dynamics of free trade as pushing, at least in principle, towards equalization of factors, and thus towards the eventual convergence between the regions.[245] This is particularly important for the EU: according to orthodox trade theory, the different countries in a customs union will eventually converge as a consequence of trade and factor mobility.[246]

The convergence assumption, however, was not matched by the economic reality of many countries and regions after WWII. Rather than converging, the most advanced nations pulled even further ahead of the rest of the world, though with the well-known exceptions of countries like Japan, Korea and Taiwan. Commenting on this dynamic, Gunnar Myrdal held in 1957 that 'the play of the forces in the market normally tends to increase, rather than to decrease, the inequalities between regions.'[247] And: '[T]rade does not by itself necessarily work for equality. It may, on the contrary, have strong backwash effects on under-developed countries.'[248] More recently, Rodríguez and Rodrik emphasized that there is no empirically identifiable relation between trade liberalization and economic convergence.[249] In regard to the EU, Rodríguez and Rodrik argued: 'European convergence seems to be the result of factors largely unrelated to trade liberalization.'[250] Slaughter, after analysing four sets of trade liberalization (EEC, EFTA, liberalization between

[243] Ohlin (n 185), 29: '[T]he mobility of goods to some extent compensates for the lack of inter-regional mobility of the factors; or (which is really the same thing), trade mitigates the disadvantages of the unsuitable geographical distribution of the productive facilities.'

[244] ibid, 77.

[245] Modern representatives of the convergence thesis are, inter alia: Robert Barro and Xavier Sala-i-Martin, 'Convergence' (1992) 100 *Journal of Political Economy* 223; Gregory Mankiw, David Romer and David Weil, 'A Contribution to the Empirics of Economic Growth' (1992) 107 *Quarterly Journal of Economics* 407; Robert Barro, Gregory Mankiw and Xavier Sala-I-Martin, 'Capital Mobility in Neoclassical Models of Growth' (1995) 85 *American Economic Review* 103; Xavier Sala-i-Martin, 'The Classical Approach to Convergence Analysis' (1996) 106 *Economic Journal* 1019.

[246] Kallioras and Petrakos (n 242), 669.

[247] Myrdal (n 29), 26; see also Gene Grossman and Elhanan Helpman, 'Endogenous Innovation in the Theory of Growth' (1994) 8 *Journal of Economic Perspectives* 23, 23.

[248] Myrdal (n 29), 51.

[249] Rodríguez and Rodrik (n 237), 308.

[250] ibid, 308.

EEC and EFTA, GATT Kennedy Round), failed to identify any systematic effect of trade liberalization on regional convergence.[251] Factor mobility may equally foster divergence rather than convergence: new classical scholar Robert Lucas argued that financial capital tends to flow from the poor to the rich regions, not vice versa.[252] The same was claimed by Easterly and Levine to be the case for human capital, which flows towards the core, not the periphery.[253] As a consequence of such movements, peripheral countries may lose out in the integration process. As Marques explains, '[i]n the long run ... integration may induce concentration of activity away from the least efficient partners and towards the most efficient ones.'[254] Similarly, Davis and Weinstein held: 'It is well known that [factor price equalization] fails. Wages differ strongly across regions within countries and enormously across countries.'[255]

One reason for the increased divergence between regions may be economies of scale. As already discussed, economic theorists found that industries of the same kind would often form clusters in high-cost countries. This could not be explained by factor prices; instead, they concluded, higher concentrations of industries must lead to increased returns to scale: the benefits arise through network effects, knowledge transfer, specialized services, and reduced transportation costs.[256] Specialization, concentration and network effects are path-dependent: they tend to be self-reinforcing, which means that regional divergence is likely to remain intact or even widen.[257] In this respect, Gunnar Myrdal argued:

> A widening of markets often strengthens in the first instance the rich and progressive countries whose manufacturing industries have the lead and are already fortified by the surrounding external economies.[258]

[251] Matthew Slaughter, 'Trade liberalization and per capita income convergence: a difference-in-differences analysis' (2001) 55 *Journal of International Economics* 203, 225–27.

[252] Lucas (n 241); see also Myrdal (n 29), 28: 'Studies in many countries have shown how the banking system, if not regulated to act differently, tends to become an instrument for siphoning off the savings from the poorer regions to the richer and more progressive ones where returns on capital are high and secure.'

[253] William Easterly and Ross Levine, 'What have we learned from a decade of empirical research on growth? It's Not Factor Accumulation: Stylized Facts and Growth Models' (2001) 15 *The World Bank Economic Review* 177, 180; see also Myrdal (n 29), 27–28.

[254] Helena Marques, 'Trade and Factor Flows in a Diverse EU: What Lessons for the Eastern Enlargement(s)?' (2008) 22 *Journal of Economic Surveys* 364, 377.

[255] Davis and Weinstein (n 214), 6.

[256] Ohlin recognized this possibility, but believed that 'they are probably not very important'. Ohlin (n 185), 39.

[257] See on this Myrdal (n 29), 26–27: 'the power of attraction today of a centre has its origin mainly in the historical accident that something was once started there, and not in a number of other places where it could equally well or better have been started, and that the start met with success. Thereafter the ever-increasing internal and external economies—interpreted in the widest sense of the word to include, for instance, a working population trained in various crafts, easy communications, the feeling of growth and elbow room and the spirit of new enterprise—fortified and sustained their continuous growth at the expense of other localities and regions where instead relative stagnation or regression became the pattern.'

[258] ibid, 51. And: 'If things were left to market forces unhampered by any policy interferences, industrial production, commerce, banking, insurance, shipping and, indeed, almost all those economic

As we have already mentioned a couple of times, the question of whether European integration would lead to convergence or divergence among the regions was controversially discussed in the 1950s and 1960s. Jelle Zijlstra's important Commission study from the 1960s emphasized that the observable effects of European integration were different on different regions: whereas, for example, the previously underdeveloped northern region of the Netherlands appeared to benefit from integration, southern Italy was adversely affected.[259] In particular, the report argued that integration would be followed by a concentration process, which was assumed to have negative effects on peripheral regions.[260] The study further held that such development had to be outbalanced by regional industrial policy, which would make use of tax breaks and invest in infrastructure and transport.[261] A few decades later, Kallioras and Petrakos argued that the gains from economic integration were still unequally distributed between the core and the periphery of the EU. According to Kallioras and Petrakos, the EU's the core is constituted by Germany, France, UK, Benelux, Austria and the Scandinavian countries, whereas the South and the East constitute the periphery. Kallioras and Petrakos argued:

> Proponents of the neoclassical theory … argue that economic integration is a long-term process that eventually leads to a reduction of regional inequalities … Yet, the EU experience … does not seem to support the neoclassical claim. Core EU regions generate advantages related to agglomeration economies and increasing returns to scale that lead to differential growth performance. Conversely, peripheral EU regions, facing higher transaction costs, host, mainly, economic activities associated with constant returns to scale. Engaged in an integration process with distant and more advanced partners, peripheral EU regions tend to develop inter-industry type of trade relations, typically specializing in labour-intensive or resource-intensive activities. This specialization is the outcome of the inability of peripheral and less advanced regions to compete with their more advanced counterparts in the markets for capital-intensive and knowledge-intensive economic activities … Even though it provides an alternative (and perhaps the only feasible) route for the exploitation of the locally available skills, it is doubtful whether such a structural differentiation can produce long-term income convergence.[262]

Kallioras and Petrakos described the development in the new Member States as follows:

> Capital regions and western regions that border the EU-15 area seem to be the relative winners since they have managed to combine a set of positive, structural and

activities which in a developing economy tend to give a bigger than average return—and, in addition, science, art, literature, education and higher culture generally—would cluster in certain localities and regions, leaving the rest of the country more or less in a backwater.' (ibid, 26.) Myrdal further argued that trade equally favoured the richer regions over the others, as their competitive advantage, most notably increasing returns to scale, become even greater in an enlarged market (ibid, 28).

[259] Zijlstra (n 11), 70.
[260] ibid, 69.
[261] ibid, 69.
[262] Kallioras and Petrakos (n 242), 669.

> geographical initial conditions with market dynamics. The majority of the EU [new Member States] regions, however, have followed a rather different path. Endowed with an unfavourable set of initial conditions and being peripheral in the national and the European setting, these regions have been faced in the new economic environment with fewer opportunities and more threats. Unable to attract (or maintain) a critical scale of industrial activities, they have witnessed the collapse of large parts of their industrial bases, drastically cutting local demand and setting real restrictions to efforts and policies of indigenous growth.[263]

To conclude this section it can be held that orthodox theory tends to assume eventual convergence between the Member States of the EU, whereas alternative views hold that—and believe that real-world development supports the claim—the future may also bring continued divergence. These two views on economic integration imply radically different policy recommendations: if EU-wide convergence is believed to be an automatic consequence of trade and factor mobility, all there is to do is to remove supposed restrictions, perhaps bolstered by short-term adaptive measures. Critical trade scholars, on the other hand, see much more contingency in the process of economic development. Whether a region becomes core or periphery is path-dependent, and much more conditional on policy than orthodox theory would assume.[264] Some argue that European integration harbours both tendencies that push the regions towards convergence, as well as such that lead to greater convergence. The Padoa-Schioppa report, for example, subscribed to this view.[265] While market integration had the potential to close the gap between the European regions, adequate policy was required to counteract forces that moved in the opposite direction: 'adequate accompanying measures are required to speed adjustment in the structurally weak regions and countries, and counter tendencies towards divergence.'[266]

We have seen on the previous pages that radically different views on trade exist. While orthodox theory assumes that differences in factor endowment or in productivity are the reason why trade is beneficial, heterodox schools assume that other aspects may in fact be decisive. These include factors like network effects, specialization, proximity, innovation, the institutional setting, and path dependency. Orthodox and heterodox theory also differs in regard to how they view the effects of trade. While orthodox theory holds that trade is always beneficial on the aggregate level,[267] heterodox theory assumes that trade can have positive as well as negative effects, depending on the circumstances. This holds true, for example,

[263] ibid, 678.

[264] Ron Martin and Peter Sunley, 'The new economic geography and policy relevance' (2011) 11 *Journal of Economic Geography* 357, 359.

[265] Tommaso Padoa-Schioppa, 'Efficiency, Stability and Equity. A Strategy for the Evolution of the Economic System of the European Community' (Padoa-Schioppa Report) (1987), 4.

[266] ibid, 4.

[267] Samuelson (n 191), 1209.

for the issue of regional convergence: orthodox scholars tend to assume that trading regions will eventually converge, whereas heterodox scholars believe that trade can also lead to increased divergence, again depending on the circumstances. An important distinction between orthodox and heterodox trade theory is how they conceptualize the role of policy. National policies, from an orthodox view, have no effect at best and a detrimental effect on trade at worst. Only a market not disturbed by government action would allocate resources efficiently. Capital would flow to the 'right' place, and create growth and eventual convergence. From a heterodox view, on the other hand, the institutional setting of a country may be the exact reason for its economic success, and therefore for thriving trade. Rodrik, for example, argues that the potential benefits of economic openness can only be reaped, and disruptions connected to this openness to the world markets only dealt with, if countries have 'complementary institutions at home—in the areas of governance, judiciary, civil and political liberties, social insurance, and of course education'.[268] Only a strong institutional setting—politically, judicially and socially—can counterbalance external shocks from the world market. This calls for the development not only of the institutions connected with the liberalist state (police, judiciary), but also public bureaucracy, anti-corruption, democracy, trade unions, and parties. In particular, social insurances and social safety are a necessary correlate to an open economy: 'What is clear ... is that the provision of social insurance is an important component of market reforms—it cushions the blow on those most severely affected, it helps maintain the legitimacy of these reforms, and it avoids a backlash against the distributional and social consequences of globalization.'[269]

GROWTH AND PROSPERITY

Under what circumstances does a society become more productive, ie, when does the output per head grow? This question was one of the central topics of economic debate in the twentieth century, and continues to be so in the twenty-first century. In this section, we look at some of the competing answers to that question provided by economists, and discuss their respective implications for European law.

Classical economists had tended to address the topic of productivity growth in relation to capital accumulation.[270] Although capital was not seen as productive in itself, it was, according to Prendergast, employed as an analytical means to 'accommodate the learning processes and productive structures associated with round-about methods of production and advanced division of labour.'[271]

[268] Rodrik (n 232), 156.
[269] ibid, 157.
[270] Robinson (n 18), 109; Renee Prendergast, 'Accumulation of knowledge and accumulation of capital in early "theories" of growth and development' (2010) 34 *Cambridge Journal of Economics* 413.
[271] Prendergast (n 270), 420.

The importance ascribed to capital accumulation in relation to productivity growth can still be identified in the post-war development strategies: economists of the 1940s and 1950s identified under-accumulation of capital as a key reason for underdevelopment, and propagated large-scale investment projects as a remedy.[272] However, classical and early neoclassical economists were mainly concerned with questions relating to the distribution of present resources rather than productivity growth, for with a systematic analytical interest developed only in the wake of the Great Depression.[273] The earliest systematic growth theories attempted to model a dynamic version of Keynes' theory, which focused on the investment decisions of market actors under conditions of uncertainty. Harrod's growth model showed that a stable growth path of a society was possible only under the unlikely condition that the actual aggregate growth in output and capital stock matched the output that firms had planned for.[274] If that was not the case, subsequent investment decisions would create an unstable growth path that was not self-correcting.[275] Against this backdrop, Robert Solow proposed in the 1950s what later came to be termed the 'old' or 'exogenous' neoclassical growth theory. Solow showed that only a small fraction of productivity growth could in fact be explained by capital accumulation.[276] Instead, Solow proposed that productivity growth was mainly an effect of 'technological progress'.[277] According to Solow, 'the permanent rate of growth of output per unit of labour input is independent of the saving (investment) rate and depends entirely on the rate of technological

[272] Ramesh Chandra and Roger Sandilands, 'Does modern endogenous growth theory adequately represent Allyn Young?' (2005) 29 *Cambridge Journal of Economics* 463. See also Solow, 'Growth theory and after' (1988) 78 *American Economic Review* 307, 308: 'I believe I remember that writings on economic development often asserted that the key to a transition from slow growth to fast growth was a sustained rise in the savings rate.' For an example see Walt Rostow, *The stages of economic growth* (CUP, 1960). Some influential scholars in the 1990s revived an 'augmented' form of the old growth models which focused on capital accumulation and population growth: see Mankiw, Romer and Weil (n 245); see however Easterly and Levine (n 253); Ben Bernanke and Refet Gürkaynak, 'Is Growth Exogenous? Taking Mankiw, Romer, and Weil Seriously' (2001) 16 *NBER Macroeconomics Annual* 11.

[273] Describing Marshall's economic views, Schumpeter pointed out that 'progress is thought of as a continuous and almost automatic process that does not harbor any phenomena or problems of its own.' Schumpeter (n 192), 892–93.

[274] Roy Harrod, 'An Essay in Dynamic Theory' (1939) 49 *Economic Journal* 14. On this see for example Eckhard Hein, *Distribution and growth after Keynes* (Edward Elgar, 2014) 59.

[275] Hein (n 274), 32.

[276] Solow argued that only one-eighth of growth could be attributed to increases in capital intensity. Solow (n 272), 313. A key policy implication seems to be that policies increasing the savings (investment) rate would not raise growth in the long term. Solow argued: 'it turned out to be an implication of diminishing returns that the equilibrium rate of growth is not only not proportional to the saving (investment) rate, but is independent of the saving (investment) rate. A developing economy that succeeds in permanently increasing its saving (investment) rate will have a higher level of output than if it had not done so, and must therefore grow faster for a while. But it will not achieve a permanently higher rate of growth of output.' ibid, 308.

[277] Robert Solow, 'A Contribution to the Theory of Economic Growth' (1956) 70 *Quarterly Journal of Economics* 65; Robert Solow, 'Technical Change and the Aggregate Production Function' (1957) 39 *Review of Economics and Statistics* 312; Solow (n 272), 313.

progress in the broadest sense.'[278] In Solow's model, the rate of technological progress is conceptualized as quasi-automatic, unrelated to the factual investment decisions of market actors.[279] Because growth depends on the rate of technological progress, which in turn is unconnected to factual market processes, Solow's growth model has been termed 'exogenous'. Contrary to Harrod's early Keynesian model, which predicted an unstable growth path based on firm investment decisions under conditions of uncertainty that was not self-correcting, Solow's model predicted the self-correction of the system towards a natural growth path.[280] This, in turn, implies completely different roles for policy: whereas policy interventions leave the growth path unaffected in Solow's model, Harrod's model suggests that policy has a potentially important role to play to secure optimal development.

Against the backdrop of Solow's ('old' or 'exogenous') neoclassical growth theory we will look at three contemporary perspectives on growth and discuss their policy implications: 1) ('new' or 'endogenous') neoclassical growth theory; 2) Schumpeterian theory; and 3) post-Keynesian growth theories. New neoclassical growth theory attempted to reconceptualize technological progress as based on actual investment decisions of market actors. In Solow's model, technological progress remained a largely unexplained phenomenon, and Solow essentially assumed a steady rate of technological progress.[281] A central implication of this view was that fluctuations of the economy—caused by firm behaviour, policy, etc—were believed to affect the business cycle only, but not the long-run growth path.[282] This view was criticized by new neoclassical growth theorists,[283] who assumed that decisions of market actors to invest in innovation in fact constituted the driving force of growth.[284] For example, it was argued that the choice of households to refrain from present consumption and to spend on education instead would

[278] Solow (n 272), 309.

[279] Growth is not attributed to investment, but to factors that are extraneous to the workings of the economy, namely population growth and abstract technological progress: Hein (n 274), 60. However, Solow of course recognizes at least in principle that technical progress requires investment by firms. See Solow (n 272), 316.

[280] Hein (n 274), 59–60.

[281] Solow (n 277), 85.

[282] See on this for example Gilberto Libânio, 'Aggregate demand and the endogeneity of the natural rate of growth: evidence from Latin American economies' (2009) 33 *Cambridge Journal of Economics* 967, 972; Paul Romer, 'Increasing Returns and Long-Run Growth' (1986) 94 *Journal of Political Economy* 1002, 1003.

[283] Kenneth Arrow, 'The Economic Implications of Learning by Doing' (1962) 29 *The Review of Economic Studies* 155: 'Nevertheless a view of economic growth that depends so heavily on an exogenous variable, let alone one so difficult to measure as the quantity of knowledge, is hardly intellectually satisfactory.' Baldwin ridiculed Solow's model as assuming 'mana-from-heaven technological advances'. Baldwin (n 205), 4.

[284] Romer argued: 'While exogenous technological change is ruled out, the model here can be viewed as an equilibrium model of endogenous technological change in which long-run growth is driven primarily by the accumulation of knowledge by forward-looking, profit-maximizing agents.' Romer (n 282), 1003.

push up the long-term growth rate.[285] In the 1980s, scholars like Grossman and Helpman,[286] Lucas[287] and Romer[288] tried to show that the short-run decisions of companies to innovate would affect the long-run development of the economy, influencing the rise in productivity. This approach is termed 'endogenous' growth theory, as growth is conceptualized as the direct consequence of decisions of market participants: individual decisions to invest in education or innovation spills over in the general economy, having positive external effects.[289] The endogenous growth model has important policy consequences. These are described by Hein as follows:

> [A]s is well known from neoclassical microeconomics, the existence of positive external effects implies that private investment in human capital will fall short of the socially optimal amount of human capital accumulation. This kind of market failure can be tackled by government intervention in the market process, for example by subsidizing human capital accumulation or providing (partly) public education and training.[290]

Moreover, as endogenous growth theory does not assume a natural growth path, the long-term growth path is dependent on the short-term choices of firms and households to invest in innovation and education. This leaves significant room for policy, as a broad variety of factors may constitute incentives or disincentives for firms to innovate, including the market structure, the non-market framework, and government-funded incentives like R&D subsidies.[291] Some scholars claim that policy even trumps private investment decisions. In this regard, Helpman argued:

> Countries that start with similar endowments can follow different developmental paths as a result of differences in institutional structures, because institutions affect the incentives to innovate and to develop new technologies, the incentives to reorganize production and distribution in order to exploit new opportunities, and the incentives to accumulate

[285] More generally speaking, the important factor in innovation-based growth models is total 'human capital', as opposed to the accumulation of 'physical capital'; Paul Romer, 'Endogenous Technological Change' (1990) 98 *Journal of Political Economy* 71, 99. Hein comments: 'So far, the human capital model has demonstrated that the long-run equilibrium growth rate of the economy depends on the growth rate of human capital, which is itself determined by the technology in the education and training sector and by the share of human capital devoted to education and training. Therefore, the more households are willing to refrain from present consumption and to invest in human capital, the higher will be the long-run equilibrium growth rate of the economy.' Hein (n 274), 80.

[286] Gene Grossman and Elhanan Helpman, 'Endogenous Product Cycles' (1991) 101 *Economic Journal* 1214; Gene Grossman and Elhanan Helpman, 'Quality Ladders in the Theory of Growth' (1991) 58 *Review of Economic Studies* 43.

[287] Robert Lucas, 'On the mechanics of economic development' (1988) 22 *Journal of Monetary Economics* 3.

[288] Romer (nn 282, 285).

[289] Hein (n 274) 80.

[290] ibid, 80.

[291] See Helpman (n 184), 49–50; Endogenous growth scholars also see a complex relationship between innovation, growth and the level of trade. According to Helpman, the theory 'does not predict a simple relationship between exposure to foreign trade and productivity growth. In theory, trade can encourage or discourage the growth of income per capita.' ibid, 69. However, Helpman emphasized

> physical and human capital. For these reasons institutions are more fundamental determinants of economic growth than R&D or capital accumulation, human or physical.[292]

However, Helpman conceptualized market and non-market innovators (eg universities) as symbiotic: even though technological change may originate from government-funded research, firms 'translate' new knowledge into products of practical value.[293]

Different from neoclassical scholars, Schumpeter emphasized the discontinuities, rather than the continuities of the process of economic development. While capital accumulation plays a relevant role in economic history, he argued,[294] the decisive phenomena are innovations based on new combinations of productive means, eg new products, new means of production, new markets, new transport routes, new sources of primary products, or new forms of organization of production.[295] Schumpeter associated these functions with the figure of the 'entrepreneur', a term that encapsulates the creative and the leadership aspects that he thought to be decisive (as opposed to the function of the financier, the inventor or the owner of the productive means). Schumpeter described a process of growth where companies try to gain temporary monopolies through innovation, which allow them to reap in monopoly gains.[296] After some time, other competitors imitate the innovative product or process, and the entrepreneur's monopoly profit vanishes.[297] The innovation will dissipate into general knowledge.[298] Schumpeter understood the process of change through innovation as 'creative destruction'.[299] He described the discontinuous process of innovation as 'long waves of economic activity … each of them consists of an "industrial revolution" and the absorption of its effects.'[300] The development 'progressively raises the standard of living of the masses'.[301] Schumpeterian growth requires a certain legal and institutional framework for entrepreneurs to reap monopoly gains from their innovations; otherwise they would not have the incentive to invest in innovation. This may require, for example, well-structured intellectual property (IP) laws. However, an IP system that is too strict may protect the incumbent firm and thereby suffocate, not foster innovation. Beyond that, innovation may also require industrial policy to thrive. Development economists Dani Rodrik and Ricardo Hausmann argued

that while trade can both hinder or promote growth in theory, it has largely had pro-growth effects in practice.

292 ibid, 139.
293 Romer (n 285), 72; Grossman and Helpman (n 247), 26.
294 Joseph Schumpeter, *Theorie der wirtschaftlichen Entwicklung* (Duncker und Humblot, 1934) 103.
295 ibid, 101.
296 ibid, 212; see ibid 234 about the entrepreneur's profit as monopoly profit.
297 ibid, 229.
298 ibid, 230.
299 Schumpeter (n 38), 81.
300 ibid, 67.
301 ibid, 68.

that specialization may ensue as the result of a entrepreneurial discovery process that cannot be protected by IP law: once pioneering entrepreneurs have discovered that a certain production is specially beneficial in a country, others will copy this.[302] The positive externalities of the first entrepreneur's (potentially costly) search project thus cannot be monetized. Rodrik proposed that such situation justifies temporary subsidization of new, non-traditional industries, eg through the provision of venture capital.[303] It can thus generally be said that in Schumpeterian growth theory, institutions and policy have a potentially important role to play.[304]

(Post-)Keynesian growth theories share with new neoclassical growth theory the view that there is no automatic, exogenous growth.[305] Keynesian economics emphasizes that the future economic development is completely uncertain;[306] this means that Keynesians tend to dismiss the existence of long-run 'natural' growth trends.[307] Instead, the (investment and innovation) decisions of economic agents in the face of uncertainty shape the future trajectory. Consequently, radically different growth trajectories are possible.[308] From this perspective, the short-run business cycle is not a mere fluctuation around a general growth path; rather, short-term developments that form part of the business cycle 'cast shadows' on the long-term development, so that the growth trajectory is path-dependent.[309] Fitoussi and Saraceno argued, for example:

> [A] modicum of historical sensitivity suffices to understand that long spells of depressed economy may have long-lasting effects on the growth potential of the economy. For example, firm bankruptcies can spread to the financial sector, resulting in a credit crunch that causes a shortage of working capital for the production sector and serious negative effects on investment and the capital stock. Hysteresis effects of unemployment may further worsen the scenario.[310]

302 Rodrik (n 212), 9–11.

303 ibid, 11.

304 See for example Philippe Aghion and Peter Howitt, 'Appropriate growth policy: A unifying framework' (2006) 4 *Journal of the European Economic Association* 269.

305 There is no uniform Keynesian growth theory. As Stockhammer explains, there are in fact different (post-) Keynesian growth theories, 'with different, sometimes contradictory assumptions'. However, Stockhammer defines the following as the common features of a Keynesian growth model: 'At the very core are an independent investment function and saving propensities that differ between income classes (Kaldor savings equation). Thus the distribution of income between capital and labor plays a crucial role.' Stockhammer (n 78), 3; an extensive overview of the different versions of Keynesian growth theory is provided by Hein (n 274).

306 Keynes (n 34), 213–15.

307 Robinson argued: 'There is no law of nature that the 'natural' rate of growth should prevail. This marks the distinction between a Keynesian and a neo-neoclassical growth model.' Robinson (n 18), 118; see also Davidson (n 17), 8.

308 Libânio (n 282), 974; Hein (n 274) 182.

309 Libânio (n 282), 968.

310 Jean-Paul Fitoussi, and Francesco Saraceno, 'European economic governance: the Berlin–Washington Consensus' (2013) 37 *Cambridge Journal of Economics* 479, 487.

Keynesian growth theory differs from neoclassical growth theory, however, insofar as it assumes that the demand side plays a decisive role.[311] Keynesians argue that growth is driven by investment, but that investment is not determined by previous savings, but by future business outlooks. In Keynesian theory, saving is the decision to hold on to financial assets, whereas neoclassical theory assumes that all saving is invested, so that the demand-side is an irrelevant concern.[312] Investment decisions are driven by the investors' outlook on an uncertain future, which may be shaped by what Keynes called the 'animal spirits'.[313] If investors have a negative business outlook, they will hoard the money or acquire financial products rather than invest their assets productively, which in turn will lead to an economic downturn.[314] Producers will spend and invest less and lay off employees, which further depresses growth. In such a situation, the direct or indirect stimulation of demand by the government may be beneficial: increased demand induces firms to spend and invest more, which in turn stimulates growth.[315] Thus, aggregate demand ultimately influences the growth rate.[316] For Keynesians, the 'quality' of demand is important as well: it is assumed that the functional distribution of income (essentially the equity of distribution)[317] has an influence on demand, and thereby on growth.[318] Persons with a lower income are believed to have a higher propensity to consume, ie, they spend a larger share of their income on consumption. By contrast, richer people have a higher propensity to save, ie, to put their income into financial assets.[319] This means that if a higher income share goes

[311] Stockhammer (n 78), 4; the importance of aggregate demand for the functioning of the economy has also been emphasized by some ordoliberalist scholars, such as Alfred Müller-Armack, *Wirtschaftsordnung und Wirtschaftspolitik* (Verlag Rombach, 1966) 359.

[312] Stockhammer (n 78), 7.

[313] Keynes (n 12), 161.

[314] See Stockhammer (n 78), 8: 'In the most general formulation investment is determined by the present value of the expected future income stream—where "expected" is the critical word. Since the future is fundamentally uncertain and open, there is no objective way of forming expectations, rather it is animal spirits, conventions and psychology that determine profit expectations and thus investment spending. Hence the crucial question in Keynesian theory of investment becomes: What determines expectations about future revenues?'

[315] Mario Cassetti, 'Bargaining power, effective demand and technical progress: a Kaleckian model of growth' (2003) 27 *Cambridge Journal of Economics* 449, 450.

[316] See Hein (n 274), who argued: 'As is well known, the core finding of the theory of effective demand is that, in a monetary production economy, investment demand is independent from prior saving and that investment generates the appropriate amount of saving via the multiplier' (ibid, 25). See also Robinson, who held: 'The Keynesian models (including our own) are designed to project into the long period the central thesis of the General Theory, that firms are free, within wide limits, to accumulate as they please, and that the rate of saving of the economy as a whole accommodates itself to the rate of investment that they decree.' Joan Robinson, *Economic Philosophy* (Penguin Books, 1962) 82–83.

[317] Hein defines functional income distribution as 'the distribution of income between social classes (workers, capitalists, landowners) and/or between different types of income (wages, profits, rents), whereas the personal or household distribution looks at the distribution between house-holds and individuals regardless of the functional source of the income.' Hein (n 274), 2–3.

[318] Stockhammer (n 78), 3.

[319] ibid, 5.

to the relatively poorer part of society, a greater part of it is directed into consumption, which in turn stimulates the economy. Thus, a more equitable distribution of income may ultimately lead to higher growth.[320] From a Keynesian perspective, then, policy has a potentially significant effect on growth: it may stimulate demand in an economic downturn and thereby influence the long-term growth rate, and may implement a more equitable income distribution, which in turn is associated with higher growth.

It should be clear that the existence of competing views on economic growth has significant implications for European economic law. In internal market law, the (old) neoclassical growth model, which essentially assumes a "natural" and stable growth path, would translate into significant skepticism about any type of national policy aimed at fostering growth, as well as about redistributive policies. By contrast, from the perspective of a Schumpeterian, new neoclassical or Keynesian growth theory, industrial policy (such as investment in R&D or in public education) or redistributive policies may be seen as growth-enhancing, and thereby in line with the Union's regulatory objectives.

INTERMEDIATE FINDINGS

We may conclude the chapter by stating that economic theory displays a stunning breadth of beliefs, which makes a functional interpretation of the Treaty provisions in the light of the Union's socio-economic objectives difficult. We encountered fundamentally contradicting views both in regard to more conceptual questions such as whether the economy is better described in terms of equilibrium or of disequilibrium, as well as more practical questions such as the preconditions of growth. It has been shown that these different economic assumptions imply completely different approaches as to how the Union's objectives are best achieved, which in turn is of high relevance for the purposive interpretation of European law. Depending on the chosen economic assumptions, European law may be interpreted in completely different ways. Described in negative terms, this means that a functional interpretation of European law in the light of the Union's objectives will routinely deliver conflicting results. Put in positive terms, it means that the Treaty is best conceptualized as pluralist in the light of competing socio-economic paradigms.

[320] Eckhard Hein and Lena Vogel, 'Distribution and growth reconsidered: empirical results for six OECD countries' (2008) 32 *Cambridge Journal of Economics* 479, 481.

5

Monetary Union, the Measures Enacted Since 2008 and the 'European Macroeconomic Constitution'

INTRODUCTION

WE HAVE SEEN in the previous chapters that the macroeconomic dimension of European integration had been a core concern since the Union's earliest days. Economic union as envisioned by the Treaty of Rome was held to require a certain macroeconomic environment, such as, most notably, a stable exchange rate system. It was expected that, over time, the Member States would have to increasingly coordinate their macroeconomic policies in order to realize the potential gains from integration. Beyond that, many economists and policymakers believed that European integration would also create unwanted dynamics, most notably for Europe's peripheral regions, which would in turn make increased coordination and ultimately the adoption of common policies necessary. However, the degree to which such coordination of economic policies, as well as the adoption of common policies on the European level, were necessary remained controversial. In the Union's first decades there was some form of factual coordination of the Member States' macroeconomic policies, because the Member States' currencies were pegged within the Bretton Woods system. As the Member States all followed the dollar as the anchor currency, this also implied, incidentally, policy coordination among themselves.[1] Over time, the Union developed a limited institutional framework performing tasks of macroeconomic governance, ranging from the Monetary Committee, provided for under the Treaty of Rome, to the European Monetary System (EMS). Monetary coordination in the context of fully liberalized capital movements as implemented in the late 1980s significantly increased the need for deeper synchronization, and ultimately for common policies. The European Monetary Union (EMU), enacted by the Treaty of Maastricht, established the ECB as a supranational body with extensive regulatory competences; and the Stability and Growth Pact (SGP) created as a binding framework

[1] Robert Mundell, 'A Plan for a European Currency' (Paper Prepared for Discussion at the American Management Association Conference on Future of the International Monetary System, New York, 10–12 December, 1969) 25.

was vested, in principle, with punitive force. As compared to monetary unions coinciding with federal states such as the United States or Canada, however, the European system of macroeconomic governance that was in existence before the 2008 crisis had remained extremely limited.

Since the 2008 crisis the Union has faced an intense conflict over the orientation of its socio-economic policies, and in particular over the new tools of macroeconomic governance that were enacted in response to the crisis.[2] This conflict is characterized by two interlocked aspects, one political and the other legal. The political dimension of the conflict concerns the question of which socio-economic policies are considered preferable: should, for example, the European banks be rescued at taxpayers' expense? Should the Member States whose debt exploded as a consequence be supported by the other Member States? And should the economic slump be fought with austerity, or with a counter-cyclical investment policy? In the existing European system of macroeconomic governance with its limited institutional setup this political dimension is intertwined with a second aspect, which is of a legal nature: even if a certain socio-economic policy is assumed to be politically desirable, is it also legal? This issue found expression in numerous lawsuits in national courts as well as the CJEU, most notably in regard to the European Stability Mechanism (ESM) and the ECB's Outright Monetary Transactions (OMT) programme.[3] The question as to the legality of the crisis measures can be further separated into a substantive aspect—which measures are prohibited in substantive terms?—and a procedural-institutional aspect, ie, what form can such measures take, what procedures are available? This chapter will mostly focus on the first question, and ask whether the Treaty establishes significant constraints on policymaking from a substantive perspective. However, the procedural-institutional question will be addressed at various points as well, as the two questions are often intertwined: the competences of the Union and their limits may put restrictions on the options that are available in substantive terms. Moreover, the legal-institutional setup of the Union's macroeconomic policies has, explicitly or tacitly, often been assumed to express a comprehensive regulatory choice for a specific socio-economic paradigm, which in turn is believed to restrain the policy options available for the Union lawmakers.[4] The question as to the substantive orientation of the Treaty can thus not be fully separated from institutional and procedural issues.

[2] For an extensive literature overview, see Thomas Beukers, 'Legal writing(s) on the eurozone crisis' (2015) EUI Working Papers Law No 11.

[3] See Case C-370/12, *Thomas Pringle v Government of Ireland, Ireland and The Attorney General* [2012] ECLI:EU:C:2012:75 (hereinafter *Pringle*); Case C-62/14, *Peter Gauweiler and Others v Deutscher Bundestag* [2015] ECLI:EU:C:2015:400 (hereinafter *Gauweiler*); For an overview of the various national lawsuits, see Fabian Amtenbrink, 'New Economic Governance in the European Union: Another Constitutional Battleground?' in Kai Purnhagen and Peter Rott (eds), *Varieties of European Economic Law and Regulation* (Springer, 2014).

[4] Such assumption can be found, for example, in Paul Craig's description of what he terms the 'Maastricht settlement'. Paul Craig, 'Article Review: Pringle and the nature of legal reasoning' (2014) 21 *Maastricht Journal of European and Comparative Law* 205, 206–08.

The EMU must be analysed within the context of the advent of neoliberalism as the dominant socio-economic paradigm in the 1980s. As already discussed at the beginning of Chapter 2 on the 1992 reforms, Wolfgang Streeck has described the macroeconomic instabilities experienced since the 1970s as a consequence of the unravelling of the post-war compromise between labour and capital. In order to uphold the (impression of) growing popular prosperity despite stagnating wages and falling tax receipts from capital, various, ultimately unsuccessful, strategies were employed: whereas the 1970s saw significant inflation that upheld the illusion of wage increases for a while, the 1980s brought a considerable increase of public debt as a consequence of governments attempting to protect the existing levels of public services in the broadest sense. Finally, financial market deregulation of the 1990s brought a build-up of private debt, which was one of the key triggers of the crisis in 2008. Since the crisis, it has been the acquisition of both private and public debt by the central banks and the corresponding expansion of money that has become the main strategy to uphold the prosperity illusion, as Streeck argues.[5] Within the context of this development, the present chapter asks whether the parts of the Treaty that establish what some have called the Union's *macro*economic constitution must be interpreted as expressing a choice in favour of a specific socio-economic paradigm that is of normative relevance in the interpretation and application of its provisions. Attempting this, the present chapter proceeds as follows: we will first review the different socio-economic views on monetary union, and look at the arguments that were mobilized in support of the limited institutional setup of the EMU prior to 2008. It will be shown that this setup found backing in then-dominant economic thinking, which emphasized the ability of integrated markets to buffer asymmetrical shocks in a monetary union, and questioned the ability of governments to influence economic developments through monetary and fiscal policy. Along these lines, Fitoussi and Saraceno have argued that '[e]mbedding neoliberal principles in the treaties defining its governance, the EU has enshrined a peculiar doctrine within its constitution.'[6] Thus, prior to the crisis it might have been assumed that, as the factual EMU setup corresponded to the recommendations of the then-dominant socio-economic paradigm,[7] the Treaty had in fact to be interpreted along its lines. However, the EU's poor economic performance in the past two decades[8] as well as the economic crisis of 2008 has thrown doubt on the validity of this previously dominant paradigm,

[5] Wolfgang Streeck, *Gekaufte Zeit* (Suhrkamp, 2013), 15.

[6] Jean-Paul Fitoussi and Francesco Saraceno, 'European economic governance: the Berlin–Washington Consensus' (2013) 37 *Cambridge Journal of Economics* 479.

[7] Fitoussi and Saraceno (n 6), 480, held: 'The EU institutional set-up is no accident. It reflects the neoliberal doctrine that prevailed in the early 1990s, which posited government intervention to be useless, if not harmful, to fostering growth. The policy prescriptions are coherent with the objective of minimising obstacles to aggregate supply growth: increasing competition through deregulation and privatisation; price stability; and budget balance. Each objective has to be pursued independently from the others, as if the model of the economy was linear.'

[8] Fitoussi and Saraceno (n 6), 481, argued that the neoliberal policy consensus that was able to shape the European Union over the past decades must be judged to be unsuccessful, most notably because

which in turn shakes the assumption that the Treaty should interpreted exclusively on its basis. At the same time the measures enacted in the wake of the crisis have again altered the system of macroeconomic governance to a considerable extent.[9] This all suggests that the question as to the socio-economic orientation of the Union's macroeconomic constitution should be discussed anew.

The process that the Union embarked on in the wake of the 2008 crisis has been severely criticized for what can essentially be understood as a suspension of the rule of law. The crisis measures have been faulted for their disregard for established procedures for Treaty amendment,[10] the circumvention of procedural safeguards and parliamentary participation,[11] the disruption of the Union's institutional balance,[12] the marginalization of smaller and less rich countries,[13] the undermining of national parliamentary sovereignty,[14] the way clear procedural requirements in the Treaty were altered through secondary law,[15] the creation of unaccountable modes of governance,[16] and the shielding of the conditionality instruments from fundamental rights scrutiny.[17] Parts of the crisis measures must simply be considered to be illegal; this is the case, in particular, for the Treaty on Stability, Coordination and Governance in the Economic and Monetary Union (TSCG), the alterations made to the sanctions regime in the 'preventive' arm of the

'[i]n the past two decades the EU growth performance has been considerably lower than that of the USA'.

[9] Joerges speaks of a 'transformation' of the European economic constitution; Christian Joerges, 'The European economic constitution and its transformation through the financial crisis' (2015) ZenTra Working Papers in Transnational Studies No 47; Menéndez identifies a 'process of constitutional mutation that has consecrated the subordination of the normative values of the Social and Democratic *Rechtsstaat* to the protection of the value of capital assets.' Augustín-José Menéndez, 'The Existential Crisis of the European Union' (2013) 14 *German Law Journal* 453, 521.

[10] See on the role of EU institutions in treaties like the ESM or the TSCG Treaty: Steve Peers, 'Towards a New Form of EU Law? The Use of EU Institutions outside the EU Legal Framework' (2013) 9 *European Constitutional Law Review* 37; Paul Craig, 'The stability, coordination and governance treaty: principle, politics and pragmatism' (2012) 37 *European Law Review* 231; on the illegality of the TSCG see Andreas Fischer-Lescano and Lukas Oberndorfer, 'Fiskalvertrag und Unionsrecht' [2013] 66 *Neue Juristische Wochenschrift* 9.

[11] On the crisis measures from a perspective of parliamentary democracy see eg Amtenbrink (n 3); criticizing the circumvention of the community method: Rudolf Streinz, 'Reform der EU-Wirtschaftsverfassung: Kompetenzen und Institutionen' (58. Bitburger Gespräche, Trier, 8–9 January 2015), 15.

[12] Mark Dawson and Floris de Witte, 'Constitutional Balance in the EU after the Euro-Crisis' (2013) 76 *Modern Law Review* 817, 828–36.

[13] ibid, 836–42.

[14] See Kaarlo Tuori and Klaus Tuori, *The Eurozone Crisis* (Cambridge University Press, 2014) 209–16.

[15] Rainer Palmstorfer, 'The Reverse Majority Voting under the "Six Pack": A Bad Turn for the Union?' (2014) 20 *European Law Journal* 186; Andreas Fischer-Lescano, 'The European TSCG and EU law', guengl.eu/uploads/_old_cms_files/2012_09_06_Fischer-Lescano_Gutachten-kurz_Fiskalpakt_060912%20-%20EN.pdf, 12.

[16] See eg Claus Offe, 'The Europolis experiment and its lessons for deliberation on Europe' (2014) 15 *European Union Politics* 430, 431.

[17] See Claire Kilpatrick, 'Are the Bailouts Immune to EU Social Challenge Because They Are Not EU Law?' (2014) 10 *European Constitutional Law Review* 393; Claire Kilpatrick, 'On the Rule of Law and Economic Emergency: The Degradation of Basic Legal Values in Europe's Bailouts' (2015) 35 *Oxford Journal of Legal Studies* 325.

SGP, and the introduction of reversed qualified majority voting in both the SGP and the Macroeconomic Imbalance Procedure (MIP).[18] More generally, the evolving regime of macroeconomic governance has been held to undermine important tenets of the European legal order, including the rule of law, the institutional balance and fundamental rights. The form of Treaty interpretation employed to construct the legality of the crisis measures, consisting of a 'text, background and purposive reasoning', has turned, in Michelle Everson's words, into a 'blunt and legally meaningless melange, masking a programme that dispenses with all legal restraint in order to enable immediate political goals'.[19] The Union's competence provisions have in some instances been read as authorizing the alteration of clear Treaty requirements through secondary law (most notably in regard to reversing qualified majority voting and the reforms of the sanctions regime), creating a situation in which, potentially, anything can be done through one legal instrument or another. The process has been described by Lukas Oberndorfer as one of 'authoritarian constitutionalism', which is characterized by the implementation, through the authoritarian breach of law, of a neoliberal agenda in a legal form that makes it politically unassailable.[20] The foreseeable development may entail, as Oberndorfer argued, an eventual return to 'regular' constitutionalism, in which the crisis measures will receive a proper legal foundation.[21] However, such retroactive regularization will imply the ossification of a status quo shaped by neoliberal policy and ushered in through authoritarian means. Insisting on the rule of law is a highly political demand, as it means resisting the implementation of a socio-economic programme through improper means. The current situation is complex from the perspective of legal analysis, as it combines illegal law, a highly problematic form of legal interpretation, legally unrestrained decisionism, and a conflict between socio-economic worldviews. In such a situation, establishing the rule of law requires a highly reconstructive effort of legal scholarship: it entails the re-establishment of the meaning of the relevant provisions and of their scope, the recalibration of the powers of the various institutions, finding a way to deal with illegal law, the mobilization of legal instruments to enhance transparency, the mapping out of ways to re-establish democratic oversight, and the application of fundamental rights. From the perspective of this book, it means establishing whether the claim as to the pluralist character of the European economic constitution can be upheld in the light of the crisis measures. It will be argued that this is possible: insisting on the rule of law means, in our context, insisting on the Treaty's pluralist character in the face of neoliberal authoritarianism.

[18] Lukas Oberndorfer, 'Vom neuen, über den autoritären zum progressiven Konstitutionalismus' [2013] *Juridikum* 76.

[19] Michelle Everson, 'An Exercise in Legal Honesty: Rewriting the Court of Justice and the Bundesverfassungsgericht' (2015) 21 *European Law Journal* 474, 478.

[20] Oberndorfer (n 18).

[21] ibid, 85.

In the following sections we will revisit five regulatory areas relating to the Union's macroeconomic constitution, and ask whether they must be read as expressing a choice for a specific socio-economic paradigm: in particular we look at the ECB's stability mandate, the SGP, the Macroeconomic Imbalance Procedure, as well as Articles 123 and 125 TFEU. It will be shown in regard to all five policy areas that they are in fact open to different interpretations on the basis of competing socio-economic paradigms. The implication is that if these policies are nonetheless applied in a way that corresponds to a specific paradigm, then this must be conceptualized as a *political* choice (in the sense defined in the Introduction). In more practical terms it can be argued, for example, that the currently prevailing austerity-oriented policies constitute a political choice, as the European macroeconomic constitution would equally allow for the implementation of alternative policies based on different socio-economic paradigms. Consequently, austerity politics is in need of justification that goes beyond the claim that it is required by the text or spirit of the SGP. It could be argued that the de jure openness identified in this chapter is of limited significance in the light of a legal and institutional framework that seemingly makes the realization of a specific ideological programme de facto inevitable.[22] However, it makes a significant difference whether the source of the bias must be assumed to be constitutional in nature or has other causes, eg institutional dynamics, the use of biased economic theory in the application of the law, the capture of Union institutions by certain political and economic interests, etc. The difference is relevant from both an analytical and a political perspective. Regarding the first, it leads to the question of what exactly these 'other causes' are, and what the process is in which a pluralist legal framework is systematically applied in a way that produces biased outcomes. From a political perspective, it implies different political strategies for those who wish to forward an alternative socio-economic programme. If it is assumed that the observed bias follows directly from the law, a Treaty change would be required; if, however, the bias has other causes than the law in and by itself, different strategies (such as challenging the Commission's socio-economic assumptions, etc) may be warranted. Beyond that, it is possible that claims as to the de jure orientation of the European macroeconomic constitution are mobilized in political discourse to justify what is in fact a one-sided application of the law, and thereby provides one of the causes of the observed de facto bias. Challenging such reading of the law may subsequently also alter the political dynamics, and may make the previously hegemonic paradigm less inevitable. Given the fact that the legal provisions appear underdetermined in regard to the competing socio-economic paradigms, it is shown, in particular in regard to the SGP, that the project to fully inscribe the neoliberal paradigm into the legal framework has failed. While the

[22] See for example Fitoussi and Saraceno, (n 6), 483, who argue: 'The European institutional set-up de facto bans discretionary economic policy, by limiting monetary policy to inflation targeting, and fiscal policy to automatic stabilisation.'

reasons cannot be discussed in detail, it is proposed that the project to establish a fully rule-based, quasi-automatic system of deficit control for the whole eurozone suffers from what Wolfgang Streeck has called 'phantasies of controllability', and underestimates the importance to allow for deviations and discretionary policy choices if necessary. But if these possibilities are recognized—as is the case in the SGP—then the system can no longer be assumed to be determined by a specific socio-economic paradigm.

The final section will specifically address the crisis measures, and attempt to assess their implications as regards the socio-economic orientation of the Union. A distinction will be drawn between the requirements defined by the Treaty in procedural and in substantive terms. In regard to the former it will be argued that the Treaty must be considered to be fully determined; on this basis, it can be argued that measures such as the reverse majority voting requirement constitute breaches of Union law. By contrast, as shown throughout the book, the Treaty is underdetermined in substantive terms; and it will be argued that the crisis measures make this substantive openness manifest. The fact that an enormous spectrum of measures, ranging from the ESM, the OMT and the banking union, to the 'Six Pack' and 'Two Pack',[23] could be passed under the present Treaty implies that it is, in substantive terms, a very flexible constitutional framework. In fact, it appears to be so flexible that it is difficult to argue that it provides any significant limits as regards the socio-economic orientation of the measures that may be enacted. We thus encounter a rift between the Union's political practice, and its normative setup. The former is currently characterized to a considerable extent by neoliberal policy prescriptions, as is most visible in the pro-cyclical effects created by the Commission's one-sided focus on short-term deficit reduction, and the prescriptions addressed to the peripheral countries through conditionality. Nonetheless, this cannot support the inductive conclusion that these policies would also be normatively required, as will be shown in this chapter. This implies that the austerity politics that currently shapes the Union is, in legal terms, not devoid of alternatives. Though many obstacles to pursuing alternative socio-economic programmes on the Union level exist, the Treaty is not one of them.

COMPETING SOCIO-ECONOMIC VIEWS ON THE EMU

We have already discussed the economic arguments that were invoked for and against European monetary integration in the 1980s and 1990 in a previous chapter, but will briefly recap them here. The main argument brought forward against monetary integration was that the Union did not constitute an 'optimum currency area' (OCA). This means that it did not have sufficient mechanisms in place to outbalance asymmetrical shocks, which in turn implied that monetary union

[23] These measures will be discussed in detail later in this chapter.

would not be beneficial for the Member States, or at least not for all of them. By contrast, the main argument in favour of monetary union was that national monetary policy had supposedly lost its stabilizing ability, so that its abandonment would in fact not create significant adverse effects. Instead it was believed that asymmetric shocks that hit a monetary union could be outbalanced by fully integrated financial markets. Moreover, it was assumed that there was a tendency towards convergence within a monetary union, so that the differences between the regions would become less pronounced over time, and asymmetrical shocks thus less likely. These two competing views are sometimes termed Mundell I and Mundell II in the literature, as they are both drawing from texts written by Robert Mundell (who however is a strong proponent of the second approach, as we will discuss below). The two perspectives expressed, as for example De Grauwe argued, different socio-economic paradigms: whereas the first conformed to the post-war neoclassical synthesis, the latter was closer to monetarism or supply-side economics, which are currents of neo- and new classical economic thought particularly popular in the 1980s and 1990s.

The latter view prevailed in the sense that European monetary integration was pursued without the establishment of a broad complementary institutional framework, mainly relying on the stabilizing effects of markets instead.[24] In many ways, European monetary integration was thus based on an optimism about the ability of markets to provide stability and convergence, and a rejection of the belief that governments were able to satisfactorily manage the economy through monetary and fiscal policies.[25] The relationship between economic thinking that supports such assumptions and the (limited) institutional setup chosen for the EMU finds its clearest expression in the writings of Robert Mundell. Mundell was not only one of the early supporters of European monetary integration, he also was one of the proponents of a popular current in economic thinking that he described as 'supply-side economics'. Mundell described as the cornerstones of the 'supply side' approach the opposition to 'big government' and to progressive income taxation, support of public expenditure cuts and economic stimulation through tax cuts and regulatory reform,[26] as well as the rejection of any attempts of macroeconomic fine-tuning in favour of long-term, rule-based economic governance.[27] In his Nobel prize speech from 1999, Mundell lauded

[24] Paul De Grauwe, 'What Have we Learnt about Monetary Integration since the Maastricht Treaty?' (2006) 44 *Journal of Common Market Studies* 711, 724.

[25] McNamara argued in this regard that the EMU was based on a policy consensus that 'emphasizes the inherent stability and adaptability of the private sector and view traditional Keynesian efforts to manipulate the economy, particularly full employment strategies, as ineffective and possibly counterproductive.' Kathleen McNamara, *The Currency of Ideas: Monetary Politics in the European Union* (Cornell University Press, 1998) 145; quoted in Bojan Bugaric, 'Europe Against the Left? On Legal Limits to Progressive Politics' (2013) LEQS Paper No 61, 14.

[26] Robert Mundell, 'A reconsideration of the twentieth century' (2000) 90 *American Economic Review* 327, 335–36.

[27] Along similar lines, McKinnon blamed 'Keynesian activism' for the 'casino effect in foreign exchange markets', and argued that a strict price stability target for central banks would contribute to exchange rate stability. Ronald McKinnon, 'Mundell, the Euro, and Optimum Currency Areas' in Thomas Courchene (ed), *Money, Markets, and Mobility* (McGill, 2001), 46.

this approach for what he believed was its role in bringing down inflation since the 1980s, and more generally for the positive economic development that countries like the US had experienced.[28] This view was widely shared among economists and policymakers at that time: the fall in business cycle volatility that was observable since the mid-1980s, sometimes termed the 'great moderation', was ascribed by many to the new macroeconomic strategies employed, for example in central banking.[29] The optimal policy mix that had been 'discovered' was assumed to include an independent central bank exclusively concerned with price stability and operating on the basis of rules allowing predictability in the long run, restrained governments and well-integrated (financial) markets. For Mundell, such a setting provided a sufficient basis for monetary integration even on the global level: in his Nobel prize speech he identified a far-reaching convergence of inflation in the industrialized countries as a consequence of such policies, and speculated that this would enable some form of global monetary union, maybe even a 'world money'.[30] From the perspective of these economic assumptions, monetary integration appears not only possible *despite* the lack of a further-reaching institutional framework or a federal system of economic governance, but precisely *because* of it.

Views such as the one expressed by Mundell prominently shaped the Commission's approach to monetary union. Thus, an important structural element of the EMU was that it restricted discretionary fiscal policy, and instead relied on automatic stabilizers to counteract downturns.[31] Until as late as 2008, it has been maintained by the Commission that the EMU architecture was in fact mostly sufficient, eg in the Commission report 'EMU@10'.[32] On the background to one of the biggest economic downturns since the Great Depression, the report held:

> The governance structure in EMU has helped deliver macroeconomic stability in many dimensions: low and stable inflation, greater resilience to adverse shocks, major efficiency gains associated with strong integration in financial and product markets, and better fiscal behaviour.[33]

The limited instruments at the Union level were presented by the Commission as building 'on a strong tradition of "subsidiarity"'.[34] De Grauwe described the belief that the EMU was functional despite its restricted institutional framework, or that

[28] Mundell (n 26), 337–38.

[29] See Olivier Blanchard, Giovanni Dell'Ariccia and Paolo Mauro, 'Rethinking Macroeconomic Policy' (2010) 42 *Journal of Money, Credit and Banking* 199; Frederic Mishkin, 'Monetary Policy Strategy: Lessons from the Crisis' (2011) NBER Working Paper No 16755.

[30] Mundell (n 26), 338.

[31] Fitoussi and Saraceno (n 6), 492.

[32] EC, 'EMU@10. Successes and challenges after ten years of Economic and Monetary Union' (*European Economy* No 2, 2008), 11; on this see Paul De Grauwe, *Economics of Monetary Union* (OUP, 2012) 119.

[33] EC (n 32), 23.

[34] ibid, 23.

such limitation of macroeconomic governance tools on the European level was even a positive feature, as the 'Brussels-Frankfurt consensus':

> The Brussels-Frankfurt consensus is based on two academic theories. One is the monetarist theory ... in which the central bank cannot do much to stabilize the economy. If it tries too hard to 'fine-tune' the economy it will end up with more inflation. Thus the best thing a central bank can do is to stabilize the price level. This will have the incidental effect of producing the best possible outcome in terms of stability of the economic cycle. The second theory that influences the Brussels–Frankfurt consensus is the real business cycle theory. This says that the sources of economic cycles are shocks in technology (supply-side shocks) and changes in preferences (unemployment being mainly the result of workers taking more leisure). There is very little the central bank can do about these movements. The best is to keep the price level on a steady course. This will minimize the effects of these shocks. In addition, a macroeconomic policy based on the objective of price stability is the best thing the central bank can do to promote growth. As Lucas has stressed, the central bank's contribution to economic growth by maintaining price stability is immensely more important than an ephemeral success in reducing business cycle movements. It will come as no surprise that if one adheres to these theories the present governance of the euro area is the right one: a central bank that cares about price stability and in so doing makes the best possible contribution to maintaining macroeconomic stability and to fostering economic growth; and national governments that keep budgetary discipline and do their utmost to introduce market flexibility. In such a world the productivity driven shocks can best be dealt with by governments keeping budgets in balance. Furthermore, in such a world the need to have an active budgetary policy at the euro area level does not exist.[35]

The institutional setup of the EMU was thus shaped to a considerable degree by the then-dominant socio-economic paradigm, usually referred to alternatively as 'monetarism', 'supply-side economics' or 'neoliberalism'. In the light of such views it was argued that the EMU's limited institutional setup was not only sufficient, but in fact optimal. By contrast, economic views based on OCA theory (Mundell I) emphasized the 'incomplete' character of the EMU, as it lacked crucial tools that were considered indispensable for a modern system of macroeconomic governance.[36] Most notably it was criticized that the Union budget was too small.[37] An 'incomplete' monetary union was considered to be unstable because national governments would issue debt in a currency they did not control, so that liquidity crises and increasing budget deficits could arise.[38] A liquidity crisis might in turn

[35] De Grauwe (n 24), 726.

[36] See eg Fitoussi and Saraceno (n 6), 494.

[37] De Grauwe (n 32), 107; see also EC, 'A blueprint for a deep and genuine economic and monetary union—Launching a European Debate' COM(2012) 777 final, 2, 31; Herman Van Rompuy, *Towards a genuine economic and monetary union* (European Council, 2012), 9.

[38] De Grauwe held in that regard: 'Since there is a lot of uncertainty about the likelihood of default, and since investors have very little scientific foundation to calculate probabilities of default (until 2011 there had been none in Western Europe in the last 60 years), expectations are likely to be driven mainly by market sentiments of optimism and pessimism. Small changes in these market sentiments can lead to large movements from one type of equilibrium to another.' De Grauwe (n 32), 116.

affect domestic banks, triggering a banking crisis. To counter these risks, a federal budget was considered to be necessary; in the EU context this can be described as 'budgetary union.'[39] The Werner plan of 1970 had predicted the need for a substantially expanded European budget,[40] and in 1977 a Commission study found a significant increase of the EEC budget to be necessary.[41] Budgetary union is supposed to serve two functions, the so-called insurance function and the function of consolidating debt.[42] In a federal system, taxation is (at least partly) centralized, and various programmes, eg unemployment or pension insurance, may provide transfer payments.[43] These flows of tax receipts and transfer payments may outbalance asymmetrical shocks in the monetary union.[44] The second function of budgetary union is the consolidation of debt: if debt is pooled in a monetary union (eg in the form of Eurobonds), investor distrust leading to liquidity crises will be reduced (though economists warn of the possibility of moral hazard).[45] Beyond budgetary union, a broader coordination of macroeconomic policies among the Member States appeared necessary to many.[46] Along these lines David Marsh argued: 'Monetary unions tend eventually to collapse unless they are embedded in a coherent political framework that allows for effective collective action and burden-sharing, for instance through joint fiscal policy.'[47] We thus encounter two conflicting views on monetary union and on the institutional preconditions under which it would be successful. The institutional setup of the EMU prior to the crisis appears to conform in many regards to the socio-economic paradigm dominant from the 1980s onwards. The correspondence between this specific socio-economic paradigm on the one hand and the EMU's setup on the other may lead to the conclusion that the Treaty in fact *requires* the lawmakers to follow this paradigm. However, the paradigm was severely compromised during the economic crisis when the institutional setup turned out to be defective. The question thus arises whether the Treaty would allow for the setting up of an institutional and regulatory framework that conforms to a different socio-economic paradigm. In the following sections it will be argued that important elements of the Union's macroeconomic constitution in fact allow for multiple readings on the basis of different socio-economic paradigms, which suggests that the Treaty in fact provides such flexibility.

[39] See ibid, 14–15.

[40] See on this Eichengreen, 'European monetary unification' (1993) 31 *Journal of Economic Literature* 1321, 1323.

[41] See T Wilson, 'Review: Report of the Study Group on the Role of Public Finance in European Integration' (1978) 88 *Economic Journal* 858.

[42] See for example Eichengreen (n 40), 1334–39.

[43] For a contemporary representation see for example EC (n 37), 32; See also discussion in Eichengreen (n 40), 1337–39.

[44] EC (n 37), 32; Van Rompuy (n 37), 11.

[45] De Grauwe (n 32), 15–17; see also Van Rompuy (n 37), 9–10.

[46] See for example David Marsh, *Europe's Deadlock* (Yale University Press, 2013) 58.

[47] ibid, 12. The 2012 report 'Towards a genuine economic and monetary union' held in that regard: 'The sovereign debt crisis painfully exposed that the unsustainable economic policies pursued by some euro area countries in the past and the rigidities existing in their economies have negative

READING THE EU TREATY AS A PLURALIST MACROECONOMIC INSTRUMENT

Different intellectual paradigms have proposed different socio-economic responses to the crisis. Disagreement on policy responses include the question whether and how strict the deficit/debt rules should be enforced in the crisis, if a counter-cyclical public investment programme should be implemented or not, if austerity measures create a deflation risk and whether this should be combatted, if sovereign debt risk should be pooled, whether countries with a trade surplus should strive to reduce it, if the ECB should function as a lender of last resort, etc. It has been argued by many that the Union in fact pursued a specific socio-economic programme in the crisis, namely an austerity-oriented approach characterized by a pro-cyclical fiscal policy enforcing expenditure cuts in the downturn, increasing unemployment and creating deflationary tendencies.[48] Others have identified a more diverse (or contradictory) character of the crisis measures.[49] The central question from the perspective of this book is whether the pursuit of any specific socio-economic project is *legally* required. In other words, is the legal framework clear in the sense that a specific socio-economic programme is the only correct application of European law? Or, is it ambiguous to an extent that other policies could be pursued as well? As already asserted, the findings of this book so far suggest that the Treaty must be read as a pluralist framework. Against this background, any claim that the European system of macroeconomic governance must be assumed to implement a specific socio-economic paradigm that is of normative relevance in the interpretation and application of its provisions appears, prima facie, difficult to sustain. In the following sections it will be shown that the European system of macroeconomic governance is indeed characterized by considerable ambiguities and discretionary choices which ultimately support the view that very different socio-economic programmes could potentially be implemented within the framework of the European system of macroeconomic governance. In order to illustrate this claim, we will look at five examples: we will look at the ECB's price stability mandate, the SGP, the newly established Macroeconomic Imbalance Procedure, as well as Articles 123 and 125 TFEU.

repercussions for all members of the EMU. An integrated economic policy framework is necessary to guide at all times the policies of Member States towards strong and sustainable economic growth to produce higher levels of growth and employment.' Van Rompuy (n 37), 13.

[48] See eg Jeffrey Frankel, 'The Procyclicalists: Fiscal austerity vs. stimulus' (7 February, 2012), voxeuorg/article/procyclicalists-fiscal-austerity-vs-stimulus.

[49] Agustín Menendez has argued that the crisis measures were characterized by different and inconsistent diagnoses, which in turn constituted the basis for different sets of countermeasures. The EMU built, as shown, on the assumption that the financial markets are inherently stable, and early crisis measures were based on the principle that Member States were solely responsible for the debt they incurred. However, a number of subsequent measures must be understood as an acknowledgment of the fact that risk may build up within the regular workings of the financial markets, and that macroeconomic imbalances may occur even if the individual Member States act within the boundaries set by the Treaty. According to Menéndez, the newly established European Systemic Risk Board and the

Interpreting the Price Stability Rule in a Pluralist Form

Inflation describes an increase in prices, deflation a decrease. Central banks are assumed to be able to influence the price level through the instruments at their disposal, most notably through the interest rate. Monetary policy is, like any socio-economic policy, politically controversial:[50] lower interest rates may be conducive to higher growth and lower unemployment, but may under certain circumstances be associated with higher inflation. By contrast, a high interest rate increases the return on capital, and a low inflation rate protects its value, so that financial investors may favour such settings.[51] Monetary policy may also be controversial for its asymmetrical regional effects: as the Union's regions are diverse, they may face very different economic challenges. However, monetary policy can be set only for the eurozone as a whole. Accordingly, monetary policy may create asymmetrical effects: for a booming region the interest rate may be too low so that speculative bubbles develop, while at the same time it may be too high for a depressed area. Monetary policy is therefore an immensely political task, as became particularly obvious in the wake of the crisis.

Prior to 2007, a monetary paradigm that Mishkin called the 'new neoclassical synthesis' had become hegemonic among economists and policymakers alike.[52] Characteristic elements were, from a more procedural perspective, the centrality of long-term inflation targeting in order to anchor expectations, the significance ascribed to central bank independence, and the focus on rule-based decision-making. The synthesis tended to reject claims that monetary policy should support the pursuit of employment-oriented economic objectives, that financial markets were a source of instability, or that central banks had a responsibility to prevent the build-up of credit-driven bubbles. Its proponents lauded the 'synthesis' for the low inflation and low output volatility experienced prior to the crisis. After the crisis hit, ideological conflicts in monetary policy reappeared prominently. One important expression of this was that central banks started to engage in numerous forms of what is termed 'nonconventional' monetary policy, including liquidity provision to financial institutions, asset purchases and quantitative easing.[53] In Europe, the ECB considerably broadened the regulatory objectives it pursued, and started to take active steps to increase financial stability and to protect the eurozone. These new ends and means in turn faced severe criticism.[54] In the light of these erupting

Macroeconomic Imbalance Procedure (MIP) are expressions of the latte way of thinking. Menéndez (n 9), 497, 510.

[50] In this sense see *Gauweiler*, para 75.

[51] For examples of scholars who invoke the interest of capital owners against a higher inflation rate, see Hugo Hahn, 'The stability pact for European monetary union: compliance with deficit limit as a constant legal duty' (1998) 35 *Common Market Law Review* 77, 80; Hans-Werner Sinn, 'Austerity, growth and inflation: remarks on the eurozone's unresolved competitiveness problem' (2014) 37 *The World Economy* 1, 10.

[52] Mishkin (n 29), 31.

[53] ibid, 24.

[54] This is illustrated, for example, in the lawsuits that are the subjects of the *Gauweiler* decision.

conflicts we have to look at monetary policy anew. We will focus on the ECB's price stability mandate and its interpretation, most notably the alleged dichotomy between price stability and other regulatory objectives. It can be shown that, in purely normative terms, the ECB's price stability mandate in fact allows the pursuit a broad range of policies in the light of competing socio-economic paradigms, and does not lock the ECB into a specific worldview. However, this argument does not conflict with claims that the ECB pursued a one-sided reading of its mandate in practice.[55]

We start with a discussion of the ECB's regulatory objectives, which are defined by Article 127(1) TFEU as follows:

> The primary objective of the European System of Central Banks (hereinafter referred to as 'the ESCB') shall be to maintain price stability. Without prejudice to the objective of price stability, the ESCB shall support the general economic policies in the Union with a view to contributing to the achievement of the objectives of the Union as laid down in Article 3 of the Treaty on European Union.

Price stability is defined as the 'primary objective', while the Union's other regulatory goals may be supported 'without prejudice' to the former. The meaning of the term 'price stability' is ambivalent, as the ECB itself holds: 'While the Treaty clearly establishes the primary objective of the ECB, it does not give a precise definition of what is meant by price stability.'[56] Taken at its literal meaning, the term 'price stability' would have to be assumed to describe an inflation rate of 0 per cent. However, this is not how the ECB in fact interprets the term; instead, it targets an inflation rate of 'below, but close to, 2 per cent over the medium term.'[57] Thus, the ECB essentially defines the 'price stability' mandate as the opposite of the term's literal meaning, namely as ensuring consistent (though low) inflation. The ECB provides the following explanation why price stability is interpreted as an inflation rate of close to 2 per cent:

> Inflation rates of below, but close to, 2% are low enough for the economy to fully reap the benefits of price stability. It also underlines the ECB's commitment to
>
> — provide an adequate margin to avoid the risks of deflation. Having such a safety margin against deflation is important because nominal interest rates cannot fall below zero. In a deflationary environment monetary policy may thus not be able to sufficiently stimulate aggregate demand by using its interest rate instrument. This makes it more difficult for monetary policy to fight deflation than to fight inflation …
>
> — provide a sufficient margin to address the implications of inflation differentials in the euro area. It avoids that individual countries in the euro area have to structurally live with too low inflation rates or even deflation.[58]

[55] Fitoussi and Saraceno (n 6), 492.
[56] ecb.europa.eu/mopo/strategy/pricestab/html/index.en.html.
[57] ibid.
[58] ibid.

The ECB's explanation of why the goal of achieving 'price stability' is, contrary to the literal meaning of the term, in fact defined as an inflation target of about 2 per cent reveals the complex preconditions of a seemingly straightforward policy objective. Six points are of particular interest in that regard. First, we encounter a substantive difference between inflation on the one hand and deflation on the other, which explains why the ECB aims to achieve consistent inflation rather than price stability in a literal sense. As its conventional instruments no longer function sufficiently in the case of deflation, the ECB finds it preferable to keep the price level in the inflation area. The reason is the following: with an inflation rate of 2 per cent the ECB can bring the real interest rate down to −2 per cent by setting the nominal interest rate at 0 per cent.[59] This increases the probability that capital owners move out of capital assets and spend or invest in more productive ways. With an inflation rate of 0 per cent, by contrast, the real interest rate cannot go negative, which limits the ability of the central bank to influence market behaviour. Thus, inflation is considered less problematic than deflation, which for the ECB justifies an inflation target that conflicts with the literal reading of its mandate.

The ECB's considerations show, secondly, that the inflation target is directly connected to the objective that the ECB's instruments remain functional: deflation is to be avoided because the ECB's conventional tools will no longer function under deflationary conditions. Defined in the form of an opposition, the ECB prefers to deviate from a literal definition of the 'price stability' objective if this increases the bank's capability to influence the inflation rate. This in turn implies that the part of Article 127 TFEU which holds that price stability is the ECB's 'primary objective' cannot mean that other objectives are set aside in order to pursue price stability in all situations;[60] in fact, the situation might well be the opposite, and the price stability mandate (in a literal sense) is set aside in the pursuit of other objectives (such as ensuring the functionality of the ECB's instruments). It is along these lines that Fitoussi and Saraceno asked: 'How credible can a central bank be if it refuses to lower rates because of a largely undemonstrated inflationary threat, when the eurozone economy is on the brink of a recession?'[61] Third, the ECB specifies that the 2 per cent target is to be reached only in the 'medium term'. This implies that certain factors may require the ECB to postpone reaching the inflation target immediately, which essentially means that in the short run other objectives may well outweigh the price stability target.

This leads to a fourth point, namely that the ECB's inflation target must be viewed within the broader context of the Union's socio-economic objectives.

[59] With an inflation rate of 2 per cent and an interest rate of 0 per cent, financial assets lose value by −2 per cent.

[60] See in this regard *Gauweiler* at paras 46–56. The Court confirmed that the ECB's pursuit of the 'objective of safeguarding an appropriate transmission of monetary policy', which it defines as the 'ability of the ESCB to influence price developments by means of its monetary policy', is legitimate.

[61] Fitoussi and Saraceno (n 6), 492.

On the one hand, the functionality of the ECB's instruments depends on their broader socio-economic effects, as the ECB itself acknowledges: it holds that, in order to push the price level up, the ECB has to be able to 'stimulate aggregate demand' by lowering the interest rate. On the other hand, questions of regional equity are held to be of relevance: the objective is not simply to keep a certain average inflation target for the eurozone as a whole, but also to prevent situations in which Member States have to 'structurally live with too low inflation rates or even deflation'. Beyond that, the CJEU has confirmed in the OMT decision that protecting the future existence of the eurozone constitutes a regulatory objective of the ECB as well.[62] Such contextual reading is, as we saw, also suggested by Article 127(1) TFEU, which holds that the ECB 'shall support the general economic policies in the Union', though 'without prejudice to the objective of price stability'. This brings us, fifthly, to the question of what it actually means in practice that price stability is the ECB's 'primary objective'. It is sometimes described as the ECB's 'only mandate'.[63] However, this is clearly an incorrect view: the provision requires the ECB to support the pursuit of other regulatory objectives as well; that this shall be done '[w]ithout prejudice to the objective of price stability' merely establishes a hierarchy of objectives in case they come into conflict. In practice, the number of situations in which the price stability mandate will unambiguously be in conflict with other objectives is likely very limited, probably restricted to the (from today's perspective unlikely) situation in which the eurozone as a whole is in a boom that exhibits inflationary tendencies (in which case the primacy of the price stability mandate would presumably require the ECB to dampen the upswing by raising the interest rate, though it would still be unclear within which timeframe this should happen). In any other situation the ECB is faced with far more complex questions: what, for example, if the core is depressed while credit-driven bubbles build up in the periphery (the pre-crisis situation)? What if the core is booming but the periphery experiences high unemployment (the post-crisis situation)? Such scenarios require the ECB to consider questions of financial stability, regional balance, aggregate demand in conjunction with price stability, because all of these factors have direct implications on the latter. A dichotomic conception in which price stability is viewed in opposition to other regulatory objectives such as employment, growth or financial stability thus does not follow from Article 127 TFEU. Instead, such reading must be recognized as a version of the 'two sphere fallacy' that we have encountered numerous times, and which we identified as ideologically coded. As the ECB is free to define the strategy it deems most promising to pursue its price stability mandate, it may—depending on the socio-economic assumptions it employs—come to the conclusion that healthy growth, financial stability or regional equity may in fact be relevant factors to consider.

62 *Gauweiler*, para 77; the Court speaks of safeguarding 'the singleness of monetary policy'.
63 Sinn (n 51), 10.

A sixth point of interest is the ECB's practice to target a specific nominal value, namely 2 per cent. In recent decades, inflation targeting has become a key element of monetary policy, which is based on the assumption that expectations about future inflation shape the development of the price level.[64] A nominal anchor to which the central bank commits in a credible form is assumed to be an important tool for shaping such expectations. While the ECB binds itself to a specific numerical target as a matter of practice, the Treaty does not in fact oblige it to do so; other regulatory techniques to achieve the price stability objective could similarly be justified under the Treaty. For example, not all central banks commit to a specific target number;[65] and some economists have proposed that a price level *path* target would in fact be a superior method.[66] Moreover, the 2 per cent number is itself an arbitrary choice. As Krugman points out, no clear economic rationale supports it; rather, it developed as a convention among central banks only in the 1990s.[67] Since the outbreak of the crisis, economists like Blanchard, Dell'Ariccia and Mauro have argued that a different inflation target—eg 4 per cent—may in fact be more beneficial.[68] We can conclude, however, that from both a legal and economic perspective there is no necessity to set the inflation target at 2 per cent (rather than at, eg, 1 per cent or 5 per cent). This is of very practical relevance in the ongoing political conflict in relation to the crisis measures. Authors such as Hans-Werner Sinn have argued that the 'price stability' mandate would prohibit strategies to rectify trade imbalances in which the surplus countries would inflate without corresponding deflation by the deficit countries.[69] However, Sinn's argument conflicts with both theory and practice of monetary policy as well as the ECB's own interpretation of the 'price stability' mandate. In a fictional example provided by Sinn, Germany would have to inflate by 5.5 per cent per year, with the average eurozone inflation rate at 3.6 per cent over 10 years. On this, Sinn comments that '[i]f fluctuations in relative prices in the eurozone are always realised without any country being driven to deflation, average inflation would necessarily violate the treaty.'[70] This, however, is incorrect: not only does a specific inflation rate not, per se, 'violate the treaty'; the Treaty also does not hold that the ECB would be prevented from targeting an overall inflation rate of 3.6 per cent. While such an inflation rate surely lies above the ECB's current target rate

[64] Ben Bernanke, Thomas Laubach and Frederic Mishkin, *Inflation targeting: lessons from the international experience* (Princeton University Press, 2001) 4ff.

[65] See Mishkin (n 29), 14–15.

[66] See on this ibid, 34–35.

[67] Paul Krugman, 'Inflation targets reconsidered' in ECB (ed), *ECB Forum on central banking—Conference proceedings* (2014) 110; Ubide reports that the inflation rate in Germany in the period 1980–95—ie, still under the management of the Bundesbank—averaged 3 per cent. Angel Ubide, 'Is the European Central Bank Failing Its Price Stability Mandate?' (2014) Peterson Institute for International Economics Policy Brief No 5, 6.

[68] Blanchard, Dell'Ariccia and Mauro (n 29), 207–08.

[69] Sinn (n 51), 10.

[70] ibid, 10.

as well as above the inflation rate convention that developed since the 1990s, it is important to emphasize that there is no legal reason why 'price stability' should be interpreted as 2 per cent as opposed to, for example, 3.6 per cent. This brief discussion of the ECB's price stability mandate indicates that, far from locking in a specific ideological view on inflation, Article 127 TFEU as well as its interpretation by the ECB in fact exhibit considerable ambiguities and discretionary choices. Ultimately, it is for the ECB to decide on the strategy it wishes to employ to pursue price stability. This in turn depends on the underlying socio-economic assumptions: for example, in the current crisis situation with price level development in or close to the deflationary area, expansionary, demand-oriented policies may in fact be the most successful strategy to pursue the ECB's price stability mandate. Rather than restricting the spectrum of discretionary choice, Article 127 TFEU allows, in principle, for the implementation of a variety of monetary strategies in the light of different socio-economic paradigms. This finding of course does not undermine demands to alter the ECB's written mandate, and add, for example, an explicit obligation for the ECB to also pursue the objectives of financial stability and high employment.[71] In fact, the preceding analysis shows that a strict focus on price stability is not a realistic demand, which in turn supports the demand that the ECB's mandate should also express this plurality of objectives pursued.

Interpreting the Maastricht Rules in a Pluralist Form

The Member States face three key substantive obligations in relation to their national budgets: first, the requirement to keep the yearly deficit under 3 per cent; second, the obligation to achieve a balanced budget over the medium term; and third, the objective that the overall debt remains under 60 per cent (or at least moving towards that objective). These obligations are laid down in Article 126 TFEU and Protocol 12, the 'Treaty on Stability, Coordination and Governance in the Economic and Monetary Union' (TSCG),[72] as well as Regulations 1466/97 and 1467/97 as reformed by the 'Six Pack'.[73] These obligations are commonly referred to as the 'Maastricht criteria' and the 'Stability and Growth Pact' (SGP). It has been argued that the SGP corresponds to an ordoliberal regulatory programme, insofar as it institutes a quasi-automated and juridified

71 Many authors advocate an explicit change of the ECB's mandate. De Grauwe has proposed, for example, a dual mandate that includes both price and financial stability. De Grauwe (n 32), 206.

72 consilium.europa.eu/european-council/pdf/Treaty-on-Stability-Coordination-and-Governance-TSCG.

73 Council Regulation No 1466/97 on the strengthening of the surveillance of budgetary positions and the surveillance and coordination of economic policies [1997] OJ L 209/1, as amended by Regulation No 1175/2011 [2011] OJ L 306/12; Council Regulation No 1467/97 on speeding up and clarifying the implementation of the excessive deficit procedure [1997] OJ L 209/6 as amended by Council Regulation (EU) No 1177/2011 [2011] OJ L 306/33.

surveillance mechanism, and thereby limits discretionary choice by the (national and European) institutions.[74] In conjunction with other Treaty provisions[75] and Union policies as well as with its procedural structure,[76] the SGP has been faulted for enforcing ideologically biased policies, and in particular for making Keynesian counter-cyclical policies difficult in economic downturns, and generally for restricting public investment.[77] Along these lines, Fitoussi and Saraceno argue that '[t]he European institutional set-up de facto bans discretionary economic policy, by limiting monetary policy to inflation targeting, and fiscal policy to automatic stabilisation.'[78] It has in fact been shown that since 2007, public investment dropped markedly in the EU (and much more so in the periphery than in the core), whereas it rose in countries like the United States, Canada or Japan.[79] By contrast, between the 1970s and 2007 public investment levels in the EU had corresponded to those of other Western countries, though a significant overall drop in investment levels is observable during that period. This finding supports the argument that the SGP is in fact liable to undermine counter-cyclical policies, at least since 2007. In this section we will inquire whether the observed bias is a legally required consequence of the SGP rules. It will be argued that this is not the case: despite the clear regulatory attempt to restrict discretionary budgetary choices by the Member States and to automate the excessive deficit procedure, a considerable degree of discretion is retained, which would allow, in principle, for the pursuit of different socio-economic paradigms.

Public Debt as a Controversial Issue

Public debt is a highly contentious issue. In particular, there are significant differences in the evaluation of the causes of government debt, and regarding the question how to deal with debt in times of crisis. To clarify these disagreements, we will define two paradigmatic positions, which could be described as the pro- and the anti-austerity views. While the pro-austerity view has been around for a long time, the intellectual foundation for the most recent austerity efforts was a 2010 article by Reinhart and Rogoff. The authors argued, based on historical case studies, that 'the relationship between government debt and real GDP growth is weak for debt/GDP ratios below a threshold of 90 percent of GDP.'[80] However, once the debt rate exceeds 90 per cent, the adverse effects on growth become significant, as 'median growth rates fall by one percent, and average growth falls considerably

[74] See for example Streeck (n 5), 154–55.
[75] Most notably Arts 122, 125 and 127 TFEU.
[76] For example reverse majority voting in the Council.
[77] Streeck (n 5), 170.
[78] Fitoussi and Saraceno (n 6), 483.
[79] Francesca Barbiero and Zsolt Darvas, 'In sickness and in health: protecting and supporting public investment in Europe' (2014) Bruegel Policy Contribution No 02, 4.
[80] Carmen Reinhart and Kenneth Rogoff, 'Growth in a time of debt' (2010) NBER Working Paper No 15639, 1.

more.'[81] The reason for this threshold, according to Reinhart and Rogoff, lies in the psychology of investors, a phenomenon they term 'debt intolerance':

> [A]s debt levels rise towards historical limits, risk premia begin to rise sharply, facing highly indebted governments with difficult tradeoffs. Even countries that are committed to fully repaying their debts are forced to dramatically tighten fiscal policy in order to appear credible to investors and thereby reduce risk premia.[82]

The underlying policy argument of their paper is that the cost of bank bailouts and countercyclical government spending employed to fight downturns may have adverse long-term effects.[83] According to Reinhart and Rogoff: 'At the very minimum … traditional debt management issues should be at the forefront of public policy concerns.'[84] However, this position is highly controversial. The alleged correlation between debt and growth was questioned for example by Stiglitz, who argued:

> America left World War II with a debt of 130% of GDP, and yet in the ensuing decades the country experienced its fastest rate of growth (and the growth was shared growth). So too … if debt held back growth, England would never have experienced the industrial revolution, for it emerged from its wars with France with massive debts. The wide range of experiences shows at the minimum that debt is not destiny.[85]

More generally it has been proposed that the pro-austerity view confused cause and effect: according to this view, the current debt level is a consequence of the economic crisis, not its source.[86] The arguments of Reinhart and Rogoff were also put into question when significant calculation errors were uncovered.[87]

The theoretical backbone of the anti-austerity view is the demand-oriented position forwarded by scholars working in the Keynesian tradition. Keynesians assume that, as a crisis is characterized by a fall in private demand, a reduction of public expenditure would further increase the downturn, which in turn would lead to falling public receipts, thereby ultimately increasing public debt rather than lowering it.[88] Keynesians thus forward two key propositions: first, that austerity policies during an economic downturn end up creating higher public deficits than counter-cyclical policies would; and second, that public spending in a downturn (ranging from automatic stabilizers, such as an unemployment insurance, to

[81] ibid, 1.
[82] ibid, 23.
[83] ibid, 3, 4 and 23.
[84] ibid, 23.
[85] Joseph Stiglitz, 'Reconstructing macroeconomic theory to manage economic policy' (2014) NBER Working Paper No 20517, 19.
[86] ibid, 19; see also Streeck (n 5), 109–39; this point is recognized, in principle, by Reinhart and Rogoff, though only in relation to wartime debt. Reinhart and Rogoff (n 80), 6.
[87] Thomas Herndon, Michael Ash and Robert Pollin, 'Does high public debt consistently stifle economic growth? A critique of Reinhart and Rogoff' (2014) 38 *Cambridge Journal of Economics* 257.
[88] Nina Dodig and Hansjörg Herr, 'EU policies addressing current account imbalances in the EMU: An assessment' (2015) Institute for International Political Economy Berlin Working Paper No 46, 10–11.

discretionary investment policies) will pave the way for future deficit reduction if it succeeds in fostering growth. The two sides—the pro- and the anti-austerity views—have significant implications for the application of the SGP, which is, as we will see, characterized by ambivalent provisions that require further interpretation. Depending on which of the views is taken, radically different interpretations of the provisions are possible.

The Flexibility of the Debt Rules in the Light of Competing Views on Public Debt in Times of Crisis

In this section we will focus on the specific question whether the SGP rules enforce a priority of debt reduction over other policy objectives in times of economic downturns, which would correspond to the pro-austerity view sketched above. It will be argued that this is not necessarily the case: while the SGP aims to establish a rule-based path towards the debt limit, it acknowledges the need for a comprehensive analysis of the situation of a Member State that exceed the deficit and debt thresholds, and recognizes the need to alter or abrogate such path in exceptional circumstances. This dichotomy essentially mirrors the conflict between the pro- and the anti-austerity views: while the two sides do not necessarily differ as regards the objective of reducing debt in the long run, they do disagree as to the strategy to achieve it in the short run. The following section will show that, by granting discretion at various points, the SGP remains open towards the competing strategies on dealing with debt in times of crisis. Moreover, the SGP exhibits considerable ambiguities in regard to some of its central legal concepts (such as the notion of the 'structural deficit' or the presence of exceptional circumstances), which consequently also allow for different readings.[89] The flexibility of the SGP system has been addressed, though in a very limited form, by a recent Commission communication.[90] In early 2015, the Commission issued an interpretative Communication termed 'making the best use of the flexibility within the existing rules of the stability and growth pact'. While the Communication seems to portray the SGP's flexibility as mere leniency towards Member States that face a particularly dire situation, and does not catch the full extent to which the SGP is open to different debt-related strategies, it nonetheless provides support for the thesis that the SGP is a potentially flexible instrument. We will take a closer look at the Communication further below. Of course, the constructive nature of the present section should be manifest: at this point of time, the SGP is certainly not applied in ways that would enable a forceful counter-cyclical policy. However, the point that I try to make is that this bias stems, inter alia, from a specific *interpretation* of the SGP,

[89] On the flexibility of the SGP rules, see for example Stefano Micossi and Fabrizia Peirce, 'Flexibility clauses in the Stability and Growth Pact: No need for revision' (2014) CEPS Policy Brief No 260.

[90] EC, 'Making the best use of the flexibility within the existing rules of the stability and growth pact' COM(2015) 12 final.

Overview of relevant primary, secondary and international law

Instrument	Provision or measure	Content (excerpt)	Legal basis (secondary law)	Main ambiguities/ discretionary choices discussed in this chapter
TFEU	Article 121	Surveillance procedure	—	—
	Article 126	Prohibition of excessive deficits and debt	—	Exception clause
	Protocol 12	Definition of deficit and debt limit	—	—
TSCG	—	Balanced budget requirement	—	Calculation of structural balance
Six Pack	Reg 1466/97 (amended by Reg 1175/2011)	Balanced budget requirement	Article 121(6) TFEU	Calculation of structural balance; exception clause
	Reg 1467/97 (amended by Reg 1177/2011)	Excessive deficit procedure	Article 126(14) TFEU	Exception clause
	Reg 1173/2011	Sanctions for breach of balanced budget and deficit requirements	Articles 121(6) and 136 TFEU	Prescription of 'necessary policy measures'
	Reg 1174/2011	Sanctions relating to the Macroeconomic Imbalance Procedure	Articles 121(6) and 136 TFEU	—
	Reg 1176/2011	Macroeconomic Imbalance Procedure	Article 121(6) TFEU	Definition of 'macroeconomic imbalances'
	Dir 2011/85/EU	Rules for national budgets	Article 126(14) TFEU	—
Two Pack	Reg 472/2013	Common framework for conditionality	Articles 121(6) and 136 TFEU	Substantive openness of conditionality
	Reg 473/2013	Surveillance of national budgets and economic policies by Commission	Articles 121(6) and 136 TFEU	Discretion implied in Commission evaluation

and does not follow unambiguously from the legal provisions themselves. This finding helps to bring the various possible other factors into focus that facilitate austerity-oriented outcomes. We will briefly discuss one seemingly technical, yet highly relevant issue that has been highlighted in recent debate at the end of the section, namely the calculation of public debt.

The Balanced-Budget Requirement (Reg 1466/97)

We will first look at the balanced budget requirement, and then turn to the deficit/debt limits prescribed by the Treaty. We will focus on the provisions applying to eurozone countries alone, though the section's general claim—ie, that the SGP can be conceptualized as a pluralist instrument—also extends to the rules applicable to non-euro Member States. Regulation 1466/97 provides for the establishment of 'medium-term budgetary objectives' (MTBO) for the Member States. According to its Article 2a, 'the country-specific medium-term budgetary objectives shall be specified within a defined range between −1 % of GDP and balance or surplus, in cyclically adjusted terms, net of one-off and temporary measures.' The MTBO forms part of the so-called 'stability programmes' that Member States have to submit to the EU 'for the purpose of multilateral surveillance',[91] and which is an element of the 'European Semester'. The legal basis for this surveillance procedure is Article 121 TFEU. The stability programmes are assessed by the Council on the basis of evaluations by the Commission and the Economic and Financial Committee as to 'whether the economic assumptions on which the programme is based are plausible, whether the adjustment path towards the medium-term budgetary objective is appropriate, including consideration of the accompanying path for the debt ratio, and whether the measures being taken or proposed to respect that adjustment path are sufficient to achieve the medium-term budgetary objective over the cycle.'[92] The assessment is thus explicitly based on an evaluation of the plausibility of the 'economic assumptions' that enter the stability programmes, which will obviously depend on the models and suppositions employed. The central factor of ambiguity in the stability programmes is the notion of the 'structural deficit' that underlies the MTBOs: the Member States are supposed to achieve a balanced budget (between −1 per cent and a surplus) in the medium term, which is assumed to cover a whole business cycle. The 'structural deficit' is calculated on the basis of the gap between a country's actual and its potential output, ie, the output a country would have if all its resources were fully employed.[93] The part of the deficit that is the consequence of the country's economic underperformance will not be considered, whereas the part that would be incurred even if the economy

[91] Art 3, Reg 1466/97.
[92] Art 5, Reg 1466/97.
[93] See Achim Truger and Henner Will, 'The German "debt brake": a shining example for European fiscal policy?' (2013) Working Paper, Institute for International Political Economy Berlin, No 15, 6–8.

were at full productivity will. The latter constitutes the 'structural deficit', ie, the deficit that exists even if business cycle fluctuations are taken into account. The concept of the 'potential output' relies on a counterfactual assessment, which in turn relies on the models applied and the chosen assumptions. If the output gap is calculated to be small, a larger part of the observed deficit is considered to be 'structural', and the other way around. Consequently, the way the potential output is established provides a significant entry point for discretionary choices. Darvas argued in this regard that the concept of the 'structural balance' is 'intuitive', but 'not observable', and instead depends on estimations, which 'implicates difficulties, uncertainties and controversies'.[94] It has been argued that the Commission tends to significantly underestimates the output gap, and thereby assumes that a large part of the observed deficit is structural in nature.[95] The TSCG equally prescribes a 'structural balance' (though with −0.5 per cent as the lower limit)[96], and is thereby burdened by the same problems. Observing that the balanced budget requirement of the TSCG has not been invoked since its inception, despite the fact that most eurozone countries exceeded the limit prescribed, Gro and Alcidis argued that the imprecise character of this variable may render the requirement largely ineffective.[97] Thus, the balanced budget requirement relies centrally on an ambiguous concept which can be substantiated only on the basis of economic assumptions that may often be controversial, and of forecasts that are uncertain. Depending on the socio-economic paradigm underlying the calculations of the structural deficit and the evaluation of the MTBO more generally, Regulation 1466/97 may thus be interpreted along the lines of either the anti- or the pro-austerity view: if the output gap is calculated to be high, then there is greater room available for counter-cyclical policies.

Beyond this, the Regulation entails important additional discretionary choices, thereby further underlining the instrument's pluralist potential. In particular, the Regulation holds that '[t]he Council and the Commission shall take into account whether a higher adjustment effort is made in economic good times, whereas the effort might be more limited in economic bad times. In particular, revenue windfalls and shortfalls shall be taken into account.'[98] Explicit mention is given to the temporary budgetary effects of 'the implementation of major structural reforms which have direct long-term positive budgetary effects, including by raising potential sustainable growth, and therefore a verifiable impact on the

[94] Zsolt Darvas, 'Mind the gap! And the way structural budget balances are calculated' (18 October, 2013) bruegel.org/2013/10/mind-the-gap-and-the-way-structural-budget-balances-are-calculated/; Truger and Will identify 'substantial margins of interpretation': Truger and Will (n 93), 8.

[95] Hugo Radice, 'Enforcing austerity in Europe: The structural deficit as a policy target' (2014) 22 *Journal of Contemporary European Studies* 318, 320.

[96] Art 3(1)(b), TSCG.

[97] Daniel Gros and Cinzia Alcidi, 'The case of the disappearing Fiscal Compact' (*CEPS Commentary*, 5 November 2014) 2; for further ambiguities in the TSCG see Craig (n 10), 237.

[98] Art 9(1), Reg 1466/97.

long-term sustainability of public finances'. The evaluation of the trade-off between short- and long-term budgetary effects, in particular in conjunction with the notoriously contested question of economic growth (which we discussed in an earlier chapter), implies significant political choices by the Commission. Finally, the Regulation also provides for an exception for an 'unusual event outside the control of the Member State concerned which has a major impact on the financial position of the general government or in periods of severe economic downturn for the euro area or the Union as a whole.'[99] This begs the question of what is considered a 'severe', as opposed to a regular, economic downturn. It is this very question that is a central point of contention between the pro- and the anti-austerity views. But the Regulation does not define the dividing line between 'regular' and 'severe' downturns, leaving them to the evaluation of the European institutions. Thus, the central conflict between the pro- and the anti-austerity views—ie, under what conditions may the regular deficit rules be suspended—is not answered. This problem can also not be circumvented by reference to the general rule of interpretation that exceptions should be interpreted strictly, as it does not help to answer the question what a 'severe' downturn is: is a once-in-a-decade downturn severe enough, or does it have to be a once-in-a-century crisis? (As regards the 2008 crisis, the distinction would be of little relevance, as it would qualify either way.)[100]

Finally, we take a brief look at the aspect of sanctions. Based on a Commission recommendation, the Council may advise the Member States 'on necessary policy measures'.[101] Given the complexity of the issues in consideration, the question of which measures are considered 'necessary' is again one that is dependent on the socio-economic assumptions chosen. Sanctions can be issued on the basis of Regulation 1173/2011, which forms part of the 'Six Pack'. They are paired with a reverse majority voting requirement in the Council, in which the Commission's recommendation is considered to be adopted unless it is rejected by a qualified majority. Following a 'reasoned request' by the Member State, the sanction may be reduced or cancelled upon recommendation of the Commission, which has discretionary choice in that regard.[102]

'Excessive Deficits' (Article 126 TFEU, Regulation 1467/97)

According to Article 126 TFEU, the Council decides on the basis of a Commission opinion whether the deficit of a Member State is excessive.[103] The deficit threshold of 3 per cent and the debt limit of 60 per cent is set by Protocol 12, but can be

[99] Art 9(1), Reg 1466/97.
[100] Heather Stewart, 'We are in the worst financial crisis since Depression, says IMF' *The Guardian* (10 April 2008), theguardian.com/business/2008/apr/10/useconomy.subprimecrisis.
[101] Art 10(2), Reg 1466/97.
[102] Art 4(4), Reg 1173/2011.
[103] Art 126(3) and (6) TFEU.

altered on the basis of Article 126(14) TFEU.[104] The Commission issues a report to that effect if the Member State exceeds the 3 per cent deficit and the 60 per cent debt threshold, except when:

— the *deficit* ratio 'has declined substantially and continuously and reached a level that comes close to the reference value'; or
— the excess over the *deficit* threshold 'is only exceptional and temporary and the ratio remains close to the reference value'; or
— the *debt* ratio is 'sufficiently diminishing and approaching the reference value at a satisfactory pace'.

Article 126 TFEU is thus characterized by considerable ambiguity, expressed in the choice—to be made by the Commission—whether one of the three conditions is applicable.[105] The ambivalent provisions are further defined in the Regulation 1467/97:

— a deficit is considered to be 'exceptional' if it is 'resulting from an unusual event outside the control of the Member State concerned and with a major impact on the financial position of general government, or when resulting from a severe economic downturn' (Article 2(1));
— it is considered 'temporary' if 'budgetary forecasts as provided by the Commission indicate that the deficit will fall below the reference value following the end of the unusual event or the severe economic downturn' (Article 2(1));
— the deficit may also be considered 'exceptional' if 'the excess over the reference value results from a negative annual GDP volume growth rate or from an accumulated loss of output during a protracted period of very low annual GDP volume growth relative to its potential' (Article 2(2));
— debt is considered to be 'sufficiently diminishing and approaching the reference value at a satisfactory pace' if it either (past oriented) 'has decreased over the previous three years at an average rate of one twentieth per year as a benchmark' or (future oriented) if the reduction 'will occur over the three-year period encompassing the two years following the final year for which the data is available' (Article 2(1a)).

The ambiguity is thereby further structured, but not eliminated. In particular, it is unclear what a 'severe downturn' is and at what point it is ending (ie, how temporary is 'temporary'?), how close is 'close to the reference value', and at what point would negative or low GDP growth justify a higher deficit? Beyond that, Article 2(3) requires the Commission to provide a holistic analysis, as it 'shall take into account all relevant factors as indicated [in Article 126 TFEU].' The provision

[104] Jens Hamer, 'Article 126' in Hans Von der Groeben, Jürgen Schwarze and Armin Hatje (eds), *Europäisches Unionsrecht* (Nomos, 2015), para 157.

[105] See ibid, paras 75–85; see also Häde, who holds that the Commission and the Council have a considerable scope of evaluation and discretion in the excessive deficit procedure. Ulrich Häde, 'Article 126' in Christian Calliess and Matthias Ruffert (eds), *EUV/AEUV* (Beck, 2011), para 17.

then provides a long list of issues for the Commission to consider. Article 126(3) TFEU emphasizes that the Commission 'shall also take into account whether the government deficit exceeds government investment expenditure'. Thus, in principle, public investments that exceed the deficit and debt benchmarks may be justified.[106] Article 2(4) of the Regulation holds that '[t]he Council and the Commission shall make a balanced overall assessment of all the relevant factors, specifically, the extent to which they affect the assessment of compliance with the deficit and/or the debt criteria as aggravating or mitigating factors.'[107] With the need of such general evaluation, the institutions are obviously granted considerable discretion.[108] We can thus see that significant flexibility exists prior to entering the excessive deficit procedure; it hinges, in particular, on the scope assigned to the exceptions provided for in Article 126 TFEU, and further defined by the Regulation.

Within the excessive deficit procedure itself, new ambiguities open up. The Council issues a recommendation to the Member State, which is supposed to 'establish a deadline for the correction of the excessive deficit, which shall be completed in the year following its identification unless there are special circumstances.'[109] While the Regulation requests 'a minimum annual improvement of at least 0,5 % of GDP as a benchmark', deviations from the benchmark are possible in the presence of 'special circumstances', which remain undefined. The recommendation may be revised in the presence of 'unexpected adverse economic events with major unfavourable consequences for government finances occur after the adoption of that recommendation', and the deadline may be extended 'by one year as a rule.' A revision is also possible '[i]n the case of a severe economic downturn in the euro area or in the Union as a whole.'[110] If the Member State 'persists in failing to put into practice the recommendations', the Council gives 'notice to the Member State to take, within a specified time limit, measures for the deficit reduction which is judged necessary by the Council in order to remedy the situation.'[111] The notice can be adapted in case of 'unexpected adverse economic events with major unfavourable consequences for government finances', and the deadline may be extended.[112] Further ambivalences arise in the sanctions phase: Article 11 holds that a fine shall 'as a rule' be required, implying that exceptions are possible.[113] According to Article 12(2), it is for the Council to decide whether the Member State has 'taken effective action'. Sanctions can be abrogated 'depending on the significance of the progress made by the participating Member State'.[114] Thus, like the balanced-budget requirement, the debt/deficit rules are, in principle, open to

[106] Hamer (n 104), para 93.
[107] Art 2(4), Reg 1467/97.
[108] See Häde (n 105), para 10.
[109] Art 3(4), Reg 1467/97.
[110] Art 3(5), Reg 1467/97.
[111] Art 126(9) TFEU.
[112] Art 5(2), Reg 1467/97.
[113] Hamer (n 104), para 130.
[114] Art 14, Reg 1467/97; see on this Micossi and Peirce (n 89), 7.

different readings, and could accommodate both the pro- and the anti-austerity view.[115] Regulation 473/2013, which forms part of the 'Two Pack', did not alter the situation in substantive terms. It requires Member States to submit their draft budgets to a review by the Commission. The Commission may request a Member State to submit a revised draft if it 'identifies particular serious non-compliance with the budgetary policy obligations laid down in the SGP'.[116] The Regulation also prescribes that Member States subject to an 'excessive deficit' procedure have to establish an 'economic partnership programme', in which it lays out 'policy measures and structural reforms that are needed to ensure an effective and lasting correction of the excessive deficit'.[117] On this, an opinion is issued by the Council on the basis of a Commission proposal.[118] The evaluation of both the draft budgets and of the 'economic partnership programmes' is obviously again dependent on the socio-economic assumptions and methods employed by the Commission.

A close look at the SGP procedure thus reveals significant discretionary space. Room for interpretation arises from both an ambivalence of terms (eg 'temporary'), which constitute an implicit discretion, as well as discretion explicitly granted to the institutions at multiple points. The central ambiguity in the SGP arises in relation to the question of when downturns are severe enough to justify a deviation from the debt/deficit rules, for how long, and what the circumstances are that need to be taken into account. As already mentioned in regard to the balanced-budget requirement, it is precisely this ambiguity that reflects in key aspects the conflict between the pro- and the anti-austerity positions. The anti-austerity position holds that, in a severe downturn, deficit reduction cannot be the primary objective, as it would undermine economic recovery and thereby ultimately increase the deficit instead of reducing it. By contrast, from a pro-austerity perspective the suspension of these rules may appear unwarranted. The central point, however, is that the exception itself remains undefined, and thus open to readings based on different socio-economic paradigms. It is clear that the SGP aims at reducing public debt; but whether the path out of high debt is the pro- or the anti-austerity strategy is simply not determined. This ambiguity of the SGP is also touched upon in the Commission's Communication, which holds:

> Since 2011, the Pact has provided, in cases of a severe economic downturn in the euro area or the Union as a whole, for the pace of fiscal consolidation to be adapted for all Member States, as long as this does not endanger fiscal sustainability in the medium-term. This provision has so far never been applied—although it de facto reflects the logic used at the time of the 2008 financial crisis when the adjustment paths were re-designed for several Member States. The activation of this provision would not mean putting on hold the fiscal adjustment, but rather re-designing the adjustment path on a country-specific

[115] Arguing that the SGP provides considerable flexibility: Hamer (n 104), paras 161–63.
[116] Art 7(2), Reg 473/2013.
[117] Art 9(1), Reg 473/2013.
[118] Art 9(4), Reg 473/2013

> basis, both in terms of the adjustment effort and the deadlines to achieve the targets, to take into account the exceptional circumstances of the severe economic downturn in the euro area or the Union as a whole. The use of this provision should remain limited to exceptional, carefully circumscribed situations to minimise the risk of moral hazard.[119]

The Communication essentially expresses the view that the automatism the SGP proposes for debt and deficit reduction cannot be upheld in the light of a severe economic downturn; and that, instead, it requires an evaluation that takes a broad view on the circumstances of a country. The Communication thus articulates the fundamental dilemma underlying the SGP: on the one hand it is recognized that an event such as the 2008 crisis may occur, and that such exceptional circumstances may justify deviating from the plans made for more regular times. There is thus an acknowledgment of the need to provide space for responses to exceptional circumstances. At the same time, there is a manifest attempt to restrict the exceptions to situations defined in advance, which quite clearly is a conceptual contradiction to the recognition of the possibility that exceptional circumstances may occur. The Commission's communication also points towards another factor that essentially undermines any belief that the SGP could plausibly implement a rule-based system with automated responses to excessive deficits: the economic crisis showed that Member States may incur significant deficits for reasons that have nothing to do with their own policies. Moreover, even the most dedicated and ambitious policy responses may fail to achieve budgetary consolidation because of factors beyond the government's control. The fact that Member States are embedded not only in a highly financialized world economy and a very tight common market, but are also connected in a common monetary union means that Member States have only limited control over the factors that influence their budgets. There is thus an inherent contradiction between the notion of Member State responsibility for their own budget, on which the SGP builds, and the economic reality that Member States face. This contradiction is addressed by the Commission as follows in its Communication:

> Acknowledging the need to distinguish between fiscal consolidation actions and fiscal consolidation outcomes, with the latter often being influenced by developments outside the control of the authorities concerned, the rules envisage the possibility to take into account an unexpected deterioration of the economic situation.[120]

The Commission thus recognizes that the Member States may face situations in which their well-intended policies do not lead to the desired outcome because of factors they have no control over. Unless the Member States are to be punished for something they are not factually responsible for, the governments' efforts must be

[119] EC, 'Making the best use of the flexibility within the existing rules of the stability and growth pact' COM(2015) 12 final 17.

[120] ibid, 15.

recognized in some form.[121] This, however, means that the idea of an automatic SGP is untenable. The same applies to large structural reform efforts, which the SGP attempts to account for:[122] while they may pay off in the long run, there is no guarantee for this. For example, a market-based reorganization of the pension system may lead to lower debt in the long run, but it may also turn out to be actually more costly for the government. Similarly, taxation of capital gains (eg in conjunction with tax relief on labour) may have positive effects on both the budget and on employment, but these benefits may just as well be neutralized by capital flight. Because reforms take place against the backdrop of a complex international environment and an uncertain future, the Commission will frequently have to evaluate intentions and effort, rather than measurable developments. The 2015 Recommendation on France provides a telling example. Here, the Commission held:

> The Communication clarifies that the Commission will take into account the existence of a dedicated structural reform plan, providing detailed and verifiable information, as well as credible timelines for adoption and delivery, when recommending a deadline for the correction of the excessive deficit or the length of any extension to that deadline …
>
> The Commission will consider in May, taking into account the level of ambition of the National Reform Programme.[123]

The vocabulary employed—'dedicated structural reform plan', 'detailed and verifiable information', 'credible timelines', and, above all, the 'level of ambition'—speaks of the difficulties the Commission faces in establishing objective criteria for its evaluation. The automatic and fully rule-based SGP is more illusion than fact, and the multiple instances where the SGP grants discretionary choice identified on the preceding pages illustrate this clearly. If the SGP was intended as an implementation of an ordoliberal regulatory project, then it failed. The reasons behind this go beyond the scope of this book; however, a possibility is that a constitutional framework that governs the macroeconomic processes of 28 countries must be able to react to complex dynamics, which no regulatory structure can anticipate and fully regulate in advance. In this sense the ordoliberal vision resembles the belief in the possibility to 'fine-tune' the economy that characterized the neoclassical synthesis of the 1950s and 1960s. This is despite the fact that they appear to be located at the opposite ends of the spectrum of regulatory possibilities, with one side emphasizing rules, and the other side discretion. However, the interpretation

121 See on this Franco and Zollino, who argue: 'Structural reform is particularly challenging, in that the beneficial impact on macroeconomic imbalances is hard to assess and may be slow in emerging, and possibly even with an adverse impact in the short run.' Daniele Franco and Francesco Zollino, 'Macroeconomic imbalances in Europe: institutional progress and the challenges that remain' (2014) 46 *Applied Economics* 589, 598.

122 Art 5(1), Reg 1466/97.

123 EC, 'Recommendation for a Council Recommendation with a view to bringing an end to the excessive government deficit in France' COM(2015) 115 final, 9, 22.

of the SGP as a fully rule-based and automated system relies on the assumption that total control of the economic processes by policymakers in Europe could be possible. In this sense the ordoliberal vision shares what Streeck termed the 'phantasies of controllability' with the fine-tuners of a few decades ago.[124]

Whether an 'ambitious' and 'dedicated' consolidation plan based on anti-austerity thinking would pass the Commission's scrutiny is an open question at this point of time; but the preceding analysis of the SGP shows that, from a legal perspective, there is no reason to give precedence to the pro- over the anti-austerity perspective. We can conclude that, despite the manifest intention to provide a detailed and automated path of deficit/debt reduction, the SGP at the same time retains a significant room for discretionary choice. This, in turn, can be read as an ambiguity or openness towards different socio-economic paradigms. We thus encounter a rift between the SGP's normative setup, which is pluralist, and the Union's practice, which, as discussed briefly in the introduction, appears to favour the pro-austerity agenda. One of the reason for such bias may lie in the socio-economic assumptions the Union institutions subscribe to. Another factor that is certainly important is, as mentioned in the beginning, the seemingly technical question how public debt is calculated. If a Member States borrows money to finance investment, only the liability will be registered for the purposes of the SGP, but not the corresponding assets.[125] Surely there are reasons that support the current calculation method.[126] However, it also has significant downsides, which have become virulent in the crisis: most notably, investment cuts have been found to be particularly damaging during a downturn; this is because the fiscal multiplier of public investment (ie, the economic stimulation it triggers) would have been particularly high at that point.[127] Moreover, it has been found that in the present crisis, governments were inclined to cut capital investment rather than current spending.[128] Thus, as Member States scaled down public investment to reduce their deficit to meet the SGP criteria, their growth potential was damaged, which in turn impedes their long-term ability to reduce their deficit. The way debt is calculated for the purpose of the SGP thus seems to create a dynamic that is particularly troublesome from an anti-austerity perspective. The peculiar way of calculating government debt employed by the Union has faced growing criticism in recent years.[129] It was demanded, for example by the European Parliament, that debt taken out for capital investment should be excluded, a practice corroborated by Article 126 TFEU, which allows the Commission, as already mentioned, to 'take into account whether the government deficit exceeds government investment

[124] Streeck (n 5), 213–14.
[125] Hamer (n 104), para 82.
[126] For a summary see Barbiero and Darvas (n 79), 8.
[127] ibid, 8.
[128] ibid, 8–9.
[129] See on the recent debate ibid, 6–10.

expenditure'.[130] As the accounting standards the Commission relies on are laid down in the ESA2010, which has been passed in the form of a Regulation, it could be changed on the basis of the ordinary legislative procedure.[131] To conclude this section it can be argued that the SGP can be read in a pluralist form, supporting, in principle, both pro- and anti-austerity strategies of debt reduction. Such a finding helps focus the attention on those factors that may be responsible for the Union's current pro-austerity leaning. This may include, as discussed, biased economic assumptions adopted by the Commission, as well as the seemingly technical question of how public debt is calculated.

Interpreting the Macroeconomic Imbalances Procedure in a Pluralist Form

The Macroeconomic Imbalance Procedure (MIP) was introduced in 2011 as part of the 'Six Pack' reforms.[132] The task of the MIP is to identify emerging imbalances early through a surveillance procedure, which, in the case of the euro countries, is fortified with a system of sanctions. The assumption underlying the MIP is that, in the EU as an integrated market and in particular in the eurozone as a monetary union, numerous factors other than public debt may exert a destabilizing influence.[133] The MIP deals with highly contested questions: different socio-economic views exist as to which economic trends are liable to create adverse effects for Member States and for the Union as a whole, and which policies should be adopted in response. It will be argued that, while the MIP aims to detect macroeconomic imbalances and correct such imbalances that are deemed 'excessive', it is agnostic as to which economic trends this actually entails. Consequently, the MIP is open to different readings, and can thus be described as pluralist in the light of competing socio-economic paradigms. We will also take a brief look at how MIP has been interpreted and applied by the Commission in practice. It will be argued that the implementation by the Commission reflects this pluralism not in all respects; in particular, the Commission does not confront the problem of consistent trade surpluses the same way it confronts trade deficits. However, it will be argued that such application does not normatively follow from the MIP, and must be conceptualized as a political choice of the Commission.

[130] European Parliament resolution of 8 October 2013 on effects of budgetary constraints for regional and local authorities regarding the EU's Structural Funds expenditure in the Member States (2013/2042(INI)).

[131] Regulation (EU) No 549/2013 of the European Parliament and of the Council on the European system of national and regional accounts in the European Union [2013] OJ L 174/1.

[132] Regulation No 1176/2011 on the prevention and correction of macroeconomic imbalances [2011] OJ L 306/25; Regulation No 1174/2011 on enforcement measures to correct excessive macroeconomic imbalances in the euro area [2011] OJ L 306/8.

[133] For a brief overview of the main causes for the current imbalances in the Union, see Stefan Ederer, 'Macroeconomic imbalances and institutional reforms in the EMU' (2015) WWWforEurope Working Paper No 87, 3–8.

Overview of the MIP

The MIP complements the SGP by expanding the system of surveillance to additional macroeconomic indicators. The MIP rests on two measures, Regulation 1176/2011 'on the prevention and correction of macroeconomic imbalances', and Regulation 1174/2011 'on enforcement measures to correct excessive macroeconomic imbalances in the euro area.' Whereas the former measure lays down the general system, the latter adds a stricter regime—including sanctions—for the eurozone countries. The two measures form part of a more general attempt to pull together the binding and non-binding instruments at the disposal of the EU in the 'European semester' to create a more systematic framework of European macroeconomic governance. 'Imbalances' are defined as 'any trend giving rise to macroeconomic developments which are adversely affecting, or have the potential adversely to affect, the proper functioning of the economy of a Member State or of the economic and monetary union, or of the Union as a whole'; and 'excessive imbalances' as 'severe imbalances, including imbalances that jeopardise or risks jeopardising the proper functioning of the economic and monetary union'.[134] Imbalances are identified on the basis of economic indicators, which are defined by the Commission in the 'scoreboard'.[135] The definition of 'imbalances' is very broad, and may cover any kind of trend that is capable of having an adverse effect on a Member State or on the Union. The Regulation proposes that the scoreboard's indicators should be able to measure both internal and external imbalances, which are described the following way:

> (a) internal imbalances, including those that can arise from public and private indebtedness; financial and asset market developments, including housing; the evolution of private sector credit flow; and the evolution of unemployment; (b) external imbalances, including those that can arise from the evolution of current account and net investment positions of Member States; real effective exchange rates; export market shares; changes in price and cost developments; and non-price competitiveness, taking into account the different components of productivity.[136]

The scoreboard may be complemented with additional indicators, as the term 'including' indicates. The Regulation remains silent as to the weight that should be assigned to the various indicators. On the basis of an in-depth review, the Commission may propose recommendations to the Council to address imbalances, or initiate the 'excessive imbalance procedure'.[137] The Council establishes the existence of an excessive imbalances on recommendation by the Commission.[138] The recommendation 'shall set out the nature and implications of the imbalances and shall specify a set of policy recommendations to be followed and a deadline within

[134] Art 2(1), Reg 1176/2011.
[135] Art 4(1), Reg 1176/2011.
[136] Art 4(3), Reg 1176/2011.
[137] Arts 7–12, Reg 1176/2011.
[138] Art 7(2), Reg 1176/2011.

which the Member State concerned is to submit a corrective action plan.' Based on a Commission recommendation, the Council subsequently votes on whether the corrective action plan proposed by the Member State is sufficient, and lists specific actions required as well as a timetable for surveillance.[139] The corrective action plan is monitored by the Commission. If the Commission finds that the Member State has not taken the recommended corrective action, it advises the Council to establish non-compliance. On this vote, the Regulation stipulates what is termed 'reverse qualified majority voting': the measure is deemed adopted unless the Council, by qualified majority, rejects the recommendation within 10 days.[140] Regulation 1174/2011 establishes sanctions for non-compliance by euro countries. If the Council concludes that the Member State has not taken the corrective action recommended by the Council, an interest-bearing deposit shall be imposed.[141] Moreover, an annual fine can be levied if two successive recommendations are adopted in the same imbalance procedure, and the corrective action plan is considered to be insufficient, or non-compliance is established.[142] The sanctions mechanism also prescribes reversed voting in the Council.[143]

Different Socio-economic Perspectives on Macroeconomic Imbalances

The MIP deals with highly contested socio-economic questions.[144] Depending on the underlying socio-economic paradigm, macroeconomic trends may be evaluated in rather different ways. The question of current account imbalances, which constitutes a central parameter in the MIP, provides a clear illustration for this claim. Current account imbalances have always been considered to be among the key problems of international economic relations. As we saw in previous chapters, they were also considered a central concern in European integration. Current account imbalances are an ambivalent indicator because they may have a variety of different causes, and may, for that reason, point to either a positive or a negative economic development.[145] For example, if saving is understood as future consumption, then a current account surplus—which, in simplified terms, can be conceptualized as a surplus country lending money to a deficit country—may represent a preference of the population for future over present consumption, a situation that might, for example, be plausible for aging populations. Conversely,

[139] Art 8(2), Reg 1176/2011.
[140] Art 10(4), Reg 1176/2011.
[141] Art 3(1), Reg 1176/2011.
[142] Art 3(2), Reg 1176/2011.
[143] Art 3(3), Reg 1176/2011.
[144] See for example Stefano Micossi, 'Misguided policies risk breaking up the eurozone and the EU' (2011) CEPS Working Paper No 260, 3–4; Dariusz Adamski, 'National power games and structural failures in the European macroeconomic governance' (2012) 49 *Common Market Law Review* 1319, 1353–54.
[145] See Maurice Obstfeld, 'Financial flows, financial crises, and global imbalances' (2012) 31 *Journal of International Money and Finance* 469, 474–79.

a current account deficit may indicate the opposite situation, and characterize expanding economies: credit-financed investment may have positive economic effects in the future. Current account deficits or surpluses are thus not necessarily problematic; however, they *may* indicate underlying structural problems.[146] The current account deficits accrued by the peripheral countries in the 2000s illustrate their ambivalent nature. As then-dominant economic theory predicted convergence between the core and the peripheral countries in an integrated market, the latter were expected to consume and invest more than they saved. The observed surplus in core countries and the deficit in peripheral countries therefore seemed to conform to these predictions.[147] Before the 2008 crisis, current account deficits were thus largely viewed as a by-product of the ongoing convergence process in the EMU.[148] When the crisis hit, however, current account imbalances became liabilities for the peripheral countries in ways unexpected by then-dominant theory. The current account deficit is financed through credit; it had been expected that, in an integrated monetary union, robust private borrowers could always access credit, regardless of the current account balance. However, for a number of reasons, interest rates hikes affected all borrowers in the peripheral countries indiscriminately, making the current account deficit unviable.

These problems now inform today's views on the current account, which no longer perceive surpluses and deficits as benign side-products of the convergence process. Current account deficits are now viewed with suspicion; but there are competing explanations as to why they have arisen. From one perspective, current account surpluses tend to be interpreted as a sign of a successful, export-oriented economy that kept wage increases in check in order to improve its competitive position. From the same perspective, deficits are understood as an indication of excessive consumption, debt-making and wage increases. From another perspective, however, current account surpluses indicate a lack of domestic consumption, caused by subdued wage developments.[149] As wages stagnated over the past decade in countries like Germany while productivity increased, domestic demand was no longer absorbing production. Wage depression increased the competitive position of the surplus countries, but only at the expense of the other European countries; the surplus countries are seen as engaging in a 'beggar-thy-neighbour' strategy. Moreover, trade surpluses have also been faulted for creating the mobile capital which in turn fuelled speculative bubbles in the peripheral countries.[150] These two perspectives imply different ways out of the current imbalances, which could

[146] ibid, 478.

[147] See Nils Holinski, Clemens Kool and Joan Muysken, 'Persistent macroeconomic imbalances in the euro area: Causes and consequences' (2012) 94 *Federal Reserve Bank of St Louis Review* 1, 3–4 and 12, with further references.

[148] 'State-of-play in implementing macroeconomic adjustment programmes in the euro area' (Study at the request of the Economic and Monetary Affairs Committee, 2014), 12–13.

[149] Dodig and Herr (n 88), 1.

[150] Obstfeld (n 145), 478, with further references.

be termed 'symmetrical' and 'asymmetrical' strategies, respectively. The 'asymmetrical' perspective assumes that the imbalances in the eurozone are caused by negative deviations from a 'correct' development or a baseline, such as high public or private debt, rising labour costs, etc, which find expression in the difficulties experienced by the governments and the private sector in the deficit countries. The thrust of the convergence efforts to rectify these imbalances is assumed to rest on those countries that experienced refinancing problems on the capital market during the crisis, and is thus 'asymmetrical' in nature. By contrast, the 'symmetrical' view assumes that imbalances arise not through a deviation from some absolute baseline, but through relative differences between the development of the Member States. In this sense, the fault lies not necessarily with one country or the other, but in the fact that their developments diverge. For example, the wage increases one Member State experienced create an imbalance only because the wage development in another Member State was depressed at the same time. If both Member States had experienced the same wage increases, competitiveness towards the world could be retained through a euro devaluation. With a diverging development, however, the wage development will have to be adapted in a symmetrical way by both deficit and surplus countries. The standard for wage-setting is often held to be productivity gains: wages should rise in the same proportion as productivity. From this perspective, it is usually assumed that the wage levels in the surplus countries should rise in order to catch up with productivity gains in the past decade. This would increase domestic demand in the surplus countries, reduce their surpluses, and, indirectly, reduce the deficits in the deficit countries as well. The example of the current account thus illustrates the ambivalent nature of the indicators of macroeconomic imbalances. Depending on the socio-economic assumptions applied, different interpretations of the parameters may be possible, which in turn indicate different policy strategies. Regarding the current crisis, a significant difference exists regarding the question as to whether the adjustment efforts should be shouldered by the peripheral countries alone, or whether this should be a shared effort between the core and the periphery. Micossi asked in that regard: '[W]ould an exogenous increase in the propensity to save in Germany always have to be met by a deflationary adjustment in Italy?'[151]

The Pluralist Nature of the MIP Regulation

The different views on macroeconomic imbalances discussed in the previous section raise the question of how the MIP relates to these positions. The answer is that the Regulations remain, in principle, agnostic as regards the different socio-economic views on macroeconomic imbalances. The central indicator for this agnosticism is the extremely broad definition of the concept of 'macroeconomic imbalances'. These are defined as 'any trend' that has the potential to adversely

[151] Micossi (n 144), 5.

affect a Member State, the eurozone or the EU.[152] 'Excessive imbalances' are defined (in what is essentially a tautological form) as 'severe imbalances, including imbalances that jeopardise or risks jeopardising the proper functioning of the economic and monetary union'. Because of its broad reach, this definition of macroeconomic imbalances supports both a 'symmetrical' and an 'asymmetrical' reading.[153] Moreover, we have already mentioned that the list of indicators provided by the Regulation is not exhaustive. Beyond that, the Regulation remains silent as to the weight that should be assigned to the various indicators. The Regulations must thus be considered to be pluralist in the sense that they do not give preference to any specific view on macroeconomic imbalances.

Of course, there are certain aspects of the Regulation that might be read as an implicit bias towards a specific view on macroeconomic imbalances. For example, while recognizing the problems associated with both current account surpluses and deficits, the Regulation's preamble holds that 'the need for policy action is particularly pressing in Member States showing persistently large current-account deficits and competitiveness losses.'[154] Another potential cause for potential biases identified by some commentators is that the MIP is based on single-country analyses, and does not engage in an overall evaluation.[155] According to Moschella, this 'may lead to missing (or downplaying) important systemic macroeconomic and financial developments.'[156] And Franco and Zollino argue:

> Since multilateral factors are increasingly affecting national current accounts, a challenging issue is making sure that policy recommendations to one country take account of the externalities in other Member States, to enhance the coherence of domestic policies with the area-wide objectives of growth and stability. In this framework, proper domestic policy stands confirmed as a primary and necessary condition for reducing vulnerabilities both nationally and area-wide. Yet a country-by-country approach may lose sight of the area-wide risks, which are mostly rooted in feedback effects and can aggravate all the problems of macroeconomic sustainability. The systemic impact of the risks of imbalance in one country makes the shared value of their prevention and correction all the greater.[157]

Thus, the country-based structure of the MIP may create outcomes that are biased in favour of the asymmetrical approach to combating imbalances. At the same time, while the structure of the MIP is indeed based on a country-by-country approach, this does not necessarily mean that the analysis that informs it could not, in principle, draw from a general, systematic perspective on imbalances in the Union. As a preliminary finding, it can thus be held that that the Regulation remains extremely

[152] Art 2, Reg 1176/2011.
[153] Adamski (n 144), 1353, fn 106.
[154] Reg 1176/2011, preamble, clause 17.
[155] See for example Dodig and Herr (n 88), 12.
[156] Manuela Moschella, 'Monitoring Macroeconomic Imbalances: Is EU Surveillance More Effective than IMF Surveillance?' (2014) 52 *Journal of Common Market Studies* 1273, 1284.
[157] Franco and Zollino (n 121), 599.

general as regards the interpretation of the imbalances observed, and is thus open towards different socio-economic approaches.

Application of MIP by the Commission: Scoreboard and Recommendations

We will now look at the implementation of the MIP by the Commission in the scoreboard as well as the country-specific recommendations. As already mentioned, the regulation proposes a number of indicators to be included in the scoreboard, which may, however, be amended. The indicators shall be equipped with 'indicative thresholds … to serve as alert levels'.[158] The scoreboard is defined as a 'tool to facilitate early identification and monitoring of imbalances'.[159] Given the different perspectives on macroeconomic imbalances discussed above, the choice of indicators as well as the definition of thresholds is potentially controversial. In this regard, Franco and Zollino held:

> The challenge is arduous, because macroeconomic stability depends on a difficult combination of economic, social and institutional factors. Unlike fiscal policy, for which it was agreed that the sustainability assessment is based on numerical targets under the virtually full control of governments, measures to prevent macroeconomic vulnerability are quite controversial … In this respect, developments that can be considered growth-enhancing and welfare-improving today may harbour the seeds of harmful imbalances if the general situation changes, due to either domestic or, more problematically, external shocks.[160]

The indicators and thresholds defined by the Commission in the scoreboard on the basis of the Regulation are listed in the following table.

MIP scoreboard indicators[161]

Indicator	**Threshold**
3 year backward moving average of the current account balance as percentage of GDP	+6% and −4%
net international investment position as percentage of GDP	−35%
5 years' percentage change of export market shares measured in values	−6%
3 years' percentage change in nominal unit labour cost	+9% for euro area countries and +12% for non-euro area countries

(continued)

[158] Art 4(4), Reg 1176/2011.
[159] Art 4(1), Reg 1176/2011.
[160] Franco and Zollino (n 121), 597.
[161] ec.europa.eu/economy_finance/economic_governance/macroeconomic_imbalance_procedure/mip_scoreboard/index_en.htm.

MIP scoreboard indicators (*Continued*)

Indicator	Threshold
3 years' percentage change of the real effective exchange rates based on HICP/CPI deflators, relative to 41 other industrial countries, with thresholds	−/+5% for euro area countries and −/+11% for non-euro area countries
private sector debt (consolidated) in % of GDP	133%
private sector credit flow in % of GDP	15%
year-on-year changes in house prices relative to a Eurostat consumption deflator	6%
general government sector debt in % of GDP	60%
3-year backward moving average of unemployment rate	10%
year-on-year changes in total financial sector liabilities	16.5%

A detailed discussion of the individual indicators cannot be undertaken here; however, a few observations can be made. A key criticism of the indicators is that they are not defined in a symmetrical way. This becomes manifest as regards the current account balance, where the scoreboard sets the threshold levels at −4 and +6 per cent, implying that surpluses are less problematic than deficits.[162] While this is certainly true for individual countries who are member of a monetary union (but not necessarily for countries with an independent monetary policy, as the example of the United States or the United Kingdom shows), this is a questionable assumption in regard to the stability of the monetary union as a whole. As we saw, the build-up of surpluses in the eurozone is frequently held to be as problematic as that of deficits. A symmetrical definition of the indicator would suggest no difference between the positive and the negative threshold levels. Beyond that it is curious that the nominal unit labour costs are set with an upwards threshold only, implying that a significant drop in wages would not constitute a source of instability, whereas a wage increase would.[163] Such a view is hardly shared across the board, with many economists assuming that demand—which largely depends on wages—is a key factor in economic growth. A more symmetrical definition of the

[162] See Moschella (n 156), 1283–84; however, the Regulation expressly holds that surpluses and deficits do not necessarily need to be treated the same way: 'The assessment of Member States showing large current-account deficits may differ from that of Member States that accumulate large current-account surpluses' (Art 3(2)). The reason for such differential evaluation of surpluses and deficits presumably lies in the fact that surpluses do not create market distrust. In a recent study the Commission held in this regard: '[C]urrent account surpluses do not raise concerns about the sustainability of external debt or financing capacity.' EC, 'Current account surpluses in the EU' (*European Economy* No 9, 2012), 10.

[163] Dodig and Herr (n 88), 6.

indicator would define a downwards threshold corresponding to the upper limit. Based on these two critiques it may be argued that the scoreboard seems to implement an asymmetrical, rather than a symmetrical approach, thereby suggesting a bias in favour of a specific socio-economic paradigm.[164] Of course, the Commission has wide discretion in interpreting the scoreboard indicators; it emphasized in that regard that the 'scoreboard indicators are neither policy targets nor policy instruments' and that 'the reading of the scoreboard results is not mechanical but takes into account other relevant information as well as the broad economic context'.[165] At the same time, however, the biases inscribed into the indicators may have practical relevance; as the Commission itself states, 'the scoreboard has an important communication role'.[166] Consequently, the scoreboard may be viewed as indicating a biased implementation of the MIP. From the perspective of this book this leads to the question whether such biased application is legally *required* or merely *enabled*. In the light of our previous discussion, it can be argued that the MIP itself does not suggest a preference for a reading in the light of any specific socio-economic paradigm. Thus, the asymmetrical definition of indicators and thresholds in the scoreboard does not follow from the MIP, and must instead be considered to be a political choice by the Commission.

We will now turn to the Commission's country-specific evaluations. The country-specific analyses illustrate the complexity of identifying excessive imbalances. The alert mechanism reports show that all countries exceed the thresholds defined by the scoreboard with some value or another.[167] As an example, we will discuss the 2014 report on Germany. Germany is beyond the threshold with its current account surplus (6.5 per cent) and a falling REER (−8.9 per cent), but also suffered from falling export share (−13.1 per cent) and high government debt (81 per cent).[168] Most interestingly for our purposes, Germany has recorded a consistently high current account surplus of over 6 per cent since 2007. We have already discussed that the current account is an ambivalent indicator, and may have a wide spectrum of possible underlying causes. The 'in-depth review' of Germany emphasizes these multiple causes; it argues that, on the one hand, the 'current account surplus is in line with the structural characteristics of the German economy'.[169] On the other hand, however, it holds that 'the pace at which it has been accumulated and its persistence even during a time of adjustment within the euro area cannot be explained by factors that usually drive the current account. This is a priori a sign that the country's economic resources are not being allocated fully efficiently, which ultimately could

[164] Ederer argued in this context: 'The macroeconomic imbalances procedure (MIP) which was established in 2011 to target these developments is not adequate to eliminate these imbalances. It is not based on the understanding of these imbalances as a symmetric phenomenon, which can only be dealt with by a coordinated cross-national approach.' Ederer (n 133), 15.

[165] EC, 'Scoreboard for the surveillance of macroeconomic imbalances' (2012) Occasional Papers No 92, 3.

[166] ibid, 4.

[167] ec.europa.eu/economy_finance/economic_governance/documents/alert_mechanism_report_2014_statistical_annex_en.pdf.

[168] EC, 'Alert Mechanism Report 2014' (COM 790 final), 4.

[169] EC, 'Macroeconomic Imbalances Germany 2014'(2014) Occasional Papers No 174, 11.

be to the detriment of German economic welfare.'[170] Germany's current account surplus is a symptom for a number of underlying problems, as the Commission held in the Alert Mechanism Report: according to the Commission, it essentially indicates 'inefficient levels of savings and investments'. Moreover, it may lead to an appreciation of the euro, which would make it 'more difficult for the peripheral countries to recover competitiveness through internal depreciation'.[171] In the 2014 report, the Commission acknowledged recent wage increases, but emphasized that the effects were 'small compared to the gains recorded in the pre-crisis decade'.[172] At the same time, the Commission emphasized an alleged difference between the risk of surpluses and of deficits, respectively. In the report on Germany, the Commission held that the current account surpluses 'do not raise risks similar to large deficits'.[173] Given the fact that the thresholds are already defined in an asymmetrical form (−4 per cent vs +6 per cent), such argument in the light of a country exceeding even the higher limit seems to grant a double-relief for surplus countries as opposed to countries featuring a deficit: the threshold is already higher, presumably because surpluses are less of a problem, but even if the higher threshold is crossed, the alleged difference between surplus and deficits is again invoked. Despite this overly hands-off approach to current account surpluses, the Commission made a cautious argument in favour of a symmetrical adjustment of the trade imbalances, in which German domestic demand should be strengthened. Recommended policies include infrastructure investment and the creation of a climate beneficial for wage growth. According to my own evaluation, of the total of seven policy recommendations proposed by the report, four conform in a broad sense to the symmetrical view towards trade imbalances, and the other three appear ambivalent.[174] In this sense we may identify a symmetrical approach of the Commission in the country-specific report for Germany, assuming that it is required, even though it is a surplus country, to participate in the adjustment effort.[175] Despite this, there is cause to question whether the Commission would

[170] ibid, 11.

[171] EC, 'Alert Mechanism Report 2014' COM(2013) 790 final, 14.

[172] ibid, 14.

[173] EC, 'Recommendation for a Council Recommendation on Germany's 2014 national reform programme' COM(214) 406 final, 3 (para 7).

[174] I consider the following recommendations in the 2014 Alert Mechanism Report on Germany as confirming the symmetrical perspective: 1) 'identify and implement measures that help strengthen domestic demand and the economy's growth potential'; 2) 'additional measures appear needed to address the backlog in public investment and in particular to step up infrastructure investment'; 3) 'appropriate conditions should be secured in order to enable wage growth to further contribute to domestic demand'; 4) 'an increase in aggregate demand in Germany would raise growth domestically, but would also entail an additional benefit of helping the economic recovery in the euro area'. By contrast, I view the following recommendations as neutral or ambivalent in regard to the symmetrical and the asymmetrical view: 1) 'steps to further reduce disincentives to work would be welcome, with a view to supporting labour supply and raising the income of workers, in particular those at the bottom of the income distribution'; 2) 'more efficient corporate taxation'; 3) 'ensure that the banking sector has sufficient loss absorption capacity to withstand economic and financial shocks.'

[175] It was reported that the Commission's recommendation for a more symmetrical adjustment met with resistance from Germany, most notably by Bundesbank president Jens Weidmann. Dodig and Herr (n 88), 6–7.

> with severe difficulties caused by natural disasters or exceptional occurrences beyond its control. However, as emphasised by the European Council in recital 4 of the preamble to Decision 2011/199, Article 122(2) TFEU does not constitute an appropriate legal basis for the establishment of a stability mechanism of the kind envisaged by that decision. The fact that the mechanism envisaged is to be permanent and that its objectives are to safeguard the financial stability of the euro area as a whole means that such action cannot be taken by the Union on the basis of that provision of the FEU Treaty.[184]

The Court thus holds that Article 122(2) TFEU does not constitute an appropriate legal basis the ESM for two reasons: because the ESM is a 'permanent' institution, and because its objective is to safeguard the stability of the eurozone as a whole, rather than that of a particular Member State. While the provision does not actually define the time period for which financial assistance may be granted, it has been argued that it had to be 'temporary' because, according to the provision, support could be granted only in the presence of 'exceptional' occurrences.[185] However, such interpretation has been rightfully questioned.[186] The term 'exceptional' qualifies the likelihood of an occurrence; whether an event, once occurred, would then justify assistance only in the short or also in the long run is not defined by the provision.[187] Moreover, as Borger argues, the ESM does in fact grant assistance merely on a temporal basis; while it is correct that the ESM has been established in permanence, there seems no indication in the Treaty why the Union could not establish a permanent body to grant temporal support.[188] Similarly, the argument that Article 122(2) TFEU is not an appropriate legal basis because the ESM's objective is to 'safeguard the financial stability of the euro area as a whole', whereas Article 122(2) TFEU is targeted at individual Member States in difficulties, is unconvincing. It is not inconceivable that severe difficulties experienced by one Member State may cause problems for others as well, which motivates them to support the former. Article 122(2) TFEU in no way precludes the Council from granting aid for ulterior motives, such as protecting the eurozone's financial stability; in fact, it does not require any particular motivation at all.[189] Finally, it has been argued that the crisis—at least in Greece—had not been beyond the country's control, because it was the result of irresponsible fiscal policies, so that Article 122(2) TFEU could not be applicable.[190]

[184] *Pringle*, 65.

[185] Merino (n 176), 1634.

[186] Vestert Borger, 'The ESM and the European Court's Predicament in Pringle' (2013) 14 *German Law Journal* 113, 128–29.

[187] In fact, the provision does not further define the assistance that can be granted in any way. See Jean-Victor Louis, 'The no-bailout clause and rescue packages' (2010) 47 *Common Market Law Review* 971, 983.

[188] In this sense Borger (n 186), 128–29.

[189] Arguing that 'the Council is granted a very wide margin of discretion' in assessing whether Art 122(2) TFEU is applicable to the situation of a Member State: Merino (n 176), 1634.

[190] Kai Hentschelmann, 'Finanzhilfen im Lichte der No Bailout-Klausel Eigenverantwortung und Solidarität in der Währungsunion' [2011] *Europarecht* 282, 297.

However, such an argument applies an isolated perspective and ignores the restraints that the eurozone countries were subjected to. Beyond that, it appears that the criterion can hardly serve as a sharp legal delineating line, and rather constitutes a political evaluation best left to the Council. Thus, Article 122 TFEU could have well served as a basis for establishing an institution such as the ESM, and for granting loans to Member States in financial difficulties.[191]

The main discussion in *Pringle* concerned the question whether Article 125 TFEU prohibited the granting of loans to Member States in difficulties. The provision holds that neither the Union nor a Member State shall 'be liable for or assume the commitments' of another Member State or its institutions.[192] Right since its inception, Article 125 TFEU has routinely been referred to, by commentators and European institutions alike, as the 'no-bailout clause'.[193] This description implies an extremely broad meaning; a 'bailout' in common usage entails any kind of support, including loans. It is along these lines that for example Beck argued that Article 125 TFEU 'strictly prohibit[s] any de facto transfer of the financial risk of public debt between Member States save where expressly provided for in the Treaties and strictly limited to the purposes of those exceptional provisions'.[194] And Van Malleghem held that 'the Member States were thought to have irrevocably committed themselves to not helping other members of the monetary union, thereby reinforcing the fiscal discipline of all of its members.'[195] However, the provision text itself appears to be much more limited than these commentators suggest: most notably, it does not speak of a 'bailout'. In fact, it merely seems to prohibit a specific situation, namely one where the Union or the Member States

[191] While the European Council has declared it will no longer use Art 122 TFEU for providing assistance to ensure the stability of the eurozone, the provision remains a valid legal basis. European Council Decision amending Art 136 of the Treaty on the Functioning of the European Union with regard to a stability mechanism for Member States whose currency is the euro [2011] OJ L 91/1, preamble, para 4.

[192] For a legislative history of Art 125 TFEU see Bernardus Smulders and Jean-Paul Keppenne, 'AEUV Artikel 125' in Hans von der Groeben, Jürgen Schwarze and Armin Hatje (eds), *Europäisches Unionsrecht* (Nomos, 2015), paras 2–10.

[193] See ibid, paras 2–10; Merino (n 176), 1625.

[194] Gunnar Beck, 'The Court of Justice, the Bundesverfassungsgericht and Legal Reasoning during the Euro Crisis: The Rule of Law as a Fair-Weather Phenomenon' (2014) 20 *European Public Law* 539, 549.

[195] Pieter-Augustijn Van Malleghem, 'Pringle: A Paradigm Shift in the European Union's Monetary Constitution' (2013) 14 *German Law Journal* 141, 161; See also Tomkin, who argues: 'Moreover, in practice, the provision of financial assistance on the scale envisaged by the ESMT will always be subject to conditions. It is practically and politically inconceivable that Member States would directly and fully assume such financial burden without imposing any conditions on the recipient Member State. To suggest that Article 125 TFEU was only intended to prohibit unconditional indemnities that fully absolve a debtor Member State of its liability for debts would significantly restrict its scope of application.' Jonathan Tomkin, 'Contradiction, circumvention and conceptual gymnastics: the impact of the adoption of the ESM Treaty on the State of European Democracy' (2013) 14 *German Law Journal* 169, 182. For further references to literature that interprets Art 125 TFEU in this sense see Merino (n 176), 1626, fn 37.

become liable for another Member State's debts, or take them over altogether.[196] Would this also prohibit repayable loans? A textual interpretation of Article 125 TFEU would suggest that this is not the case:[197] if person X loans money to person Y, it would be incorrect to say that X has became 'liable' for Y's 'commitments', or that X 'assumed' them: X has not become liable to Y's creditors in any meaningful use of the term. In this sense, the common practice of describing Article 125 TFEU as the 'no-bailout clause' appears misguided: if at all, the provision can be assumed to prohibit certain forms of bailout, but certainly not everything that could fall under this overly broad term.[198] However, many commentators have argued that a historical and functional interpretation of the provision would lead to a different result. Essentially it is held that Article 125 TFEU forms part of a macroeconomic governance system in which certain forms of financing of public institutions are prohibited: Article 123(1) TFEU prohibits the ECB from directly financing them, and Article 125 TFEU prohibits the Union or other Member States from taking over commitments. The objective is to force Member States to refinance themselves through the financial market alone (additional to tax receipts). This, in turn, is supposed to enforce budgetary discipline. The Court itself subscribes to this view:

> It is apparent from the preparatory work relating to the Treaty of Maastricht that the aim of Article 125 TFEU is to ensure that the Member States follow a sound budgetary policy … The prohibition laid down in Article 125 TFEU ensures that the Member States remain subject to the logic of the market when they enter into debt, since that ought to prompt them to maintain budgetary discipline. Compliance with such discipline contributes at Union level to the attainment of a higher objective, namely maintaining the financial stability of the monetary union. Given that that is the objective pursued by Article 125 TFEU, it must be held that that provision prohibits the Union and the Member States from granting financial assistance as a result of which the incentive of the recipient Member State to conduct a sound budgetary policy is diminished.[199]

The historical and functional interpretation of Article 125 TFEU advanced by the Court holds that the provision should be interpreted more broadly than its wording would suggest, so that 'no-bailout clause' may be a fitting name after all. Thus, the Treaty exhibits a tension: on the one hand, Article 125 TFEU seems to prohibit Member States from refinancing themselves in ways other than through the financial market; on the other hand, Article 122 TFEU allows for financial assistance if a Member State is in difficulty.[200] During the economic crisis, these two provisions came into apparent conflict, and the question arose as to how the conflict should be resolved. Some authors claimed a primacy of the prohibition of any support

[196] In this sense Van Malleghem (n 195), 160.
[197] In this sense Merino (n 176), 1627.
[198] See however Hentschelmann (n 190), 293.
[199] *Pringle*, paras 135–36.
[200] In this sense Hentschelmann (n 190), 287–88.

over the possibility to grant financial assistance.[201] Others authors, like Louis, opposed such a view; reviewing the relevant legislative history, Louis held: 'The exclusion of co-responsibility does not automatically rule out assistance interventions in favour of Member States in difficulty.' According to Louis, Article 122(2) TFEU 'must be interpreted as a "counterweight" to the no-bailout clause.'[202] And Pipkorn, writing already in 1994, explained Article 122(2) TFEU in this way:

> This reflects a compromise in a debate in which some Member States held that they should not be left without means of financial assistance as provided hitherto by Article 108 EEC, while others feared that the mechanism would be open to misuse for unjustified transfers of resources from those States which were performing well to those which were not.[203]

It has been pointed out that the Member States explicitly affirmed the compatibility of Article 122(2) TFEU with Article 125 TFEU in an amendment to the Treaty of Nice.[204] Thus, two distinct principles seem to characterize the Treaty: Member States are responsible for their own debt; and Member States may receive support if they face certain difficult situations. How these two relate to each other is ultimately not answered.[205] It is in this context that the Court comes to the conclusion that Article 125 TFEU does not in fact prohibit financial assistance in the form of repayable loans granted under conditionality. Pointing first at Articles 122(2) TFEU, which, as already discussed, allows the Union to provide financial assistance in case of 'severe difficulties caused by natural disasters or exceptional occurrences beyond its control', the Court argues that Article 125 TFEU cannot be read as prohibiting all forms of financial assistance.[206] The same follows, according to the Court, from a comparative reading of Articles 123 and 125 TFEU.[207] According to the Court, financial assistance granted in the form of a repayable loan linked to conditions does not undermine the objective of sound budgetary policy, and therefore does not conflict with Article 125 TFEU.[208]

[201] ibid, 287–88.

[202] Louis (n 187), 983; Louis asserts that '[o]ne should not conclude that loans by Member States are excluded. The no-bailout clause does not prohibit these' (ibid, 985); see in a similar sense Merino (n 176), 1633.

[203] Jörn Pipkorn, 'Legal Arrangements in the Treaty of Maastricht for the Effectiveness of the Economic and Monetary Union' (1994) 31 *Common Market Law Review* 263, 273.

[204] The 'Declaration on Article 100 of the Treaty establishing the European Community' holds: 'The Conference recalls that decisions regarding financial assistance, such as are provided for in Article 100 and are compatible with the no bail-out rule laid down in Article 103, must comply with the 2000–2006 financial perspective, and in particular paragraph 11 of the Interinstitutional Agreement of 6 May 1999 between the European Parliament, the Council and the Commission on budgetary discipline and improvement of the budgetary procedure, and with the corresponding provisions of future interinstitutional agreements and financial perspectives.' Treaty of Nice amending the Treaty on European Union, the Treaties establishing the European Communities and certain related acts [2001] OJ C80/1.

[205] See in this sense Smulders and Keppenne (n 192), para 19.

[206] *Pringle*, paras 130–31.

[207] ibid, para 132.

[208] ibid, para 137.

medium-term effects of broad and disruptive structural reforms may often outweigh the long-run potential of such measures.[219] Finally, the memorandum pays relatively little regard to the demand side, which is a fundamental concern from a standpoint of Keynesian economics. The relevant question from our perspective is whether the Union institutions are legally *required* to implement such neoliberal programmes through the instrument of conditionality. The answer is quite clearly in the negative: neither Articles 143 or 122 TFEU, the EFSF Agreement nor the ESM Treaty provide any substantive specification as to the conditions that can be attached to financial assistance. The EFSF Agreement, for example, simply speaks of 'appropriate policy conditionality' that shall be imposed by the memorandum of understanding. Thus, conditionality appears to be largely undefined in substantive terms. This implies, on the one hand, that the Union institutions could, in principle, impose reforms based on different socio-economic paradigms; on the other it means that reforms imposed by the Union institutions constitute political choices, which thereby must be justified on political grounds. If, as many argue, austerity politics has produced adverse socio-economic effects in the countries that are or have been subject to conditionality, then the Commission and the ECB must provide a justification on which grounds it would be appropriate to nonetheless continue such policy.[220]

Gauweiler and the OMTs: Interpreting Article 123 TFEU in a Pluralist Form

In 2012, the ECB announced its Outright Monetary Transactions (OMT) programme. Once activated, the ECB would acquire eurozone government bonds on the secondary bond market to a potentially unlimited extent.[221] The announcement that the ECB was willing to engage in OMTs if necessary was intended to bring down the interest rate for bonds of the troubled eurozone countries. The announcement was challenged as conflicting with Article 123 TFEU, and the CJEU ruled on the question in the *Gauweiler* decision. Article 123 TFEU holds:

> Overdraft facilities or any other type of credit facility with the [ECB] or with the central banks of the Member States … in favour of Union institutions, bodies, offices or agencies, central governments, regional, local or other public authorities, other bodies governed by public law, or public undertakings of Member States shall be prohibited, as shall the purchase directly from them by the European Central Bank or national central banks of debt instruments.

[219] See eg Dani Rodrik, 'The Mirage of Structural Reform' (*Project Syndicate*, 8 October 2015), project-syndicate.org/commentary/greece-structural-reform-mirage-by-dani-rodrik-2015-10.

[220] See eg Alberti Nardello, 'IMF: austerity measures would still leave Greece with unsustainable debt' *The Guardian* (30 June 2015), theguardian.com/business/2015/jun/30/greek-debt-troika-analysis-says-significant-concessions-still-needed.

[221] ECB, 'Technical features of Outright Monetary Transactions' (Press release, 6 September 2012), ecb.europa.eu/press/pr/date/2012/html/pr120906_1.en.html.

Article 123 TFEU prohibits the ECB from granting credits to the Member States, or from directly acquiring government debt instruments like bonds. The central legal question in *Gauweiler* was whether this also prohibits bond acquisitions on the secondary market. In economic terms, a key issue touched upon by *Gauweiler* is whether the ECB is allowed to serve as a 'lender of last resort' in the sovereign bond market. The term 'lender of last resort' describes the ability of an institution to provide liquidity to the market in a 'solvency crisis', ie, if no other sources are available because of an economic shock.[222] The ECB had functioned as a 'lender of last resort' since the crisis hit in 2008, but only for financial institutions.[223] By contrast, the ECB has been reluctant to perform the same function on the sovereign bond market,[224] such intervention presumably being prohibited under Article 123(1) TFEU. The ECB's reluctance to adopt a lender of last resort role on the sovereign bond market has been faulted for extending the sovereign debt crisis: only the announcement of OMTs ended the high interest rates on the bonds of some eurozone countries, and stabilized the financial market.[225] Like any other economic issue, the question of whether central banks should act as lenders of last resort to governments is a conflicted one. Opponents warn of the inflation risk that such intervention would allegedly entail, and argue that it would facilitate moral hazard.[226] Proponents argue that this function is necessary to prevent solvency crises as described above, and point to the fact that the central banks of all Western countries perform this function, without the risks that opponents warn about being realized.[227]

The OMT announcement was challenged in the German Constitutional Court, which referred the question to the CJEU as to whether the announcement had infringed Article 123 TFEU.[228] The CJEU first emphasized that the provision text prohibits only the 'direct' purchase of public debt instruments, whereas the OMT announcement is concerned with acquisitions on the secondary market.[229] It then argued that 'the ESCB does not have authority to purchase government bonds on secondary markets under conditions which would, in practice, mean that its action has an effect equivalent to that of a direct purchase of government bonds from the public authorities and bodies of the Member States, thereby undermining the effectiveness of the prohibition in Article 123(1) TFEU.'[230] Thus, the prohibition is interpreted more broadly than the provision text would suggest. The Court

[222] De Grauwe (n 32), 204.
[223] ibid, 202–05.
[224] ibid, 205.
[225] Fitoussi and Saraceno (n 6), 491.
[226] See on these points and for a critique thereof De Grauwe (n 32), 121–23.
[227] Fitoussi and Saraceno (n 6), 491.
[228] On the legal discussion on OMTs and on the German lawsuit see Helmut Siekmann, 'The legality of outright monetary transactions (OMT) of the European system of central banks' (2015) IMFS Working Paper Series No 90.
[229] *Gauweiler*, para 95.
[230] ibid, para 97.

justified this interpretation by reference to the objectives pursued by the provision. According to the Court, 'the aim of Article 123 TFEU is to encourage the Member States to follow a sound budgetary policy, not allowing monetary financing of public deficits or privileged access by public authorities to the financial markets to lead to excessively high levels of debt or excessive Member State deficits.'[231] From this, according to the Court, follows the need to build in 'safeguards' to prevent bond acquisitions that have 'an effect equivalent to that of a direct purchase of government bonds on the primary market', which is what the ECB had done. The list of safeguards attached to the OMTs by the ECB is long, and includes:

— the ECB has full discretion in the execution of the OMT; only the ECB decides on the start, scope, and end of OMTs;[232]
— a minimum period between the issue of a security on the primary market and the acquisition on the secondary market will be respected;
— the ECB will not make any prior announcement whether it will engage in OMTs.

More conditions follow from the fact that interventions must not 'lessen the impetus of the Member States concerned to follow a sound budgetary policy'.[233] Against this, further safeguards attached to the OMTs are spelled out:

— the OMTs are temporal, and will end as soon as the objectives are achieved;[234]
— the ECB acquires only certain types of bonds;
— the ECB acquires only bonds from countries undergoing a 'structural adjustment programme',[235] which means that they are already subject to an obligation to pursue structural reforms, so that they cannot rely on OMTs instead of pursuing 'fiscal consolidation'.[236]

Under such conditions, the OMT announcement was found to be legal. The Court essentially held that the partial lender-of-last-resort role the ECB had decided to assume did not conflict with the prohibition of direct bond acquisitions laid down in Article 123 TFEU. Whether all such conditions are indeed necessary to prevent an effect similar to the direct acquisition of government bonds and to safeguard fiscal discipline seems questionable. Given that such operations are in fact a common tool in the toolbox of central banks, an over-restrictive interpretation of Article 123 TFEU that reaches significantly beyond its textual content seems hard to justify. However, the Court's decision in *Gauweiler* illustrates that Article 123 TFEU in fact provides a considerable scope for interpretation, and potentially supports both views on whether the ECB should take up a role as a lender of last

[231] ibid, para 100.
[232] On these conditions see ibid, para 106.
[233] ibid, para 109.
[234] ibid, para 112.
[235] ibid, para 116.
[236] ibid, para 120.

resort on the sovereign bond market. The provision text suggest a possibly rather large role (excluding only direct acquisitions), whereas the contextual analysis employed by the CJEU is obviously more restricted. In this sense the provision appears to be open in the light of competing socio-economic paradigms.

The previous sections have shown that significant aspects of what may be called the Union's *macro*economic constitution—including both new measures and those existing prior to the crisis—provides a considerable scope of interpretation, which provides the doctrinal support for the book's claim that the Treaty must be considered to be a pluralist instrument. The preceding analysis has mapped out the scope of discretionary choice available in the interpretation of the various Treaty provisions relating to macroeconomic governance. However, such inductive approach will necessarily remain incomplete, in particular in the current, dynamic situation of the European polity. In the following, last section, I will attempt a more general assessment of what the passage of the crisis measures imply in regard to the overall socio-economic orientation of the Treaty. It will be argued that the breadth of these measures imply a significant flexibility of the Treaty in substantive terms.

THE PLURALIST CHARACTER OF THE TREATY IN THE LIGHT OF THE CRISIS MEASURES

The 2008 economic crisis confronted the Union with a situation for which it had only a limited set of institutions and tools readily available. New policies and institutions were developed on an ad-hoc basis, and moved in uncharted terrain, thus raising a question as to their conformity with European law. The Commission's state aid decisions on the bank rescues, the Irish challenge to the ESM and the German lawsuit on the ECB's OMT programme that were the subject in the *Pringle* and *Gauweiler* cases, respectively, as well as numerous other national challenges, are all expressions of this uncertainty.[237] By and large, the crisis measures were found to be in conformity with European law when challenged, and the European institutions, the Member States and their courts mostly acquiesced even though, as already discussed, there was and continues to be considerable resistance and criticism. In political terms this can be explained by the immense pressure to which the national and European institutions were subjected since 2008.[238] It is surely plausible to argue that most, if not all, of the instruments of macroeconomic governance of the past years passed only because of the exceptional circumstances posed by the crisis. Had the crisis not occurred, Member States might not have agreed to the banking union, the sharpened SGP or the MIP, and if they had, the measures may yet have been halted by the various national constitutional courts.

[237] For an overview of the various national challenges to the crisis measures, see Amtenbrink (n 3).
[238] See in this sense Streinz (n 11), 17; Tuori and Tuori (n 14), 120.

provision's open substantive character, it seems out of the question that a clear procedural requirement in the Treaty may be turned on its head through secondary legislation.[244] Similarly, while the Union institutions are not bound to implement any specific socio-economic paradigm through conditionality, this does not mean that their acts should be exempt from fundamental rights scrutiny on the basis of Article 51(1) FRC. Thus, we essentially encounter a legal framework that is, not unlike how many national constitutions are interpreted, open from a substantive perspective, but fully determined in procedural terms. It defines procedural requirements, delineates competences and establishes certain substantive guarantees, but ultimately cannot be considered to restrict substantive regulatory choices in the socio-economic realm in any significant way.[245] Given the fully determined character of the Treaty in procedural terms, many aspects of the crisis measures passed since 2008 appear deeply problematic, or simply illegal. The latter is the case, in particular, for the TSCG, the sanctions attached to the 'preventive' arm, and reverse qualified majority voting.[246]

Given the deeply problematic consequences of employing a state-of-emergency logic discussed above, insisting on the full applicability of the Treaty's rules in times of crisis is imperative. This is true, in principle, also for the Treaty's substantive restrictions. However, as shown in this chapter, the Treaty remains relatively open as to which socio-economic project may be pursued. Consequently, it is not implausible to read, for example, the Treaty as not generally prohibiting financial assistance to Member States in need, or for the ECB to engage in the whole spectrum of tools available to a central bank and to pursue objectives beyond an implausibly narrow reading of its mandate. Surely the CJEU's reading of Articles 123 or 125 TFEU show a willingness to interpret the legal system dynamically with an eye to the challenges posed by the crisis, but it can, from a substantive perspective, hardly be claimed that it exceeds accepted forms of legal interpretation to an extent that it suspends the rule of law.[247] Thus, within the

[244] See Palmstorfer (n 15); Andreas Fischer-Lescano and Steffen Kommer, 'EU in der Finanzkrise: Zur Leistungsfähigkeit des Verfahrens der verstärkten Zusammenarbeit für eine Intensivierung der Wirtschafts- und Sozialpolitik' (2011) 44 *Kritische Justiz* 412, 427–28.

[245] Fritz Scharpf has recently demanded a 'de-constitutionalisation of European law', explaining: 'In comparison to the present Treaty, the coverage of a European constitution should be greatly reduced. In addition to rules for the organisation and procedures of European governing institutions and the allocation of legislative competences between the Union and its Member States, the constitution should ensure the protection of individual civic and civil rights, but it should not include rules amounting to an economic constitution.' I believe that, correctly interpreted, the European economic constitution boils down to exactly that. Scharpf, 'After the crash: A perspective on multilevel European democracy' (2015) 21 *European Law Journal* 384, 400.

[246] See Lukas Oberndorfer, 'Economic Governance rechtswidrig? Eine Krisenerzählung ohne Kompetenz' 3 *AK-Infobrief eu & international* 7, 10–12.

[247] This, however, is the argument for example of Gunnar Beck. See Beck (nn 194 and 209).

tight procedural framework established by the Treaty, a broad range of socio-economic programmes can be pursued, thereby providing considerable flexibility also during times of crisis. If any form of state-of-emergency justification of the crisis measures is rejected, then the crisis measures must be seen as speaking to the considerable openness of the Treaty in substantive terms. By this I mean that a constitutional framework that allows for the passage of a broad spectrum of measures ranging from financial assistance to the Member States to the 'Six Pack' and from OMTs to the banking union without a specific enabling provision must, in substantive terms, be truly open in nature. Insisting on the full applicability of the Treaty in times of crisis and in regular times alike implies that the substantive openness the Treaty showed during the crisis must be understood as a general feature of the Treaty, and not one that merely applies when it is deemed expedient. This implies that the Treaty may, in principle, also support the enactment of many other instruments of macroeconomic governance, with potentially different ideological pedigrees. In the light of the crisis measures it is difficult to imagine, prima facie, any substantive limits to the socio-economic programmes that can potentially be pursued on the European level.[248] Of course, whether a specific instrument, eg a European unemployment insurance,[249] a 'Green New Deal',[250] or Eurobonds,[251] can be passed under the Treaty requires a careful, separate analysis. But while the European Treaty certainly imposes numerous restrictions and limitations on the lawmakers, the spectrum of measures that can be enacted under the Treaty must nonetheless be considered a rather broad one.[252]

The openness of the Treaty as manifested in the crisis measures makes generalized, abstract statements about the substantive scope and limits of the current Treaty framework highly suspicious, as they are likely shaped by hegemonic political or economic narratives, rather than following from the Treaty itself. For example, the claim that the Treaty would prohibit the establishment of a 'transfer union'

[248] Streinz argued that the transfer of additional competences to the Union institutions require a Treaty change once they reach a certain intensity (*gewisse Intensität*). However, such a metaphor of quantity is problematic: the crisis measures indicate that the transfer has already taken place. Given the broad character of the enabling clauses, as testified by their application, it cannot be argued that the enactement of qualitatively similar measures based on a similar interpretation of the Treaty provisions would constitute an unwarranted transfer of competences if this was not the case previously. Streinz (n 11), 8.

[249] See eg László Andor, 'Basic European unemployment insurance: Countering divergences within the Economic and Monetary Union' (Speech at the University of Economics and Business, Vienna, 29 September 2014); Fischer-Lescano and Kommer (n 244), 432.

[250] See eg Hilary French, Michael Renner and Gary Gardner, *Auf dem Weg zu einem Green New Deal* (Heinrich-Böll-Stiftung, 2009).

[251] See eg Jaques Delpla and Jakob Von Weizsäcker, 'Eurobonds: The blue bond concept and its implications' (2011) Bruegel policy contribution No 2; Stijn Claessens, Ashoka Mody and Shahin Vallée, 'Paths to Eurobonds' (2012) IMF Working Paper No 172.

[252] Whether a further federalization would be a beneficial thing is a different question. For critical voices see for example Giandomenico Majone, *Rethinking the Union of Europe Post-Crisis — Has Integration Gone Too Far?* (CUP, 2014); Alexander Somek, 'What Is Political Union' (2013) 14 *German Law Journal* 561.

must clearly be rejected as an ideologically coded argument:[253] not only has the Union pursued policies with considerable transfer elements for decades, most notably its cohesion, agricultural and social policies (as represented in the respective funds such as the ESF); the crisis also showed that the ability to grant financial assistance to Member States if necessary is a prerequisite for the very functioning of the eurozone and the internal market as a whole. Beyond that it cannot be denied that market integration per se has redistributive effects between the Member States, given the fact that these have been a central concern for the Union since its very inception.[254] From this perspective it hardly makes sense, in legal terms, to claim that the current Treaty framework would prohibit the creation of a 'transfer union'. Rather, a measure that finds a plausible legal basis and serves the regulatory objectives of the Union may well be legal under the current Treaty even if it implies considerable transfer elements. Generalized statements such as the one just discussed obscure the substantive openness of the European legal system that became manifest during the economic crisis, and project ideologically coded assumptions onto the legal framework. The same applies to arguments that the Treaty would not support, for example, broad European fiscal, wage, tax or social policies,[255] or the establishment of a European 'social union.'[256] While, as already mentioned, the Treaty obviously defines numerous conditions and limitations in regard to the regulatory projects that can be pursued on the Union level, these can only be established on the basis of a concrete legal analysis in relation to the specific measure in question. Generalized statements as to which types of policies or projects can or cannot be pursued within the present Treaty framework will almost certainly be shaped by implicit economic or political narratives, and should thus not uncritically be adopted into legal discourse.[257] Instead, it seems most plausible to start an inquiry into the substantive scope and limits of the Treaty framework from the general assumption—as substantiated throughout this book—that the Treaty is a pluralist instrument in the light of competing socio-economic paradigms, and does not, prima facie, prohibit the implementation of any specific programme.

It should be clear that the distinction drawn here between the underdetermined character of the Treaty's substance on the one hand and what I described as its

[253] For a version of this claim from political debate see Patrick Adenauer, 'Solidarität ist keine Einbahnstraße' *The European*, 26 August 2010, theeuropean.de/patrick-adenauer/4097-warnung-vor-der-transferunion; for an example from academic debate see Ruffert (n 210), 1792.

[254] See in particular the discussion on the potential adverse effects of European integration on peripheral regions such as the Italian South.

[255] See Fischer-Lescano and Kommer (n 244), 423.

[256] See ibid, 433.

[257] The same is true from a perspective of national law, which also defines restraints on how European law—for example open-ended enabling provisions—is to be applied. These limitations are equally susceptible to be read along ideologically coded lines. On the limits as defined by national law see for example Christian Calliess and Christopher Schoenfleisch, 'Auf dem Weg in die europäische "Fiskalunion"—Europa- und verfassungsrechtliche Fragen einer Reform der Wirtschafts- und Währungsunion im Kontext des Fiskalvertrages' (2012) 67 *JuristenZeitung* 477, 486–87; see also Tuori and Tuori (n 14), 194–204.

fully determined 'procedural' character on the other is not a completely stable one; however, it is nonetheless an important analytical distinction in order to identify the various implicit assumptions that enter the interpretation process. Surely procedural rules—most notably relating to the distribution of competences between the Union and the Member States—may have an impact on the policies that can be pursued on the European level, and thereby potentially on the Union's socio-economic orientation. However, as has been suggested in this section, these limitations are liable to be read along ideologically coded terms, especially when they are defined in the abstract. I contend that we tend to understand the distribution of competences between the Union and the Member States in the light of implicit substantive assumptions: in this sense our view of the substantive orientation of the Union is liable to shape our understanding of the procedural limitations, and not the other way around. Of course, this claim employs a reading of the European Treaty that is based on a broad view of the Union's regulatory competences, and relies on (often contextual and teleological) interpretations of the Treaty provisions that differ considerably from those predominant before the crisis. Even though this is, as shown, a valid perspective in legal terms, it will surely have problematic political implications. The dynamic reading of the Treaty has enabled the development of a political and institutional structure on the Union level that, at least from today's perspective, is of precarious political legitimacy (even though I do not believe that the application of a conservative interpretative approach—in the sense of preferring the *status quo ante*—would have fared better in the light of the factual difficulties the Union faced in the past years).[258] The European constitutional settlement today looks abysmal from a perspective of democratic control, institutional balance, and fundamental rights. A reform process that remedies this troubling situation is overdue: full democratic control must be established, the applicability of fundamental rights must be ensured, and the federal settlement between the Member States and the Union reframed. However, the Union's present deficiencies in all these questions do not alter the fact that the Treaty, as it now stands, is a pluralist framework that seems to establish, in purely legal terms, few limitations as to which socio-economic paradigms can be pursued. Repeating a claim made in the introduction, it can be argued that, prima facie, the Treaty must be assumed to not prohibit the pursuit of any specific socio-economic programme. Whether, for example, a Keynesian, a libertarian or even a post-capitalist programme can be enacted on the Union level cannot be excluded in the abstract.

INTERMEDIATE FINDINGS

The debate on the socio-economic orientation of the European economic constitution has been led, in recent years, most intensively in regard to the European system of macroeconomic governance. Until the outbreak of the crisis, it might have

[258] See Dawson and de Witte (n 12).

been assumed that the European macroeconomic constitution would implement a specific socio-economic paradigm, based on supply-side or neoliberal economic assumptions as well as on an ordoliberal regulatory programme. However, the measures enacted in the wake of the crisis undermine such reading.[259] The Treaty cannot be held to require the implementation of any specific socio-economic programme, and must instead be conceptualized as pluralist, also in regard to macroeconomic governance. It has been shown in relation to five policy areas how a pluralist reading of the macroeconomic framework may look like. In the final section I have suggested that the policies realized since the outbreak of the crisis—if they are accepted as legal—imply that the Treaty must be an extremely flexible constitutional framework. It has been argued that, if measures like the EMS, OMT, the banking union, 'Six Pack' and 'Two Pack' can be enacted under the Treaty, then it is plausible that a broad spectrum of other measures could be enacted on the basis of the Treaty as well. While this claim must be developed in detail elsewhere, I suggest that the crisis measures generally speak to the pluralist character of the European (macro)economic constitution. In the light of the crisis measures it is implausible to argue that the Treaty would provide a significant substantive limitation as to the measures that can, in principle, be enacted. In other words, whether the Union is developed on the basis of, say, a left Keynesian, or a right neoclassical (or, possibly, a libertarian or a post-capitalist) socio-economic paradigm is not considerably restricted by the Treaty.

[259] For a similar argument see Tuori and Tuori (n 14), 181–87.

Conclusion

THIS BOOK HAS made the claim that the European economic constitution is a pluralist framework in the light of competing socio-economic paradigms. Defined in negative terms, this means that we cannot assume that European law has to be interpreted on the basis of any specific socio-economic worldview; in positive terms it means that a multitude of socio-economic projects may be pursued within the framework of the Treaty. From a doctrinal perspective such openness finds expression in generally termed enabling provisions (such as Article 114 TFEU) as well as in the fact that the Treaty provisions are often ambivalent, and allow for different interpretations. Where law does not fully determine its application, it grants discretion to those applying it. From a legal perspective, the discretion granted to executive institutions or to courts is no different in qualitative terms than the discretion granted to a legislator. Within a discretionary space the institution makes a choice that is not further determined by law, and may thus be considered to be 'political' in nature. It is in this sense that authors like Hans Kelsen or, more recently, Alec Stone Sweet, have described executive institutions and courts as lawmakers.[1] Identifying the European economic constitution as a pluralist framework in the light of competing socio-economic paradigms implies that the European institutions are often not restrained as to whether they follow a specific worldview or paradigm when they exercise their discretion under European law, ie, when they act as legislative, executive or judicial lawmakers. Consequently, if their decisions are biased in favour of a specific socio-economic paradigm, this usually is not because it is legally required by the Treaty, but because of choices made in the application of the law. In many ways this is a liberating result: the European economic constitution does not force the European institutions to pursue any specific socio-economic programme, as it cannot be assumed that the European polity has bound itself to a specific worldview. However, the result is also burdensome, because it means that the European institutions—from the (European) Council and the EP to the Commission, the CJEU and the ECB—as well as the Member States are fully responsible in a political sense for their regulatory choices. Of course, these choices are likely to be, more often than not, not fully conscious ones; it has been argued throughout the book that hegemonic narratives eg in legal doctrine, economics and history

[1] It is in this sense that authors like Hans Kelsen or, more recently, Alec Stone Sweet, have described executive institutions and courts as lawmakers. Kelsen held that 'The judicial function is thus, like legislation, both creation and application of law.' Hans Kelsen, *General Theory of Law and State* (Harvard University Press, 1949) 134; see also Alec Stone Sweet and Jud Mathews, 'Proportionality balancing and global constitutionalism' (2008) 47 *Columbia Journal of Transnational Law* 73 87.

routinely shape our understanding of the law, so that ambiguities and discretionary choices which allow for competing readings of the Treaty are often not recognized as such. In order to fully realize the extent to which European law allows for different interpretations in the light of competing socio-economic paradigms, such hegemonic narratives must be identified, as we did in this book. Only then will the pluralist character of the European economic constitution become fully manifest: the Treaty essentially defines only few substantive limitations as regards to which socio-economic programmes may be pursued within its framework. We thus encounter a divide between the Union's constitutional setup, which is pluralist, and the prevailing political practice on the Union level, which is neoliberal in many respects. From a legal perspective it is important to emphasize this divide, and prevent the latter from analytically collapsing into the former.

Bibliography

LEGISLATION AND OTHER DOCUMENTS

Resolution adopted by the Ministers of Foreign Affairs of the Member States of the ECSC at their meeting at Messina (1955).

Council Regulation (EEC) No 25 on the financing of the common agricultural policy [1962] OJ 30/991.

General Programme for the abolition of restrictions on freedom of establishment [1962] OJ 2/36.

General Programme for the abolition of restrictions on freedom to provide services [1962] OJ 2/32.

Council Directive 64/221/EEC on the co-ordination of special measures concerning the movement and residence of foreign nationals which are justified on grounds of public policy, public security or public health [1964] OJ 56/850.

Décision du Conseil 64/247/CEE créant un Comité de politique économique à moyen terme [1964] OJ 64/1031.

Commission Directive 66/683/EEC eliminating all differences between the treatment of national products and that of products which, under Articles 9 and 10 of the Treaty, must be admitted for free movement, as regards laws, regulations or administrative provisions prohibiting the use of the said products and prescribing the use of national products or making such use subject to profitability [1966] OJ 220/3748.

Ergänzende Antwort der Kommission der Europäischen Wirtschaftsgemeinschaft auf die schriftliche Anfrage Nr 118 von Herrn Deringer [1967] OJ 59/901.

Schriftliche Anfrage Nr 64 von Herrn Deringer an die Kommission der Europäischen Wirtschaftsgemeinschaft [1967] OJ 169/11.

Schriftliche Anfrage Nr 118 von Herrn Deringer an die Kommission der Europäischen Wirtschaftsgemeinschaft [1967] OJ 9/122.

Richtlinie 70/32/EWG der Kommission über die Lieferungen von Waren an den Staat, seine Gebietskörperschaften und die sonstigen juristischen Personen des öffentlichen Rechts [1969] L13/1.

Commission Directive 70/50/EEC on the abolition of measures which have an effect equivalent to quantitative restrictions on imports and are not covered by other provisions adopted in pursuance of the EEC Treaty [1969] OJ L 013/29.

Council Directive 70/157/EEC on the approximation of the laws of the Member States relating to the permissible sound level and the exhaust system of motor vehicles [1970] OJ L 42/16.

Council Directive 73/23/EEC on the harmonization of the laws of Member States relating to electrical equipment designed for use within certain voltage limits [1973] OJ L 77/29.

Council Directive 74/150/EEC on the approximation of the laws of the Member States relating to the type-approval of wheeled agricultural or forestry tractors [1974] OJ L 84/10.

Council Directive 74/151/EEC on the approximation of the laws of the Member States relating to certain parts and characteristics of wheeled agricultural or forestry tractors [1974] OJ L 84/25.
Council Directive 74/152/EEC on the approximation of the laws of the Member States relating to the maximum design speed of and load platforms for wheeled agricultural or forestry tractors [1974] OJ L 84/33.
Annex to the Conclusions of the Presidency of the European Council (Bremen, 6 and 7 July, 1978).
Conclusions of the Presidency of the European Council on 6 and 7 July (*Bulletin of the European Communities* No 6, 1978).
Council Regulation (EEC) No 3181/78 of 18 December 1978 relating to the European monetary system [1978] OJ L 379/2.
Draft European Act—German-Italian Initiative (*Bulletin of the European Communities* No 11, 1981).
European Council, Presidency's Conclusions (Copenhagen 3–4 December, 1982).
Council Directive 83/189/EEC laying down a procedure for the provision of information in the field of technical standards and regulations [1983] OJ L 109/8.
Solemn Declaration on European Union (*Bulletin of the European Communities* No 6, 1983).
Draft Treaty establishing the European Union (*Bulletin of the European Communities* No 2, 1984).
Council Resolution on a new approach to technical harmonisation and standards [1985] OJ C 136/1.
Council Directive 78/404/EEC on the harmonization of the laws of the Member States relating to simple pressure vessels [1987] OJ L 220/48.
Council Directive 88/361/EEC for the implementation of Article 67 of the Treaty [1988] OJ L 178/5.
Hanover European Council, Conclusions of the Presidency (*Bulletin of the European Communities* No 6, 1988).
Community Charter of the fundamental social rights of workers, adopted at the Strasbourg European Council on 9 December 1989.
Regulation (EC) No 883/2004 of the European Parliament and of the Council on the coordination of social security systems [2004] L 166/1.
Council Directive 2006/112/EC on the common system of value added tax [2006] OJ L 347/1.
Regulation No 1174/2011 on enforcement measures to correct excessive macroeconomic imbalances in the euro area [2011] OJ L 306/8.
Council Regulation No 1466/97 on the strengthening of the surveillance of budgetary positions and the surveillance and coordination of economic policies [1997] OJ L 209/1, as amended by Regulation No 1175/2011 [2011] OJ L 306/12.
Council Regulation No 1467/97 on speeding up and clarifying the implementation of the excessive deficit procedure [1997] OJ L 209/6 as amended by Council Regulation (EU) No 1177/2011 [2011] OJ L 306/33.
European Parliament resolution of 23 March 2011 on the draft European Council decision amending Article 136 of the Treaty on the Functioning of the European Union with regard to a stability mechanism for Member States whose currency is the euro (2011).
Regulation No 1176/2011 on the prevention and correction of macroeconomic imbalances [2011] OJ L 306/25.

Communication from the Commission: 'A blueprint for a deep and genuine economic and monetary union—Launching a European Debate' COM(2012) 777 final/2.
'State-of-play in implementing macroeconomic adjustment programmes in the euro area' (Study on the request of the Economic and Monetary Affairs Committee, 2014).

ESSAYS, PAPERS, BOOKS AND OTHER SOURCES

Adamski, D, 'National power games and structural failures in the European macroeconomic governance' (2012) 49 *Common Market Law Review* 1319.
Adenauer, P, 'Solidarität ist keine Einbahnstraße', *The European* theeuropean.de/patrick-adenauer/4097-warnung-vor-der-transferunion.
Aghion, P and Howitt, P, 'Appropriate growth policy: A unifying framework' (2006) 4 *Journal of the European Economic Association* 269.
Akerlof, G, 'The market for "lemons": Quality uncertainty and the market mechanism' (1970) *Quarterly Journal of Economics* 488.
Albrecht, K, *Planifikateure am Werk. Wirtschaft zwischen Zwang und Freiheit* (Econ-Verlag, 1964).
Aleinikoff, A, 'Constitutional Law in the Age of Balancing' (1987) 96 *Yale Law Journal* 943.
Alexy, R, *A Theory of Constitutional Rights* (Oxford University Press, 2002).
Amtenbrink, F, 'New Economic Governance in the European Union: Another Constitutional Battleground?' in Purnhagen, K and Rott, P (eds), *Varieties of European Economic Law and Regulation* (Springer, 2014).
Anderson, P and Hall, S, 'The Politics of the Common Market' (1961) I/10 *New Left Review* 1.
Andor, L, 'Basic European unemployment insurance: Countering divergences within the Economic and Monetary Union' (Speech at the University of Economics and Business, Vienna, 29 September 2014).
Antal, KV, 'Harmonisation of Turnover Taxes in the Common Market' (1963) 1 *Common Market Law Review* 41.
Arrow, K, 'A difficulty in the concept of social welfare' (1950) 58 *Journal of Political Economy* 328.
——, 'The Economic Implications of Learning by Doing' (1962) 29 *The Review of Economic Studies* 155.
Arrow, K and Debreu, G, 'Existence of an Equilibrium for a Competitive Economy' (1954) 22 *Econometrica* 265.
Artis, M, 'The Maastricht Road to Monetary Union' (1992) 30 *Journal of Common Market Studies* 299.
Atkinson, A, Piketty, T and Saez, E, 'Top incomes in the long run of history' (2009) NBER Working Paper No 15408.
Balassa, B, *The Theory of Economic Integration* (George Allen & Unwin Ltd, 1961).
——, 'Planning in an open economy' (1967) 2 *Intereconomics* 75.
——, 'Planning and programming in the European Common Market' (1973) 4 *European Economic Review* 217.
——, 'Trade Creation and Trade Diversion in the European Common Market: An appraisal of the evidence' (1974) 42 *The Manchester School* 93.
Baldwin, R, 'Gottfried Haberler's Contributions to International Trade Theory and Policy' (1982) 97 *Quarterly Journal of Economics* 141.

——, 'The growth effects of 1992' (1989) NBER Working Paper No 3119.
Barak, A, 'Proportionality and Principled Balancing' (2010) 4 *Law & Ethics of Human Rights* 1.
Barbiero, F and Darvas, Z, 'In sickness and in health: protecting and supporting public investment in Europe' (2014) Bruegel Policy Contribution No 02.
Barents, R, 'New developments in measures having equivalent effect' (1981) 18 *Common Market Law Review* 271.
Barnard, C, 'Derogations, Justifications and the Four Freedoms: Is State Interest Really Protected?' in Barnard C and Odudu O (eds), *The Outer Limits of European Union Law* (Hart, 2009).
Barro, R, Mankiw, G and Sala-i-Martin, X, 'Capital Mobility in Neoclassical Models of Growth' (1995) 85 *American Economic Review* 103.
Barro, R and Sala-i-Martin, X, 'Convergence' (1992) 100 *Journal of Political Economy* 223.
Bartl, M, 'Internal Market Rationality, Private Law and the Direction of the Union: Resuscitating the Market as the Object of the Political' (2015) 21 *European Law Journal* 572.
——, 'The Way We Do Europe: Subsidiarity and the Substantive Democratic Deficit' (2015) 21 *European Law Journal* 23.
Baum, F, *The Wonderful Wizard of Oz* (GM Hill Co, 1900).
Beck, G, 'Article Review: The Legal Reasoning of the Court of Justice and the Euro Crisis—The Flexibility of the Court's Cumulative Approach and the Pringle Case' (2013) 20 *Maastricht Journal of European and Comparative Law* 635.
——, 'The Court of Justice, the Bundesverfassungsgericht and Legal Reasoning during the Euro Crisis: The Rule of Law as a Fair-Weather Phenomenon' (2014) 20 *European Public Law* 539.
Bentham, J, *A fragment on goverment* (Eighteenth Century Collections Online, 1776).
Béraud, RC, 'Les mesures d'effet équivalent au sens des articles 30 et suivants du Traité de Rome' [1968] *Revue trimestrielle de droit europeen*, 265.
Bercusson, B, 'The European Community's Charter of Fundamental Social Rights of Workers' (1990) 53 *Modern Law Review* 624.
Berg, A and Ostry, J, 'Equality and Efficiency' (2011) 48 *Finance & Development* 12.
Bermann, G, 'The Single European Act: A New Constitution for the Community' (1988) 27 *Columbia Journal for Transnational Law* 529.
Bernanke, B and Gürkaynak, R, 'Is Growth Exogenous? Taking Mankiw, Romer, and Weil Seriously' (2001) 16 *NBER Macroeconomics Annual* 11.
Bernanke, B, Laubach, T and Mishkin, F, *Inflation targeting: lessons from the international experience* (Princeton University Press, 2001).
Beukers, T, 'The Eurozone crisis and the legitimacy of differentiated integration' (2013) EUI Working Papers MWP No 36.
——, 'Legal writing(s) on the Eurozone crisis' (2015) EUI Working Papers Law No 11.
Blanchard, O, Dell'Ariccia, G and Mauro, P, 'Rethinking Macroeconomic Policy' (2010) 42 *Journal of Money, Credit and Banking* 199.
Böhm, F, *Die Ordnung der Wirtschaft als geschichtliche Aufgabe und rechtsschöpferische Leistung* (Kohlhammer, 1937).
——, 'Die Idee des ORDO im Denken Walter Euckens: Dem Freunde und Mitherausgeber zum Gedächtnis' [1950] *ORDO: Jahrbuch für die Ordnung von Wirtschaft und Gesellschaft* 15.

——, 'Das Janusgesicht der Konzentration' in Böhm F (ed), *Freiheit und Ordnung in der Marktwirtschaft* (Nomos, 1980).

——, 'Die Kapitalgesellschaft als Instrument der Unternehmenszusammenfassung' in Böhm, F (ed), *Freiheit und Ordnung in der Marktwirtschaft* (Nomos, 1980).

Böhm, F, Eucken, W and Grossmann-Doerth, H, 'Unsere Aufgabe' in Böhm F (ed), *Die Ordnung der Wirtschaft als geschichtliche Aufgabe und rechtsschöpferische Leistung* (Kohlhammer, 1937).

Borger, V, 'The ESM and the European Court's Predicament in Pringle' (2013) 14 *German Law Journal* 113.

Bork, R, *The Antitrust Paradox* (Basic Books, 1978).

Boyer, F and Sallé, JP, 'The Liberalization of Intra-European Trade in the Framework of OEEC' (1955) 4 IMF Staff Papers 179.

Brown, E, 'Regent Developments in the Social Policy of the European Economic Community' (1966) 3 *Common Market Law Review* 184.

Buchanan J and Tullock, G, *The calculus of consent: logical foundations of constitutional democracy* (University of Michigan Press, 1965).

Buckel, S, *Subjektivierung und Kohäsion* (Velbrück Wissenschaft, 2007).

Buckel, S and Oberndorfer, L, 'Die lange Inkubationszeit des Wettbewerbs der Rechtsordnungen—Eine Genealogie der Rechtsfälle Viking/Laval/Rüffert/Luxemburg aus der Perspektive einer materialistischen Europarechtstheorie' in Fischer-Lescano, A, Rödl, F and Schmid, C (eds), *Europäische Gesellschaftsverfassung Zur Konstitutionalisierung sozialer Demokratie in Europa* (Nomos, 2009).

Bugaric, B, 'Europe Against the Left? On Legal Limits to Progressive Politics' (2013) LEQS Paper No 61.

Burrows, N, 'Harmonisation of technical standards: reculer pour mieux sauter?' (1990) 53 *Modern Law Review* 597.

Calabresi, G, 'The Pointlessness of Pareto: Carrying Coase Further' (1991) 100 *Yale Law Journal* 1211.

Calliess, C and Schoenfleisch, C, 'Auf dem Weg in die europäische "Fiskalunion"—Europa- und verfassungsrechtliche Fragen einer Reform der Wirtschafts- und Währungsunion im Kontext des Fiskalvertrages' (2012) 67 *JuristenZeitung* 477.

Camps, M, *Britain and the European community* (Princeton University Press, 1964).

Cantore, N, Page, S and te Velde, DW, 'Making the EU's Common Agricultural Policy coherent with development goals' (2011) ODI Briefing Paper 69.

Capeta, T, 'Legal Framework of the European Monetary System and the European Monetary Union' (Fourth Biennial International Conference European Community Studies Association, Charleston, 11/14 May 1995).

Caporaso, J and Tarrow, S, 'Polanyi in Brussels. European institutions and the embedding of markets in society' (2008) RECON Online Working Paper 01.

Caruso, D, 'The Missing View of the Cathedral: The Private Law Paradigm of European Legal Integration' (1997) 3 *European Law Journal* 3.

——, 'Private Law and Public Stakes in European Integration: the Case of Property' (2004) 10 *European Law Journal* 751.

Cassetti, M, 'Bargaining power, effective demand and technical progress: a Kaleckian model of growth' (2003) 27 *Cambridge Journal of Economics* 449.

Catalano, N, *Manuel de droit des Communautés européennes* (Dulloz et Sirey, 1962).

Chalmers, D, 'The European Redistributive State and a European Law of Struggle' (2012) 18 *European Law Journal* 667.

Chamberlin, E, *The theory of monopolistic competition* (Harvard University Press, 1935).
Chandra, R and Sandilands, R, 'Does modern endogenous growth theory adequately represent Allyn Young?' (2005) 29 *Cambridge Journal of Economics* 463.
Chang, H-J, *Kicking away the ladder* (Anthem Press, 2007).
Chesné, G, *L'Établissement des Étrangers en France et la Communauté Économique Européenne* (R Pichon et R Durand-Auzias, 1962).
Cimoli, M and Porcile, G, 'Global growth and international cooperation: a structuralist perspective' (2011) 35 *Cambridge Journal of Economics* 383.
Claessens, S, Mody, A and Vallée, S, *Paths to Eurobonds* (2012) IMF Working Paper No 172.
Clifton, J, Comín, F and Díaz Fuentes, D, *Privatisation in the European Union* (Kluwer, 2003).
Coase, R, 'The Problem of Social Cost' (1960) 3 *Journal of Law and Economics* 1.
Cohen-Eliya, M and Porat, I, 'Proportionality and the Culture of Justification' (2011) 59 *American Journal of Comparative Law* 463.
Collins, D, 'Towards a European Social Policy' (1966) 5 *Journal of Common Market Studies* 26.
Commons, J, *Institutional economics* (University of Wisconsin Press, 1959).
——, *Legal Foundations of Capitalism* (University of Wisconsin Press, 1968).
Cooper, CA and Massell, BF, 'A New Look at Customs Union Theory' (1965) 75 *Economic Journal* 742.
Corden, W, 'Economies of Scale and Customs Union Theory' (1972) 80 *Journal of Political Economy* 465.
——, 'Monetary Integration' (1972) Princeton University, Essays in International Finance, No 93.
Craig, P, 'The stability, coordination and governance treaty: principle, politics and pragmatism' (2012) 37 *European Law Review* 231.
——, 'Article Review: Pringle and the nature of legal reasoning' (2014) 21 *Maastricht Journal of European and Comparative Law* 205.
Crouch, C, *The strange non-death of neoliberalism* (Polity, 2011).
Currie, D, 'European Monetary Union: Institutional structure and economic performance' (1992) 102 *Economic Journal* 248.
Dam, K, *The GATT. Law and International Economic Organization* (University of Chicago Press, 1970).
Dani, M, 'Rehabilitating Social Conflicts in European Public Law' (2012) 18 *European Law Journal* 621.
Darvas, Z, 'Mind the gap! And the way structural budget balances are calculated' (18 October, 2013) bruegel.org/2013/10/mind-the-gap-and-the-way-structural-budget-balances-are-calculated/.
Dauses, M, 'The System of the Free Movement of Goods in the European Community' (1985) 33 *American Journal of Comparative Law* 209.
Davidson, I, 'Prospects for Monetary Reform' (1972) 28 *The World Today* 377.
Davidson, P, *Money and the Real World* (Macmillan, 1978).
Davies, G, 'Democracy and Legitimacy in the Shadow of Purposive Competence' (2015) 21 *European Law Journal* 2.
Davis, D and Weinstein, D, 'What role for empirics in international trade?' (2001) NBER Working Paper No 8543.
Dawson M and de Witte, F, 'Constitutional Balance in the EU after the Euro-Crisis' (2013) 76 *Modern Law Review* 817.

——, 'Self-Determination in the Constitutional Future of the EU' (2015) 21 *European Law Journal* 371.

De Crayencour, J-P, 'Propos sur le Droit d'Établissement dans le Traité de Rome' [1968] *Cahiers de Droit Europeén* 420.

De Grauwe, P, 'What Have we Learnt about Monetary Integration since the Maastricht Treaty?' (2006) 44 *Journal of Common Market Studies* 711.

——, *Economics of Monetary Union* (OUP, 2012).

De Grauwe, P, Rebelo, S and Von Hagen, J, 'Towards European Monetary Union without the EMS' (1994) 9 *Economic Policy* 149.

De Witte, F, 'The Architecture of a "Social Market Economy"' (2015) LSE Law, Society and Economy Working Papers 13.

De Zwaan, J, 'The single European act: Conclusion of a unique document' (1986) 23 *Common Market Law Review* 747.

Dehousse, R, 'Integration v. regulation? On the dynamics of regulation in the European Community' (1992) 30 *Journal of Common Market Studies* 383.

Dekker, W, *Europe 1990: An Agenda for Change* (1985).

Delors, J, 'The Commission's programme for 1989. Address by Jacques Delors, President of the Commission, to the European Parliament and his reply to the debate' (1989), Supplement 2 *Bulletin of the European Communities*.

——, *Report on economic and monetary union in the European Community* (Delors Report) (1989).

——, 'The Future of Free Trade in Europe and the World' (1994) 18 *Fordham International Law Journal* 715.

Delpla, J and Von Weizsäcker, J, 'Eurobonds: The blue bond concept and its implications' (2011) Bruegel policy contribution No 2.

Dodig, N and Herr, H, 'EU policies addressing current account imbalances in the EMU: An assessment' (2015) Institute for International Political Economy Berlin Working Paper No 46.

Dornbusch, R, 'Expectations and exchange rate dynamics' (1976) 84 *Journal of Political Economy* 1161.

Dougan, M, 'The Bubble that burst: Exploring the Legitimacy of the Case Law on the Free Movement of Union Citizens' in Adams M et al (eds), *Judging Europe's Judges* (Hart, 2013).

Drijber, B, 'The country of origin principle' Hearing before the Committee Internal Market and Consumer Protection on the Proposed Directive on Services in the Internal Market (2004) europarl.europa.eu/hearings/20041111/imco/contributions_en.htm.

Easterly, W and Levine, R, 'What have we learned from a decade of empirical research on growth? It's Not Factor Accumulation: Stylized Facts and Growth Models' (2001) 15 *The World Bank Economic Review* 177.

EC (European Commission), '25 Years of Digital Europe' ec.europa.eu/information_society/doc/digitaleurope-historial.pdf.

——, 'First General Report on the Activities of the Community (January 1958 to September, 1958)' (1958).

——, 'Memorandum of the Commission on the action programme of the Community for the second stage' COM(62) 300.

——, 'First General Report on the Activities of the Communities 1967' (1968).

——, 'General programme for elimination of technical barriers to trade due to disparities in national legislation' COM(68) 138 final.

——, 'Industrial Policy in the Community' (Colonna Report) (Brussels, 1970).
——, 'The Community's industrial policy. Commission Memorandum to the Council' COM(70) 100; Supplement to Bulletin 4/1970 of the European Communities.
——, 'Harmonization of legislation pertaining to beer' (Newsletter on the common agricultural policy No 6, 1970).
——, 'First communication of the Commission about the Community's policy on the environment' SEC (71) 2616 final.
——, 'Elimination des entraves techniques aux échanges dans la CEE: Le point de la situation' (Information Memo, 1972).
——, 'Etude du Comité économique et social sur les problemes concernant le rapprochement des législations relatives aux entraves techniques' CES 469/72.
——, 'Etat d'avancement des travaux relatifs au programme général pour l'élimination des entraves techniques aux échanges dans le domaine industriel' (1973).
——, 'A preliminary Community programme for consumer information and protection' COM(73) 2108 final.
——, 'Programme of action in the field of technological and industrial policy' SEC (73) 3824 final.
——, 'Programme of Action of the European Communities on the Environment' [1973] OJ C112/1.
——, 'Scientific and Technological Policy Programme' COM(73) 1250.
——, 'A new approach to the approximation of legislation' (Information Interior Market, 1974).
——, 'Abolition of technical barriers to trade in industrial products during 1974: the present situation' (Information Memo P-7/75, 1975).
——, 'Communication from the Commission concerning the consequences of the judgment given by the Court of Justice in case 120/78' ('Cassis de Dijon') [1979] OJ C 256/2.
——, 'The removal of technical barriers to trade' (Office for Official Publications of the European Communities, 1979).
——, 'Programme of the Commission for 1985. Statement by Jacques Delors, President of the Commission, to the European Parliament and His Reply to the Ensuring Debate' (Strasbourg, 12 March 1985, *Bulletin of the European Communities*, Supplement 4/85).
——, 'Completing the Internal Market' (White Paper from the Commission to the European Council (Milan, 28–29 June), COM(85) 310 final.
——, 'Television and Broadcasting' (Background Note, 1986).
——, 'The Regions of the Enlarged Community, Third Periodic Report on the social and economic situation and development of the regions of the Community' (1987), aei.pitt.edu/31139/1/Third_periodic_report.pdf.
——, 'The Single Act: A New Frontier for Europe. Communication from the Commission to the Council' COM(87) 100 final.
——, 'Towards a Dynamic European Community. Green Paper on the Development of the Common Market for Telecommunications Services and Equipment' COM(87) 290 final.
——, 'Europe 1992. The overall challenge' SEC (88) 524 final.
——, 'One Market, One Money' (*European Economy* No 44, 1990).
——, 'From the Single Act to Maastricht and beyond. The means to match our ambitions' COM(92) 2000 final.
——, 'Growth, competitiveness, employment. The challenges and ways forward into the 21st century' (White paper) COM(93) 700.

——, 'EMU@10. Successes and challenges after ten years of Economic and Monetary Union' (*European Economy* No 2, 2008).
——, 'Current account surpluses in the EU' (*European Economy* No 9, 2012).
——, 'Scoreboard for the surveillance of macroeconomic imbalances' (2012) Occasional Papers No 92.
——, 'Alert Mechanism Report 2014' COM(2013) 790 final.
——, 'Macroeconomic Imbalances Germany 2014' (2014) Occasional Papers No 174.
——, 'Recommendation for a Council Recommendation on Germany's 2014 national reform programme' COM(2014) 406 final.
——, 'Making the best use of the flexibility within the existing rules of the stability and growth pact' COM(2015) 12 final.
——, 'Recommendation for a Council Recommendation with a view to bringing an end to the excessive government deficit in France' COM(2015) 115 final.
ECB, 'Technical features of Outright Monetary Transactions' (Press release, 6 September, 2012), ecb.europa.eu/press/pr/date/2012/html/pr120906_1.en.html.
Ederer, S, 'Macroeconomic imbalances and institutional reforms in the EMU' (2015) WWWforEurope Working Paper No 87.
Editorial, 'The Single European Act' (1986) 23 *Common Market Law Review* 249.
——, 'After Maastricht—and what now?' (1992) 29 *Common Market Law Review* 443.
——, 'Post-Maastricht' (1992) 29 *Common Market Law Review* 199.
——, 'Growth, competitiveness and unemployment: the challenges facing the Union' (1994) 31 *Common Market Law Review* 1.
Ehle, D, 'Massnahmen gleicher Wirkung wie mengenmässige Beschränkungen und ihre Abschaffung im Gemeinsamen Markt' [1967] *Aussenwirtschaftsdienst des Betriebs-Beraters* 453.
Ehle, D and Meier, G, *EWG-Warenverkehr: Außenhandel—Zölle—Subventionen* (Schmidt, 1971).
Ehlermann, C-D, 'The internal market following the Single European Act' (361) 24 *Common Market Law Review* 361.
Eichengreen, B, *Should the Maastricht Treaty be Saved?* (1992) Princeton University, Studies in International Finance No 74.
——, 'European monetary unification' (1993) 31 *Journal of Economic Literature* 1321.
——, *The European economy since 1945. Coordinated capitalism and beyond* (Princeton University Press, 2007).
Eichengreen, B, Tobin, J and Wyplosz, C, 'Two cases for sand in the wheels of international finance' (1995) 105 *Economic Journal* 162.
Emerson, M et al, *The Economics of 1992* (Oxford University Press, 1988).
Emminger, O, *The D-Mark in the conflict between internal and external equilibrium, 1948–75* (1977) Princeton University, Essays in International Finance No 122.
Etzioni, A, 'European Unification: A Strategy of Change' (1963) 16 *World Politics* 32.
Eucken, W, *Grundsätze der Wirtschaftspolitik* (Mohr/Siebeck, 1952).
Evans, A, 'Economic Policy and the Free Movement of Goods in EEC Law' (1983) 32 *International and Comparative Law Quarterly* 577.
Everling, U, 'Die Allgemeine Ermächtigung der EG zur Zielverwirklichung nach Art 235 EWGV' [1967] *Europarecht Sonderheft* 2.
——, *Die Koordinierung der Wirtschaftspolitik in der Europäischen Wirtschaftsgemeinschaft als Rechtsproblem* (Mohr, 1964).
——, *The Right of Establishment in the Common Market* (Commerce Clearing House, 1964).

——, 'The Court of Justice as a decisionmaking authority' (1984) 82 *Michigan Law Review* 1294.
Everson, M, 'An Exercise in Legal Honesty: Rewriting the Court of Justice and the Bundesverfassungsgericht' (2015) 21 *European Law Journal* 474.
Everson, M and Joerges, C, 'Reconfiguring the Politics–Law Relationship in the Integration Project through Conflicts–Law Constitutionalism' (2012) 18 *European Law Journal* 644.
Feldstein, M, 'The political economy of the European economic and monetary union: political sources of an economic liability' (1998) NBER Working Paper No 6150.
Fennelly, N, 'Legal Interpretation at the European Court of Justice' (1996) 20 *Fordham International Law Journal* 656.
Ferrera, M, *The Boundaries of Welfare: European Integration and the New Spatial Politics of Social Protection* (Oxford University Press, 2005).
Fischer-Lescano, A, 'The European TSCG and EU law', guengl.eu/uploads/_old_cms_files/2012_09_06_Fischer-Lescano_Gutachten-kurz_Fiskalpakt_060912%20- %20EN.pdf.
Fischer-Lescano, A and Kommer, S, 'EU in der Finanzkrise: Zur Leistungsfähigkeit des Verfahrens der verstärkten Zusammenarbeit für eine Intensivierung der Wirtschafts- und Sozialpolitik' (2011) 44 *Kritische Justiz* 412.
Fischer-Lescano, A and Möller, K, 'Soziale Rechtspolitik in Europa' Friedrich Ebert Stiftung, library.fes.de/pdf-files/id/ipa/09344.pdf.
Fischer-Lescano, A and Oberndorfer, L, 'Fiskalvertrag und Unionsrecht' [2013] 66 *Neue Juristische Wochenschrift* 9.
Fitoussi, J-P and Saraceno, F, 'European economic governance: the Berlin–Washington Consensus' (2013) 37 *Cambridge Journal of Economics* 479.
Fligstein, N and Mara-Drita, I, 'How to Make a Market: Reflections on the Attempt to Create a Single Market in the European Union' (1996) 102 *American Journal of Sociology* 1.
Forsythe, J, 'Legislative History of the Fair Labor Standards Act' (1939) 6 *Law and Contemporary Problems* 464.
Franco, D and Zollino, F, 'Macroeconomic imbalances in Europe: institutional progress and the challenges that remain' (2014) 46 *Applied Economics* 589.
Frankel, J, 'The Procyclicalists: Fiscal austerity vs. stimulus', wwwvoxeuorg/article/procyclicalists-fiscal-austerity-vs-stimulus.
Frankel, J and Romer, D, 'Does trade cause growth?' (1999) 89 *American Economic Review* 379.
Frankel, J and Rose, A, 'The endogenity of the optimum currency area criteria' (1998) 108 *Economic Journal* 1009.
French, H, Renner, M and Gardner, G, *Auf dem Weg zu einem Green New Deal* (Heinrich-Böll-Stiftung, 2009).
Fried, C, 'Two Concepts of Interests: Some Reflections on the Supreme Courts Balancing Test' (1962) 76 *Harvard Law Review* 755.
Friedman, M, 'The Case for Flexible Exchange Rates' in Friedman M (ed), *Essays in Positive Economics* (University of Chicago Press, 1953).
——, *Capitalism and Freedom* (University of Chicago Press, 1982).
Galbraith JK, *American Capitalism. The Concept of Countervailing Power* (Hamish Hamilton, 1952).
——, *The Affluent Society* (Houghton Mifflin Company, 1998).

Galbraith, J, *Inequality and instability: a study of the world economy just before the Great Crisis* (OUP, 2013).

Gardiner, R, *Treaty Interpretation* (Oxford University Press, 2010).

GATT, 'The Possible Impact of the European Economic Community, in Particular, the Common Market, upon World Trade' (1957) Trade Intelligence Papers No 6, Geneva.

Gehrels, F and Johnston, B, 'The Economic Gains of European Integration' (1955) 63 *Journal of Political Economy* 275.

Gellner, M, 'Relations between the Six and the Seven: A Survey of Recent Developments' (1960) 16 *The World Today* 278.

Gibb, R and Treadgold, A, 'Completing the internal market: implications for the regions' (1989) *Area* 75.

Gill, S, 'European governance and new constitutionalism: economic and monetary union and alternatives to disciplinary neoliberalism in Europe' (1998) 3 *New Political Economy* 5.

Giubboni, S, *Social Rights and Market Freedom in the European Constitution* (Cambridge University Press, 2006).

Glyn, A (ed), *Social democracy in neoliberal times: the left and economic policy since 1980* (Oxford University Press, 2001).

Goldman, B, 'The Convention Between the Member States of the European Economic Community on the Mutual Recognition of Companies and Legal Persons' (1969) 6 *Common Market Law Review* 104.

Gordon, L, 'The Organization for European Economic Cooperation' (1956) 10 *International Organization* 1.

Gormley, L, 'Cassis de Dijon and the Communication from the Commission' (1981) 6 *European Law Review* 454.

Grabitz, E, 'Das Recht auf Zugang zum Markt nach dem EWG-Vertrag' in Stödter R and Thieme W (eds), *Hamburg—Deutschland—Europa (Festschrift Ipsen)* (JCB Mohr (Paul Siebeck), 1977).

Graf, M, *Der Begriff "Maßnahmen gleicher Wirkung wie mengenmäßige Einfuhrbeschränkungen" in dem EWG-Vertrag* (Heymann, 1972).

Groetzinger, J, 'The New GATT Code and the International Harmonization of Products Standards' (1974) 8 *Cornell International Law Journal* 168.

Gros, D and Alcidi, C, 'The case of the disappearing Fiscal Compact' (2014) CEPS Commentary, 5 November.

Gros, D and Thygesen, N, 'The institutional approach to monetary union in Europe' (1990) 100 *Economic Journal* 925.

Grossman, G and Helpman, E, 'Endogenous Product Cycles' (1991) 101 *Economic Journal* 1214.

——, 'Quality Ladders in the Theory of Growth' (1991) 58 *Review of Economic Studies* 43.

——, 'Endogenous Innovation in the Theory of Growth' (1994) 8 *Journal of Economic Perspectives* 23.

Gundelach, F, 'Closing speech', European Symposium on Trends in the Regulations concerning motor vehicle design (1975).

Haack, W, 'The Selectivity of Economic Integration Theories: A Comparison of Some Traditional and Marxist Approaches' (1983) 21 *Journal of Common Market Studies* 365.

Häde, U, 'Article 126' in Calliess, C and Ruffert, M (eds), *EUV/AEUV* (Beck, 2011).

Hahn, H, 'The stability pact for European monetary union: compliance with deficit limit as a constant legal duty' (1998) 35 *Common Market Law Review* 77.

Hale, R, 'Coercion and Distribution in a Supposedly Non-Coercive State' (1923) 38 *Political Science Quarterly* 470.

——, 'Force and the State: A Comparison of "Political" and "Economic" Compulsion' (1935) 35 *Columbia Law Review* 149.

——, 'Bargaining, Duress and Economic Liberty' (1943) 43 *Columbia Law Review* 603.

Hall, P and Soskice, D, 'An Introduction to Varieties of Capitalism' in Hall, P and Soskice, D (eds), *Varieties of Capitalism The Institutional Foundations of Comparative Advantage* (Oxford University Press, 2001).

Hamer, J, 'Article 126' in von der Groeben, H, Schwarze J and Hatje A (eds), *Europäisches Unionsrecht* (Nomos, 2015).

Harrod, R, 'An Essay in Dynamic Theory' (1939) 49 *Economic Journal* 14.

Hatje, A, 'Wirtschaftsverfassung im Binnenmarkt' in von Bogdandy A and Bast J (eds), *Europäisches Verfassungsrecht Theoretische und dogmatische Grundzüge* (Springer, 2009).

Hatzopoulos, V, *Regulating Services in the European Union* (2012).

Hayek, F, *Law, Legislation and Liberty*, vol I: Rules and Order (Routledge, 1973).

——, *Law, Legislation and Liberty*, vol II: The Mirage of Social Justice (Routledge, 1976).

Hayes, M, *The economics of Keynes* (Elgar, 2006).

Heckscher, E, 'The Effect of Foreign Trade an the Distribution of Income' in Allen W (ed), *International trade theory Hume to Ohlin* (Random House, 1967).

Heilperin, M, 'European Integration: Commercial and Financial Postulates' in Haines G (ed), *European Integration* (Johns Hopkins Press, 1957).

——, 'Freer Trade and Social Welfare: Some Marginal Comments on the Ohlin report' (1957) 75 *International Labour Review* 173.

Hein, E, *Distribution and growth after Keynes* (Edward Elgar, 2014).

Hein, E and Vogel, L, 'Distribution and growth reconsidered: empirical results for six OECD countries' (2008) 32 *Cambridge Journal of Economics* 479.

Helpman, E, 'A Simple Theory of International Trade with Multinational Corporations' (1984) 92 *Journal of Political Economy* 451.

——, 'Imperfect competition and international trade: Evidence from fourteen industrial countries' (1987) 1 *Journal of the Japanese and International Economies* 62.

——, *The mystery of economic growth* (Harvard University Press, 2010).

Helpman, E and Krugman, P, *Market structure and foreign trade* (Harvester Wheatsheaf, 1985).

Hentschelmann, K, 'Finanzhilfen im Lichte der No Bailout-Klausel Eigenverantwortung und Solidarität in der Währungsunion' [2011] *Europarecht* 282.

Herndon, T, Ash, M and Pollin, R, 'Does high public debt consistently stifle economic growth? A critique of Reinhart and Rogoff' (2014) 38 *Cambridge Journal of Economics* 257.

Hicks, J, 'Mr. Keynes and the "Classics"; A Suggested Interpretation' (1937) 5 *Econometrica* 147.

Hirsch, E, 'French planning and its European application' (1962) 1 *Journal of Common Market Studies* 117.

Hofmann, H and Pantazatou, K, 'The Transformation of the European Economic Constitution' (2015) University of Luxembourg Law Working Paper 01.

Holinski, N, Kool, C and Muysken, J, 'Persistent macroeconomic imbalances in the euro area: Causes and consequences' (2012) 94 *Federal Reserve Bank of St Louis Review* 1.

Höpner, M and Schäfer, A, 'A New Phase of European Integration: Organised Capitalisms in Post-Ricardian Europe' (2010) 33 *West European Politics* 344.
——, 'Embeddedness and Regional Integration: Waiting for Polanyi in a Hayekian Setting' (2012) 66 *International Organization* 429.
Horwitz, M, *The Tranformation of American Law, 1780–1860* (Harvard University Press, 1977).
——, *The Transformation of American Law 1870–1960. The Crisis of Legal Orthodoxy* (Oxford University Press, 1992).
Hovenkamp, H, 'Antitrust policy after Chicago' (1985) 84 *Michigan Law Review* 213.
Howse, R, 'From Politics to Technocracy—and Back Again: The Fate of the Multilateral Trading Regime' (2002) 96 *American Journal of International Law* 94.
Hu, Y-S, 'German agricultural power: the impact on France and Britain' (1979) 35 *The World Today* 453.
Imbs, J and Wacziarg, R, 'Stages of diversification' (2003) 93 *American Economic Review* 63.
IMF, *World Economic Outlook. Globalization and Inequality* (2007).
Ingram, JC, *The case for European monetary integration* (1973) Princeton University, Essays in International Finance No 89.
Ioannidis, M, 'EU Financial Assistance Conditionality after "Two Pack"' (2014) 74 *Zeitschrift für ausländisches öffentliches Recht und Völkerrecht* 1.
Irwin, D, 'The GATT in Historical Perspective' (1995) 85 *American Economic Review* 323.
Italianer, A, 'Whither the Gains from European Economic Integration?' (1994) 45 *Revue économique* 689.
Jacquemin, A and Wright, D, 'Corporate Strategies and European Challenges Post 1992' (1993) 31 *Journal of Common Market Studies* 525.
Jans, J, 'Proportionality revisited' (2000) 27 *Legal Issues of Economic Integration* 239.
Joerges, C, 'What is left of the European Economic Constitution? A melancholic eulogy' (2005) 30 *European Law Review* 461.
——, 'The European economic constitution and its transformation through the financial crisis' (2015) ZenTra Working Papers in Transnational Studies No 47.
Joerges, C and Rödl, F, 'Informal Politics, Formalised Law and the 'Social Deficit' of European Integration: Reflections after the Judgments of the ECJ in Viking and Laval' (2009) 15 *European Law Journal* 1.
Johnson, H, 'The Criteria of Economic Advantage' (1957) 19 *Bulletin of the Oxford University Institute of Economics & Statistics* 33.
Kaldor, N, 'The Irrelevance of Equilibrium Economics' (1972) 82 *Economic Journal* 1237.
Kalecki, M, 'The Distribution of the National Income' in Kalecki M (ed), *Essays in the Theory of Economic Fluctuations* (Russell & Russell, 1938).
Kallioras, D and Petrakos, G, 'Industrial growth, economic integration and structural change: evidence from the EU new member-states regions' (2010) 45 *Annals of Regional Science* 667.
Kalman, L, 'Law, Politics, and the New Deal(s)' (1999) 108 *Yale Law Journal* 2165.
Kapteyn, PJG and verLoren van Themaat, P, *Introduction to the Law of the European Communities* (Sweet & Maxwell, 1973).
Kaupa, C 'Maybe not activist enough? On the Court's alleged neoliberal bias in its recent labor cases' in De Witte, B, Dawson M and Muir E (eds), *Judicial Activism at the European Court of Justice: Causes, Responses and Solutions* (Edward Elgar, 2013).

Kelsen, H, *Über Grenzen zwischen juristischer und soziologischer Methode* (Mohr, 1911).
——, *Reine Rechtslehre* (Deuticke, 1934).
——, *General Theory of Law and State* (Harvard University Press, 1949).
Kennedy, D, 'Three Globalizations of Law and Legal Thought: 1850–2000' in Trubek D and Santos A (eds), *The New Law and Economic Development* (Cambridge University Press, 2006).
Keynes, JM, 'The General Theory of Employment' (1937) 51 *Quarterly Journal of Economics* 209.
——, *The General Theory of Employment, Interest, and Money* (First Harvest/Harcourt, 1964).
——, *A treatise on money*, Vol II (Macmillan, 1965).
——, 'Proposals for an International Currency (or Clearing) Union [February 11, 1942]' in Horsefield K (ed), *The International Monetary Fund 1945–1965, Volume III: Documents* (IMF, 1969).
Kilpatrick, C, 'Are the Bailouts Immune to EU Social Challenge Because They Are Not EU Law?' (2014) 10 *European Constitutional Law Review* 393.
——, 'On the Rule of Law and Economic Emergency: The Degradation of Basic Legal Values in Europe's Bailouts' (2015) 35 *Oxford Journal of Legal Studies* 325.
Kindleberger, C, 'French Planning' in Millikan M (ed), *National Economic Planning* (National Bureau of Economic Research, 1967).
——, *The World in Depression* (University of California Press, 2013).
Kitzinger, U, *The European common market and community* (Routledge, 1967).
Klisch C-M, *Die Konjunkturpolitik in der Europäischen Wirtschaftsgemeinschaft* (Nomos, 1974).
Kornai, J, *Anti-Equilibrium. On economic systems theory and the task of research* (North-Holland, 1971).
Krauss, M, 'Recent Developments in Customs Union Theory: An Interpretive Survey' (1972) 10 *Journal of Economic Literature* 413.
Kreinin, M, 'On the "Trade-Diversion" Effect of Trade-Preference Areas' (1959) 67 *Journal of Political Economy* 398.
——, 'On the dynamic effects of a customs union' (1964) 72 *Journal of Political Economy* 193.
Krugman, P, 'Lessons of Massachusetts for EMU' in Torres F and Giavazzi F (eds), *Adjustment and growth in the European Monetary Union* (CUP, 1993).
——, 'The Increasing Returns Revolution in Trade and Geography' (2009) 99 *American Economic Review* 561.
——, 'The new Economic Geography, now Middle-Aged' Presentation to the Association of American Geographers (2010), princeton.edu/~pkrugman/aag.pdf.
——, 'Inflation targets reconsidered' in ECB (ed), *ECB Forum on central banking—Conference proceedings* (ECB, 2014).
Kumm, M, 'Constitutional rights as principles: On the structure and domain of constitutional justice' (2004) 2 *International Journal of Constitutional Law* 574.
——, 'Institutionalising Socratic Contestation: The Rationalist Human Rights Paradigm, Legitimate Authority and the Point of Judicial Review' (2007) 1 *European Journal of Legal Studies* 2.
Küsters, H, *Die Gründung der Europäischen Wirtschaftsgemeinschaft* (Nomos Verlagsgesellschaft, 1982).

Lambert, J, 'The Constitutional Crisis 1965–66' (1966) 4 *Journal of Common Market Studies* 195.

Lane, R, 'New community competences under the Maastricht Treaty' (1993) 30 *Common Market Law Review* 939.

Lanyi, A, *The case for floating exchange rates reconsidered* (1969) Princeton University, Essays in International Finance No 72.

Leibenstein, H, 'Allocative Efficiency vs. "X-Efficiency"' (1966) 56 *American Economic Review* 392.

Leibfried, S and Pierson, P, *Prospects for Social Europe* (Center for European Studies, Harvard University, 1992).

Lell, H-J, *Die soziale Harmonisierung in der Europäischen Wirtschaftsgemeinschaft und ihre wirtschaftlichen Auswirkungen* (Duncker & Humblot, 1966).

Levi Sandri, L, 'The Social Policy of the European Economic Community' Address to the Fifth General Assembly of Free Trade Union of the Member States of the European Communities, 10 November 1966, aei.pitt.edu/14299/.

Lewin, K, 'The Free Movement of Workers' (1965) 2 *Common Market Law Review* 300.

Libânio, GA, 'Aggregate demand and the endogeneity of the natural rate of growth: evidence from Latin American economies' (2009) 33 *Cambridge Journal of Economics* 967.

Licari, J, 'The European Investment Bank' (1969) 8 *Journal of Common Market Studies* 192.

Lindberg, L, *The political dynamics of European economic integration* (Stanford University Press, 1963).

Lintott, H, 'The Organization for European Economic Cooperation' (1949) 3 *International Organization* 269.

Lipsey, R, 'The Theory of Customs Unions: A General Survey' (1960) 70 *Economic Journal* 496.

Lipsey, R and Lancaster, K, 'The General Theory of Second Best' (1956) 24 *Review of Economic Studies* 11.

Lodge, J, 'The Single European Act: Towards a New Euro-Dynamism?' (1986) 24 *Journal of Common Market Studies* 203.

Looper, R, 'The Significance of Regional Market Arrangements' (1959) *University of Illinois Law Forum* 364.

Louis, J-V, 'The no-bailout clause and rescue packages' (2010) 47 *Common Market Law Review* 971.

Loussouarn, Y, 'L'harmonisation du droit d'établissement' [1969] *Revue trimestrielle de droit europeen* 275.

Lucas, R, 'On the mechanics of economic development' (1988) 22 *Journal of Monetary Economics* 3.

——, 'Why Doesn't Capital Flow from Rich to Poor Countries?' (1990) 80 *American Economic Review* 92.

——, 'The Industrial Revolution: Past and Future' (2003) Annual Report Essay, Federal Reserve Bank of Minneapolis.

Ludlow, NP, 'The making of the CAP: towards a historical analysis of the EU's first major policy' (2005) 14 *Contemporary European History* 347.

Luhmann, N, *Das Recht der Gesellschaft* (Suhrkamp, 1995).

Lutz, F, 'Europäische Währungsprobleme: 1946–1950' [1951] *ORDO: Jahrbuch für die Ordnung von Wirtschaft und Gesellschaft* 299.

Machlup, F, 'Three Concepts of the Balance of Payments and the so-called Dollar Shortage' (1950) 60 *Economic Journal* 46.

Majone, G, *Rethinking the Union of Europe Post-Crisis—Has Integration Gone Too Far?* (Cambridge University Press, 2014).

Mak, V, 'Standards of Protection: In Search of the "Average Consumer" of EU Law in the Proposal for a Consumer Rights Directive' (2010) 19 *European Review of Private Law* 25.

Makower, H and Morton, G, 'A Contribution Towards a Theory of Customs Unions' (1953) 63 *Economic Journal* 33.

Mankiw, G, 'Defending the one percent' (2013) 27 *Journal of Economic Perspectives* 21.

Mankiw, G, Romer, D and Weil, D, 'A Contribution to the Empirics of Economic Growth' (1992) 107 *Quarterly Journal of Economics* 407.

Manzella, GP and Mendez, C, 'The turning points of EU Cohesion policy' (2009) Report Working Paper, ec.europa.eu/regional_policy/archive/policy/future/pdf/8_manzella_final-formatted.pdf.

Marjolin, R, 'Prospects for the European Common Market' (1957) 36 *Foreign Affairs* 131.

——, 'A Plan for Europe?' Speech at the Congress of the Confédération nationale de la Mutualité, de la Coopération et du Crédit agricoles, aei.pitt.edu/14820/1/S88.pdf.

——, 'Summary of M. Marjolin's closing address in the colloquy on "European Planning"' Rome, 30 November–2 December 1962, aei.pitt.edu/14861/1/S141.pdf.

Marques, H, 'Trade and Factor Flows in a Diverse EU: What Lessons for the Eastern Enlargement(s)?' (2008) 22 *Journal of Economic Surveys* 364.

Marsh, D, *The Euro: the politics of the new global currency* (Yale University Press, 2009).

——, *Europe's Deadlock* (Yale University Press, 2013).

Marshall, T, 'The Constitution: A Living Document' (1987) 30 *Howard Law Journal* 915.

Martin, R and Sunley, P, 'The new economic geography and policy relevance' (2011) 11 *Journal of Economic Geography* 357.

Martin, R and Tyler, P, 'Evaluating the impact of the structural funds on objective 1 regions: An exploratory discussion' (2006) 40 *Regional Studies* 201.

Marx, K, *Das Kapital*, vol 1 (Dietz Verlag, 1962).

——, *Das Kapital*, vol II (Dietz Verlag, 1963).

Massé, P, 'The French Plan and economic theory' (1965) 33 *Econometrica* 265.

Mathews, C, 'Non-Tariff Import Barriers and the Kennedy Round' (1965) 2 *Common Market Law Review* 403.

Mattei, U and Nicola, F, 'A "Social Dimension" in European Private Law? The Call for Setting a Progressive Agenda' (2006) 41 *New England Law Review* 1.

Mayes, D, 'The Effects of Economic Integration on Trade' (1978) 17 *Journal of Common Market Studies* 1.

McCarthy, J, 'Protectionism and Product Harmonization in the EEC' (1979) 10 *Economic and Social Review* 187.

McDowell, M and Hudson, W, 'Social Democrats Choose Europe: Comparing the European Policies of the British Labour and French Socialist Parties' (Biennial Conference of the European Community Studies Association, George Mason University, Fairfax, Virginia, May 22–24, 1991).

McGee, A and Weatherill, S, 'The Evolution of the Single Market–Harmonisation or Liberalisation' (1990) 53 *Modern Law Review* 578.

McKenzie, L, 'On the Existence of General Equilibrium for a Competitive Market' (1959) 27 *Econometrica* 54.

McKinnon, R, 'Optimum currency areas' (1963) 53 *American Economic Review* 717.

——, 'Mundell, the Euro, and optimum currency areas', in Courchene T (ed), *Money, Markets and Mobility* (McGill, 2001).

——, 'Optimum Currency Areas and Key Currencies: Mundell I versus Mundell II' (2004) 42 *Journal of Common Market Studies* 689.

McLachlan, D and Swann, D, *Competition policy in the European Community: the rules in theory and practice* (Oxford University Press, 1967).

McNamara, K, *The Currency of Ideas: Monetary Politics in the European Union* (Cornell University Press, 1998).

Meade, J, *Planning and the price mechanism: the liberal-socialist solution* (Allen & Unwin, 1948).

——, *The theory of international economic policy*, vol 1: The Balance of Payments (Oxford University Press, 1954).

——, 'The Balance-of-Payments Problems of a European Free-Trade Area' (1957) 67 *Economic Journal* 379.

Meij, AWH and Winter, JA, 'Measures having an effect equivalent to quantitative restrictions' (1976) 13 *Common Market Law Review* 79.

Menéndez, AJ, 'The Existential Crisis of the European Union' (2013) 14 *German Law Journal* 453.

Merino, AdG, 'Legal developments in the Economic and Monetary Union during the debt crisis: The mechanisms of financial assistance' (2012) 49 *Common Market Law Review* 1613.

Merton, P, 'Industrial Organization and the Gains from Europe 1992' (1989) Brookings Papers on Economic Activity 277.

Mestmäcker E-J, *Europäisches Wettbewerbsrecht* (Beck'sche Verlagsbuchhandlung, 1974).

——, 'Auf dem Wege zu einer Ordnungspolitik für Europa' in Mestmäcker E-J, Möller H and Schwarz H-P (eds), *Eine Ordnungspolitik für Europa: Festschrift für Hans von der Groeben zu seinem 80 Geburtstag* (Nomos, 1987).

——, 'On the Legitimacy of European law' (1994) 58 *Rabels Zeitschrift für ausländisches und internationales Privatrecht/The Rabel Journal of Comparative and International Private Law* 615.

Micossi, S, 'Misguided policies risk breaking up the eurozone and the EU' (2011) CEPS Working Paper No 260.

Micossi, S and Peirce, F, 'Flexibility clauses in the Stability and Growth Pact: No need for revision' (2014) CEPS Policy Brief No 260.

Milward, A, *The European Rescue of the Nation-state* (Routledge, 2000).

Minsky, H, 'Capitalist financial processes and the instability of capitalism' (1980) 14 *Journal of Economic Issues* 505.

——, 'The Financial Instability Hypothesis: A Restatement' in Minsky H (ed), *Can 'it' happen again? Essays on Instability and Finance* (ME Sharpe, 1982).

——, *Stabilizing an unstable economy* (Yale University Press, 1986).

——, 'The financial instability hypothesis' (1992) Jerome Levy Economics Institute Working Paper No 74.

Mishkin, F, 'Monetary Policy Strategy: Lessons from the Crisis' (2011) NBER Working Paper No 16755.

Moens, G, 'Freedom of Movement of Goods in the European Community' (1989) 17 *Melbourne University Law Review* 733.

Montgomery, S, 'The Potential Economic Effects of the European Economic Community' (1965) 6 *Boston College Law Review* 425.

Moravcsik, A, 'Negotiating the Single European Act: national interests and conventional statecraft in the European Community' (1991) 45 *International Organization* 19.
Moschella, M, 'Monitoring Macroeconomic Imbalances: Is EU Surveillance More Effective than IMF Surveillance?' (2014) 52 *Journal of Common Market Studies* 1273.
Mosley, H, 'The social dimension of Europe integration' (1990) 129 *International Labour Review* 147.
Müller-Armack, A, *Wirtschaftsordnung und Wirtschaftspolitik* (Verlag Rombach, 1966).
Mundell, R, 'The Pure Theory of International Trade' (1960) 50 *American Economic Review* 67.
——, 'A Theory of Optimum Currency Areas' (1961) 51 *American Economic Review* 657.
——, 'A Plan for a European Currency' (Paper Prepared for Discussion at the American Management Association Conference on Future of the International Monetary System, New York, 10–12 December, 1969).
——, 'Uncommon arguments for common currencies' in Johnson H and Swoboda A (eds), *The economics of common currencies* (1973).
——, 'A reconsideration of the twentieth century' (2000) 90 *American Economic Review* 327.
Myrdal, G, *An international economy: problems and prospects* (Harper & Brothers, 1956).
——, *Economic theory and under-developed regions* (Duckworth, 1957).
N.N., 'Die bisherigen Massnahmen der Gemeinschaft zur Verwirklichung der Niederlassungsfreiheit und des freien Dienstleistungsverkehrs im Gemeinsamen Markt' [1967] *Aussenwirtschaftsdienst des Betriebs-Beraters* 437.
Nardello, A, 'IMF: austerity measures would still leave Greece with unsustainable debt' *The Guardian* (30 June, 2015), theguardian.com/business/2015/jun/30/greek-debt-troika-analysis-says-significant-concessions-still-needed.
Neal, L, *The economics of Europe and the European Union* (Cambridge University Press, 2007).
Nemes, L and Aversa, A, 'Legal Aspects of the European Economy since World War II' (1961) 36 *Notre Dame Lawyer* 111.
Nicola, F, 'Another View on European Integration: Distributive Stakes in the Harmonization of European Law' Progressive Lawyering, Globalization and Markets: Rethinking Ideology and Strategy—American University, WCL Research Paper No 08-28 (2007) ssrn.com/paper=1090244.
——, 'Transatlanticisms: Constitutional Asymmetry and Selective Receptions of U.S. Law and Economics in the Formation of European Private Law' (2008) 16 *Cardozo Journal of International & Comparative Law* 101.
——, 'Decentralization and Harmonization in the Construction of Europe: Structural Comparisons and Distributive Consequences' (Dissertation, Harvard Law School, 2009).
Nicolaïdis, K and Schmidt, S, 'Mutual recognition "on trial": the long road to services liberalization' (2007) 14 *Journal of European Public Policy* 717.
Nicoll, W, 'The Luxembourg Compromise' (1984) 23 *Journal of Common Market Studies* 35.
Oberndorfer, L, 'Post-neoliberale Integrationsweise der EU. Perspektivenwechsel an der Schnittstelle Politik / Ökonomie / Recht' in Blaha B and Weidenholzer J (eds), *Freiheit Beiträge für eine demokratische Gesellschaft* (Braumüller, 2010).
——, 'Economic Governance rechtswidrig? Eine Krisenerzählung ohne Kompetenz' 3 *AK-Infobrief eu & international* 7.

——, 'Die Renaissance des autoritären Liberalismus? Carl Schmitt und der deutsche Neoliberalismus vor dem Hinrergrund des Eintritts der "Massen" in die europäische Politik' (42) 168 *Prokla* 413.
——, 'Vom neuen, über den autoritären zum progressiven Konstitutionalismus' [2013] *Juridikum* 76.
Obstfeld, M, 'Financial flows, financial crises, and global imbalances' (2012) 31 *Journal of International Money and Finance* 469.
OECD, *Divided we stand: why inequality keeps rising* (OECD Publishing, 2011).
OEEC, *The organisation for European Economic Co-operation: history and structure* (Paris, 1953).
Offe, C, 'Advanced capitalism and the welfare state' (1972) 2 *Politics & Society* 479.
——, 'The Europolis experiment and its lessons for deliberation on Europe' (2014) 15 *European Union Politics* 430.
Ohlin, B, *Interregional and International Trade* (Harvard University Press, 1967).
Ohlin, B et al, 'Social Aspects of European Economic Co-operation (Ohlin-Report, Summary)' (1956) 74 *International Labour Review* 99.
Okun, A, *Equality and Efficiency: The Big Tradeoff* (The Brookings Institution, 1975).
Oliver, P, *Free Movement of Goods in the E.E.C.* (European Law Centre, 1982).
——, 'Measures of equivalent effect: a reappraisal' (1982) 19 *Common Market Law Review* 217.
Olson, M, *The Logic of Collective Action* (Harvard University Press, 1965).
Ostrom, E, *Governing the commons* (Cambridge University Press, 1990).
——, 'Collective Action and the Evolution of Social Norms' (2000) 14 *Journal of Economic Perspectives* 137.
——, *Understanding institutional diversity* (Princeton University Press, 2005).
Ostry, J, Berg, A and Tsangarides, C, 'Redistribution, inequality, and growth' IMF Staff Discussion Note, February 2014.
Overturf, S, 'The Economics of the Renewed Integration Movement' (1994) *Annals of the American Academy of Political and Social Science* 84.
Padoa-Schioppa, T, 'Efficiency, Stability and Equity. A Strategy for the Evolution of the Economic System of the European Community' (Padoa-Schioppa Report) (1987).
Palk, W, 'Harmonization of the Laws of the European Common Market Countries' (1966) 2 *Manitoba Law Journal* 173.
Palmstorfer, R, 'The Reverse Majority Voting under the "Six Pack": A Bad Turn for the Union?' (2014) 20 *European Law Journal* 186.
Parfitt, T, 'The EEC's Common Agricultural Policy' (1965) 21 *The World Today* 308.
——, 'The EEC: Mansholt in Transition' (1970) 26 *The World Today* 344.
Paulson, S, 'Book review on Überlegungen zu Hans Kelsens "Allgemeine Theorie der Normen" by Kazimierz Opalek, and "Untersuchungen zur Stufenbaulehre Adolf Merkls und Hans Kelsens", by Jürgen Behrend' (1982) 27 *American Journal of Jurisprudence* 159.
Peers, S, 'Towards a New Form of EU Law?: The Use of EU Institutions outside the EU Legal Framework' (2013) 9 *European Constitutional Law Review* 37.
Pelkmans, J, 'The new approach to technical harmonization and standardization' (1987) 25 *Journal of Common Market Studies* 249.
——, 'Mutual recognition in goods. On promises and disillusions' (2007) 14 *Journal of European Public Policy* 699.
Pescatore, P, 'Some critical remarks on the "Single European Act"' (1987) 24 *Common Market Law Review* 9.

Petersmann, E-U, 'Grundprobleme der Wirtschaftsverfassung der EG' (1994) 48 *Aussenwirtschaft* 389.

Peterson, J, 'Technology Policy in Europe: Explaining the Framework Programme and Eureka in Theory and Practice' (1991) 29 *Journal of Common Market Studies* 269.

Philip, A, 'Social Aspects of European Economic Co-operation' (1957) 76 *International Labour Review* 244.

Piketty, T, *Capital in the twenty-first century* (The Belknap Press of Harvard University Press, 2014).

Piketty, T and Saez, E, 'Top incomes and the great recession: Recent evolutions and policy implications' (2013) 61 *IMF Economic Review* 456.

Pinder, J, 'Positive Integration and Negative Integration: Some Problems of Economic Union in the EEC' (1968) 24 *The World Today* 88.

Pipkorn, J, 'Legal Arrangements in the Treaty of Maastricht for the Effectiveness of the Economic and Monetary Union' (1994) 31 *Common Market Law Review* 263.

Poiares Maduro, M, *We the Court. The European Court of Justice and the European Economic Constitution: a critical reading of Article 30 of the EC Treaty* (Hart, 1998).

Polanyi, K, *The great transformation* (Beacon, 1957).

Pollack, M, 'Integrating Left and Right: Studying EU Politics' (1998) 11 *ECSA Review* 2.

Pomfret, R, 'What is the Secret of the EMS's Longevity?' (1991) 29 *Journal of Common Market Studies* 623.

Posner, R, *Economic Analysis of Law* (Aspen Publishers, 2007).

Prebisch, R, 'Commercial Policy in the Underdeveloped Countries' (1959) 49 *American Economic Review* 251.

Prendergast, R, 'Accumulation of knowledge and accumulation of capital in early 'theories' of growth and development' (2010) 34 *Cambridge Journal of Economics* 413.

Radice, H, 'Enforcing austerity in Europe: The structural deficit as a policy target' (2014) 22 *Journal of Contemporary European Studies* 318.

Reinhart, C and Rogoff, K, *Growth in a time of debt* (2010) NBER Working Paper No 15639.

Ricardo, D, *Principles of Political Economy and Taxation* (Prometheus Books, 1996).

Riesenfeld, S, 'Common Market for Agricultural Products and Common Agricultural Policy in the European Economic Community' (1965) *University of Illinois Law Review* 658.

Rivers, J, 'Proportionality and Variable Intensity of Review' (2006) 65 *Cambridge Law Journal* 174.

Robinson, J, *Economic Philosophy* (Penguin Books, 1962).

——, 'Review of Money, Trade and Economic Growth by H. G. Johnson' (1962) 72 *Economic Journal* 690.

——, *Essays in the theory of economic growth* (Macmillan, 1963).

——, *The economics of imperfect competition* (Macmillan, 1969).

——, *Economic heresies* (Basic Books, 1971).

Robinson, N, 'The European Investment Bank: The EU's Neglected Institution' (2009) 47 *Journal of Common Market Studies* 651.

Rodríguez-Pose, A and Fratesi, U, 'Between Development and Social Policies: The Impact of European Structural Funds in Objective 1 Regions' (2004) 38 *Regional Studies* 97.

Rodríguez, F and Rodrik, D, 'Trade Policy and Economic Growth: A Skeptic's Guide to the Cross-National Evidence' (2000) 15 *NBER Macroeconomics Annual* 261.

Rodrik, D, 'The Mirage of Structural Reform' (*Project Syndicate*, 8 October, 2015) project-syndicate.org/commentary/greece-structural-reform-mirage-by-dani-rodrik-2015-10.

——, 'Globalisation, Social Conflict and Economic Growth' (1998) 21 *World Economy* 143.
——, 'Industrial policy for the twenty-first century' (2004) CEPR Discussion Paper No 4767.
——, *One economics, many recipes* (Princeton University Press, 2007).
Rodrik, D, Subramaninan A and Trebbi, F, 'Institutions Rule: The Primacy of Institutions over Geography and Integration in Economic Development' (2002) NBER Working Paper No 9305.
Romer, P, 'Increasing Returns and Long-Run Growth' (1986) 94 *Journal of Political Economy* 1002.
——, 'Endogenous Technological Change' (1990) 98 *Journal of Political Economy* 71.
Röpke, W, 'Wirtschaftssystem und internationale Ordnung Prolegomena' (1951) 4 *ORDO: Jahrbuch für die Ordnung von Wirtschaft und Gesellschaft* 261.
——, *Die Lehre von der Wirtschaft* (Eugen Rentsch Verlag, 1961).
Ross, G, *Jacques Delors and European Integration* (Polity Press, 1995).
Rostow, W, *The stages of economic growth* (CUP, 1960).
Roth, W-H, 'The European Economic Community's Law on Services: Harmonisation' (1988) 25 *Common Market Law Review* 35.
Ruffert, M, 'The European debt crisis and European Union law' (2011) 48 *Common Market Law Review* 1777.
Ruggie, J, 'International regimes, transactions, and change: embedded liberalism in the postwar economic order' (1982) 36 *International Organization* 379.
Rüstow, A, 'Kritik des technischen Fortschritts' (1951) 4 *ORDO: Jahrbuch für die Ordnung von Wirtschaft und Gesellschaft* 373.
Sala-i-Martin, X, 'The Classical Approach to Convergence Analysis' (1996) 106 *Economic Journal* 1019.
Samuelson, P, 'A Note on the Pure Theory of Consumer's Behaviour' (1938) 5 *Economica* 61.
——, 'The Gains from International Trade' (1939) 5 *The Canadian Journal of Economics and Political Science/Revue canadienne d'Economique et de Science politique* 195.
——, 'International Trade and the Equalisation of Factor Prices' (1948) 58 *Economic Journal* 163.
——, 'A Ricardo-Sraffa Paradigm Comparing Gains from Trade in Inputs and Finished Goods' (2001) 39 *Journal of Economic Literature* 1204.
Sandholtz, W and Zysman, J, '1992: Recasting the European Bargain' (1989) 42 *World Politics* 95.
Sands, P, 'European Community Environmental Law: Legislation, the European Court of Justice and Common Interest Groups' (1990) 53 *Modern Law Review* 685.
Saraceno, F, 'High Inequality and its Impact on the Economy: Issues and Solutions' (Paper presented at workshop "Réformer l'Europe," Paris, 9 January, 2014).
Sauter, W, *Competition law and industrial Policy in the EU* (OUP, 1997).
——, 'The Economic Constitution of the European Union' (1998) 4 *Columbia Journal of European Law* 27.
Scharpf, F, 'The Joint-Decision Trap: Lessons From German Federalism and European Integration' (1988) 66 *Public Administration* 239.
——, 'Community and autonomy: multi-level policy-making in the European Union' (1994) 1 *Journal of European Public Policy* 219.
——, 'Introduction: the problem-solving capacity of multi-level governance' (1997) 4 *Journal of European Public Policy* 520.

——, *Governing in Europe: effective and democratic?* (OUP, 1999).
——, 'The Joint-decision Trap Revisited' (2006) 44 *Journal of Common Market Studies* 845.
——, 'The asymmetry of European integration, or why the EU cannot be a "social market economy"' (2010) 8 *Socio-Economic Review* 211.
——, 'After the crash: A perspective on multilevel European democracy' (2015) 21 *European Law Journal* 384.
Scherer, J, *Die Wirtschaftsverfassung der EWG* (Nomos, 1970).
Schiller, K-V, 'Gewährt Art. 30 des EWG-Vertrages dem Gemeinschaftsbürger neben einem subjektiven Abwehrrecht auch ein subjektives Leistungsrecht?' [1980] *Recht der internationalen Wirtschaft* 569.
Schlink, B, 'Proportionality in Constitutional Law: Why Everywhere but Here' (2011) 22 *Duke Journal of Comparative & International Law* 291.
Schloss, H, 'The European Payments Union' (1951) 17 *Southern Economic Journal* 465.
Schmidt, S, 'Mutual recognition as a new mode of governance' (2007) 14 *Journal of European Public Policy* 667.
Schopflin, G, 'EFTA: The Other Europe' (1964) 40 *International Affairs* 674.
Schumpeter, J, *Theorie der wirtschaftlichen Entwicklung* (Duncker und Humblot, 1934).
——, *Capitalism, Socialism, and Democracy* (Harper Colophon Books, 1975).
——, *History of Economic Analysis* (OUP, 1996).
Schwartz, I, '30 Jahre EG-Rechtsangleichung' in Mestmäcker, E-J, Möller, H and Schwarz, H-P (eds), *Eine Ordnungspolitik für Europa: Festschrift für Hans von der Groeben zu seinem 80 Geburtstag* (Nomos, 1987).
Scitovsky, T, 'A Reconsideration of the Theory of Tariffs' (1942) 9 *The Review of Economic Studies* 89.
——, *Economic theory and Western European integration* (Allen & Unwin, 1958).
Screpanti, E and Zamagni, S, *An outline of the history of economic thought* (OUP, 2005).
Seidel, M, 'The Harmonization of Laws Relating to Pharmaceuticals in the EEC' (1969) 6 *Common Market Law Review* 309.
Sen, A, 'Rational fools: A critique of the behavioral foundations of economic theory' (1977) *Philosophy & Public Affairs* 317.
Servan-Schreiber, J-J, *Le défi américain* (Denoel, 1967).
Sherwood, M, 'Eurobeer' *New Scientist* (21 February, 1974) 494.
Siekmann, H, 'The legality of outright monetary transactions (OMT) of the European system of central banks' (2015) IMFS Working Paper Series No 90.
Sinn, HW, 'Austerity, growth and inflation: remarks on the Eurozone's unresolved competitiveness problem' (2014) 37 *The World Economy* 1.
Slaughter, M, 'Trade liberalization and per capita income convergence: a difference-in-differences analysis' (2001) 55 *Journal of International Economics* 203.
Slynn, G, 'Aspects of the Law of the European Economic Community' (1985) 18 *Cornell International Law Journal* 1.
Smith, A, *Wealth of Nations* (Prometheus Books, 1991).
Smulders, B and Keppenne, J-P, 'AEUV Artikel 125' in von der Groeben, H, Schwarze, J and Hatje, A (ed), *Europäisches Unionsrecht* (Nomos, 2015).
Solow, R, 'A Contribution to the Theory of Economic Growth' (1956) 70 *Quarterly Journal of Economics* 65.
——, 'Technical Change and the Aggregate Production Function' (1957) 39 *Review of Economics and Statistics* 312.

——, 'Growth theory and after' (1988) 78 *American Economic Review* 307.
——, *Monopolistic Competition and Macroeconomic Theory* (CUP, 1998).
Somek, A, *Individualism. An Essay on the Authority of the European Union* (Oxford University Press, 2008).
——, 'The Argument from Transnational Effects I: Representing Outsiders through Freedom of Movement' (2010) 16 *European Law Journal* 315.
——, 'From Workers to Migrants, from Distributive Justice to Inclusion: Exploring the Changing Social Democratic Imagination' (2012) 18 *European Law Journal* 711.
——, 'What Is Political Union' (2013) 14 *German Law Journal* 561.
Spaak, F and Jaeger, J, 'The Rules of Competition within the European Common Market' (1961) 26 *Law and Contemporary Problems* 485.
Spaak, P-H et al, *Rapport des Chefs de Délégation aux Ministres des Affaires Etrangères* (Spaak Report) (1956).
Spence, M, 'Product Selection, Fixed Costs, and Monopolistic Competition' (1976) 43 *Review of Economic Studies* 217.
Steindorff, E, *Der Gleichheitssatz im Wirtschaftsrecht des Gemeinsamen Marktes* (Walter De Gruyter & Co, 1965).
Stewart, H, 'We are in the worst financial crisis since Depression, says IMF' *The Guardian* (10 April, 2008), theguardian.com/business/2008/apr/10/useconomy.subprimecrisis.
Stiglitz, J, 'Information and the Change in the Paradigm of Economics' Prize Lecture, 8 December 2001, www.nobelprize.org/nobel_prizes/economics/laureates/2001/stiglitz-lecture.pdf.
——, *Globalization and its Discontents* (Norton, 2002).
——, *The Price of Inequality* (Norton, 2013).
——, 'Reconstructing macroeconomic theory to manage economic policy' (2014) NBER Working Paper No 20517.
Stiglitz, J, Sen, A and Fitoussi, J-P, 'Report by the Commission on the Measurement of Economic Performance and Social Progress' (2009), www.stiglitz-sen-fitoussi.fr/documents/rapport_anglais.pdf.
Stockhammer, E, 'Robinsonian and Kaleckian growth. An update on post-Keynesian growth theories' (1999) WU Working Paper No 67.
Stone Sweet, A and Mathews, J, 'Proportionality balancing and global constitutionalism' (2008) 47 *Columbia Journal of Transnational Law* 73.
Streeck, W, *Gekaufte Zeit* (Suhrkamp, 2013).
Streinz, R, 'Reform der EU-Wirtschaftsverfassung: Kompetenzen und Institutionen' (58. Bitburger Gespräche, Trier, 8–9 January, 2015).
Streit, M and Mussler, W, 'The economic constitution of the European community: From Rome to Maastricht' (1994) 5 *Constitutional Political Economy* 319.
Stuart, JM, 'The Court of Justice of the European Communities: The Scope of its Jurisdiction and the Evolution of its Case Law under the EEC Treaty' (1981) 3 *Northwestern Journal of International Law & Business* 415.
Swann, D, *The Economics of the Common Market* (Penguin Books, 1992).
Swann, D and McLachlan, D, 'Programming and Competition in the European Communities' (1964) 74 *Economic Journal* 85.
Taylor, P, 'Interdependence and autonomy in the European Communities: the case of the European monetary system' (1980) 18 *Journal of Common Market Studies* 370.

Teasdale, A, 'The life and death of the Luxembourg Compromise' (1993) 31 *Journal of Common Market Studies* 567.
Thompson, D, 'Harmonization of Laws' (1965) 3 *Journal of Common Market Studies* 302.
Thomson, G, *Address to the Birmingham Chamber of Commerce and Industry* (Birmingham, 5 November, 1974).
——, *Address to the Pharmaceutical Society of Great Britain* (Dundee, 15 September, 1976).
Tietmeyer, W, 'Die Gründung des Sachverständigenrates aus der Sicht der Wirtschaftspolitik' in Sachverständigenrat (ed), *Vierzig Jahre Sachverständigenrat* (Sachverständigenrat, 2003).
Tinbergen, J, *International Economic Integration* (Elsevier, 1954).
Tomkin, J, 'Contradiction, circumvention and conceptual gymnastics: the impact of the adoption of the ESM Treaty on the State of European Democracy' (2013) 14 *German Law Journal* 169.
Tridimas, T, *The General Principles of EU Law* (Oxford University Press, 2006).
Triffin, R, *Monopolistic Competition and General Equilibrium Theory* (Harvard University Press, 1949).
Truger, A and Will, H, 'The German "debt brake": a shining example for European fiscal policy?' (2013) Working Paper, Institute for International Political Economy Berlin, No 15.
Tsoukalis, L, 'Is the re-launching of economic and monetary union a feasible proposal?' (1976) 15 *Journal of Common Market Studies* 231.
Tumlir, J and La Haye, L, 'The Two Attempts at European Economic Reconstruction After 1945' (1981) 137 *Zeitschrift für die gesamte Staatswissenschaft/Journal of Institutional and Theoretical Economics* 367.
Tuori, K and Tuori, K, *The Eurozone Crisis* (Cambridge University Press, 2014).
Ubide, A, *Is the European Central Bank Failing Its Price Stability Mandate?* (2014) Peterson Institute for International Economics Policy Brief No 5.
Ulmer, P, 'Zum Verbot mittelbarer Einfuhrbeschränkungen im EWG-Vertrag' (1973) *GRUR Int* 502.
——, 'Zum Verbot mittelbarer Einfuhrbeschränkungen im EWG-Vertrag' [1973] *Aussenwirtschaftsdienst des Betriebs-Beraters* 349.
UN, *Economic planning in Europe* (prepared by the secretariat of the Economic Commission for Europe, 1965).
——, *The European economy from the 1950s to the 1970s* (prepared by the secretariat of the Economic commission for Europe, 1972).
Ungerer, H, 'The European monetary system and the international monetary system' (1989) 27 *Journal of Common Market Studies* 231.
USITC, *Implementing the European Community Single Market: Sixth Followup Report* (USITC Publication, 1994).
Van Gerven, W, 'Droit d'Établissement' [1965] *Cahiers de Droit Europeén* 125.
——, *Principes du droit des ententes de la Communauté Économique Européenne* (Bruylant, 1966).
——, 'The recent case law of the Court of Justice concerning Articles 30 and 36 of the EEC Treaty' (1977) 14 *Common Market Law Review* 5.
Van Malleghem, P-A, 'Pringle: A Paradigm Shift in the European Union's Monetary Constitution' (2013) 14 *German Law Journal* 141.

Van Rompuy, H, *Towards a genuine economic and monetary union* (2012).
Vaubel, R, 'Currency Competition and European Monetary Integration' (1990) 100 *Economic Journal* 936.
Veblen, T, 'The Limitations of Marginal Utility' (1909) 17 *Journal of Political Economy* 620.
verLoren van Themaat, P, 'Bevat Artikel 30 van het EEG-Verdrag slechts een non-discriminatie-bedingsel ten aanzien van invoerbeperkingen?' [1967] *Sociaal Economische Wetgeving* 632.
——, 'Competition and Planning in the EEC and the Member States' (1970) 7 *Common Market Law Review* 311.
——, 'E.E.G.-richtlijnen betreffende discriminerende aankoop-politiek overheidsinstellingen, discriminerende prijsvoorschriften en andere maatregeln van gelijke werking als kwantitatieve invoerbeperkingen' [1970] *Sociaal Economische Wetgeving* 258.
——, *The changing structure of international economic law: a contribution of legal history, of comparative law and of general legal theory to the debate on a new international economic order* (Nijhoff, 1981).
verLoren van Themaat, P and Gormley, L, 'Prohibiting Restriction of Free Trade within the Community: Articles 30-36 of the EEC Treaty' (1981) 3 *Northwestern Journal of International Law & Business* 577.
Viner, J, *The customs union issue* (Carnegie Endowment for International Peace, 1950).
——, 'Conflicts of Principle in Drafting a Trade Charter' in Viner, J (ed), *International Economics* (The Free Press, 1951).
——, 'Economic Foundations of International Organization' in Viner, J (ed), *International Economics* (The Free Press, 1951).
——, 'Professor Taussig's Contribution to the Theory of International Trade' in Viner, J (ed), *International Economics* (The Free Press, 1951).
Vogelaar, T, 'The Approximation of the laws of Member States under the Treaty of Rome' (1975) 12 *Common Market Law Review* 211.
von der Groeben, H, 'Competition Policy in the Common Market and in the Atlantic Partnership' (1965) 10 *Antitrust Bulletin* 125.
——, 'Deutschland, Europäische Gemeinschaft, Atlantische Partnerschaft' in von der Groeben, H (ed), *Europa—Plan und Wirklichkeit* (Nomos, 1967).
——, 'Die Bedeutung der EWG für Europa' in von der Groeben H (ed), *Europa—Plan und Wirklichkeit* (Nomos, 1967).
——, 'Die nächsten zehn Jahre' in von der Groeben H (ed), *Europa—Plan und Wirklichkeit* (Nomos, 1967).
——, 'Gemeinsamer Markt und Euratom—Stand der Entwicklung' in von der Groeben, H (ed), *Europa—Plan und Wirklichkeit* (Nomos, 1967).
——, 'Nationalstaat und Europäische Gemeinschaft im Lichte sozialen Wandels' in von der Groeben, H (ed), *Europa—Plan und Wirklichkeit* (Nomos, 1967).
——, 'Vier Jahre Gemeinsamer Markt' in von der Groeben H (ed), *Europa—Plan und Wirklichkeit* (Nomos, 1967).
——, 'Zur Politik der Rechtsangleichung in der Europäischen Wirtschaftsgemeinschaft' (1967) 8 *Zeitschrift für Rechtsvergleichung* 129.

——, 'Mitbestimmung in the Europäischen Aktiengesellschaft—der Vorschlag der Kommission der EG' in Von der Groeben, H, Vetter H and Friedrich O (eds), *Europäische Aktiengesellschaft: Beitrag zur sozialen Integration?* (Europa Union Verlag, 1972).
——, *Aufbaujahre der Europäischen Gemeinschaft. Das Ringen um den Gemeinsamen Markt und die Politische Union (1958–1966)* (Nomos, 1982).
von der Groeben, H, von Boeckh, H and Thiesing, J, *Kommentar zum EWG-Vertrag* (Nomos, 1974).
Wade, R, 'Capitalism and Democracy at Cross-Purposes' (2013) 56 *Challenges* 1.
Waelbroeck, M, *Les reglementations nationales de prix et le droit communautaire* (Ed. de l'Univ. de Bruxelles, 1975).
Watson, P, 'Freedom of establishment and freedom to provide services: some recent developments' (1983) 20 *Common Market Law Review* 767.
Weatherill, S, *EU consumer law and policy* (Edward Elgar, 2013).
Wellisz, S, 'Economic planning in the Netherlands, France, and Italy' (1960) 68 *Journal of Political Economy* 252.
Werner, P, 'Realisation by Stages of Economic and Monetary Union in the Community' (Werner Report) (*Bulletin of the European Communities*, Supplement 11/1970).
White, E, 'In Search of the Limits to Article 30 of the EEC Treaty' (1989) 26 *Common Market Law Review* 235.
Wilkinson, M, 'Authoritarian Liberalism in the European Constitutional Imagination: Second Time as Farce?' (2015) 21 *European Law Journal* 313.
Wilkinson, R and Pickett, K, *The spirit level: why equality is better for everyone* (Penguin, 2010).
Williams, J, *Economic stability in a changing world* (OUP, 1953).
Wilson, T, 'Review: Report of the Study Group on the Role of Public Finance in European Integration' (1978) 88 *Economic Journal* 858.
Wohlfarth, E et al, *Die Europäische Wirtschaftsgemeinschaft: Kommentar zum Vertrag* (Vahlen, 1960).
Wonnacott, P and Wonnacott, R, 'Is Unilateral Tariff Reduction Preferable to a Customs Union? The Curious Case of the Missing Foreign Tariffs' (1981) 71 *American Economic Review* 704.
Young, A, 'Increasing Returns and Economic Progress' (1928) 38 *Economic Journal* 527.
Zijlstra, J, *Möglichkeiten und Grenzen der Konjunkturpolitik* (Universität Kiel, 1962).
——, *Economische politiek en concurrentieproblematiek in de EEG en de lid-staten* (Staatsdrukkerij- en Uitgeversbedrijf, 1966).
Ziltener, P, *Strukturwandel der europäischen Integration: die Europäische Union und die Veränderung der Staatlichkeit* (Westfälisches Dampfboot, 1999).
Zines, L, 'Balancing of Community and National Interests by the European Court' (1972) 5 *Federal Law Review* 171.
Zis, G, 'The European Monetary System 1979–84: An Assessment' (1984) 23 *Journal of Common Market Studies* 45.
Zuleeg, M, 'Relationship of Community Law to National Law' (1977) 5 *International Journal of Law Libaries* 5.

Index

www.ingramcontent.com/pod-product-compliance
Ingram Content Group UK Ltd.
Pitfield, Milton Keynes, MK11 3LW, UK
UKHW020132290926
15471UKWH00003B/430

9 781509 926442